DOCUMENTS OF
WESTERN CIVILIZATION

❧

VOLUME II: SINCE 1500

Candace Gregory
California State University, Sacramento

THOMSON
™
WADSWORTH

Australia • Canada • Mexico • Singapore • Spain • United Kingdom • United States

Documents of Western Civilization Volume II: Since 1500
Candace Gregory, California State University, Sacramento

Publisher: Clark Baxter
Assistant Editor: Paul Massicotte
Editorial Assistant: Lucinda Bingham
Technology Project Manager: David Lionetti
Marketing Manager: Lori Grebe Cook
Marketing Assistant: Theresa Jessen
Project Manager, Editorial Production: Katy German

Art Director: Maria Epes
Print Buyer: Judy Inouye
Permissions Editor: Joohee Lee
Compositor: Candace Gregory
Cover Designer: tani hasegawa
Cover Image: Smithsonian American Art Museum, Washington, DC, USA / Art Resource, NY
Printer: Webcom

Library of Congress Control Number: 2005925746

ISBN 0-495-03011-2

Thomson Higher Education
10 Davis Drive
Belmont, CA 94002-3098
USA

Printed in Canada
1 2 3 4 5 6 7 09 08 07 06 05

For more information about our products,
contact us at:
Thomson Learning Academic Resource Center
1-800-423-0563
For permission to use material from this text
or product, submit a request online at
http://www.thomsonrights.com.
Any additional questions about permissions
can be submitted by email to
thomsonrights@thomson.com.

CONTENTS

VOLUME II: SINCE 1500

PREFACE

History is a lived experience. Reading the primary sources — the original thoughts, spoken words, opinions, and experiences of the people of the past — is one way for the student in the present to hope to understand history and, in a sense, relive it. Textbooks and other secondary studies are an indispensable tool of historical understanding, yet they can only convey the basic facts as we now understand them. It is from the original documents that the past gains color and dimension, and becomes the lives of real people rather than just a list of dates, events, and figures.

Documents of Western Civilization brings together a wide array of primary sources from across the spectrum of Western (i.e., European) history, illustrating the formation and development of Western cultures and states. The guiding principles of selection were twofold: to include documents that represented the most fundamental aspects of Western history, and to include documents that also represented the wide variety of cultures and peoples that have made up the West. Defining what was important and fundamental for each period of Western history was itself a challenge. The kinds of texts included in this source reader, and thus defined as important, are diverse. They include texts of law, politics, religion, science, philosophy and myth; testimonials; biographies; poetry and literature; speeches; and proclamations. Selections include lesser known works as well as "classic" texts. Women, marginal groups, outsiders, and other groups normally silent in the historical record are revealed through these documents to have been crucial to the development of the West. These groups, who are less often reflected in primary source readers, are clearly represented here, but are not segregated on their own. They are incorporated into the larger scope of their own particular part of Western civilization. For instance, there is no section on "Women in the Reformation," but the section on the Reformation includes Teresa of Avila's counter-reformation mysticism. Documents were also chosen for their user-friendliness. None of them are so esoteric or removed from our own culture so as to be impossible for students to understand. If anything, most students will probably find — in how people lived and felt — that the past is remarkably like the present.

The sources in this reader have been arranged in both a chronological and thematic manner. Although each source can be used individually to illustrate characteristics of a particular culture and period in Western civilization, they are arranged to reflect general trends in the development of the West. Each document is followed by a few discussion questions, while each section of documents concludes with questions that compare and contrast the individual documents in relation to the overall theme of the section.

A brief introduction precedes each document; these introductions place the documents in the larger context of Western history, and provide a background against which the aforementioned questions of interpretation and discovery can be addressed. However, these introductions are deliberately brief, so as not to distract from the reader's discovery of the past. While this sourcebook can be read on its own, it is perhaps best approached with a textbook in hand for further information on chronology and the broader historical picture. *Documents of Western Civilization* is intended to be a supplement to *Western Civilization* by Jackson J. Spielvogel. However, it is designed to be of use to any general survey of Western European history.

ACKNOWLEDGEMENTS

Thanks are due to the editors at Wadsworth Group/Thomson Learning, particularly Paul Massicotte; to my colleagues of the History Department of California State University, Sacramento, who provided advice and support in assembly of this reader, especially Barbara Keys, Mona Siegel, Afshin Marashi, and Katerina Lagos; the professors of history from whom I took classes over the years; and to my mother for her support as well. Thanks are also due to Larry Brooks. More importantly, thanks are due to all the students I have taught over the years for their responses, reactions, and reflections on the use of primary source material in history classes.

HOW TO READ
A PRIMARY SOURCE DOCUMENT

Every primary source should be approached like a puzzle, the solution of which builds a small picture of a Western culture piece-by-piece, word-by-word. All primary sources are both puzzles in themselves and clues to larger puzzles. Knowing how to read a document, how to decode it for clues and decipher its meaning, is a learnable skill. Most importantly, it is an entertaining exercise in puzzle solving.

Every primary source is shaped by a particular context and contains specific content. Each is equally important, yet in different ways and in different situations. Answering the questions that establish the context is your first priority as a reader, though you will find that you must decipher the content to do so. Furthermore, answering one question may help answer another question, but will more than likely lead to more questions. Here is a list of five general questions that should be asked about the context of any primary source:

1. *What is the content of the document? (What does it say?)*
2. *Who created/wrote it?*
3. *Where did it originate?*
4. *When was the source created/written?*
5. *Why was the source created/written down?*

The first question is that of content, which must be deciphered and interpreted. It is important to recognize and to remember that every act of reading a primary source document, whether from a recent period or the ancient past, is an act of interpretation. It is essential that you, as the reader, recognize your own context and biases, but not allow them to overpower your understanding of the document at hand. In other words, we use primary sources to understand the past, not to judge it. Furthermore, it is important to read a document for all levels of content: explicit and implicit. It is also important to use, whenever possible, other sources than the document itself in interpreting it. Comparison with other primary source documents and research into secondary sources is useful, and often necessary.

Secondly, perhaps the simplest question to ask of a primary source: who wrote it? Sometimes the author of the primary source is known explicitly, but as one goes further back into the historical record such information becomes scarce. Details (such as gender, occupation, social class, education level, biases, intentions, etc.) about the author or authors can often be discerned from the primary source itself, if one reads it carefully enough. Similar details about the culture (political system, religious beliefs, etc.) that produced the primary source can often also be detected in the documents.

The third question any reader should ask: where did the primary source originate? The "West" is a bit of a misnomer; the term has always referred to a wide geographic region of diverse peoples and cultures, although the primary focus of this sourcebook is the development of Western Europe. This diversity is reflected in the array of primary sources produced since the beginning of Western civilization. The context of each primary source reveals unique details about the specific region and culture that created it.

The fourth question relates to situating the document in time: when was it created? In what ways was this document shaped by the concerns of a particular era? There is second part to this question, in that one must also consider when the source was written down. The distinction between acts of creation and acts of writing — distinct from one another — is particularly important to consider for the earliest periods of Western history, when oral transmission of sources occurred before then act of writing down those sources. The reader must always consider hat there may be a gap in time between creation and writing.

The fifth question concerns purpose. Content alone usually provides answers to the riddle of why, although the why is not always clear or simple to explain. Nor is there necessarily only one answer to the question of purpose.

Consider the following example of how to read a primary source document, *The Sixty-Seven Articles of Zwingli*:

The articles and opinions below, I, Ulrich Zwingli, confess to have preached in the worthy city of Zurich as based upon the Scriptures which are called inspired by God, and I offer to protect and conquer with the said articles, and where I have not now correctly understood said Scriptures I shall allow myself to be taught better, but only from said Scriptures.

I. *All who say that the Gospel is invalid without the confirmation of the Church err and slander God.*

II. *The sum and substance of the Gospel is that our Lord Jesus Christ, the true Son of God, has made known to us the will of his heavenly Father, and has with his innocence released us from death and reconciled God.*

III. *Hence Christ is the only way to salvation for all who ever were, are, and shall be.*

IV. *Who seeks or points out another door errs, yea, he is a murderer of souls and a thief.*

V. *Hence all who consider other teachings equal to or higher than the Gospel err, and do not know what the Gospel is.*

VI. *For Jesus Christ is the guide and leader, promised by God to all human beings, which promise was fulfilled.*

VII. *That he is an eternal salvation and head of all believers, who are his body, but which is dead and can do nothing without him.*

VIII. *From this follows first that all who dwell in the head are members and children of God, and that is the church or communion of saints, the bride of Christ, Ecclesia catholica.*

IX. *Furthermore, that as the members of the head, so no one in the body of Christ can do the least without his head, Christ.*

X. *As that man is mad whose limbs (try to) do something without his head, tearing, wounding, injuring himself; thus when the members of the Church undertake something without their head, Christ, they are mad, and injure and burden themselves with unwise ordinances.*

XI. Hence we see in the clerical (so-called) ordinances, concerning their splendor, riches, classes, titles, laws, a cause of all foolishness, for they do not also agree with the head.

What can be known about and from this document? How does research into sources help us read this document?

1. *What is the content of the document? What does it say?* Here you would summarize what the text states. It begins by identifying who the author is, Ulrich Zwingli, who proclaims that this is a confession of preaching he has done in the city of Zurich. This particular excerpt includes eleven articles of faith and the administration of that faith, covering such topics as what a Christian should believe and who should determine what doctrines should be, and simultaneously dismisses "clerical" ordinance, which implies that this is a rejection of some existing church.

2. *Who created/wrote it?* The authorship is clearly stated in the first line; it was written by Ulrich Zwingli. Even if you did not know before reading the document that Zwingli was a Protestant reformer, his religious beliefs are evident from the text. Thus, authorship is more than just determining the name of the person who wrote it, it is also about the character of the person that wrote it, the author's educational background (what he or she learned, how they learned, for example), what his or her profession was, his or her social class, and his or her motivation. In the preceding example, the frequency with which the author (Zwingli) invokes God and Jesus Christ clearly identifies him as a Christian. That he specifically refers to Jesus Christ as the Son of God marks him as a Trinitarian Christian, one who believes in the trinity of Father, Son, and Holy Spirit. His Protestant sympathies are indicated by the frequent reference to the Gospels; Protestantism was based on the reliance on scripture as the primary authority for faith, whereas the Catholic Church recognized the importance of scripture but restricted to itself the right to interpret scripture. However, it is also clear that Zwingli had some training in Catholic doctrine. In Article II above he refers to Jesus Christ as the "true Son of God" which echoes the doctrinal claim of the Nicene Creed, the basic statement of faith for the Catholic Church.

3. *Where did it originate?* Again, this document tells us explicitly that it was written in Zurich. However, many of the clues mentioned above about authorship would also indicate that someone of Western culture wrote it.

4. *When was the source created/written?* There is no date in the document itself to answer this question. You could look up the life dates of Zwingli and estimate a range of dates in which he could have written it. Internal evidence indicates that it was written during or shortly after the Reformation began in the early sixteenth century. The author (Zwingli) is careful to distinguish himself as a Christian whose faith is based entirely on Scripture, a commonly held belief among Protestants. Furthermore he criticizes those who follow "clerical (so-called) ordinances," clearly distinguishing himself from the Catholic clergy and its hierarchy. This kind of direct confrontation between scriptural based Christianity and a hierarchical faith of law, clerics, and titles (i.e., Roman Catholicism) was typical of the early Reformation. Furthermore, Zwingli uses the phrase "to have preached." According to canon law and the medieval Catholic Church, only ordained priests (those who followed the "clerical ordinances") were legally allowed to preach. Zwingli's articles are so critical of the Catholic Church that he is either an ordained cleric preaching against his own superiors or a layperson who is preaching without church authority. Neither one would have been tolerated by the medieval church for very long. If this text were typical of Zwingli's writing, without

any clear retribution from the Catholic Church, it indicates that the Protestant schism has already begun, and that there is now the potential for preaching without the papal approval. It is also more than likely that Zwingli was speaking in a place that was at least sympathetic to his beliefs.

There is one very interesting phrase in the above that illustrates why *close* and careful reading of every primary source document is necessary. In Article VIII above, the author uses the phrase *Ecclesia catholica* to refer to the Church; it is a Latin phrase and is a sign of a faith in transition. The medieval Catholic Church which Zwingli grew up in, but which he is trying to reform, was a Latin-based church; although he wants to introduce a vernacular church, he still slips and reveals his own religious background. Couple this clue with the reference earlier to Zwingli's use of "true Son of God" and it becomes clear that this source dates from a period in Western history that was still influenced by Catholic belief, even as it is clear that Zwingli was moving away from it.

5. *Why was the source created/written down?* Actually, the answers to who, where, and when, above, are probably also the answers to the why. Zwingli used his list of *Sixty-Seven Articles* as a way to establish the authority of his own belief over that of the Roman Catholic Church he opposed. The *Articles* are a way for Zwingli to establish several of the tenets of his own particular sect of Christianity. He is a Trinitarian Christian and thus believes in a tri-partite God that is Father, Son, and Holy Spirit. He believes in the basic story of Christianity; that Jesus Christ was the Son of God, and that he was born and died in order to ensure the salvation of his believers. Zwingli has a thorough understanding of Catholic doctrines and the hierarchical nature of the Catholic Church, yet rejects both in favor of scripture and faith without mediation. He also believes in the necessity (he sees it as a requirement from God) that the state and church be one and the same identity; for him, the city of Zurich is to be run as not as a secular society but as a Christian city, a community of the faithful. In rejecting the hierarchy of the Church, Zwingli in effect authorizes himself to preach; thus in the *Articles* he empowers himself to issue said *Articles* in the first place.

PART 15

REFORMATION AND THE WARS OF RELIGION

There were many Reformations in the sixteenth century. Some of the movement's leaders began as reformers and became protesters, while others remained reformers. Furthermore, these Reformations did not appear without precedent or cause; humanism and renaissance ideas also contributed to the Reformations. Martin Luther's objections to particular Catholic practices in 1517 was certainly one starting point of one Reformation, but it had inherited fifteenth-century humanism and movements that emphasized personal piety. John Calvin and Ulrich Zwingli introduced their own Reformations in the decade after Luther's, and while they both agreed with Luther (and each other) on some doctrines and beliefs, they disagreed with Luther (and each other) on many more. All three, as well as other reformers were influenced by emerging national awareness. It seemed as if every European country had its own version of a Reformation. The Catholic Church had its own as well, although it did so without changing any doctrine; instead it underwent an internal renewal and rid itself of abuses.

All Reformations, whether Protestant or Catholic, ended up the period embroiled in violence. Religious wars swept across Europe in the mid-sixteenth century and would continue into the seventeenth. One particularly horrific manifestation of the religious violence was the witch hunts, which admittedly began in the Late Middle Ages, but which increased in both scope and degree of violence as the Reformation progressed. Reformation and religious violence were both aided by the new technology of printing, which made ideas more readily available to a wider audience than ever before.

15.1

NINETY-FIVE THESES, MARTIN LUTHER

The most important document of the Protestant Reformation was the Ninety-Five Theses *of Martin Luther. Luther (1483-1546) was an intensely devout monk with legal training and humanist interests who was obsessed with salvation. In 1517 Luther was teaching at the university in Wittenberg when the Dominican Tetzel arrived to preach a special indulgence. Indulgences were papal dispensations (releases) from either penance or time in purgatory in exchange for an act of faith. The Crusades are an example of how indulgences had been used by the Church; Crusaders had been promised full remission of their sins in exchange for fighting. Tetzel promised salvation if people donated money for the construction of St. Peter's in Rome. Luther was confused by the theology of the indulgence and offended by the apparent "sale" of salvation preached by Tetzel. Luther posited ninety-five points on penance, indulgences, and salvation; he proposed this topic for discussion in the traditional university manner by posting his theses on the church door.*

———— ✦ ————

QUESTIONS

1. How does Luther's legal background reveal itself in how he thinks about indulgences?
2. Find an example of how Luther uses scripture to argue against the theory of indulgence.
3. How is Luther using this opportunity to criticize papal abuses?

NINETY-FIVE THESES
or
DISPUTATION ON THE POWER AND EFFICACY OF INDULGENCES

1. When our Lord and Mater Jesus Christ said, "Repent" [Matt. 4:17], he willed the entire life of believers to be one of repentance.
2. This word cannot be understood as referring to the sacrament of penance, that is, confession and satisfaction, as administered by the clergy.
3. Yet it does not mean solely inner repentance; such inner repentance is worthless unless it produces various outward mortifications of the flesh.
4. The penalty of sin remains as long as the hatred of self, that is, true inner repentance, until our entrance into the kingdom of heaven.
5. The pope neither desires nor is able to remit any penalties except those imposed by his own authority or that of the canons.
6. The pope cannot remit any guilt, except by declaring and showing that it has been remitted by God; or, to be sure, by remitting guilt in cases reserved to his judgment. If his right to grant remission in these cases were disregarded, the guilt would certainly remain unforgiven.
7. God remits guilt to no one unless at the same time he humbles him in all things and makes him submissive to his vicar the priest.
8. The penitential canons are imposed only on the living, and, according to the canons themselves, nothing should be imposed on the dying.
9. Therefore the Holy Spirit through the pope is kind to us insofar as the pope in his decrees always makes exception of the article of death and of necessity.
10. Those priests act ignorantly and wickedly who, in the case of the dying, reserve canonical penalties for purgatory.
11. Those tares of changing the canonical penalty to the penalty of purgatory were evidently sown while the bishops slept [Matt. 13:25].
12. In former times canonical penalties were imposed, not after, but before absolution, as tests of true contrition.
13. The dying are freed by death from all penalties, are already dead as far as the canon laws are concerned, and have a right to be released from them.

14. Imperfect piety or love on the part of the dying person necessarily brings with it great fear; and the smaller the love, the greater the fear.
15. This fear or horror is sufficient in itself, to say nothing of other things, to constitute the penalty of purgatory, since it is very near the horror of despair.
16. Hell, purgatory, and heaven seem to differ the same as despair, fear, and assurance of salvation.
17. It seems as though for the souls in purgatory fear should necessarily decrease and love increase.
18. Furthermore, it does not seem proved, either by reason or Scripture, that souls in purgatory are outside the state of merit, that is, unable to grow in love.
19. Nor does it seem proved that should in purgatory, at least not all f them, are certain an assured of their own salvation, even if we ourselves may be entirely certain of it.
20. Therefore the pope, when he uses the words "plenary remission of all penalties," does not actually mean "all penalties," but only those imposed by himself.
21. Thus those indulgence preachers are in error who say that a man is absolved from every penalty and saved by papal indulgences.
22. As a matter of fact, the pope remits to souls in purgatory no penalty which, according to canon law, they should have paid in this life.
23. If remission of all penalties whatsoever could be granted to anyone at all, certainly it would be granted only to the most perfect, that is, to very few.
24. For this reason most people are necessarily deceived by that indiscriminate and high-sounding promise of release from penalty.
25. That power which the pope has in general over purgatory corresponds to the power which any bishop or curate has in a particular way in his own diocese and parish.
26. The pope does very well when he grants remission to souls in purgatory, not by the power of the keys, which he does not have, but by way of intercession for them.
27. They preach only human doctrines who say that as soon as the money clinks into the money chest, the soul flies out of purgatory.
28. It is certain that when money clinks in the money chest, greed and avarice can be increased; but when the church intercedes, the result is in the hands of God alone.
29. Who knows whether all souls in purgatory wish to be redeemed, since we have exceptions in St. Severinus and St. Paschal, as related in a legend.
30. No one is sure of the integrity of his own contrition, much less of having received plenary remission.
31. The man who actually buys indulgences is as rare as he who is really penitent; indeed, he is exceedingly rare.
32. Those who believe that they can be certain of their salvation because they have indulgence letters will be eternally damned, together with their teachers.
33. Men must especially be on guard against those who say that the pope's pardons are that inestimable gift of God by which man is reconciled to him.
34. For the graces of indulgences are concerned only with the penalties of sacramental satisfaction established by man.
35. They who teach that contrition is not necessary on the part of those who intend to buy souls out of purgatory or to buy confessional privileges preach unchristian doctrine.
36. Any truly repentant Christian has a right to full remission of penalty and guilt, even without indulgence letters.
37. Any true Christian, whether living or dead, participates in all the blessings of Christ and the church; and this is granted him by God, even without indulgence letters.

38. Nevertheless, papal remission and blessing are by no means to be disregarded, for they are, as I have said (Thesis 6), the proclamation of the divine remission.

39. It is very difficult, even for the most learned theologians, at one and the same time to commend to the people the bounty of indulgences and the need of true contrition.

40. A Christian who is truly contrite seeks and loves to pay penalties for his sins; the bounty of indulgences, however, relaxes penalties and causes men to hate them -- at least it furnishes occasion for hating them.

41. Papal indulgences must be preached with caution, lest people erroneously think that they are preferable to other good works of love.

42. Christians are to be taught that the pope does not intend that the buying of indulgences should in any way be compared with works of mercy.

43. Christians are to be taught that he who gives to the poor or lends to the needy does a better deed than he who buys indulgences.

44. Because love grows by works of love, man thereby becomes better. Man does not, however, become better by means of indulgences but is merely freed from penalties.

45. Christians are to be taught that he who sees a needy man and passes him by, yet gives his money for indulgences, does not buy papal indulgences but God's wrath.

46. Christians are to be taught that, unless they have more than they need, they must reserve enough for their family needs and by no means squander it on indulgences.

47. Christians are to be taught that they buying of indulgences is a matter of free choice, not commanded.

48 Christians are to be taught that the pope, in granting indulgences, needs and thus desires their devout prayer more than their money.

49. Christians are to be taught that papal indulgences are useful only if they do not put their trust in them, but very harmful if they lose their fear of God because of them.

50. Christians are to be taught that if the pope knew the exactions of the indulgence preachers, he would rather that the basilica of St. Peter were burned to ashes than built up with the skin, flesh, and bones of his sheep.

51. Christians are to be taught that the pope would and should wish to give of his own money, even though he had to sell the basilica of St. Peter, to many of those from whom certain hawkers of indulgences cajole money.

52. It is vain to trust in salvation by indulgence letters, even though the indulgence commissary, or even the pope, were to offer his soul as security.

53. They are the enemies of Christ and the pope who forbid altogether the preaching of the Word of God in some churches in order that indulgences may be preached in others.

54. Injury is done to the Word of God when, in the same sermon, an equal or larger amount of time is devoted to indulgences than to the Word.

55. It is certainly the pope's sentiment that if indulgences, which are a very insignificant thing, are celebrated with one bell, one procession, and one ceremony, then the gospel, which is the very greatest thing, should be preached with a hundred bells, a hundred processions, a hundred ceremonies.

56. The true treasures of the church, out of which the pope distributes indulgences, are not sufficiently discussed or known among the people of Christ.

57. That indulgences are not temporal treasures is certainly clear, for many indulgence sellers do not distribute them freely but only gather them.

58. Nor are they the merits of Christ and the saints, for, even without the pope, the latter always work grace for the inner man, and the cross, death, and hell for the outer man.
59. St. Lawrence said that the poor of the church were the treasures of the church, but he spoke according to the usage of the word in his own time.
60. Without want of consideration we say that the keys of the church, given by the merits of Christ, are that treasure.
61. For it is clear that the pope's power is of itself sufficient for the remission of penalties and cases reserved by himself.
62. The true treasure of the church is the most holy gospel of the glory and grace of God.
63. But this treasure is naturally most odious, for it makes the first to be last (Mt. 20:16).
64. On the other hand, the treasure of indulgences is naturally most acceptable, for it makes the last to be first.
65. Therefore the treasures of the gospel are nets with which one formerly fished for men of wealth.
66. The treasures of indulgences are nets with which one now fishes for the wealth of men.
67. The indulgences which the demagogues acclaim as the greatest graces are actually understood to be such only insofar as they promote gain.
68. They are nevertheless in truth the most insignificant graces when compared with the grace of God and the piety of the cross.
69. Bishops and curates are bound to admit the commissaries of papal indulgences with all reverence.
70. But they are much more bound to strain their eyes and ears lest these men preach their own dreams instead of what the pope has commissioned.
71. Let him who speaks against the truth concerning papal indulgences be anathema and accursed.
72. But let him who guards against the lust and license of the indulgence preachers be blessed.
73. Just as the pope justly thunders against those who by any means whatever contrive harm to the sale of indulgences.
74. Much more does he intend to thunder against those who use indulgences as a pretext to contrive harm to holy love and truth.
75. To consider papal indulgences so great that they could absolve a man even if he had done the impossible and had violated the mother of God is madness.
76. We say on the contrary that papal indulgences cannot remove the very least of venial sins as far as guilt is concerned.
77. To say that even St. Peter if he were now pope, could not grant greater graces is blasphemy against St. Peter and the pope.
78. We say on the contrary that even the present pope, or any pope whatsoever, has greater graces at his disposal, that is, the gospel, spiritual powers, gifts of healing, etc., as it is written, 1 Co 12[:28].
79. To say that the cross emblazoned with the papal coat of arms, and set up by the indulgence preachers is equal in worth to the cross of Christ is blasphemy.
80. The bishops, curates, and theologians who permit such talk to be spread among the people will have to answer for this.
81. This unbridled preaching of indulgences makes it difficult even for learned men to rescue the reverence which is due the pope from slander or from the shrewd questions of the laity.
82. Such as: "Why does not the pope empty purgatory for the sake of holy love and the dire need of the souls that are there if he redeems an infinite number of souls for the sake of miserable money with which to build a church?" The former reason would be most just; the latter is most trivial.

83. Again, "Why are funeral and anniversary masses for the dead continued and why does he not return or permit the withdrawal of the endowments founded for them, since it is wrong to pray for the redeemed?"

84. Again, "What is this new piety of God and the pope that for a consideration of money they permit a man who is impious and their enemy to buy out of purgatory the pious soul of a friend of God and do not rather, because of the need of that pious and beloved soul, free it for pure love's sake?"

85. Again, "Why are the penitential canons, long since abrogated and dead in actual fact and through disuse, now satisfied by the granting of indulgences as though they were still alive and in force?"

86. Again, "Why does not the pope, whose wealth is today greater than the wealth of the richest Crassus, build this one basilica of St. Peter with his own money rather than with the money of poor believers?"

87. Again, "What does the pope remit or grant to those who by perfect contrition already have a right to full remission and blessings?"

88. Again, "What greater blessing could come to the church than if the pope were to bestow these remissions and blessings on every believer a hundred times a day, as he now does but once?"

89. "Since the pope seeks the salvation of souls rather than money by his indulgences, why does he suspend the indulgences and pardons previously granted when they have equal efficacy?"

90. To repress these very sharp arguments of the laity by force alone, and not to resolve them by giving reasons, is to expose the church and the pope to the ridicule of their enemies and to make Christians unhappy.

91. If, therefore, indulgences were preached according to the spirit and intention of the pope, all these doubts would be readily resolved. Indeed, they would not exist.

92. Away, then, with all those prophets who say to the people of Christ, "Peace, peace," and there is no peace! (Jer 6:14)

93. Blessed be all those prophets who say to the people of Christ, "Cross, cross," and there is no cross!

94. Christians should be exhorted to be diligent in following Christ, their Head, through penalties, death and hell.

95. And thus be confident of entering into heaven through many tribulations rather than through the false security of peace (Acts 14:22).

Source: *Luther's Works, Volume 31, Career of the Reformer: 1*, ed. Harold J. Grimm (Philadelphia: Muhlenberg Press, 1957), pp. 25-33.

15.2

✦

SIXTY-SEVEN ARTICLES, ULRICH ZWINGLI

With the Ninety-Five Theses *of Luther, the Protestant Reformation had begun. Luther had probably not intended to break away from the church when he first questioned the practice of indulgences, but that was the end result. Particularly appealing to many Christians across Europe was Luther's insistence that scripture alone should be the source of Christian doctrine. Ulrich Zwingli (1484-1531) began preaching on the centrality of scripture in 1523 and was immediately controversial; a town council was called after much debate proclaimed Zwingli to be the spiritual leader of the city and encouraged him to continue his preaching. The Reformation begun by Luther in Germany had spread to Switzerland.*

Although he was influenced by Luther, Zwingli was no Lutheran. The two theologians differed greatly on certain doctrines, particularly their interpretation of the nature of the sacraments and the relationship between church and state. Zwingli envisioned Zurich as a "Christian" city, and theorized that the civil authority came from God.

The following source lists Zwingli's plan for Zurich.

---- ✣ ----

QUESTIONS

1. What is Zwingli's view of the papacy?
2. According to Zwingli, what is the relationship between the individual and God?
3. How does Zwingli define the priesthood?

The articles and opinions below, I, Ulrich Zwingli, confess to have preached in the worthy city of Zurich as based upon the Scriptures which are called inspired by God, and I offer to protect and conquer with the said articles, and where I have not now correctly understood said Scriptures I shall allow myself to be taught better, but only from said Scriptures.

I. All who say that the Gospel is invalid without the confirmation of the Church err and slander God.

II. The sum and substance of the Gospel is that our Lord Jesus Christ, the true Son of God, has made known to us the will of his heavenly Father, and has with his innocence released us from death and reconciled God.

III. Hence Christ is the only way to salvation for all who ever were, are and shall be.

IV. Who seeks or points out another door errs, yea, he is a murderer of souls and a thief.

V. Hence all who consider other teachings equal to or higher than the Gospel err, and do not know what the Gospel is.

VI. For Jesus Christ is the guide and leader, promised by God to all human beings, which promise was fulfilled.

VII. That he is an eternal salvation and head of all believers, who are his body, but which is dead and can do nothing without him.

VIII. From this follows first that all who dwell in the head are members and children of God, and that is the church or communion of the saints, the bride of Christ, *Ecclesia catholica.*

IX. Furthermore, that as the members of the body can do nothing without the control of the head, so no one in the body of Christ can do the least without his head, Christ.

X. As that man is mad whose limbs (try to) do something without his head, tearing, wounding, injuring himself; thus when the members of Christ undertake something without their head,

Christ, they are mad, and injure and burden themselves with unwise ordinances.

XI. Hence we see in the clerical (so-called) ordinances, concerning their splendor, riches, classes, titles, laws, a cause of all foolishness, for they do not also agree with the head.

XII. Thus they still rage, not on account of the head (for that one is eager to bring forth in these times from the grace of God,) but because one will not let them rage, but tries to compel them to listen to the head.

XIII. Where this (the head) is hearkened to one learns clearly and plainly the will of God, and man is attracted by his spirit to him and changed into him.

XIV. Therefore all Christian people shall use their best diligence that the Gospel of Christ be preached alike everywhere.

XV. For in the faith rests our salvation, and in unbelief our damnation; for all truth is clear in him.

XVI. In the Gospel one learns that human doctrines and decrees do not aid in salvation.

ABOUT THE POPE

XVII. That Christ is the only eternal high priest, wherefrom it follows that those who have called themselves high priests have opposed the honor and power of Christ, yea, cast it out.

ABOUT THE MASS

XVIII. That Christ, having sacrificed himself once, is to eternity a certain and valid sacrifice for the sins of all faithful, wherefrom it follows that the mass is not a sacrifice, but is a remembrance of the sacrifice and assurance of the salvation which Christ has given us.

XIX. That Christ is the only mediator between God and us.

XX. That God desires to give us all things in his name, whence it follows that outside of this life we need no mediator except himself.

XXI. That when we pray for each other on earth, we do so in such fashion that we believe that all things are given to us through Christ alone.

ABOUT GOOD WORKS

XXII. That Christ is our justice, from which follows that our works in so far as they are good, so far they are of Christ, but in so far as they are ours, they are neither right nor good.

CONCERNING CLERICAL PROPERTY

XXIII. That Christ scorns the property and pomp of this world, whence from it follows that those who attract wealth to themselves in his name slander him terribly when they make him a pretext for their avarice and wilfullness.

CONCERNING THE FORBIDDING OF FOOD

XXIV. That no Christian is bound to do those things which God has not decreed, therefore one may eat at all times all food, wherefrom one learns that the decree about cheese and butter is a Roman swindle.

ABOUT HOLIDAY AND PILGRIMAGE

XXV. That time and place is under the jurisdiction of Christian people, and man with them, wherefrom is learnt that those who fix time and place deprive the Christians of their liberty.

ABOUT HOODS, DRESS, INSIGNIA

XXVI. That God is displeased with nothing so much as with hypocrisy; whence is learnt that all is gross hypocrisy and profligacy which is mere show before men. Under this condemnation fall hoods, insignia, plates, etc.

ABOUT ORDER AND SECTS

XXVII. That all Christian men are brethren of Christ and brethren of one another, and shall create no father (for themselves) on earth. Under this condemnation fall orders, sects, brotherhoods, etc.

ABOUT THE MARRIAGE OF ECCLESIASTS

XXVIII. That all which God has allowed or not forbidden is righteous, hence marriage is permitted to all human beings.

XXIX. That all who are called clericals sin when they do not protect themselves by marriage after they have become conscious that God has not enabled them to remain chaste.

ABOUT THE VOW OF CHASTITY

XXX. That those who promise chastity [outside of matrimony] take foolishly or childishly too much upon themselves, whence is learnt that those who make such vows do wrong to the pious being.

ABOUT THE BAN

XXXI. That no special person can impose the ban upon any one, but the Church, that is the congregation of those among whom the one to be banned dwells, together with their watch man, *i.e.*, the pastor.

XXXII. That one may ban only him who gives public offence.

ABOUT ILLEGAL PROPERTY

XXXIII. That property unrighteously acquired shall not be given to temples, monasteries, cathedrals, clergy or nuns, but to the needy, if it cannot be returned to the legal owner.

ABOUT MAGISTRY

XXXIV. The spiritual (so-called) power has no justification for its pomp in the teaching of Christ.

XXXV. But the lay has power and confirmation from the deed and doctrine of Christ.

XXXVI. All that the spiritual so-called state claims to have of power and protection belongs to the lay, if they wish to be Christians.

XXXVII. To them, furthermore, all Christians owe obedience without exception.

XXXVIII. In so far as they do not command that which is contrary to God.

XXXIX. Therefore all their laws shall be in harmony with the divine will, so that they protect the oppressed, even if he does not complain.

XL, They alone may put to death justly, also, only those who give public offence (if God is not offended let another thing be commanded).

XLI. If they give good advice and help to those for whom they must account to God, then these owe to them bodily assistance.

XLII. But if they are unfaithful and transgress the laws of Christ they may be deposed in the name of God.

XLIII. In short, the realm of him is best and most stable who rules in the name of God alone, and his is worst and most unstable who rules in accordance with his own will.

ABOUT PRAYER

XLIV. Real petitioners call to God in spirit and truly, without great ado before men.

XLV. Hypocrites do their work so that they may be seen by men, also receive their reward in this life.

XLVI. Hence it must always follow that church-song and outcry without devoutness, and only for reward, is seeking either fame before the men or gain.

ABOUT OFFENCE

XLVII. Bodily death a man should suffer before he offend or scandalize a Christian.

XLVIII. Who through stupidness or ignorance is offended without cause, he should not be left sick or weak, but he should be made strong, that he may not consider as a sin which is not a sin.

XLIX. Greater offence I know not than that one does not allow priests to have wives, but permits them to hire prostitutes. Out upon the shame!

ABOUT REMITTANCE OF SIN

L. God alone remits sin through Jesus Christ, his Son, and alone our Lord.

LI. Who assigns this to creatures detracts from the honor of God and gives it to him who is not God; this is real idolatry.

LII. Hence the confession which is made to the priest or neighbor shall not be declared to be a remittance of sin, but only a seeking for advice.

LIII. Works of penance coming from the counsel of human beings (except the ban) do not cancel sin; they are imposed as a menace to others.

LIV. Christ has borne all our pains and labor. Hence whoever assigns to works of penance what belongs to Christ errs and slanders God.

LV. Whoever pretends to remit to a penitent being any sin would not be a vicar of God or St. Peter, but of the devil.

LVI. Whoever remits any sin only for the sake of money is the companion of Simon and Balaam, and the real messenger of the devil personified.

ABOUT PURGATORY

LVII. The true divine Scriptures know naught about purgatory after this life.

LVIII. The sentence of the dead is known to God only.

LVIX. And the less God has let us know concerning it, the less we should undertake to know about it.

LX. That man earnestly calls to God to show mercy to the dead I do not condemn, but to determine a period of time therefor (seven years for a mortal sin), and to lie for the sake of gain, is not human, but devilish.

ABOUT THE PRIESTHOOD.

LXI. About the consecration which the priests have received in late times the Scriptures know nothing.

LXII. Furthermore, they know no priests except those who proclaim the word of God.

LXIII. They command honor should be shown, i.e., to furnish them with food for the body.

ABOUT THE CESSATION OF MISUSAGES

LXIV. All those who recognize their errors shall not be allowed to suffer, but to die in peace, and thereafter arrange in a Christian manner their bequests to the Church.

LXV. Those who do not wish to confess, God will probably take care of. Hence no force shall be used against their body, unless it be that they behave so criminally that one cannot do without that.

LXVI. All the clerical superiors shall at once settle down, and with unanimity set up the cross of Christ, not the money-chests, or they will perish, for I tell thee the ax is raised against the tree.

LXVII. If any one wishes conversation with me concerning interest, tithes, unbaptized children or confirmation, I am willing to answer.

Let no one undertake here to argue with sophistry or human foolishness, but come to the

Scriptures to accept them as the judge (foras cares! the Scriptures breathe the Spirit of God), so that the truth either may be found, or if found, as I hope, retained.

Amen.

Thus may God rule.

The basis and commentary of these articles will soon appear in print.

Sources: *Ulrich Zwingli (1484-1531): Selected Works*, ed. Samuel Macauley Jackson (Philadelphia: University of Philadelphia Press, 1901, 1972), pp. 111-117.

15.3

✣

"RAPTURE OF THE SOUL," TERESA OF AVILA

The Catholic Church was not unresponsive to the charges of reformers such as Luther and Zwingli. There were two stages to the Counter-Reformation that took place within the Catholic Church. One was the official response by both pope and emperor, which were to condemn Luther and the Protestants, and to summon a church council at Trent in 1545-1563, which confirmed all Catholic doctrines and practices. The second response was a movement of spiritual renewal, which promoted a more personal relationship between humanity and God. New religious orders such as the Society of Jesus (the Jesuits) and the Capuchins (a reformed Franciscan order) emerged. Missionary activity also increased, helped by the discovery of the Americas and new access to Asia. Mysticism had a resurgence in popularity, which incorporated personal piety and traditional Catholic faith. Teresa of Avila (1515-1582) was a Carmelite nun who had intense visions of God. In the following excerpt from her mystical text, the Interior Castle, *she discusses the soul's rapturous union with God.*

✣

QUESTIONS

1. How is Teresa's understanding of rapture related to her gender?
2. Compare this with Luther's Ninety-Five Theses. How do the two differ in their description of how the soul knows God?
3. Who do you think was the intended audience of this mystical text?

. . . I want to put down here some kinds of rapture that I've come to understand because I've discussed them with so many spiritual persons. But I don't know whether I shall succeed as I did when I wrote elsewhere about them and other things that occur in this dwelling place. On account of certain reasons it seems worthwhile to speak of these kinds of rapture again — if for no other reason, so that everything related to these dwelling places will be put down here together.

3. One kind of rapture is that in which the soul even though not in prayer is touched by some word it remembers or hears about God. It seems that His Majesty from the interior of the soul makes the spark we mentioned increase, for He is moved with compassion in seeing the soul suffer so long a time from its desire. All burnt up, the soul is renewed like the phoenix, and one can devoutly believe that its faults are pardoned. Now that it is so pure, the Lord joins it with Himself, without anyone understanding what is happening except these two; nor does the soul itself understand in a way that can afterward be explained. Yet, it does have interior understanding, for this experience is not like that of fainting or convulsion; in these latter nothing is understood inwardly or outwardly.

4. What I know in this case is that the soul was never so awake to the things of God nor did it have such deep enlightenment and knowledge of His Majesty. This will seem impossible, for if the faculties are so absorbed that we can say they are dead, and likewise the senses, how can a soul know that it

understands this secret? I don't know, nor perhaps does any creature but only the Creator. And this goes for many other things that take place in this state — I mean in these two dwelling places, for there is no closed door between the one and the other. Because there are things in the last that are not revealed to those who have not yet reached it, I thought I should divide them.

5. When the soul is in this suspension, the Lord likes to show it some secrets, things about heaven, and imaginative visions. It is able to tell of them afterward, for these remain so impressed on the memory that they are never forgotten. But when the visions are intellectual, the soul doesn't know how to speak of them. For there must be some visions during these moments that are so sublime that it's not fitting for those who live on this earth to have the further understanding necessary to explain them. However, since the soul is in possession of its senses, it can say many things about these intellectual visions.

It could be that some of you do not know what a vision is, especially an intellectual one. I shall explain at the proper time, for one who has the authority ordered me to do so. And although the explanation may not seem pertinent, it will perhaps benefit some souls.

6. Well now you will ask me: If afterward there is to be no remembrance of these sublime favors granted by the Lord to the soul in this state, what benefit do they have? O daughters, they are so great one cannot exaggerate! For even though they are unexplainable, they are well inscribed in the very interior part of the soul and are never forgotten.

But, you will insist, if there is no image and the faculties do not understand, how can the visions be remembered? I don't understand this either; but I do understand that some truths about the grandeur of God remain so fixed in this soul that even if faith were not to tell it who God is and of its obligation to believe that He is God, from that very moment it would adore Him as God, as did Jacob when he saw the ladder. By means of the ladder Jacob must have understood other secrets that he didn't know how to explain, for by seeing just a ladder on which angels descended and ascended he would not have understood such great mysteries if there had not been deeper interior enlightenment. I don't know if I'm guessing right in what I say, for although I have heard this story about Jacob, I don't know if I'm remembering it correctly.

7. Nor did Moses know how to describe all that he saw in the bush, but only what God wished Him to describe. But if God had not shown secrets to his soul along with a certitude that made him recognize and believe that they were from God, Moses could not have entered into so many severe trials. But he must have understood such deep things among the thorns of that bush that the vision gave him the courage to do what he did for the people of Israel. So, sisters, we don't have to look for reasons to understand the hidden things of God. Since we believe He is powerful, clearly we must believe that a worm with as limited a power as ours will not understand His grandeurs. Let us praise Him, for He is pleased that we come to know some of them.

8. I have been wanting to find some comparison by which to explain what I'm speaking about, and I don't think there is any that fits. But let's use this one: You enter into the room of a king or great lord, or I believe they call it the treasure chamber, where there are countless kinds of glass and earthen vessels and other things so arranged that almost all of these objects are seen upon entering. Once I was brought to a room like this in the house of the Duchess of Alba where, while I was on a journey, obedience ordered me to stay because of this lady's insistence with my superiors. I was amazed on entering and wondered what gain could be gotten from that conglomeration of things, and I saw that one could praise the Lord at seeing so many different kinds of objects, and now I laugh to myself on realizing how the experience has helped me here in my explanation. Although I was in that room for a while, there was so much there to see that I soon forgot it all; none of those pieces has remained in my memory any more than if I had never seen them, nor would I know how to explain the workmanship of any of them. I can

only say in general that I remember seeing everything. Likewise with this favor, the soul, while it is made one with God, is placed in this empyreal room that we must have interiorly. For, clearly, the soul has some of these dwelling places since God abides within it. And although the Lord must not want the soul to see these secrets every time it is in this ecstasy, for it can be so absorbed in enjoying Him that a sublime good like that is sufficient for it, sometimes He is pleased that the absorption decrease and the soul see at once what is in that room. After it returns to itself, the soul is left with that representation of the grandeurs it saw; but it cannot describe any of them, nor do its natural powers grasp any more than what God wished that it see supernaturally.

9. You, therefore, might object that I admit that the soul sees and that the vision is an imaginative one. But I'm not saying that, for I'm not dealing with an imaginative vision but with an intellectual one. Since I have no learning, I don't know how in my dullness to explain anything. If what I have said up to now about this prayer is worthwhile, I know clearly that I'm not the one who has said it.

I hold that if at times in its raptures the soul doesn't understand these secrets, its raptures are not given by God but are caused by some natural weakness. It can happen to persons with a weak constitution, as is so with women, that any spiritual force will overcome the natural powers, and the soul will be absorbed as I believe I mentioned in reference to the prayer of quiet. These experiences have nothing to do with rapture. In a rapture, believe me, God carries off for Himself the entire soul, and, as to someone who is His own and His spouse, He begins showing it some little part of the kingdom that it has gained by being espoused to Him. However small that part of His kingdom may be, everything that there is in this great God is magnificent. And He doesn't want any hindrance from anyone, neither from the faculties nor from the senses, but He immediately commands the doors of all these dwelling places to be closed; and only that door to His room remains open so that we can enter. Blessed be so much mercy; they will be rightly cursed who have not wanted to benefit by it and who have lost this Lord.

10. O my sisters, what nothingness it is, that which we leave! Nor is what we do anything, nor all that we could do for a God who thus wishes to communicate Himself to a worm! And if we hope to enjoy this blessing even in this present life, what are we doing? What is causing us to delay? What is enough to make us, even momentarily, stop looking for this Lord as did the bride in the streets and in the squares? Oh, what a mockery everything in the world is if it doesn't lead us and help us toward this blessing even if its delights and riches and joys, as much of them as imaginable, were to last forever! It is all loathsome dung compared to these treasures that will be enjoyed without end. Nor are these anything in comparison with having as our own the Lord of all the treasures of heaven and earth.

11. O human blindness! How long, how long before this dust will be removed from our eyes! Even though among ourselves the dust doesn't seem to be capable of blinding us completely, I see some specks, some tiny pebbles that if we allow them to increase will be enough to do us great harm. On the contrary, for the love of God, Sisters, let us benefit by these faults so as to know our misery, and they will give us clearer vision as did the mud to the blind man cured by our Spouse. Thus, seeing ourselves so imperfect, let us increase our supplications that His Majesty may draw good out of our miseries so that we might be pleasing to Him.

12. I have digressed a great deal without realizing it. Pardon me, Sisters, and believe me that having reached these grandeurs of God (I mean, reached the place where I must speak of them), I cannot help but feel very sorry to see what we lose through our own fault. Even though it is true that these are blessing the Lord gives to whomever He wills, His Majesty would give them all to us if we loved Him as He loves us. He doesn't desire anything else than to have those to whom to give. His riches do not lessen because He gives them away.

13. Well now, to get back to what I was saying, the Spouse commands that the doors of the dwelling places be closed and even those of the castle and the outer wall. For in desiring to carry off this soul, He takes away the breath so that, even though the other senses sometimes last a little longer, a person cannot speak at all; although at other times everything is taken away at once, and the hands and the body grow cold so that the person doesn't seem to have any life; nor sometimes is it known whether he is breathing. This situation lasts but a short while, I mean in its intensity; for when this extreme suspension lets up a little, it seems that the body returns to itself somewhat and is nourished so as to die again and give more life to the soul. Nevertheless, so extreme an ecstasy doesn't last long.

15.4

THE EDICT OF NANTES

The Wars of Religion began in 1524 with a peasant rebellion in Germany. In France, the religious divisions turned into a civil war between noble families. John Calvin (1509-1564) began preaching in Paris in 1533, although he fled in 1536 to avoid persecution. Many people (including nobles) were still drawn to Calvinism (known in France as Huguenots) for spiritual reasons; others saw this as a chance to demand social and political reforms. In 1559 the monarchy faced another crisis: a series of weak kings, whose state was run by their mother Catherine de' Medici and the fanatically anti-Protestant Guise family. By 1562 the powerful Bourbons, relatives of the king and rivals of the Guise, were Huguenots. War broke out in 1562 when the Duc of Guise massacred Huguenots. In 1572 a larger massacre of Huguenots occurred on St. Bartholomew's Day, ordered by the king, Catherine, and Guise family. Huguenots had been invited to Paris to celebrate the marriage of Henry of Navarre (a Huguenot himself) to the king's sister.

But Henry did marry Margaret, the king's sister. When her two remaining brothers died, Henry became the next king of France (1594). He agreed to convert to Catholicism, but remained sympathetic to the Huguenots. In 1598 he issued this Edict.

QUESTIONS

1. Does the Edict offer full toleration to the Huguenots? Explain why or why not.
2. How does Henry think the state should best deal with the recent violence?
3. How much freedom is actually promised to the Huguenots?

Henry, by the grace of God king of France and of Navarre, to all to whom these presents come, greeting:

Among the infinite benefits which it has pleased God to heap upon us, the most signal and precious is his granting us the strength and ability to withstand the fearful disorders and troubles which prevailed on our advent in this kingdom. The realm was so torn by innumerable factions and sects that the most legitimate of all the parties was fewest in numbers. God has given us strength to stand out against this storm; we have finally surmounted the waves and made our port of safety, — peace for our state. For which his be the glory all in all, and ours a free recognition of his grace in making use of our instrumentality in the good work.... We implore and await from the Divine Goodness the same protection and favor which he has ever granted to this kingdom from the beginning....

We have, by this perpetual and irrevocable edict established and proclaimed and do establish and proclaim:

I. First, that the recollection of everything done be one party or the other between March, 1585, and our accession to the crown, and during all the preceding period of troubles, remain obliterated and forgotten, as if no such things had ever happened.

III. We ordain that the Catholic Apostolic and Roman religion shall be restored and reestablished in all places and localities of this our kingdom and countries subject to our sway, where the exercise of the same has been interrupted, in order that it may be peaceably and freely exercised, without any trouble or hindrance: forbidding very expressly all persons, of whatsoever estate, quality, or condition, from troubling, molesting, or disturbing ecclesiastics in the celebration of divine service, in the enjoyment or collection of tithes, fruits, or revenues of their benefices, and all other rights and dues belonging to them: and that all those who during the troubles have taken possession of churches. Houses, goods or revenues, belonging to the said ecclesiastics, shall surrender to them entire possession and peaceable enjoyment of such rights, liberties, and sureties as they had before they were deprived of them.

VI. And in order to leave no occasion for troubles or differences between our subjects, we have permitted, and herewith permit, those of the said religion called Reformed to live and abide in all the cities and places of this our kingdom and countries of our sway, without being annoyed, molested, or compelled to do anything in the matter of religion contrary to their consciences, . . . upon condition that they comport themselves in other respects according to that which is contained in this our present edict.

VII. It is permitted to all lords, gentlemen, and other persons making profession of the said religion called Reformed, holding the right of high justice [or a certain feudal tenure], to exercise the said religion in their houses.

IX. We also permit those of the said religion to make and continue the exercise of the same in all villages and places of our dominion where it was established by them and publicly enjoyed several and divers times in the year 1597, up to the end of the month of August, notwithstanding all decrees and judgments to the contrary.

XIII. We very expressly forbid to all those of the said religion its exercise, either in respect to ministry, regulation, discipline, or the public instruction of children, or otherwise, in this our kingdom and lands of our dominion, otherwise than in the places permitted and granted by the present edict.

XIV. It is forbidden as well to perform any function of the said religion in our court or retinue, or in our lands and territories beyond the mountains, or in our city of Paris. or within five leagues of the said city.

XVIII. We also forbid all our subjects, of whatever quality and condition, from carrying off be force or persuasion, against the will of their parents, the children of the said religion, in order to cause them to be baptized or confirmed in the Catholic Apostolic and Roman Church; and the same is forbidden to those of the said religion called Reformed, upon penalty of being punished with especial severity.

XXI. Books concerning the said religion called Reformed may not be printed and publicly sold, except in cities and places where the public exercise of the said religion is permitted.

XXII. We ordain that there shall be no difference or distinction made in respect to the said religion, in receiving pupils to be instructed in universities, colleges, and schools; nor in receiving the sick and poor into hospitals, retreats and public charities.

XXIII. Those of the said religion called Reformed shall be obliged to respect the laws of the Catholic Apostolic and Roman Church, recognized in this our kingdom, for the consummation of marriages contracted, or to be contracted, as regards the degrees of consanguinity and kinship.

Source: James Harvey Robinson, ed., *Readings in European History*, Vol. II, (Boston: Ginn and Company, 1904, 1934), pp. 183-85.

15.5

✤

MALLEUS MALEFICARUM

Another manifestation of the Wars of Religion was the witch hunts. There had been restrictions against witchcraft within the medieval Catholic Church, but active persecution of people suspected of witchcraft began in 1484 with a papal bull, which specifically allowed the inquisition to use torture on suspected witches. The witch trials begin in earnest in the mid-sixteenth century, and continue until about mid-seventeenth century. "Witches" were yet another target of religious violence: both Catholics and Protestants persecuted men and women suspected of witchcraft.

The following source is from 1486. It is an excerpt from the Malleus Maleficarum, *the "Hammer of Witches" written by two Dominican friars. It was intended to be handbook for the identification, capture, torturing, and execution of suspected witches. The* Malleus *was popular with both Catholics and Protestants. The following excerpt identifies a group that was deemed particularly susceptible to interest in witchcraft: women.*

✤

QUESTIONS

1. How exactly is "witch craft" being defined in this period?
2. Why were women supposed to be so susceptible?
3. This text was written by a Catholic, yet the basic principles of it were also used by Protestant witch hunters. What "authority" does this text have for Protestants?

Why Superstition is chiefly found in Women.

As for the first question, why a greater number of witches is found in the fragile feminine sex than among men; it is indeed a fact that it were idle to contradict, since it is accredited by actual experience, apart from the verbal testimony of credibly witnesses. And without in any way detracting from a sex in which God has always taken great glory that His might should be spread abroad, let us say that various men have assigned various reasons for this fact, which nevertheless agree in principle. Wherefore it is good, for the admonition of women, to speak of this matter; and it has often been proved by experience that they are eager to hear of it, so long as it is set forth with discretion.

For some learned men propound this reason; that there are three things in nature, the Tongue, an Ecclesiastic, and a Woman, which know no moderation in goodness or vice; and when they exceed the bounds of their condition they reach the greatest heights and the lowest depths of goodness and vice. When they are governed by a good spirit, they are most excellent in virtue; but when they are governed by an evil spirit, they indulge the worst possible vices....

Now the wickedness of women is spoken of in *Ecclesiasticus* xxv: There is no head above the head of a serpent: and there is no wrath above the wrath of a woman. I had rather dwell with a lion and a dragon than to keep house with a wicked woman. And among much which in that place precedes and follows about a wicked woman, he concludes: All wickedness is but little to the wickedness of a woman. Wherefore S. John Chrysostom says on the text, It is not good to marry (*S. Matthew* xix): What else is woman but a foe to friendship, an unescapable punishment, a necessary evil, a natural temptation, a desirable calamity, a domestic danger, a delectable detriment, an evil of nature, painted with fair colours! Therefore if it be a sin to divorce her when she ought to be kept, it is indeed a necessary torture; for either we commit adultery by divorcing her, or we must endure daily strife. Cicero in his second book of *The Rhetorics* says: The many lusts of men lead them into one sin, but the lust of women leads them into all sins; for the root of all women's vices is avarice. And Seneca says in his *Tragedies:* A woman either loves or hates; there is no third grade. And the tears of woman are a deception, for they may spring from true grief, or they may be a snare. When a woman thinks alone, she thinks evil....

And all this is made clear also in the New Testament concerning women and virgins and other holy women who have by faith led nations and kingdoms away from the worship of idols to the Christian religion. Anyone who looks at Vincent of Beauvais (*in Spe. Histo.*, XXVI. 9) will find marvellous things of the conversion of Hungary by the most Christian Gilia, and of the Franks by Clotilda, the wife of Clovis. Wherefore in many vituperations that we read against women, the word woman is used to mean the lust of the flesh. As it is said: I have found a woman more bitter than death, and good woman subject to carnal lust.

Other again have propounded other reasons why there are more superstitious women found than men. And the first is, that they are more credulous; and since the chief aim of the devil is to corrupt faith, therefore he rather attacks them. See *Ecclesiasticus* xix: He that is quick to believe is light-minded, and shall be diminished. The second reason is, that women are naturally more impressionable, and more ready to receive the influence of a disembodied spirit; and that when they use this quality well they are very good, but when they use it ill they are very evil.

The third reason is that they have slippery tongues, and are unable to conceal from the fellow-women those things which by evil arts they know; and, since they are weak, they find an easy and secret manner of vindicating themselves by witchcraft. See *Ecclesiasticus* as quoted above: I had rather dwell with a lion and a dragon than to keep house with a wicked woman. All wickedness is but little to the wickedness of a woman. And to this may be added that, as they are very impressionable, they act accordingly.

There are also others who bring forward yet other reasons, of which preachers should be very careful how they make use. For it is true that in the Old Testament the Scriptures have much that is evil to say about women, and this because of the first temptress, Eve, and her imitators; yet afterwards in the New Testament we find a change of name, as from Eva to Ave (as S. Jerome says), and the whole sin of Eve taken away by the benediction of Mary. Therefore preachers should always say as much praise of them as possible.

But because in these times this perfidy is more often found in women than in men, as we learn by actual experience, if anyone is curious as to the reason, we may add to what has already been said the following: that since they are feebler both in mind and body, it is not surprising that they should come more under the spell of witchcraft.

For as regards intellect, or the understanding of spiritual things, they seem to be of a different nature from men; a fact which is vouched for by the logic of the authorities, backed by various examples from the Scriptures. Terence says: Women are intellectually like children. And Lactantius (*Institutiones*, III): No woman understood philosophy except Temeste. And *Proverbs* xi, as it were describing a woman, says: As a jewel of gold in a swine's snout, so is a fair woman which is without discretion.

But the natural reason is that she is more carnal than a man, as is clear from her many carnal abominations. And it should be noted that there was a defect in the formation of the first woman, since she was formed from a bent rib, that is, a rib of the breast, which is bent as it were in a contrary direction to a man. And since through this defect she is an imperfect animal, she always deceives. For Cato says: When a woman weeps she weaves snares. And again: When a woman weeps, she labours to deceive a man. And this is shown by Samson's wife, who coaxed him to tell her the riddle he had propounded to the Philistines, and told them the answer, and so deceived him. And it is clear in the case of the first woman that she had little faith; for when the serpent asked why they did not eat of every tree in Paradise, she answered: Of every tree, etc. - lest perchance we die. Thereby she showed that she doubted, and had little in the word of God. And all this is indicated by the etymology of the word; for *Femina* comes from *Fe* and *Minus*, since she is ever weaker to hold and preserve the faith. And this as regards faith is of her very nature; although both by grace and nature faith never failed in the Blessed Virgin, even at the time of Christ's Passion, when it failed in all men.

Therefore a wicked woman is by her nature quicker to waver in her faith, and consequently quicker to abjure the faith, which is the root of witchcraft.

And as to her other mental quality, that is, her natural will; when she hates someone whom she formerly loved, then she seethes with anger and impatience in her whole soul, just as the tides of the sea are always heaving and boiling. Many authorities allude to this cause. *Ecclesiasticus* xxv: There is no wrath above the wrath of a woman. And Seneca (*Tragedies*, VIII): No might of the flames or the swollen winds, no deadly weapon, is so much to be feared as the lust and hatred of a woman who has been divorced from the marriage bed....

And indeed, just as through the first defect in their intelligence they are more prone to abjure the faith; so through their second defect of inordinate affections and passions they search for, brood over, and inflict various vengeances, either by witchcraft, or by some other means. Wherefore it is no wonder that so great a number of witches exist in this sex.

Women also have weak memories; and it is a natural vice in them not to be disciplined, but to follow their own impulses without any sense of what is due; this is her whole study, and all that she keeps in her memory. So Theophrastus says: If you hand over the whole management of the house to her, but reserve some minute detail to your own judgement, she will think that you are displaying a great want of faith in her, and will stir up strife; and unless you quickly take counsel, she will prepare poison for you, and consult seers and soothsayers; and will become a witch....

If we inquire, we find that nearly all the kingdoms of the world have been overthrown by women. Troy, which was a prosperous kingdom, was, for the rape of one woman, Helen, destroyed, and many thousands of Greeks slain. The kingdom of the Jews suffered much misfortune and destruction through the accursed Jezebel, and her daughter Athaliah, queen of Judah, who caused her son's sons to be killed, that on their death she might reign herself; yet each of them was slain. The kingdom of the Romans endured much evil through Cleopatra, Queen of Egypt, that worst of women. And so with others. Therefore it is no wonder if the world now suffers through the malice of women.

And now let us examine the carnal desires of the body itself, whence has arisen unconscionable harm to human life. Justly may we say with Cato of Utica: If the world could be rid of women, we should not be without God in our intercourse. For truly, without the wickedness of women, to say nothing of witchcraft, the world would still remain proof against innumerable dangers. Hear what Valerius said to Rufinus: You do not know that women is the Chimaera, but it is good that you should know it; for that monster was of three forms; its face was that of a radiant and noble lion, it had the filthy belly of a goat, and it was armed with the virulent tail of a viper. And he means that a woman is beautiful to look upon, contaminating to the touch, and deadly to keep.

Let us consider another property of hers, the voice. For as she is a liar by nature, so in her speech she stings while she delights us. Wherefore her voice is like the song of the Sirens, who with their sweet melody entice the passers-by and kill them. For they kill them by emptying their purses, consuming their strength, and causing them to forsake God. Again Valerius says to Rufinus: When she speaks it is a delight which flavours the sin; the flower of love is a rose, because under its blossom there are hidden many thorns. See *Proverbs* v, 3-4: Her mouth is smoother than oil; that is, her speech is afterwards as bitter as absinthium. [Her throat is smoother than oil. But her end is as bitter as wormwood.]

Let us consider also her gait, posture, and habit, in which is vanity of vanities. There is no man in the world who studies so hard to please the good God as even an ordinary woman studies by her vanities to please men. An example of this is to be found in the life of Pelagia, a worldly woman who was wont to go about Antioch, tired and adorned most extravagantly. A holy father, name Nonnus, saw her and began to weep, saying to his companions, that never in all his life had he used such diligence to please God; and much more he added to this effect, which is preserved in his orations.

It is this which is lamented in *Ecclesiastes* vii, and which the Church even now laments on account of the great magnitude of witches. And I have found a woman more bitter than death, who is the hunter's snare, and her heart is a net, and her hands are bands. He that pleaseth God shall escape from her; but he that is a sinner shall be caught by her. More bitter than death, that is, than the devil: *Apocalypse* vi, 8, His name was Death. For though the devil tempted Eve to sin, yet Eve seduced Adam. And as the sin of Eve would not have brought death to our soul and body unless the sin had afterwards passed on to Adam, to which he was tempted by Eve, not by the devil, therefore she is more bitter than death....

To conclude. All witchcraft comes from carnal lust, which is in women insatiable. See *Proverbs* xxx: There are three things that are never satisfied, yea, a forth thing which says not, It is enough; that is, the mouth of the womb. Wherefore for the sake of fulfilling their lusts they consort even with devils.

From Heinrich Kramer and James Sprenger, *The Malleus Maleficarum*, trans. Montague Summers, p. 41-47. Copyright © 1970 Dover Publications, Inc. Reprinted with permission.

QUESTIONS FOR PART 15

1. Did Luther and Zwingli see their Reformation as making Christianity easier for believers?
2. Was the Reformation (Protestant or Catholic) good for women?
3. How did the Reformation exacerbate the witch-hunts?

PART 16

New World Encounters

The late fifteenth and sixteenth centuries are often called the Age of Exploration or the Age of Discovery. Both were certainly two of the major themes of the period. This was also the time of the Reformation, itself an exploration of sorts, one that examined the spiritual discoveries of the period. This chapter will examine the geographic explorations. In 1492, in a story well known to most students of Western history, Christopher Columbus made the second (to the Vikings) European discovery of the American continents. In the decades prior to this, Portuguese and Spanish navigators had begun to explore the western coast of North Africa. In the century following Columbus, Portuguese, Spanish, English, French, and Dutch sailors continued these earlier explorations of Africa and the Americas, and eventually moved into Asia as well. The drive to explore was fueled by many factors: a desire to find new routes to the riches (spices, gold, goods) of the East without having to go through the usual Muslim merchants, religious fervor (increased by the keen interests in all things religious thanks to the Reformation), a strong sense of competition against those same Muslim merchants who had for so many centuries dominated trade, and a very simple craving for adventure. Exploration was also inspired by a long tradition of tales that emphasized the mysteriousness of the East and a growing sense of curiosity about these relatively unknown lands.

Europe went into the Age of Exploration confident in itself religiously, politically, and culturally. The encounters with non-European cultures that resulted from the "new world" discoveries only increased that confidence. All too quickly the interest in exploration, discovery, and adventure became the need to conquer. Exploration for Europe meant expansion; colonies were quickly founded and empires created. Western history was effectively transformed into world history at this moment.

16.1

"Court of the Great Khan," Marco Polo

Discovery of the newly Americas was not the beginning of European explorations. An earlier exploration of Asia occurred in 1271 when a Venetian merchant family followed the Silk Road, a major trade route, from Italy to China. The Polos were looking for financial gain and trading opportunities; however, the youngest member of the family, Marco took advantage of the chance to meet with various Asian cultures and peoples. When he returned to Venice in he recorded his observations in what was known alternatively as the "Wonders of the East" or the "Millions of the East" and was tremendously popular for its colorful stories and was popular with later explorers, who sometimes used Polo's text as a literal navigational guide. Columbus not only read Polo's text, he took it with him on his voyage in 1492.

The following excerpts describe the court of Kublai Khan, emperor of China in when Polo reached China.

--- ✦ ---

QUESTIONS

1. Polo's text tells of the many wives and concubines of Kublai Khan; what impression about the Far East do you think this helped to create for Europe?
2. In describing the palace of Kublai, what aspects does Polo remark upon and emphasize?
3. Does Polo have an opinion about the Khan?

[Chapter 8]

Of the figure and stature of the Great Khan — of his four principal Wives — and of the annual selection of young women for him in the province of Ungut

Kublai, who is styled Great Khan, or Lord of Lords, is of the middle stature, that is, neither tall nor short. His limbs are well formed, and in his whole figure there is a just proportion. His complexion is fair, and occasionally suffused with red, like the bright tint of the rose, which adds much grace to his countenance. His eyes are black and handsome, his nose is well shaped and prominent.

He has four wives of the first rank, who are esteemed legitimate, and the eldest born son of any one of these succeeds to the empire, upon the decease of the Great Khan. They bear equally the title of empress, and have their separate courts. None of them have fewer than three hundred young female attendants of great beauty, together with a multitude of youths as pages, and other eunuchs, as well as ladies of the bedchamber; so that the number of persons belonging to each of their respective courts amounts to ten thousand.

When his majesty is desirous of the company of one of his empresses, he either sends for her, or goes himself to her palace. Besides these, he has many concubines provided for his use, from a province of Tartary named Ungut, the inhabitants of which are distinguished for beauty of features and fairness of complexion. Every second year, or oftener, as it may happen to be his pleasure, the Great Khan sends thither his officers, who collect for him, one hundred or more, of the handsomest of the young women, according to the estimation of beauty communicated to them in their instructions.

The mode of their appreciation is as follows. Upon the arrival of these commissioners, they give orders for assembling all the young women of the province, and appoint qualified persons to examine them, who, upon careful inspection of each of them separately, that is to say, of the hair, the countenance, the eyebrows, the mouth, the lips, and other features, as well as the symmetry of these with each other, estimate their value at sixteen, seventeen, eighteen, or twenty, or more carats, according to the greater or less degree of beauty. The number required by the Great Khan, at the rates, perhaps, of twenty or twenty-one carats, to which their commission was limited, is then selected from the rest, and they are conveyed to his court.

Upon their arrival in his presence, he causes a new examination to be made by a different set of inspectors, and from amongst them a further selection takes place, when thirty or forty are retained for his own chamber at a higher valuation. These are committed separately to the care of the elderly ladies of the palace, whose duty it is to observe them attentively during the course of the night, in order to ascertain that they have not any concealed imperfections, that they sleep tranquilly, do not snore, have sweet breath, and are free from unpleasant scent in any part of the body. Having undergone this rigorous scrutiny, they are divided into parties of five, one of which parties attends during three days and three nights, in his majesty's interior apartment, where they are to perform every service that is required of them, and he does with them as he likes.

When this term is completed, they are relieved by another party, and in this manner successively, until the whole number have taken their turn; when the first five recommence their attendance. But whilst the one party officiates in the inner chamber, another is stationed in the outer apartment adjoining; in order that if his majesty should have occasion for anything, such as drink or victuals, the former may signify his commands to the latter, by whom the article required is immediately procured. In this way the duty of waiting upon his majesty's person is exclusively performed by these young females. The remainder of them, whose value had been estimated at an inferior rate, are assigned to the different lords of the household; under whom they are instructed in cookery, in dressmaking, and other suitable works; and upon any person belonging to the court expressing an inclination to take a wife, the Great Khan bestows upon him one of these damsels, with a handsome portion. In this manner he provides for them all amongst his nobility.

It may be asked whether the people of the province do not feel themselves aggrieved in having their daughters thus forcibly taken from them by the sovereign? Certainly not; but, on the contrary, they regard it as a favour and an honour done to them; and those who are the fathers of handsome children feel highly gratified by his condescending to make choice of their daughters. "If," say they, "my daughter is born under an auspicious planet and to good fortune, his majesty can best fulfill her destinies, by matching her nobly; which it would not be in my power to do." If, on the other hand, the daughter misconducts herself, or any mischance befalls her, by which she becomes disqualified, the father attributes the disappointment to the malign influence of her stars....

[Chapter 10]

...In the middle of each division of these walls is a handsome and spacious building, and consequence within the enclosure there are eight such buildings, in which are deposited the royal military stores; one building being appropriated to the reception of each class of stores. Thus, for instance, the bridles, saddles, stirrups, and other furniture serving for the equipment of cavalry, occupy one storehouse; the bows, strings, quivers, arrows, and other articles belonging to archery, occupy another; cuirasses, corselets, and other armour formed of leather, a third storehouse; and so of the rest....

Within these walls, which constitute the boundary of four miles, stands the palace of the Great Khan, the most extensive that has ever yet been known. It reaches from the northern to the southern wall, leaving only a vacant space (or court), where persons of rank and the military guards pass and re-pass. It has no upper floor, but the roof is very lofty. The paved foundation or platform on which it stands is raised ten spans above the level of the ground, and a wall of marble, two paces wide, is built on all sides, to the level of this pavement, within the line of which the palace is erected; so that the wall, extending beyond the ground plan of the building, and encompassing the whole, serves as a terrace, where those who walk on it are visible from without. Along the exterior edge of the wall is a handsome balustrade, with pillars, which the people are allowed to approach. The sides of the great halls and the apartments are ornamented with dragons in carved work and gilt, figures of warriors, of birds, and of beasts, with representations of battles. The inside of the roof is contrived in such a manner that nothing besides gilding and painting presents itself to the eye.

On each of the four sides of the palace there is a grand flight of marble steps, by which you ascend from the level of the ground to the wall of marble which surrounds the building, and which constitute the approach to the palace itself.

The grand hall is extremely long and wide, and admits of dinners being there served to great multitudes of people. The palace contains a number of separate chambers, all highly beautiful, and so admirably disposed that it seems impossible to suggest any improvement to the system of their arrangement The exterior of the roof is adorned with a variety of colors, red, green, azure, and violet, and the sort of covering is so strong as to last for many years. The glazing of the windows is so well wrought and so delicate as to have the transparency of crystal.

In the rear of the body of the palace there are large buildings containing several apartments, where is deposited the private property of the monarch, or his treasure in gold and silver bullion, precious stones, and pearls, and also his vessels of gold and silver plate. Here are likewise the apartments of his wives and concubines; and in this retired situation he dispatches business with convenience, being free from every kind of interruption.

On the other side of the grand palace, and opposite to that in which the emperor resides, is another palace, in every respect similar, appropriated to the residence of Chinghis, his eldest son, at whose court are observed all the ceremonials belonging to that of his father, as the prince who is to succeed to the government of the empire. Not far from the palace, on the northern side, and about a bow-shot distance from the surrounding wall, is an artificial mount of earth, the height of which is full a hundred paces, and the circuit at the base about a mile. It is clothed with the most beautiful evergreen trees; for whenever his Majesty receives information of a handsome tree growing in any place, he causes it to be dug up, with all its roots and the earth about them, and however large and heavy it may be, he has it transported by means of elephants to this mount, and adds it to the verdant collection. Because the trees on this hill are always green it has acquired the name of the Green Mount.

From *The Travels of Marco Polo* by Manuel Komroff. Copyright 1926 by Boni & Liveright, Inc., renewed 1953 by Manuel Komroff. Copyright 1930 by Horace Liveright, Inc., renewed © 1958 by Manuel Komroff. Used by permission of Liveright Publishing Corporation.

16.2

AZTEC ACCOUNT OF THE SPANISH CONQUEST

Hernán Cortés (1485-1547) arrived in Mexico in 1519 with a small (less than 600 men) force. Upon reaching Mexico he burned his ships so that his men had no option but to press on He found the area under the control of the Aztec Empire. Through alliances with smaller states that were under the domination of the Aztecs, Cortes soon controlled most of the central Mexico. He convinced the Aztecs that he had been sent by their gods and took over their state as well. In 1520 the Aztecs rebelled; the following excerpt is an Aztec description of the resulting massacre.

Questions

1. What explanation does Motecuhzoma (Moctezuma) offer for why his people will be conquered?
2. Why do the Spanish keep Motecuhzoma a hostage and not kill him.
3. Why do the Aztecs send out magicians and wizards to negotiate with the Spanish?

The Spaniards See the Objects of Gold

Then Motecuhzoma dispatched various chiefs. Tzihuacpopocatzin was at their head, and he took with him a great many of his representatives. They went out to meet the Spaniards in the vicinity of Popocatepetl and Iztactepetl, there in the Eagle Pass.

They gave the "gods" ensigns of gold, and ensigns of quetzal feathers, and golden necklaces. And when they were given these presents, the Spaniards burst into smiles; their eyes shone with pleasure; they were delighted by them. They picked up the gold and fingered it like monkeys; they seemed to be transported by joy, as if their hearts were illuminated and made new.

The truth is that they longed and lusted for gold. Their bodies swelled with greed, and their hunger was ravenous; they hungered like pigs for that gold. They snatched at the golden ensigns, waved them from side to side and examined every inch of them. They were like one who speaks a barbarous tongue: everything they said was in a barbarous tongue....

Motecuhzoma's Despair

When the envoys arrived in the city, they told Motecuhzoma what had happened and what they had seen. Motecuhzoma listened to their report and then bowed his head without speaking a word. For a long time he remained thus, with his head bent down. And when he spoke at last, it was only to say: "What help is there now, my friends? Is there a mountain for us to climb? Should we run away? We are Mexicanos: would this bring any glory to the Mexican nation?

"Pity the old men, and the old women, and the innocent little children. How can they save themselves? But there is no help. What can we do? Is there nothing left us?

"We will be judged and punished. And however it may be, and whenever it may be, we can do nothing but wait."...

The Statue of Huitzilopochtli

On the evening before the fiesta of Toxcatl, the celebrants began to model a statue of Huitzilopochtli. They gave it such a human appearance that it seemed the body of a living man. Yet they made the statue with nothing but a paste made of the ground seeds of chicalote, which they shaped over an armature of sticks.

When the statue was finished, they dressed it in rich feathers, and they painted crossbars over and under its eyes. They also clipped on its earrings of turquoise mosaic; these were in shape of serpents, with gold rings hanging from them. Its nose plug, in the shape of an arrow, was made of gold and was inlaid with fine stones.

They placed the magic headdress of hummingbird feathers on its head. They also adorned it with an *anecuyotl*, which was a belt made of feathers, with a cone at the back. Then they hung around its neck an ornament of yellow parrot feathers, fringed like the locks of a young boy. Over this they put its nettle-leaf cape, which was painted black and decorated with five clusters of eagle feathers.

Next they wrapped it in its cloak, which was painted with skulls and bones, and over this they fastened its vest. The vest was painted with dismembered human parts: skulls, ears, hearts, intestines, torsos, breasts, hands and feet. They also put on its *maxtlatl*, or loincloth, which was decorated with images of dissevered limbs and fringed with amate paper. This *maxtlatl* was painted with vertical stripes of bright blue.

They fastened a red paper flag at its shoulder and placed on its head what looked like a sacrificial flint knife. This too was made of red paper; it seemed to have been steeped in blood.

The statue carried a *tehuehuelli*, a bamboo shield decorated with four clusters of fine eagle feathers. The pendant of this shield was blood-red, like the knife and the shoulder flag. The statue also carried four arrows.

Finally, they put the wristbands on its arms. These bands, made of coyote skin, were fringed with paper cut into little strips....

The Spaniards Attack the Celebrants

At this moment in the fiesta, when the dance was loveliest and when song was linked to song, the Spaniards were seized with an urge to kill the celebrants. They all ran forward, armed as if for battle. They closed the entrances and passageways, all the gates of the patio: the Eagle Gate in the lesser palace, the Gate of the Canestalk and the Gate of the Serpent of Mirrors. They posted guards so that no one could escape, and then rushed into the Sacred Patio to slaughter the celebrants. They came on foot, carrying their swords and their wooden or metal shields.

They ran in among the dancers, forcing their way to the place where the drums were played. They attacked the man who was drumming and cut off his arms. Then they cut off his head, and it rolled across the floor.

They attacked all the celebrants, stabbing them, spearing them, striking them with their swords. They attacked some of them from behind, and these fell instantly to the ground with their entrails hanging out. Others they beheaded: they cut off their heads, or split their heads to pieces.

They struck others in the shoulders, and their arms were torn from their bodies. They wounded some in the thigh and some in the calf. They slashed others in the abdomen, and their entrails all spilled to the ground. Some attempted to run away, but their intestines dragged as they ran; they seemed to tangle their feet in their own entrails. No matter how they tried to save themselves, they could find no escape.

Some attempted to force their way out, but the Spaniards murdered them at the gates. Others climbed the walls, but they could not save themselves. Those who ran into the communal houses were safe there for a while; so were those who lay down among the victims and pretended to be dead. But it they stood up again, the Spaniards saw them and killed them.

The blood of the warriors flowed like water and gathered into pools. The pools widened, and the stench of blood and entrails filled the air. The Spaniards ran into the communal houses to kill those who were hiding. They ran everywhere and searched everywhere; they invaded every room, hunting and killing.

The Aztecs Retaliate

When the news of this massacre was heard outside the Sacred Patio; a great cry went up: "Mexicanos, come running!" Bring your spears and shields! The strangers have murdered our warriors!"

This cry was answered with a roar of grief and anger: the people shouted and wailed and beat their palms against their mouths. The captains assembled at once, as if the hour had been determined in advance. They all carried their spears and shields.

Then the battle began. The Aztecs attacked with javelins and arrows, even with the light spears that are used for hunting birds. They hurled their javelins with all their strength, and the cloud of missiles spread out over the Spaniards like a yellow cloak.

The Spaniards immediately took refuge in the palace. They began to shoot at the Mexicans with their iron arrows and to fire their cannons and arquebuses. And they shackled Motecuhzoma in chains....

From *Broken Spears: The Aztec Account of the Conquest of Mexico*, edited by Miguel Leon-Portilla, p. 51-52, 54-55, 72-77. Copyright © 1962 Beacon Press.

16.3

JESUIT MISSIONARY IN CHINA, MATTEO RICCI

Explorers came in many forms. Polo was a merchant. Cortés was a conquistador (conqueror). Matteo Ricci was a Jesuit missionary, who in 1583 followed a path very similar to Polo's three hundred years' earlier. As a Jesuit, Ricci had taken vows of extreme obedience to the papacy. One of the most important functions of the Jesuit order, which was created in 1540, was missionary activity to convert people (Protestant or non-Christian) to Roman Catholicism. Ricci traveled extensively in India and China, and even reached Japan. The following excerpt is from Ricci's description of the religious practices he found in China.

QUESTIONS

1. Compare this account of the Chinese with the earlier one by Polo (Source 16.1).
2. Do you think this account of the Chinese encouraged or discouraged more Europeans from going to Asia?
3. Does Ricci view the superstitions of the Chinese as a religious belief?

9. Concerning Certain Rites, Superstitious and Otherwise

In this chapter we shall treat of the superstitious rites peculiar to certain sects, and shall touch upon such as may serve as a summary of them all....

No superstition is so common to the entire kingdom as that which pertains to the observance of certain days and hours as being good or bad, lucky or unlucky, in which to act or to refrain from acting, because the result of everything they do is supposed to depend upon a measurement of time. This imposture has assumed such a semblance of truth among them that two calendars are edited every year, written by the astrologers of the crown and published by public authority. These almanacs are sold in such great quantities that every house has a supply of them. They are produced in pamphlet form, and in them one finds directions as to what should be done and what should be left undone for each particular day, and at what precise time each and every thing should be done. In this manner the entire year is carefully mapped out in exact detail. Besides these regular calendars there are other books of this kind, more complex in their contents. Then, too, a horde of deceitful directors make a living by instructing those who consult them as to the correct day and hour for doing each particular thing in a day's routine. They charge but very little for their fraudulent advice so that no one will hesitate to have an adviser....

It is a common practice also to consult the demons, the family spirits, as the Chinese call them, and there are many of them. In this, however, they imagine that there is more of divination than anything diabolical, but in this too, they are victims of fraud and deception. In such consultations, oracles are received through the voices of little children and from the sounds of brute beasts, revealing the past and the absent, as proof of the truth of what they foretell for the future. These oracles are always produced by fraud and trickery. Of course, we read that such superstitions are common to heathens in general, but the following sample is quite peculiar to the Chinese. In choosing a place to erect a public edifice or a private house, or in selecting a plot of ground in which to bury the dead, they study the location with reference to the head and the tail and the feet of the particular dragons which are supposed to dwell beneath that spot. Upon these local dragons they believe that the good and bad fortune, not only of the family but also of the town and the province and of the entire kingdom, is wholly dependent. Many of their most distinguished men are interested in this recondite science and, when necessary, they are called in for consultation, even from a great distance. This might happen when some public building or a monument is to be erected and the machines used for that purpose are to be placed so that public misfortune might be avoided and good fortune attend the undertaking. Just as their astrologers read the stars, so their geologists reckon the fate or the fortune of a place from the relative position of mountains or rivers or fields, and their reckoning is just as deceitful as the reading of the stargazers. What could be more absurd than their imagining that the safety of a family, honors, and their entire existence must depend upon such trifles as a door being opened from one side or another, as rain falling into a courtyard from the right or from the left, a window opened here or there, or one roof being higher than another?

The streets and the taverns and all other public places abound in these astrologers and geologists, diviners and fortunetellers, or, to group them all in one class, in these imposters. Their business consists in making vain promises of prosperous fortunes at a given price. Some of them are blind men, others of low station in life, and at times, women of questionable character. According to the dictum of the Gospel, they really are, "The blind leading the blind," and their number is so great that they may be said to constitute a universal nuisance. In fact, this obnoxious class is a veritable pest in the capital cities and even in the court. Such is their means of livelihood, and not a few of them are able to support a large family in luxury and at times to accumulate considerable wealth. The high and the low, the noble and the plebeian, the educated and the illiterate are counted among their victims, as are the magistrates, the dignitaries of the realm, and even the King himself. One can readily judge from what has been said, of the auguries they read into the cackling of birds, how solicitous they are about first morning meetings and about shadows cast upon a roof by the rays of the sun. In a word, whatever misfortune befalls an individual, a city, a province, or the kingdom, they attribute it to adverse fortune, or to something wrong in the person or in the realm, as the case may be. They look upon such adversity as being a just visitation for their sins, which have called down a private or a public vindication from above.

We shall add here a few shocking practices which the Chinese look upon with indifference and which, God forbid, they even seem to consider as quite morally correct, and from these one can readily conclude to others of the same category. This people is really to be pitied rather than censured, and the deeper one finds them involved in the darkness of ignorance, the more earnest one should be in praying for their salvation.

Many of them, not being able to forgo the company of women, sell themselves to wealthy patrons, so as to find a wife among his women servants, and in so doing, subject their children to perpetual slavery. Others buy a wife when they can save money enough to do so, and when their family becomes too numerous to be supported, they sell their children into slavery for about the same price that one would pay for a pig or a cheap little donkey — about one crown or maybe one and a half. Sometimes this is done when there is really no necessity, and children are separated from their parents forever, becoming slaves to the purchaser, to be used for whatever purpose he pleases. The result of this practice is that the whole country is virtually filled with slaves; not such as are captured in war or brought in from abroad, but slaves by the Portuguese and the Spaniards. These few at least have an opportunity of becoming Christian and of thus escaping the slavery of Satan. The only ameliorating feature in this traffic of children is the fact that it lessens the great multitude of the extremely poor who have to labor incessantly in the sweat of their brow to eke out a miserable living. One might add also that slavery among the Chinese is more bearable because less exacting than among any other people in the world. A Chinese slave can purchase his freedom for the same price that was paid for him, if he can manage to acquire that amount of money.

A far more serious evil here is the practice in some provinces of disposing of female infants by drowning them. The reason assigned for this is that their parents despair of being able to support them. At times this is also done by people who are not abjectly poor, for fear the time might come when they would not be able to care for these children and they would be forced to sell them to unknown or to cruel slave masters. Thus they become cruel in an effort to be considerate. This barbarism is probably rendered less atrocious by their belief in metempsychosis, or the transmigration of souls. Believing that souls are transferred from one body that ceases to exist into another that begins to exist, they cover up their frightful cruelty with a pretext of piety, thinking that they are doing the child a benefit by murdering it. According to their way of thinking, they are releasing the child from the poverty of the family into which it was born, so that it may be reborn into a family of better means. So it happens that this slaughter of the innocents is carried on not in secret but in the open and with general public knowledge.

Another more or less common custom, and still more barbarous than that aforementioned, is the practice of committing suicide in desperation of earning a living, or in utter despair because of misfortune, or still more foolishly and more cowardly, out of spite for an enemy. They say that thousands of people, women as well as men, take their own lives in the course of a year. This is frequently done by hanging or by choking oneself to death in a public place or perhaps before the home of an enemy. Jumping into rivers and swallowing poison are other common methods and they often commit suicide for very trivial reasons. If a magistrate should pass a severe sentence upon one who is accused by the parents of a suicide of having driven their son to despair, the accused will frequently see no other way out of the difficulty than by taking his own life. Many of the magistrates show great wisdom in this respect by making it a law unto themselves never to handle a case involving a suicide and they probably save many a life by doing so.

Yet another barbarity common in the northern provinces is that of castrating a great number of male children, so they may act as servants or slaves to the King. This condition is demanded for service in the royal palace, so much so, indeed, that the King will have no others nor will he consult with or even speak to any other. Almost the whole administration of the entire kingdom is in the hands of this class of semi-men, who number nearly ten thousand in the service of the royal palace alone. They are a meager-looking class, uneducated and brought up in perpetual slavery, a dull and stolid lot, as incapable of understanding an important order as they are inefficient in carrying it out....

The Chinese look upon all foreigners as illiterate and barbarous, and refer to them in just these terms. They even disdain to learn anything from books of outsiders because they believe that all true science and knowledge belongs to them alone. If perchance they have occasion to make mention of externs in their own writings, they treat them as though there was no room for doubt that they differ but little from the beasts of the field and the forest. Even the written characters by which they express the word foreigner are those that are applied to beasts, and scarcely ever do they give them a title more honorable than they would assign to their demons. One would scarcely believe how suspicious they are of a legate or an ambassador of a neighboring country, sent in to pay respect to the King, to settle a tributary tax, or to conduct any sort of business. The fact that China may have been on friendly terms with the kingdom of the visiting legates, from time immemorial, does not exempt the visiting dignitaries from being conducted along their entire route within the realm as captives or prisoners and permitted to see nothing in the course of their journey. During their whole sojourn they are lodged in buildings, constructed like cattle barns, within the limits of the palace grounds, to which they are confined under lock and key. They are never permitted to see the King, and their diplomatic or other business is carried on with selected magistrates. No one in the whole kingdom is ever permitted to do business with foreigners, excepting at certain times and in certain places, as on the peninsula of Macao where a trading mart was established with the Portuguese in 1557. Anyone carrying on foreign trade without official sanction would be subject to the severest punishment.

From *China in Sixteenth Century by Matthew Ricci*, translated by Louis J. Gallagher, S.J., p. 82-89. Copyright 1942, 1953 and renewed 1970 by Louis J. Gallagher, S.J. Used by permission of Random House, Inc.

16.4

CAPTURE AND ENSLAVEMENT, OLAUDAH EQUIANO

There are few written accounts by Africans of their enslavement and transportation to the American colonies. That scarcity makes the autobiography of Olaudah Equiano (1745-1797), published in 1791, all the more striking. Equiano had been a member of the Ibo tribe of Benin; at age ten he was kidnapped by members of a rival tribe and sold into slavery. After passing through several African hands, he was sold to European slavers and transported to Barbados and then to Virginia. Eventually he was purchased by an English sea captain and taken to England. In 1766, with his owner's help, he was able to buy his freedom and eventually became a ship owner himself. In 1791 he published his book, The Interesting Narrative of the Life of Olaudah Equiano, or Gustavus Vasso, the African, *from which this selection is taken.*

———————— ✦ ————————

QUESTIONS

1. Why is Equiano flogged for refusing to eat? Does this reveal concern on the part of the slavers?
2. How does Equiano's initial enslavement by an African family differ from his subsequent enslavement by Europeans?
3. Why does Equiano publish this narrative under both his African and European names?

Vol. I

One day, when all our people were gone out to their work as usual, and only I and my sister were left to mind the house, two men and a woman got over our walls, and in a moment seized us both; and, without giving us time to cry out, or to make resistance, they stopped our mouths, and ran off with us into the nearest wood. Here they tied our hands, and continued to carry us as far as they could, till night came on, when we reached a small house....The next morning we left the house, and continued traveling all day....

The next day proved a day of greater sorrow than I had yet experienced, for my sister and I were then separated; while we lay clasped in each other's arms. It was in vain that we besought them not to part us; she was torn from me, and immediately carried away, while I was left in a state of distraction not to be described. I cried and grieved continually; and for several days did not eat anything but what they forced into my mouth. At length, after many days' travelling, during which I had often changed masters, I got into the hands of a chieftain, in a very pleasant country. This man had two wives and some children, and they all used me extremely well....

I was there, I suppose, about a month, and they at length used to trust me some little distance from the house....I therefore determined to seize the first opportunity of making my escape, and to shape my course for that quarter; for I was quite oppressed and weighed down by grief after my mother and friends; and my love of liberty, ever great, was strengthened by the mortifying circumstance of not daring to eat with the free-born children, although I was mostly their companion....

Equiano describes the horrors of a slave ship.

The first object which saluted my eyes when I arrived on the coast was the sea, and a slave ship, which was then riding at anchor, and waiting for its cargo. These filled me with astonishment, that was soon converted into terror...when I was carried on board....

I now saw myself deprived of all chance of returning to my native country, or even the least glimpse of gaining the shore, which I now considered as friendly; and I even wished for my former slavery, in preference of my present situation, which was filled with horrors of every kind, still heightened by my ignorance of what I was to undergo. I was not long suffered to indulge my grief. I was soon put down under the decks, and there I received such a salutation in my nostrils as I had never experienced in my life: so that, with the loathsomeness of the stench, and crying together, I became so sick and low that I was not able to eat, nor had I the least desire to taste anything. I now wished for the last friend, death, to relieve me; but soon, to my grief, two of the white men offered me eatables, and, on my refusing to eat, one of them held me fast by the hands, and laid me across, I think, the windlass, and tied my feet, while the other flogged me severely. I had never experienced anything of this kind before, and although not being used to the water, I naturally feared that element the first time I saw it, yet, nevertheless, could I have got over the nettings, I would have jumped over the side, but I could not; and besides the crew used to watch us very closely who were not chained down to the decks, lest we should leap into the water; and I have seen some of these poor African prisoners most severely cut for attempting to do so, and hourly whipped for not eating. This indeed was often the case with myself.

Source: David Waldstreicher, *The Struggle Against Slavery: A History in Documents* (New York: Oxford University Press, 2001), pp. 18-20.

QUESTIONS FOR PART 16

1. Of the many reasons why Europeans explored and conquered, what do you think was the single most important?
2. What role did the Reformation and Religious Wars play in the Age of Exploration?
3. Did the Europeans treat all of the newly discovered cultures the same? Why or why not?

PART 17

SEVENTEENTH CENTURY STATE BUILDING

Europe faced many challenges as it entered the seventeenth century: the chaos of the Reformation, the Wars of Religion, and the rapid expansion of European states into world empires. There were several major trends in this new century: a weariness from the religions wars in many states (although they continued in the Holy Roman Empire), a growing secularization (coupled in part with the new scientific theories in the next section), increased economic activity (from those empires) and the beginning of trade wars, and above all else, the rise of new theories of royal government.

The seventeenth century was the true beginning of modern states, however much of it built upon centuries of political and legal traditions. Each European state took its own approach to state building, although the centrality of the monarchy remained constant in most of them. It was, in fact, the most powerful age of kings Europe had seen in a very long time. The pinnacle of royal power was found in the absolutist states of France under Louis XIV, Prussia under the Hohenzollern dynasty, and Russia under Peter the Great. For every monarch who successfully established absolute rule there were many more who attempted it and failed. The Habsburgs of the Holy Roman Empire saw their dominions reduced drastically by the Thirty Years' War (1618-1648), which revealed just how fractured the Empire was. Each independent state within the Empire gained recognized sovereignty, while small kingdoms such as Sweden emerged as true political contenders and the Dutch republic established one of the wealthiest international trade empires. The Stuart dynasty of England also wanted to achieve the royal dream of absolutism, yet failed. In 1648 a parliamentary republic replaced the monarchy; although the monarchy was restored in 1660, it was as a limited, constitutional monarch.

17.1

CARDINAL RICHELIEU ON THE RIGHTS OF THE KING

No European monarch was ever as absolute as Louis XIV (1643-1715) of France. The concept of absolutism was tied to the belief in the divine right of kings. According to the divine right theory, a king received his power directly from God and not from the people, not from any other body of government. Because his power was divine in origin, it was thus absolute and could not be limited. At least that was the theory of absolutism. The reality was usually a bit of a compromise; James I of England had been the first monarch to articulate the concept of divine right, but was actually quite limited in power by Parliament. In France, however, Louis XIV faced no such limitation. The extent of the French king's sovereignty was established by Louis XIII's administrator Cardinal Richelieu (d. 1642). Thanks to Richelieu, Louis XIV inherited a kingdom in which private armies (the bane of medieval kings) had been abolished and the separatist Huguenots were exiled or destroyed. During his reign Louis XIV took on the French peasants and aristocracy, and attempted through a series of wars to dominate all of Europe.

The following excerpt is from a letter from Cardinal Richelieu to Louis XIII outlining his accomplishments.

---- ✤ ----

QUESTIONS

1. What was the advantage to Louis XIII in destroying all the Huguenot held castles?
2. Although the letter is written to Louis XIII, how is it also a blueprint for Louis XIV's absolutism?
3. Do you see any conflict in Richelieu's position as Cardinal to the pope and his work in centralizing the French king's power?

Richelieu's account of the condition of France when he became minister in 1624.

At the time when your Majesty resorted to admit me both to your council and to an important place in your confidence for the direction of your affairs, I may say that the Huguenots shared the state with you; that the nobles conducted themselves as if they were not your subjects, and the most powerful governors of the provinces as if they were sovereign in their offices.

I may say that the bad example of all of these was so injurious to this realm that even the best regulated *parlements* were affected by it, and endeavored, in certain cases, to diminish your royal authority as far as they were able in order to stretch their own powers beyond the limits of reason.

I may say that every one measured his own merit by his audacity; that in place of estimating the benefits which they received from your Majesty at their proper worth, all valued them only in so far as they satisfied the extravagant demands of their imagination; that the most arrogant were held to be the wisest, and found themselves the most prosperous.

I may also say that the foreign alliances were unfortunate, individual interests being preferred to those of the public; in a word, the dignity of the royal majesty was so disparaged, and so different from what it should be, owing to the malfeasance of those who conducted your affairs, that it was almost impossible to perceive its existence.

It was impossible, without losing all, to tolerate longer the conduct of those to whom your Majesty had intrusted the helm of state; and, on the other hand, everything could not be changed at once without violating the laws of prudence, which do not permit the abrupt passing from one extreme to another.

The sad state of your affairs seemed to force you to hasty decisions, without permitting a choice of time or of means; and yet it was necessary to make a choice of both, in order to profit by the change which necessity demanded from your prudence.

Thoughtful observers did not think that it would be possible to escape all the rocks in so tempestuous a period; the court was full of people who censured the temerity of those who wished to undertake a reform; all well knew that princes are quick to impute to those who are near them the bad outcome of the undertakings upon which they have been well advised; few people consequently expected good results from the change which it was announced that I wished to make, and many believed my fall assured even before your Majesty had elevated me.

Notwithstanding these difficulties which I represented to your Majesty, knowing how much kings may do when they make good use of their power, I ventured to promise you, with confidence, that you would soon get control of your state, and that in a short time your prudence, your courage, and the benediction of God would give a new aspect to the realm....

Edict of 1626 ordering the demolition of the feudal castles in France.

Whereas formerly the assemblies of the estates of this realm and those of notable persons chosen to give advice to ourselves, and to the late king, our very honorable lord and father, on important affairs of this realm, and likewise the assembly of the estates of the province of Brittany held by us in the year 1614, have repeatedly requested and very humbly supplicated our said lord and father and ourselves to cause the demolition of many strongholds in divers places of this realm, which, being neither on hostile frontiers nor in important passes or places, only serve to augment our expenses by the maintenance of useless garrisons, and also serve as retreats for divers persons who on the least provocation disturb the provinces where they are located;...

For these reasons, we announce, declare, ordain, and will that all the strongholds, either towns or castles, which are in the interior of our realm or provinces of the same, not situated in places of importance either for frontier defense or other considerations of weight, shall be razed and demolished; even ancient walls shall be destroyed so far as it shall be deemed necessary for the well-being and repose of our subjects and the security of this state, so that our said subjects henceforth need not fear that the said places will cause them any inconvenience, and so that we shall be freed from the expense of supporting garrisons in them.

Letters patent establishing the French Academy in 1635.

Richelieu was much interested in the encouragement of science, art, and literature. The French Academy, which he induced the king to establish by the following order, had begun with the informal conference of a few men of letters, who met at one another's houses.

When God called us to the headship of the state we cherished the purpose not only of putting an end to the disorders caused by the civil wars which had so long distracted the realm, but we also aimed to adorn the state with all the ornaments appropriate to the oldest and most illustrious of existing monarchies. Although we have labored without intermission to realize this purpose, it has been impossible hitherto fully to accomplish it.... [But now] the confusion has at last given way to good order, which we have reestablished by the best of all means, namely, by reviving commerce, enforcing military discipline in our armies, adjusting the taxes, and checking luxury. Every one is aware of the part that our very dear and beloved cousin, the cardinal, duke of Richelieu, has had in the accomplishment of all these things.

Importance of cultivating the French language.

Consequently when we communicated our intention to him, he represented to us that one of the most glorious proofs of the happiness of a realm is that the sciences and arts flourish within it, and that letters as well as arms are held in esteem, since these constitute one of the chief ornaments of a powerful state; that, after so many memorable exploits, we had now only to add the agreeable to the essential, and to adorn the useful. He believed that we could not do better than to commence with the most noble of all arts, namely, eloquence. The French language, which has suffered much hitherto from neglect on the part of those who might have rendered it the most perfect of modern tongues, is not more capable than ever of taking its high place, owing to the great number of persons who possess a special knowledge of the advantages which it enjoys and who can augment these advantages. The cardinal informed us that, with a view of establishing fixed rules for the language, he had arranged meetings of scholars whose decisions in these matters had met with his hearty approval, and that in order to put these decisions into execution and render the French language not only elegant but capable of treating all the arts and sciences, it would only be necessary to perpetuate these gatherings. This could be done with great advantage should it please us to sanction them, to permit rules and regulations to be drawn up for the order of procedure to be observed, and to reward those who compose the association by some honorable marks of our favor.

For these reasons, and in view of the advantages which our subjects may derive from the said meetings, acceding to the desires of our said cousin:

We do permit, by our special favor, power, and royal authority, and do authorize and approve by these presents, signed by our hand, the said assemblies and conferences. We will that they continue hereafter in our good city of Paris, under the name of the *French Academy*; that our said cousin shall be designated as its head and protector; that the number of members be limited to forty persons....

Source: James Harvey Robinson, *Readings in European History,* Vol. II, (Boston: Ginn and Company, 1906, 1934), pp. 268-72.

17.2

⸙

THIRTY YEARS' WAR: DESTRUCTION OF MAGDEBURG

The Thirty Years' War was the last of the Religious Wars of the Reformation, but was also very much a war of politics and national interests. It was primarily fought within the Holy Roman Empire, but not exclusively. The war went through several stages; the combatants varied from place to place and decade to decade. In Bohemia the war was fought between Catholics and Calvinists (although it was also a response to the German Habsburg dynasty's attempt to increase its power over the state). Danish Lutherans entered the war in order to protect Protestants in Germany from the attempts by the Habsburgs to re-Catholicize the German states, as they were attempting to do in Bohemia. In contrast, the war in Sweden was clearly mostly one of politics; King Gustavus Adolphus (d. 1635) used the opportunity to try and establish his kingdom's dominance over the Baltic. The settlement to the war, the Treaty of Westphalia in 1648, ensured that politics and faith would remain intertwined. The Treaty allowed for individual rulers within the Holy Roman Empire to decide what would be the official faith of his own state.

The following excerpt describes the massacre of Protestants in the German city of Magdeburg in 1631, which brought Gustavus Adolphus renewed determination to fight German Catholic princes.

✢

QUESTIONS

1. One characteristic of the war was the improvement in guns and their efficiency; how did that affect the siege of Magdeburg?
2. Which do you think was more multinational in character, the Protestant or Catholic armies?
3. What might have been the motivation for the Imperial army sacking Magdeburg? Do you think it was about religion?

The Destruction of Magdeburg (May, 1631).

So then General Pappenheim collected a number of his people on the ramparts by the New Town, and brought them from there into the streets of the city. Von Falckenberg was shot, and fires were kindled in different quarters; then indeed it was all over with the city, and further resistance was useless. Nevertheless some of the soldiers and citizens did try to make a stand here and there, but the imperial troops kept bringing on more and more forces — cavalry, too — to help them, and finally they got the Kröckenthor open and let in the whole imperial army and the forces of the Catholic League, — Hungarians, Croats, Poles, Walloons, Italians, Spaniards, French, North and South Germans.

Thus it came about that the city and all its inhabitants fell into the hands of the enemy, whose violence and cruelty were due in part to their common hatred of the adherents of the Augsburg Confession, and in part to their being imbittered by the chain shot which had been fired at them and by the derision and insults that the Magdeburgers had heaped upon them from the ramparts.

Then was there naught but beating and burning, plundering, torture, and murder. Most especially was every one of the enemy bent on securing much booty. When a marauding party entered a house, if its master had anything to give he might thereby purchase respite and protection for himself and his family till the next man, who also wanted something, should come along. It was only when everything had been brought forth and there was nothing left to give that the real trouble commenced. Then, what with blows and threats of shooting, stabbing, and hanging, the poor people were so terrified that if they had had anything left they would have brought it forth if it had been buried in the earth or hidden away in a thousand castles. In this frenzied rage, the great and splendid city that had stood like a fair princess in the land was now, in its hour of direst need and unutterable distress and woe, given over to the flames, and thousands of innocent men, women, and children, in the midst of a horrible din of heartrending shrieks and cries, were tortured and put to death in so cruel and shameful a manner that no words would suffice to describe, nor no tears to bewail it....

Thus is a single day this noble and famous city, the pride of the whole country, went up in fire and smoke; and the remnant of its citizens, with their wives and children, were taken prisoners and driven away by the enemy with a noise of weeping and wailing that could be heard from afar, while the cinders and ashes from the town were carried by the wind to Wanzleben, Egeln, and still more distant places....

In addition to all this, quantities of sumptuous and irreplaceable house furnishings and movable property of all kinds, such as books, manuscripts, paintings, memorials of all sorts,...which money could not buy, were either burned or carried away by the soldiers as booty. The most magnificent garments, hangings, silk stuffs, gold and silver lace, linen of all sorts, and other household goods were bought by the army sutlers for a mere song and peddled about by the card load all through the archbishopric of

Magdeburg and in Anhalt and Brunswick. Gold chains and rings, jewels, and every kind of gold and silver utensils were to be bought from the common soldiers for a tenth of their real value....

Source: James Harvey Robinson, ed. *Readings in European History*, Vol. II. (Boston: Ginn and Company, 1906, 1934), pp. 211-212.

17.3

---✦---

CROMWELL'S SPEECH BEFORE PARLIAMENT

As with the Thirty Years' War, the motivations of the various sides in the English Civil War (1642-1648) were diverse and complicated. The forces of Charles I, the Cavaliers, were fighting for their certainty in monarchy as the best government. Charles was himself also fighting for his conviction that he was king by divine right. The king's main adversary was Parliament, which had convened in 1640 in order to address the abuses of its sovereignty by the King. Parliament in England was already an ancient institution by 1640; its independence had been assured through such acts as the signing of Magna Carta in 1215. By 1642 Parliament's forces, the Roundheads, were led by Oliver Cromwell, a man of devoutly Puritan beliefs. One of the reasons for Parliament's hostility was its suspicion that Charles was too sympathetic to Catholicism, perhaps to the point of planning to convert to the Roman faith. After almost seventy years of uninterrupted Protestant rule, Parliament wanted to prevent the religious upheaval that having a Catholic on the throne would cause. Religion was not the only issue of disagreement between King and Parliament (taxes were, as usual, also a factor) but it was certainly one of the most pressing.

Parliament won the Civil War when it had Charles executed for tyranny. The beheading of Charles was shocking to all of Europe; in an age when kings could claim divine favor, this was tantamount to blasphemy for many Christians. Although Parliament would later depose another king (James II) for being too Catholic, it would exile rather than execute him.

In the following speech, Cromwell defends his status as the "Lord Protector" of England.

---✦---

QUESTIONS

1. Having won the war, why does Cromwell call himself Lord Protector and not king?
2. What are the Biblical justifications for Cromwell's actions and victories?
3. How does Cromwell defend his need to raise money from taxes?

For I look at the People of these Nations as the blessing of the Lord: and they are a People blessed by God. They have been so; and they will be so, by reason of that immortal seed which hath been, and is, among them; those Regenerated Ones in the land, of several judgments; who are all the Flock of Christ and lambs of Christ. "His," though perhaps under many unruly passions, and troubles of spirit; whereby they give disquiet to themselves and others: yet they are not so to God; since to us He is a God of other patience; and He will own the least of Truth in the hearts of His People. And the People being the blessing of God, they will not be so angry but they will prefer their safety to their passions, and their real security to forms, when Necessity calls for Supplies. Had they not well been acquainted with this principle, they had never seen this day of Gospel Liberty.

But if any man shall object, "It is an easy thing to talk of Necessities when men create Necessities: would not the Lord Protector make himself great and his family great? Doth not he make these Necessities? And then he will come upon the People with his argument of Necessity!" — This was something hard indeed. But I have *not* yet known what it is to "make Necessities," whatsoever the thoughts or judgments of men are. And I say this, not only to this Assembly, but to the world, That the man liveth not who can come to me and charge me with having, in these great Revolutions, "made Necessities." I challenge even all that fear God. And as God hath said, "My glory I will not give unto another," let men take need and be twice advised how they call His Revolutions, the things of God, and His working of things from one period to another, — how, I say, they call them Necessities of men's creation! For by so doing, they do vilify and lessen the works of God, and rob Him of His glory; which He hat said He will not give unto another, nor suffer to be taken from Him! We know what God did to Herod, when he was applauded and did not acknowledge God. And God knoweth what He will do with men, when they call His Revolutions human designs, and so detract from His glory. These issues and events have not been forecast; but were sudden Providences in things: whereby carnal and worldly men are enraged; and under and at which, many, and I fear some good men, have murmured and repined, because disappointed of their mistaken fancies. But still all these things have been the wise disposings of the Almighty; though instruments have had their passions and frailties. And I think it is an honour to God to acknowledge the Necessities to have been of God's imposing, when truly they have been so, as indeed they have. Let us take our sin in our actions to ourselves; it's much more safe than to judge things so contingent, as if there were not a God that ruled the Earth!

We know the Lord hath poured this Nation from vessel to vessel, till He poured it into your lap, when you came first together. I am confident that it came so into your hands; and was not judged by you to be from counterfeited or feigned Necessity, but by Divine Providence and Dispensation. And this I speak with more earnestness, because I speak for God and not for men. I would have any man to come and tell of the Transactions that have been, and of those periods of time wherein God hath made these Revolutions; and find where he can fix a feigned Necessity! I could recite particulars, if either my strength would serve me to speak, or yours to hear. If that you would resolve the great Hand of God in His great Dispensations, you would find that there is scarce a man who fell off, at any period of time when God had any work to do, who can give God or His work at this day a good word.

"It was," say some, "the cunning of the Lord Protector," — I take it to myself, — "it was the craft of such a man, and his plot, that hath brought it about!" And, as they say in other countries, "There are five or six cunning men in England that have skill; they do all these things." Oh, what blasphemy is this! Because men that are without God in the world, and walk not with Him, know not what it is to pray or believe, and to receive returns from God, and to be spoken unto by the Spirit of God, — who speaks without a Written Word sometimes, yet *according* to it! God hath spoken heretofore in divers manners. Let Him speak as He pleaseth. Hath He not given us liberty, nay, is it not our duty, To go to the Law and the Testimony? And there we shall find that there *have* been impressions, in extraordinary cases, as well without the Written Word as with it. And therefore there is no difference in the thing thus asserted from Truths generally received, — except we will exclude the Spirit; without whose concurrence all other teachings are ineffectual. He doth speak to the hearts and consciences of men; and leadeth them to His Law and Testimony, and there "also" He speaks to them: and so gives them double teachings. According tot hat of Job: "God speaketh once, yea twice"; and to that of David: "God hath spoken once, yea twice have I heard this." These men that live upon their *mumpsimus* and *sumpsimus*, their Masses and Service-books, their dead and carnal worship, — no marvel if they be strangers to God, and to the works of God, and to spiritual dispensations. And because *they* say and believe thus, must we do so too? We, in this land, have been otherwise instructed; even by the Word, and Works, and Spirit of God.

To say that men bring forth these things when God doth them, — judge you if God will bear this? I wish that every sober heart, though he hath had temptations upon him of deserting this Cause of God, yet may take heed how he provokes and falls into the hands of the Living god by such blasphemies as these! According to the Tenth of the *Hebrews*: "If we sin wilfully after that we have received the knowledge of the truth, there remains no more sacrifice for sin." "A terrible word." It was spoken to the Jews who, having professed Christ, apostatised from Him. What then? Nothing but a fearful "falling into the hands of the Living God!" — They that shall attribute to this or that person the contrivances and production of those mighty things God hath wrought in the midst of us; and "fancy" that they have not been the Revolutions of Christ Himself, "upon whose shoulders the government is laid," — they speak against God, and they fall under His hands without a Mediator. That is, if we deny the Spirit of Jesus Christ the glory of all His works in the world; by which He rules kingdoms, and doth administer, and is the rod of His strength, — we provoke the Mediator: and He may say: I will leave you to God, I will not intercede for you; let Him tear you to pieces! I will leave thee to fall into God's bands; thou deniest me my sovereignty and power committed to me; I will not intercede nor mediate for thee; thou fallest into the hands of the Living God! — Therefore whatsoever you may judge men for, howsoever you may say, "This is cunning and politic, and subtle," — take heed again, I say, how you judge of His Revolutions as the product of men's inventions! — I may be thought to press too much upon this theme. But I pray God it may stick upon your hearts and mine. The worldly-minded man knows nothing of this, but is a stranger to it; and thence his atheisms, and murmurings at instruments, yea, repining at God Himself. And no wonder; considering the Lord hath done such things amongst us as have not been known in the world these thousand years, and yet notwithstanding is not owned by us!

There is another Necessity, which you have put upon us, and we have not sought. I appeal to God, Angels, and Men, — if I shall "now" raise money according to the Article in the Government, whether I am not compelled to do it! Which "Government" had power to call you hither; and did: — and instead of seasonably providing for the Army, you have laboured to overthrow the Government, and the Army is now upon Free-quarter! And you would never so much as let me hear a tittle from you concerning it. Where is the fault? Has it not been as if you had a purpose to put this extremity upon us and the Nation? I hope this was not in your minds. I am not willing to judge so: — but such is the state into which we are reduced. By the designs of some in the Army who are now in custody, it was designed to get as many of them as possible, — through discontent for want of money, the Army being in a barren country, near thirty weeks behind in pay, and upon other specious pretences, — to march for England out of Scotland; and, in discontent, to seize their General there [*General Monk*], a faithful and honest man, that so another [*Colonel Overton*] might head the Army. And all this opportunity taken from your delays. Whether will this be a thing of feigned Necessity? What could it signify, but "The Army are in discontent already; and we will make them live upon stones; we will make them cast-off their governors and discipline?" What can be said to this? I list not to unsaddle myself, and put the fault upon your backs. Whether it hath been for the good of England, whilst men have been talking of this thing or the other, and pretending liberty and many good words, — whether it has been as it should have been? I am confident you cannot think it has. The Nation will not think so. And if the worst should be made of things, I know not what the Cornish men nor the Lincolnshire men may think, or other Counties; but I believe they will all think *they are not safe*. A temporary suspension of "caring for the greatest liberties and privilege" (if it were so, which is denied) would not have been of such damage as the not providing against Free-quarter hath run the Nation upon. And if it be my "liberty" to walk abroad in the fields, or to take a journey, yet it is not my wisdom to do so when my house is on fire!

Source: *British Orations from Ethelbert to Churchill* (New York: E. P. Dutton, 1960), pp. 48-52.

17.4

"A Dialogue on Sovereign Power," Thomas Hobbes

Thomas Hobbes (1588-1679) was one of the major political theorists of the seventeenth century. Hobbes lived through the English Civil War, although he did not live to see another king removed from the throne (in 1688 James II is peaceably replaced by his daughter Mary and her husband William of Orange, both devoutly Protestant). His understanding of the rights of the state is particularly affected by the events of his lifetime. In many of his writings, including his most famous political treatise, The Leviathan, he argued that the all-powerful state was the only thing that stood between humanity and its own inclination toward savage primitivism. He argued for a different type of absolutism from the Louis XIV model; Hobbes believed the state should be absolute but not necessarily the king.

This source is from a dialogue Hobbes wrote on the common law of England.

Questions

1. Does Hobbes have a theory of natural law?
2. What limits does Hobbes place on the power of kings?
3. Do you think Hobbes supported Parliament during the Civil War?

La. I Grant you that the King is sole Legislator; but with this Restriction, that if he will not Consult with the Lords of Parliament, and hear the Complaints and Informations of the Commons, that are best acquainted with their own wants, he sinneth against God, though he cannot be Compell'd to any thing by his Subjects by Arms and Force.

Ph. We are Agreed upon that already. Since therefore the King is sole Legislator, I think it also Reason he should be sole Supream Judge.

La. There is no doubt of that; for otherwise there would be no Congruity of Judgments with the Laws. I Grant also that he is the Supream Judge over all Persons, and in all Causes Civil, and Ecclesiastical within his own Dominions, not only by Act of Parliament at this time, but that he has ever been so by the Common-Law: For the Judges of both the Benches have their Offices by the King's Letters Patents, and so (as to Judicature) have the Bishops. Also the Lord Chancellor hath his office by receiving from the King the Great Seal of *England*; and, to say all at once, there is no Magistrate, or Commissioner for Publick Business, neither of Judicature, nor Execution in State, or Church, in Peace, or War, but he is made so by Authority from the King.

Ph. 'Tis true; But perhaps you may think otherwise, when you Read such Acts of Parliament, as say, that the King shall have Power and Authority to do this or that by Virtue of that Act, as *Eliz. c.* I. That your Highness, your Heirs, and Successors, Kings, or Queens of this Realm, shall have full Power and Authority, by Virtue of this Act, by Letters Patents under the Great Seal of *England* to Assign, *&c.* Was it not this Parliament that gave this Authority to the Queen?

La. No; For the Statute in this Clause is no more than (as Sir *Edw. Coke* useth to speak) an Affirmance of the Common-Law; For she being Head of the Church of *England* might make Commissioners for the deciding of Matters Ecclesiastical, as freely as if she had been Pope, who did, you know pretend his right from the Law of God....

La. How would you have a Law defin'd?

Ph. Thus; A Law is the Command of him or them that have the Sovereign Power, given to those that be his or their Subjects, declaring Publickly and plainly what every of them may do, and what they must forbear to do....

La. By your Definition of a Law, the King's Proclamation under the Great Seal of *England* is a Law; for it is a Command, and Publick, and of the Sovereign to his Subjects.

Ph. Why not? If he think it necessary for the good of his Subjects: For this is a Maxim at the Common-Law Alleged by Sir *Edward Coke* himself. (2 *Inst.* p. 306), *Quando Lex aliquid concedit, concedere videtur et id per quod devenitur ad illud.* And you know out of the same Author, that divers Kings of *England* have often, to the Petitions in Parliament which they granted, annexed such exceptions as these, unless there be necessity, saving our Regality; which I think should be always understood, though they be not expressed; and are understood so by Common Lawyers, who agree that the King may recall any Grant wherein he was deceiv'd.

La. Again, whereas you make it of the Essence of a Law to be Publickly and plainly declar'd to the People, I see no necessity for that. Are not all Subjects Bound to take notice of all Acts of Parliament, when no Act can pass without their Consent?

Ph. If you had said that no Act could pass without their knowledge, then indeed they had been bound to take notice of them; but none can have knowledge of them but the Members of the Houses of Parliament; therefore the rest of the People are excus'd; Or else the Knights of the [Shires] should be bound to furnish People with a sufficient Number of Copies (at the People's Charge) of the Acts of Parliament at their return into the Country; that every man may resort to them, and by themselves, or friends, take notice of what they are obliged to; for otherwise it were impossible they should be obeyed: And that no Man is bound to do a thing Impossible is one of Sir *Edw. Cokes* Maxims at the Common-Law. I know that most of the Statutes are Printed, but it does not appear that every Man is bound to Buy the Book of Statutes, nor to search for them at *Westminster* or at the *Tower*, nor to understand the Language wherein they are for the most part Written....

Ph. But what are you better for your Right, if a rebellious Company at home, or an Enemy from abroad, take away the Goods, or dispossess you of the Lands you have a right to? Can you be defended, or repair'd, but by the strength and authority of the King? What reason therefore can be given by a man that endeavours to preserve his Propriety, why he should deny, or malignly contribute to the Strength that should defend him, or repair him? Let us see now what your Books say to this point, and other points of the Right of Sovereignty. *Bracton*, the most authentick author of the Common Law, *fol.* 55. saith thus: *Ipse Dominus Rex habet omnia jura in manu sua, sicut Dei Vicarius; habet etiam ea quæ sunt Pacis; habet etiam coercionem, ut Delinquentes puniat; item habet in potestate sua Leges; nihil enim prodest Jura condere, nisi sit qui Jura tueatur:* That is to say, Our Lord the King hath all Right in his own Hands; is God's Vicar; he has all that concerns the Peace; he has the power to punish Delinquents; all the Laws are in his power:; to make laws is to no purpose, unless there be some-body to make them obeyed. If *Bracton's* Law be Reason, as I, and you think it is; what temporal power is there which the King hath not? Seeing that at this day all the power spiritual which *Bracton* allows the *Pope*, is restored to the Crown; what is there that the King cannot do, excepting sin against the Law of God? The same *Bracton Lib.* ii. *c.* 8. saith thus; *Si autem a Rege petatur (cum Breve non currat contra ipsum) locus erit supplicationi, quod factum suum corrigat, et emendet; quod quidem si non fecerit, satis sufficit ei ad pœnam, quod Dominum expectet Ultorem; nemo quidem de factis ejus præsumat disputare, multo fortius contra factum suum venire:* That is to say, if any thing be demanded of the King (seeing a Writ lyeth not against him) he is put to his Petition, praying him to Correct and Amend his own Fact; which if he will not do, it is a sufficient Penalty for him, that he is to expect a punishment from the Lord: No Man may presume to dispute of what he does, much less to resist him. You see by this, that this Doctrine concerning the Rights of Sovereignty, so much Cryed down by the long Parliament, is the Ancient Common-Law, and that the only Bridle of the Kings of *England*, ought to be the fear of God. And again, *Bracton*, *c.* 24 of the second Book says, That the Rights of the Crown cannot be granted away; *Ea vero quæ Jurisdictionis [sunt] et Pacis, et ea quæ sunt jJustitiæ et Paci annexa, ad nullum pertinent nisi ad Coronam et Dignitatem Regiam, nec a Corona separari possunt, nec a privata persona possideri.* That is to say: those things which belong to Jurisdiction and Peace, and those things that are annexed to Justice and Peace, appertain to none, but to the Crown and Dignity of the King, nor can be separated from the Crown, nor be possest by a private Person. Again, you'l find in *Fleta* (a Law-Book written in the time of *Edw.* 2.) That Liberties though granted by the King, if they tend to the hindrance of Justice, or subversion of the Regal Power, were not to be used, nor allowed: For in that Book *c.* 20. concerning Articles of the Crown, which the jJustices Itinerant are to enquire of, the 54th Article is this, you shall inquire, *De Libertatibus concessis quæ impediunt Communem Justitiam, et Regiam Potestatem subvertunt.* Now what is a greater hindrance to Common Justice, or a greater subversion of the Regal Power, than a Liberty in Subjects to hinder the King from raising Money necessary to suppress, or prevent Rebellions, which doth destroy Justice, and subvert the power of the Sovereignty? Moreover, when a Charter is granted by the King in these words, *Dedita etc.* . . . *coram etc.* . . . *pro me et hæredibus meis*[, t]he grantor by the Common-Law (as Sir *Edw. Coke* says in his Commentaries on *Littleton*) is to warrant his Gift; and I think it Reason, especially if the Gift be upon Consideration of a price Paid. Suppose a Forraign State should lay claim to this

Kingdom ('tis no Matter as to the Question I am putting, whether the Claim be unjust), how would you have the King to warrant to every Free-holder in *England* the Lands they hold of him by such a Charter? If he cannot Levy Money, their Estates are lost, and so is the King's Estate; and if the King's Estate be gone, how can he repair the Value due upon the Warranty? I know that the King's Charters are not so meerly Grants, as that they are not also Laws; but they are such Laws as speak not to all the King's Subjects in general, but only to his Officers; implicitly forbidding them to Judge or eExecute any thing contrary to the said Grants. There be many Men that are able Judges of what is right Reason, and what not; when any of these shall know that a Man has no Superiour nor Peer in the Kingdom, he will hardly be perswaded he can be bound by any Law of the Kingdom, or that he who is Subject to none but God, can make a Law upon himself, which he cannot also as easily abrogate, as he made it. The main Argument, and that which so much taketh with the throng of People, proceedeth from a needless fear put into their minds by such Men as mean to make use of their hHands to their own ends; for if (say they) the King may (notwithstanding the Law) do what he please, and nothing to restrain him but the fear of punishment in the World to come, then (in case there come a King that fears no such punishment) he may take away from us, not only our Lands, Goods, and Liberties, but our Lives also if he will: And they say true; but they have no reason to think he will, unless it be for his own profit; which cannot be, for he loves his own Power; and what becomes of his power when his Subjects are destroyed or weakened, by whose multitude and strength he enjoys his power, and every one of his Subjects his Fortune? And lastly, whereas they sometimes say the King is bound, not only to cause his Laws to be observ'd, but also to observe them himself; I think the King causing them to be observ'd is the same thing as observing them himself: For I never heard it taken for good Law, that the King may be Indicted, or Appealed, or served with a Writ, till the long Parliament practised the contrary upon the good King *Charles*, for which divers of them were Executed, and the rest by this our present King pardoned.

Source: Thomas Hobbes, *A Dialogue Between A Philosopher and A Student of the Common Laws of England* (Chicago: University of Chicago Press, 1971), pp. 66-77.

—————— ✢ ——————

QUESTIONS FOR PART 17

1. Compare the definitions of royal power given by Richelieu and Hobbes.
2. If most states were unsuccessful in establishing absolute monarchies, why does the idea remain popular well into the eighteenth century? Is it just royal greed?
3. Is there any move to secularize politics in the seventeenth century?

PART 18

REVOLUTIONS IN SCIENCE

As Europe transitioned out of the Middle Ages and into the Modern era, it did so with an inquisitive spirit. In matters of religion, politics, trade, and the sciences, Europeans of the sixteenth and seventeenth centuries were not satisfied with the traditional answers; the unexamined life was no longer worth living. In the end, a complete shift in worldview had occurred, although it took the West several more centuries to recognize that. Many subjects of inquiry produced dramatic change (such as the Protestant Reformation and the discovery of new worlds) while others led to more traditional results (as in the witch hunts, which represented a traditionalist response to change).

The last phase of exploration was that of the sciences. Here too a revolution in thought occurred, one that shook European culture down to its core just as Lutheranism had done in 1517. Science changed both in approach and in technique, in theory and in technology, and the changes in one realm of discourse (theory or practice) led to changes in the other, and so forth. As with the religious reformations, there was no one scientific revolution; there were many and the process continues. Perhaps the greatest single legacy of the period is the very concept that science should not stand still, that it should change and seek innovative ideas and approaches.

The scientific transformations began in astronomy, spread to physics and optics, and then to the natural sciences. The change in traditional ways of viewing, explaining, and understanding the physical world was a gradual one that encompassed many new discoveries before the old order of thought changed. It was really only with hindsight that Europe realized how volatile the new scientific discoveries were. When Columbus found the Americas, Europe had to find a new way to explain its place on the earth; similarly, when Copernicus suggested the earth was not the center of the cosmos, humanity had to rethink its place in the universe.

18.1

COPERNICAN THEORY

Nicolaus Copernicus (1473-1543) was a Polish astronomer and mathematician; his revolutionary discovery that the sun was the center of the cosmos was due more to his theoretical understanding of how the stars moved than any observations of his own. Observational proof of Copernicus' heliocentric worldview would come later. Copernicus' most important contribution was simply his willingness to question the geocentric theory that had dominated Europe since the second century AD, when a Greek astronomer named Ptolemy first described the heavens has a series of perfect spheres revolving around a still earth. The Ptolemaic theory had been challenged by some pagan astronomers, but medieval theologians built their theory of a divinely order cosmos around it. Copernicus, however, recognized that mathematically the Ptolemaic system simply did not work. He also recognized that challenging the geocentric theory was dangerous, particularly in the religious climate of the early sixteenth century and did not publish his definitive work, On the Revolution of Heavenly Spheres, *until shortly before his death. The following is an excerpt, which argues that ancient astronomers have to be challenged.*

QUESTIONS

1. How does Copernicus use comets to disprove the Ptolemaic theory of an earth-centered universe?
2. Why *must* the universe be spherical?
3. How is Copernicus' revolutionary new idea a result of Renaissance humanism?

Refutation of the arguments of the ancients that the earth remains still in the middle of the universe, as if it were its center.

From this and similar reasons it is supposed that the earth rests at the center of the universe and that there is no doubt of the fact. But if one believed that the earth revolved, he would certainly be of the opinion that this movement was natural and not arbitrary. For whatever is in accord with nature produces results which are the opposite of those produced by force. Things upon which force or an outside power has acted, must be injured and cannot long endure: what happens by nature, however, preserves itself well and exists in the best condition. So Ptolemy feared without good reason that the earth and all earthly objects subject to the revolution would be destroyed by the act of nature, since this latter is opposed to artificial acts, or to what is produced by the human spirit. But why did he not fear the same, and in a much higher degree, of the universe, whose motion must be as much more rapid as the heavens are greater than the earth? Or has the heaven become so immense because it has been driven outward from the center by the inconceivable power of the revolution; while if it stood still, on the contrary, it would collapse and fall together? But surely if this is the case the extent of the heavens would increase infinitely. For the more it is driven higher by the outward force of the movement, so much the more rapid will the movement become, because of the ever increasing circle which must be traversed in 24 hours; and conversely if the movement grows the immensity of the heavens grows, so the velocity would increase the size and the size would increase the velocity unendingly. According to the physical law that the endless cannot wear away nor in any way move, the heavens must necessarily stand still. But it is said that beyond the sky no body, no place, no vacant space, in fact nothing at all exists; then it is strange that some thing should be enclosed by nothing. But if the heaven is endless and is bounded only by the inner hollow, perhaps this establishes all the more clearly the fact that there is nothing outside the heavens, because everything is within it, but the heaven must then remain unmoved. The highest proof on which one supports the finite character of the universe is its movement. But whether the universe is endless or limited we will leave to the physiologues; this remains sure for us that the earth enclosed between the poles, is bounded by a spherical surface. Why therefore should we not take the position of ascribing to a movement conformable to its nature and corresponding to it form, rather than suppose that the whole universe whose limits are not and cannot be known moves? and why will we not recognize that the appearance of a daily revolution belongs to the heavens, but the actuality to the earth; and that the relation is similar to that of which one says: "We run out of the harbor, the lands and cities retreat from us." Because if a ship sails along quietly, everything outside of it appears to those on board as if it moved with the motion of the boat, and the boatman thinks that the boat with all on board is standing still, this same thing may hold without doubt of the motion of the earth, and it may seem as if the whole universe revolved. What shall we say, however, of the clouds and other things floating, falling or raising in the air — except that not only does the earth move with the watery elements belonging with it, but also a large part of the atmosphere, and whatever else is in any way connected with the earth; whether it is because the air immediately touching the earth has the same nature as the earth, or that the motion has become imparted to the atmosphere. A like astonishment must be felt if that highest region of the air be supposed to follow the heavenly motion, as shown by those suddenly appearing stars which the Greeks call comets or bearded stars, which belong to that region and which rise and set like other stars. We may suppose that part of the atmosphere, because of it great distance from the earth, has become free from the earthly motion. So the atmosphere which lies close to the earth and all things floating in it would appear to remain still, unless driven here and there by the wind or some other outside force, which chance may bring into play; for how is the wind in the air different from current in the sea? We must admit that the motion of things rising and falling in the air is in relation to the universe a double one, being always made up of a rectilinear and a circular movement. Since that which seeks of its own weight to fall is essentially earthy, so there is no doubt that these follow the same natural law as their whole; and it results from this same principle that those things which pertain to fire are forcibly driven on high. Earthly fire is nourished with earthly stuff, and it is said that the flame is only burning smoke. But the peculiarity of the fire consists in this that it expands whatever is seizes upon, and it carries this out so consistently that it can in no way and by no machinery be prevented from breaking its bonds and completing its work. The expanding motion, however, is directed from the center outward; therefore if any earthly material is ignited it moves upward. So to each single body belongs a single motion, and this is evinced preferably in a circular direction as long as the single body remains in its natural place and its entirety. In this position the movement is the circular movement which as far as the body itself is concerned is as if it did not occur. The rectilinear motion, however, siezes upon those bodies which have wandered or have been driven from their natural position or have been in any way disturbed. Nothing is so much opposed to the order and form of the world as the displacement of one of its parts. Rectilinear motion takes place only when objects are not properly related, and are not complete according to their nature because they have separated from their whole and have lost their unity. Moreover, objects which have been driven outward or away, leaving out of consideration the circular motion, do not obey a single, simple and regular motion, since they cannot be controlled simply by their lightness or by the force of their weight, and if in falling they have at first a slow movement the rapidity of the motion increases as they fall, while in the case of earthly fire which is forced upwards — and we have no means of knowing any other kind of fire — we will see that its motion is slow as if its earthly origin thereby showed itself. The circular motion, on the other hand, is always regular, because it is not subject to an intermittent cause. Those other objects, however, would cease to be either light or heavy in respect to their natural movement if they reached their own place, and thus they would fit into that movement. Therefore if the circular movement is to be ascribed to the universe as a whole and the rectilinear to the parts, we might say that the revolution is to the straight line as the natural state is to sickness. That Aristotle divided motion into three sorts, that from the center out, that inward toward center, and that around the center, appears to be merely a logical convenience, just as we distinguish point, line and surface, although one cannot exist without the others, and one of them are found apart from bodies. This fact is also to be considered, that the condition of immovability is held to be nobler and diviner than that of change and inconstancy, which latter therefore should be ascribed rather to the earth than to the universe, and I would add also that it seems inconsistent to attribute motion to the containing and locating element rather than to the contained and located object, which the earth is. Finally since the planets plainly are at one time nearer and at another time farther from the earth, it would follow, on the theory that the universe revolves, that the movement of the one and same body which is known to take place about a center, that is the center of the earth, must also be directed toward the center from without and from the center outward. The movement about the center must therefore be made more general, and it suffices if that single movement be about its own center. So it appears from all these considerations that the movement of the earth is more probable than its fixity, especially in regard to the daily revolution, which is most peculiar to the earth.

Source: Oliver J. Thatcher, ed., *The Ideas that have Influenced Civilization in the Original Documents, Volume V* (Boston: Roberts-Manchester Publishing Co., 1901), pp. 96-101.

18.2

---- ✤ ----

CONDEMNATION AND RECANTATION OF GALILEO

Copernicus was right to worry about the repercussions of publicizing his radical new understanding of the universe. If anyone had any doubts about the danger of doing so, the difficulties Galileo Galilei (1564-1642) faced in attempting to prove the Copernican theory offers proof. Between Copernicus and Galileo stand a host of observational and theoretical astronomer, such as Tycho Brahe and Johannes Kepler, who each contributed clues to the heliocentric puzzle. Using the astronomical tables assembled by these two men, Galileo was able to conclusively disprove the Ptolemaic system. Galileo had two advantages over these earlier astronomers: he was able to use their data and build upon it, and he had a telescope. Galileo was the first astronomer to use a telescope, a Flemish invention, and with his newly magnified vision he noticed one important fact about the stars. They were not perfect. The Ptolemaic system had fit so perfectly with Christian theology because both had argued that the universe was a perfect created system, reflecting a divine plan, focused on the greatest of divine creations, humanity. By placing humanity, the earth, at the center of the universe, the Ptolemaic theory supported scriptural understanding of creation. Galileo challenged this by pointing out the imperfections of the stars and planets, their movement, and his mathematical proof that the earth was just another heavenly body, no more perfect than the other created objects.

Unlike Copernicus, Galileo did not hesitate to publicize his ideas. At the University of Padua he taught the Copernican theories, and published his observations in The Starry Messenger *in 1610. The Catholic Church responded to this challenge by condemning the Copernican system and by summoning Galileo before the Inquisition for teaching heresy. Still, Galileo continued to teach Copernicanism, and in 1632 published a second book on it. This led to a second condemnation in 1633 by the Inquisition, Galileo's full recantation, and house arrest for the astronomer for the rest of his life. He was forbidden to write on or teach astronomy.*

The following source is the text of the second Condemnation of 1633 and Galileo's Recantation.

——————— ✣ ———————

QUESTIONS

1. How does the office of the Inquisition see Copernicanism as a rejection of scripture?
2. What sentence is pronounced for the second book of Galileo, the *Dialogues*?
3. Do you think Copernicus and Galileo saw their astronomical work as an attack on Christianity?

CONDEMNATION

We...by the grace of God, cardinals of the Holy Roman Church, Inquisitors General, by the Holy Apostolic see specially deputed, against heretical depravity throughout the whole Christian Republic.

Whereas you, Galileo, son of the late Vincenzo Galilei, Florentine, aged seventy years, were in the year 1615 denounced to this Holy Office for holding as true the false doctrine taught by some that the sun is the centre of the world and immovable and that the earth moves, and also with a diurnal motion; for having disciples to whom you taught the same doctrine; for holding correspondence with certain mathematicians of Germany concerning the same; for having printed certain letters, entitled "On the Sunspots," wherein you developed the same doctrine as true; and for replying to the objections from the Holy Scriptures, which from time to time were urged against it, by glossing the said Scriptures according to your own meaning: and whereas there was thereupon produced the copy of a document in the form of a letter, purporting to be written by you to one formerly your disciple, and in this divers propositions are set forth, following the position of Copernicus, which are contrary to the true sense and authority of Holy Scripture:

This Holy Tribunal being therefore of intention to proceed against the disorder and mischief thence resulting, which went on increasing to the prejudice of the Holy Faith, by command of his Holiness and of the most eminent Lords Cardinals of this Supreme and universal Inquisition, the two propositions of the stability of the sun and the motion of the earth were by the theological "Qualifiers" qualified as follows:

The proposition that the sun is the centre of the world and does not move from its place is absurd and false philosophically and formally heretical, because it is expressly contrary to Holy Scripture.

Therefore, by our order you were cited before this Holy Office, where, being examined upon your oath, you acknowledged the book as written and published by you. You confessed that you began to write the said book about ten or twelve years ago, after the command had been imposed upon you as above; that you questioned license to print it, without however intimating to those who granted you this license that you had been commanded not to hold, defend, or teach in any way whatever the doctrine in question.

You likewise confessed that the writing of said book in its various places drawn up in such a form that the reader might fancy that arguments brought forward on the false side are rather calculated by their cogency to compel conviction than to be easy of refutation; excusing yourself for having fallen into an error, as you alleged, so foreign to your intention, by the fact that you had written in dialogue, and by the natural complacency that every man feels in regard to his own subtleties, and in showing him more clever than the generality of men, in devising, even on behalf of false propositions, ingenious and plausible arguments.

And a suitable term having been assigned to you to prepare your defence, you produced a certificate in the handwriting of his Eminence the Lord Cardinal Bellarmine, procured by you, as you asserted, in order to defend yourself against the calumnies of your enemies, who gave out that you had abjured and had been punished by the Holy Office; in which certificate it is declared that you had not abjured and had not been punished, but merely that the declaration made by his Holiness and published by the Holy Congregation of the Index, had been announced to you, wherein it is declared that the doctrine of the motion of the earth and the stability of the sun is contrary to the Holy Scriptures, and therefore cannot be defended or held. and as in this certificate there is no mention of the two articles of the injunction, namely, the order not "to teach" and "in any way," you represented that we ought to believe that in the course of fourteen or sixteen years you had lost all memory of them and that this was why you said nothing of the injunction when you requested permission to print your book. And all this you urged not by way of excuse for your error, but that it might be set down to a vainglorious ambition rather than to malice. But this certificate produced by you in your defence has only aggravated your delinquency, since although it is there stated that the said opinion is contrary to Holy Scripture, you have nevertheless dared to discuss and to defend it and to argue its probability; nor does the license artfully and cunningly extorted by you avail you anything, since you did not notify the command imposed upon you.

And whereas it appeared to us that you had not stated the full truth with regard to your intention, we thought it necessary to subject you to a rigorous examination, at which (without prejudice, however, to the matters confessed by you, and set forth as above, with regard to your said intention) you answered like a good Catholic. Therefore, having seen and maturely considered the merits of this your cause, together with your confessions and excuses above mentioned, and all that ought justly to be seen and considered, we have arrived at the underwritten final sentence against you: —

Invoking, therefore, the most holy name of our Lord Jesus Christ and of His most glorious Mother and ever Virgin Mary, by this our final sentence, which sitting in judgment, with the counsel and advice of the Reverend Masters of sacred theology and Doctors of both Laws, our assessors, we deliver in these writings, in the cause and causes presently before us between the magnificent Carlo Sinceri, Doctor of both Laws, Proctor Fiscal of this Holy Office, of the one part, and you Galileo Galilei, the defendant, here present, tried and confessed as above, have rendered yourself in the judgment of this Holy Office vehemently suspected of heresy, namely, of having believed and held the doctrine — which is false and contrary to the sacred and divine Scriptures — that the sun is the centre of the world and does not move from east to west, and that the earth moves and is not the centre of the world; and that the opinion may beheld and defended as probable after it has been declared and defined to be contrary to Holy Scriptures and that consequently you have incurred all the censures and penalties imposed and promulgated in the sacred canons and other constitutions, general and particular, against such delinquents. From which we are content that you be absolved, provided that first, with a sincere heart, and unfeigned faith, you abjure, curse, and detest the aforesaid errors and heresies, and every other error and heresy contrary to the Catholic and Apostolic Roman Church in the form to be prescribed by us.

And in order that this your grave and pernicious error and transgression may not remain altogether unpunished, and that you may be more cautious for the future, and as an example to others, that they may abstain from similar delinquencies — we ordain that the book of the *"Dialogues of Galileo Galilei"* be prohibited by public edict.

We condemn you to the formal prison of the Holy Office during our pleasure, and by way of salutary penance, we enjoin that for three years to come you repeat once a week the seven penitential Psalms.

Reserving to ourselves full liberty to moderate, commute, or take off, in whole or in part, the aforesaid penalties and penance.

And as we say, pronounce, sentence, declare, ordain, condemn and reserve, in this and any other better way and form which we can and may lawfully employ.

So we the undersigned Cardinals pronounce.

RECANTATION

"I Galileo Galilei, son of the late Vincenzo Galilei, Florentine, aged 70 years, arraigned personally before this tribunal, and kneeling before you, most Eminent and Reverend Lord Cardinals, Inquisitor general against heretical depravity throughout the whole Christian Republic, having before my eyes and touching with my hands, the holy Gospels — swear that I have always believed, do now believe, and by God's help will for the future believe, all that is held, preached, and taught by the Holy Catholic and Apostolic Roman Church. But whereas — after an injunction had been judiciously intimated to me by this Holy Office, to the effect that I must altogether abandon the false opinion that the sun is the centre of the world and immovable, and that the earth is not the centre of the world, and moves, and that I must not hold, defend, or teach in any way whatsoever, verbally or in writing, the said doctrine, and after it had been notified to me that the said doctrine was contrary to the Holy Scripture — I wrote and printed a book in which I discuss this doctrine already condemned, and adduced arguments of great cogency in its favor, without presenting any solution of these; and for this cause I have been pronounced by the Holy Office to be vehemently suspected of heresy, that is to say, of having held and believed that the sun is the centre of the world and immovable, and that the earth is not the centre and moves: —

Therefore, desiring to remove from the minds of your Eminences, and of all faithful Christians, this strong suspicion, reasonably conceived against me, with sincere heart and unfeigned faith I abjure, curse, and detest the aforesaid errors and heresies, and generally every other error and sect whatsoever contrary to the said Holy Church; and I swear that in future I will never again say or assert, verbally or in writing, anything that might furnish occasion for a similar suspicion regarding me; but that should I know any heretic, or person suspected of heresy, I will denounce him to the Holy Office, or the Inquisitor promise to fulfil and observe in their integrity all penances that have been, or that shall be, imposed upon me by this Holy Office. And, in the event of my contravening, (which God forbid!) any of these my promises, protestations, and oaths, I submit myself to the pains and penalties imposed and promulgated in the sacred canons and other constitutions, general and particular, against such delinquents. So help me God, and His holy Gospels, which I touch with my hands.

I, the said Galileo Galilei, have abjured, sworn, promised, and bound myself as above; and in witness of the truth thereof I have with my own hand subscribed the present document of my abjuration, and recited it word for word at Rome, in the Convent of Minerva, this twenty-second day of June, 1633.

I, Galileo Galilei, have abjured as above with my own hand."

Source: Oliver J. Thatcher, ed., *The Ideas that have Influenced Civilization in the Original Documents, Volume V*, (Boston: Roberts-Manchester Publishing Co., 1901), pp. 302-307.

18.3

LETTERS ON THE EXISTENCE OF GOD, ISAAC NEWTON

Isaac Newton (1642-1727) reinvented the universe. If throughout the Middle Ages the cosmos was always understood according to the Ptolemaic theory, after the publication of Newton's Principia Mathematica *in 1686, the universe would be forever understood according to a Newtonian framework. Newton's work transcends the field of astronomy. The* Principia *was not really about astronomy per se; it was about universal mechanics. With this work Newton invented the science of physics. He also theorized on optics, chemistry, economics, motion, epistemology, theology, alchemy and other magics, and of course invented a theory of universal laws (such as gravity) that explained how it all worked. Newton's influence was dramatic and widespread, then and now. As a professor at Cambridge, president of the English Royal Society of Science, and voluminous letter writer, Newton made his theories well known to a wide audience. He was also fiercely competitive and protective of his theories, and while generally promoted all scientific exploration, was known to use his influence to suppress rivals.*

Newton's purely scientific discoveries are well known, such as his laws of motion. The two letters reproduced here introduce a less familiar side of Newton, one in which he discusses the implications of his physics and the greatest enigma of his system, of whether there is a primary force or ultimate creator behind the universe as a whole. Newton wrote these letters, and two more, to Richard Bentley in 1691-92. Bentley was preparing a series of lectures at Cambridge University on proving God's existence using the new mathematical and scientific theories. Bentley to Newton and asked him to suggest what parts of the Principia might be most useful. He also asked Newton to explain to him, a non-scientist, the theory of universal forces, particularly gravity. The letters he and Newton exchanged reveal Newton thinking out his ideas further and seeking the best way to explain them to a non-specialized audience. Bentley's sermons were published as A Confutation of Atheism.

QUESTIONS

1. What implications can you draw from the fact that Newton wanted to explain his ideas to an Anglican priest, and wanted to help Bentley incorporate them into sermons?
2. What do you think Newton meant by the phrase "author of the system?"
3. Why does Newton deny knowing the ultimate cause of gravity?

To the Reverend Dr. Richard Bentley, at the Bishop of Worcester's House in Parkstreet, Westminster.

S ir,

When I wrote my Treatise about our System, I had an Eye upon such Principles as might work, with considering Men, for the Belief of a Deity, and nothing can rejoice me more than to find it useful for that

Purpose. But if I have done the Public any service this way, it is due to nothing by Industry and patient Thought.

As to your first Query, it seems to me that if the Matter of our Sun and Planets, and all the Matter of the Universe, were evenly scattered throughout all the Heavens, and every Particle had an innate Gravity towards all the rest, and the whole Space, throughout which this Matter was scattered, was but finite; the Matter on the outside of this Space would by its Gravity tend towards all the Matter on the inside, and by consequence fall down into the middle of the whole Space, and there compose one great spherical Mass. But if the Matter was evenly disposed throughout an infinite Space, it could never convene into the Mass, but some of it would convene into one Mass and some into another, so as to make an infinite Number of great Masses, scattered at great Distances from one to another throughout all that infinite Space. And thus might the Sun and fixt Stars be formed, supposing the Matter were of a lucid Nature. But how the Matter should divide itself into two sorts, and that Part of it, which is fit to compose of shining Body, should fall down into one Mass and make a Sun, and the rest, which is fit to compose an opaque Body, like the shining Matter, but into many little ones; or if the Sun at first were an opaque body like the Planets, or the Planets lucid Bodies like the Sun, how he alone should be changed into a shining Body, whilst all they continue opaque, or all they be changed into opaque ones, whilst he remains unchanged, I do not think explicable by meer natural Causes, but am forced to ascribe it to the Counsel and Contrivance of a voluntary Agent.

The same Power, whether natural or supernatural, which placed the Sun in the Center of the six primary Planets, placed *Saturn* in the Center of the Orbs of his five secondary Planets, and *Jupiter* in the Center of his four secondary Planets, and the Earth in the Center of the Moon's Orb; and therefore had this Cause been a blind one, without Contrivance or Design, the Sun would have been a Body of the same kind with *Saturn, Jupiter,* and the Earth, that is, without Light and Heat. Why there is one Body in our System qualified to give Light and Heat to all the rest, I know no Reason, but because one was sufficient to warm and enlighten all the rest. For the *Cartesian* Hypothesis of Suns losing their Light, and then turning into Comets, and Comets into Planets, can have no Place in my System, and is plainly erroneous; because it is certain that as often as they appear to us, they descend into the System of our Planets, lower than the Orb of *Jupiter*, and sometimes lower than the Orbs of *Venus* and *Mercury*, and yet never stay here, but always return from the Sun with the same Degrees of Motion by which they approached him.

To your second Query, I answer, that the Motions which the Planets now have could not spring from any natural Cause alone, but were impressed by an intelligent Agent. For since Comets descend into the Region of our Plants, and here move all manner of ways, going sometimes the contrary way, and sometimes in cross ways, in Planes inclined to the Plane of the Ecliptick, and at all kinds of angles, 'tis plain that there is no natural Cause which could determine all the Planets, both primary and secondary, to move the same way and in the same Plane, without any considerable Variation: This must have been the Effect of Counsel. Nor is there any natural Cause which could give the Planets those just Degrees of Velocity, in Proportion to their distances from the Sun, and other central Bodies, which were requisite to make them move in such concentrick Orbs about those Bodies. Had the Planets been as swift as Comets, in Proportion to their Distances from the Sun (as they would have been, had their Motion been caused by their Gravity, whereby the Matter, at the first Formation of the Planets, might fall from the remotest Regions towards the Sun) they would not move in concentrick Orbs, but in such eccentrick ones as the Comets move in. Were all the Planets as swift as *Mercury*, or as slow as *Saturn* or his Satellites; or were their several Velocities otherwise much greater or less than they are, as they might have been had they arose from any other Cause than their Gravities; or had the Distances from the Centers about which they move, been greater or less than they are with the same Velocities; or had the Quantity of Matter in the Sun, or in *Saturn*, *Jupiter*, and the Earth, and by consequence their gravitation Power been greater or less than it is; the primary Planet could not have revolved about the Sun, nor the secondary ones about *Saturn*, *Jupiter*, and the Earth, in concentrick Circles as they do, but would have moved in Hyperbolas, or Parabolas, or in Ellipses very eccentrick. To make this System therefore, with all its Motions, required a Cause which understood, and compared together, the Quantities of Matter in the several Bodies of the Sun and Planets.

Source: Isaac Newton, *Isaac Newton's Papers & Letters on Natural Philosophy, Volume I*, ed. Bernard Cohen (Cambridge: Harvard University Press, 1958), pp. 279-99.

18.4

✦

OBSERVATIONS UPON EXPERIMENTAL PHILOSOPHY, MARGARET CAVENDISH

The scientific revolution was not limited to the discoveries and theories by men. Margaret Cavendish (1623-1673) is one of several prominent female scientists of the new age. Many of these women came from aristocratic backgrounds (Cavendish was the Duchess of Newcastle) and thus had the money and education that allowed them access to the new theories of men such as Galileo, Newton, and John Locke. Another example would be Madame de Châtelet, mistress of Voltaire, who first translated Newton's *Principia* from Latin into French. In eastern Europe the new scientific women will typically come from the artisan class, which provided training for the more practical (rather than theoretical) side of scientific discovery. These women were often derided by their male contemporaries as being amateurs or hobbyists; yet these same men refused to allow female scientists in the universities or membership in the scientific societies, which would have given them "professional" status.

Here Cavendish discusses empirical observations.

✦

QUESTIONS

1. According to Cavendish, how do our external sense perceptions differ from our rational perceptions?
2. How do you think Cavendish defined the concept "nature?"
3. Does Cavendish belief empirical knowledge is true knowledge?

XXVII Of Thawing or Dissolving of Frozen Bodies

As freezing or congelation is caused by contracting, condensing, and retentive motions; so thawing is nothing else but dissolving, dilating, and extending motions: for, freezing and thawing are two contrary actions; and as freezing is caused several ways, according to the various disposition of congealable bodies, and the temper of exterior cold; so thawing, or a dissolution of frozen bodies, may be occasioned either by a sympathetic agreement, (as for example, the thawing of ice in water, or other liquors) or by some exterior imitation, as by hot dilating motions. And it is to be observed, that, as the time of freezing, so the time of dissolving, is according to the several natures and tempers both of the frozen bodies, which occasion their thawing or dissolution: for, it is not only heat that doth cause ice, or snow, or other frozen bodies to melt quicker or slower; but, according as the nature of the heat is, either more or less dilative, or more or less rarefying: for surely, an exterior actual heat, is more rarefying than an interior virtual heat; as we see in strong spirituous liquors which are interiorly contracting, but being made actually hot, become exteriorly dilating: The like of many other bodies; so that actual heat is more dissolving than virtual heat. And this is the reason why ice and snow will melt sooner in some countries or places, than in others; and is much harder in some, than in others: for we see, that neither air, water, earth, minerals, nor any other sorts of creatures are just alike in all countries or climates: The same may be said of heat and cold. Besides, it is to be observed, that oftentimes a different application of one and the same object, will occasion different effects; as for example, if salt be mixed with ice, it may cause the contracted body of ice to change its present motions into its former state or figure, viz. into water; but being applied outwardly, or on the outside of the vessel wherein snow or ice is contained, it may make it freeze harder instead of dissolving it. Also, ice will oftentimes break into pieces of its own accord, and without the application of any exterior object: And the reason, in my opinion, is, that some of the interior parts of the ice endeavouring to return to their proper and natural figure by virtue of their interior dilative motions, do break and divide some of the exterior parts that are contracted by the motions of frost, especially those which have not so great a force or power as to resist them.

But concerning thawing, some by their trials have found, that if frozen eggs, apples, and the like bodies, be thawed near the fire, they will be thereby spoiled: but if they be immersed in cold water, or wrapt into ice or snow, the internal cold will be drawn out, as they suppose, but the external; and the frozen bodies will be harmlessly, though not so quickly, thawed. And truly, this experiment stands much to reason; for, in my opinion, when frozen bodies perceive heat or fire, the motions of their frozen parts, upon the perception, endeavour to imitate the motions of heat or fire; which being opposite to the motions of cold, in this sudden and hasty change, they become irregular, insomuch as to cause in most frozen parts a dissolution of their interior natural figure: Wherefore it is very probable, that frozen bodies will thaw more regularly in water, or being wrapt into ice or snow, than by heat or fire: for, thawing is a dilating action; and water, as also ice and snow, (which are nothing but congealed water) being of a dilative nature, may easily occasion a thawing of the mentioned frozen parts, by sympathy; provided the motions of the exterior cold do not overpower the motions of the interior frozen parts: for, if a frozen body should be wrapt thus into ice or snow, and continue in an open, cold, frosty air, I question whether it would cause a thaw in the same body; it would preserve the body in its frozen state, from dissolving or disuniting, rather than occasion its thawing. But that such frozen bodies, as apples, and eggs, etc. immersed in water, will produce ice on their outsides, is no wonder, by reason the motions of water imitate the motions of the frozen bodies; and those parts of water that are nearest, are the first imitators, and become of the same mode. By which we may see, that some parts will clothe themselves, others only veil themselves with artificial dresses; most of which dresses are but copies of other motions, and not original actions: It makes also evident, that those effects are not caused by an ingress of frigorific atoms in water, or other congealable bodies, but by the perceptive motions of their own parts. And what I have said of cold, the same may be spoken of heat; for it is known, that a part of a man's body being burned with fire, the burning may be cured by the heat of the fire; which, in my opinion, proceeds from a sympathetical agreement betwixt the motions of the fire, and the motions of the burned part: for every part of a man's body hath its natural heat, which is of an intermediate temper; which heat being heightened by the burning motions of ire, beyond its natural degree, causes a burning and smarting pain in the same part: And therefore, as the fire did occasion an immoderate heat, by an intermixture of its own parts with the parts of the flesh; so a moderate heat of the fire may reduce again the natural heat of the same parts, and that by a sympathetical agreement betwixt the motions of the elemental and animal heat. But it is to be observed, first, that the burning must be done by an intermixture of the fire with the parts of the body: Next, that the burning must be but skin-deep, (as we used to call it) that is, the burned part must not be totally overcome by fire, or else it will never be restored again. Neither are all burned bodies restored after this manner, but some; for one and the same thing will not in all bodies occasion the like effects; as we may see by fire, which being one and the same, will not cause all fuels to burn alike, and this makes true the old saying, "One man's meat, is another man's poison." The truth is, it cannot be otherwise: for, though nature, and natural self-moving matter is but one body, and the only cause of all natural effects; yet nature being divided into infinite, corporeal, figurative self-moving parts; these parts, as the effects of that only cause, must needs be various, and again, proceeding from one infinite cause, as one matter, they are all but one thing, because they are infinite parts of one infinite body. But some may say, If nature be but one body, and the infinite parts are all united into that same body; how comes it that there is such an opposition, strife and war, betwixt the parts of nature? I answer: Nature being material, is composable and dividable; and as composition is made by a mutual agreement of parts, so division is made by an opposition or strife betwixt parts; which opposition or division, doth not obstruct the union of nature, but, on the contrary, rather proves, that without an opposition of parts, there could not be a union or composition of so many several parts and creatures, nor no change or variety in nature; for if all the parts did unanimously conspire and agree in their motions, and move all but one way, there would be but one act or kind of motion in nature; whenas an opposition of some parts, and a mutual agreement of others, is not only the cause of the miraculous variety in nature, but it poises and balances, as it were, the corporeal figurative motions, which is the cause that nature is steady and fixt in herself, although her parts be in a perpetual motion.

Source: Margaret Cavendish, *Observations upon Experimental Philosophy,* ed. Eileen O'Neill (Cambridge: Cambridge University Press, 2001), pp. 46-48, 117-119.

✦

QUESTIONS FOR PART 18

1. Although not everyone mentions it explicitly, how is Christian faith still inextricably linked to science even with the new discoveries?
2. Why does Newton not face the same kind of censure from the Christian churches, as does Galileo?
3. Does the heliocentric view of the universe necessarily reduce the importance of humanity?

PART 19

THE ENLIGHTENMENT

The Enlightenment was as much a revolutionary movement as the scientific discoveries of Copernicus, Galileo, Newton, and Cavendish. In fact, these scientists began the enlightenment when they moved from discussing astronomy and mechanics to debating matters of natural philosophy. The Enlightenment also owes a cultural debt to the humanists of the Renaissance, which re-oriented Europe toward an examination of human endeavor rather than mere contemplation of the divine.

The Enlightenment began with a few French philosophers, called *philosophes*, who read the works of Newton and the other new sciences; most were not scientists themselves but they read the latest scientific theories. In fact, they read everything: accounts of new world exploration, colonialism, political theories (such as those of Hobbes and Locke), and current events. The movement quickly spread out of France and throughout the rest of Europe, and then to the colonies of the Americas. The result was another intellectual revolution, this one with even more pervasive influence than the sciences. One of the most profound ideological shifts brought about by the Enlightenment was the move toward a more skeptical and more secular worldview. Whereas Copernicus and Galileo had suggested that God had created a heliocentric universe, the *philosophes* went further and questioned whether God was part of the plan at all. The Enlightenment transformed not only the intellectual arena, it also led directly to the political revolutions of the eighteenth century, the nationalist movements of the nineteenth century, and the increasing secularization of the West in the twentieth century.

19.1

SOME THOUGHTS CONCERNING EDUCATION, JOHN LOCKE

Next to Newton, John Locke probably had the most influence on the philosophes. An Englishman, Locke (1632-1704) was primarily a political theorist. In his Two Treatises on Government, *Locke argued against the absolutist model of the seventeenth century; he felt that government should only exist to link the laws of people with the higher law of nature. However, Locke was also reading the works of contemporary, natural philosophers (such as Newton) and considering what role humanity had in relation to nature. The traditional view of the Christian Middle Ages, bolstered by scripture, had been that man was created to dominate nature. The new understanding of the universe as a mechanical system revolving in imperfect ellipses around the sun called into question this view. Locke and other pre-Enlightenment philosophers argued instead that humanity was an integral part of nature, with only the capacity for reason distinguishing humanity from animals. Instead of being in charge of nature, Locke claimed, humanity was shaped by nature. He expressed this more clearly in his* Essay Concerning Human Understanding, *in which he proposed that all people were blank slates upon which nature built knowledge through experience.*

Locke was asked by a close friend to propose a plan for educating the friend's son. Locke responded with several letters on education that extended his discussion of how knowledge was acquired. He later expanded the letters into an essay, from which this passage is taken.

———————— ✢ ————————

QUESTIONS

1. Does Locke have a positive or negative view of the potential of education?
2. What role does Locke envision for religion to play in education?
3. Why does Locke insist that education be fun?

118.

Curiosity in children (which I had occasion just to mention Section 108) is but an appetite after knowledge; and therefore ought to be encouraged in them, not only as a good sign, but as the great instrument nature has provided to remove that ignorance they were born with; and which, without this busy inquisitiveness, will make them dull and useless creatures. The ways to encourage it, and keep it active and busy, are, I suppose, these following:

1. Not to check or discountenance any enquiries he shall make, nor suffer them to be laughed at; but to answer all his questions, and explain the matter he desires to know, so as to make them as much intelligible to him as suits the capacity of his age and knowledge. But confound not his understanding with explications or notions that are above it; or with the variety or number of things that are not to his present purpose. Mark what 'tis his mind aims at in the question, and not what words he expresses it in: and when you have informed and satisfied him in that, you shall see how his thoughts will enlarge themselves, and how by fit answers he may be led on farther than perhaps you could imagine. For knowledge is grateful to the understanding, as light to the eyes: children are pleased and delighted with it exceedingly, especially if they see that their enquiries are regarded, and that their desire of knowing is encouraged and commended. And I doubt not but one great reason why many children abandon themselves wholly to silly sports, and trifle away all their time insipidly, is, because they have found their curiosity baulked, and their enquiries neglected. But had they been treated with more kindness and respect, and their questions answered, as they should, to their satisfaction; I doubt not but they would have taken more pleasure in learning, and improving their knowledge, wherein there would be still newness and variety, which is what they are delighted with, than in returning over and over to the same play and playthings.

119. 2. To this serious answering their questions, and informing their understandings, in what they desire, as if it were a matter that needed it, should be added some peculiar ways of commendation. Let others whom they esteem, be told before their faces of the knowledge they have in such and such things;

and since we are all, even from our cradles, vain and proud creatures, let their vanity be flattered with things that will do them good; and let their pride set them on work on something which may turn to their advantage. Upon this ground you shall find, that there cannot be a greater spur to the attaining what you would have the eldest learn, and know himself, than to set him upon teaching it his younger brothers and sisters.

120. 3. As children's enquiries are not to be slighted; so also great care is to be taken, that they never receive deceitful and eluding answers. They easily perceive when they are slighted or deceived; and quickly learn the trick of neglect, dissimulation and falsehood, which they observe others to make use of. We are not to intrench upon truth in any conversation, but least of all with children; since if we play false with them, we not only deceive their expectation, and hinder their knowledge, but corrupt their innocence, and teach them the worst of vices. They are travelers newly arrived in a strange country, of which they know nothing; we should therefore make conscience not to mislead them. And though their questions seem sometimes not very material, yet they should be seriously answered; for however they may appear to us (to whom they are long since known) enquiries not worth the making; they are of moment to those who are wholly ignorant. Children are strangers to all we are acquainted with; and all the things they meet with, are at first unknown to them, as they once were to us: and happy are they who meet with civil people that will comply with their ignorance, and help them to get out of it.

If you or I now should be set down in Japan, with all our prudence and knowledge about us, a conceit whereof makes us, perhaps, so apt to slight the thoughts and enquiries of children; should we, I say, be set down in Japan, we should, no doubt (if we would inform our selves of what is there to be known) ask a thousand questions, which, to a supercilious or inconsiderate Japaner, would seem very idle and impertinent; though to us they would be very material and of importance to be resolved; and we should be glad to find a man so complaisant and courteous, as to satisfy our demands, and instruct our ignorance.

When any new thing comes in their way, children usually ask the common question of a stranger: *What is it?* Whereby they ordinarily mean nothing but the name; and therefore to tell them how it is called, is usually the proper answer to that demand. And the next question usually is, *What is it for?* And to this it should be answered truly and directly. The use of the thing should be told, and the way explained, how it serves to such a purpose, as far as their capacities can comprehend it. And so of any other circumstances they shall ask about it; not turning them going, till you have given them all the satisfaction they are capable of; and so leading them by your answers into farther questions. And perhaps to a grown man, such conversation will not be altogether so idle and insignificant as we are apt to imagine. The native and untaught suggestions of inquisitive children do often offer things, that may set a considering man's thoughts on work. And I think there is frequently more to be learned from the unexpected questions of a child, than the discourses of men, who talk in a road, according to the notions they have borrowed, and the prejudices of their education.

121. 4. Perhaps it may not sometimes be amiss to excite their curiosity by bringing strange and new things in their way, on purpose to engage their enquiry, and give them occasion to inform themselves about them and if by chance their curiosity leads them to ask what they should not know, it is a great deal better to tell them plainly, that it is a thing that belongs not to them to know, than to pop them off with a falsehood of a frivolous answer....

132. Children, afraid to have their faults seen in their naked colors, will, like the rest of the sons of Adam, be apt to make excuses. This is a fault usually bordering upon, and leading to untruth, and is not to be indulged in them; but yet it ought to be cured rather with shame than roughness. If therefore, when a child is questioned for any thing, his first answer be an excuse, warn him soberly to tell the truth; and

then if he persists to shuffle it off with a falsehood, he must be chastised; but if he directly confess, you must commend his ingenuity, and pardon the fault, be it what it will; and pardon it so, that you never so much as reproach him with it, or mention it to him again: for if you would have him in love with ingenuity, and by a constant practice make it habitual to him, you must take care that it never procure him the least inconvenience; but on the contrary, his own confession bringing always with it perfect impunity, should be besides encouraged by some marks of approbation. If his excuse be such at any time that you cannot prove it to have any falsehood in it, let it pass for true, and be sure not to show any suspicion of it. Let him keep up his reputation with you as high as is possible; for when once he finds he has lost that, you have lost a great, and your best hold upon him. Therefore let him not think he has the character of a liar with you, as long as you can avoid it without flattering him in it. Thus some slips in truth may be overlooked. But after he has once been corrected for a lie, you must be sure never after to pardon it in him, whenever you find and take notice to him that he is guilty of it: for it being a fault which he has been forbid, and may, unless he be willful, avoid, the repeating of it is perfect perverseness, and must have the chastisement due to that offence.

133. This is what I have thought concerning the general method of educating a young gentleman; which, though I am apt to suppose may have some influence on the whole course of his education, yet I am far from imagining it contains all those particulars which his growing years or peculiar temper may require. But this being premised in general, we shall in the next place descend to a more particular consideration of the several parts of his education.

134. That which every gentleman (that takes any care of his education) desires for his son, besides the estate he leaves him, is contained, I suppose, in these four things, *virtue, wisdom, breeding* and *learning.* I will not trouble my self whether these names do not some of them sometimes stand for the same thing, or really include one another. It serves my turn here to follow the popular use of these words, which, I presume, is clear enough to make me be understood, and I hope there will be no difficulty to comprehend my meaning.

135. I place *virtue* as the first and most necessary of those endowments that belong to a man or a gentleman; as absolutely requisite to make him valued and beloved by others, acceptable or tolerable to himself. Without that, I think, he will be happy neither in this nor the other world.

136. As the foundation of this, there ought very early to be imprinted on his mind a true notion of God, as of the independent Supreme Being, Author and Maker of all things, from Whom we receive all our good, Who loves us, and gives us all things. And consequent to this, instill into him a love and reverence of this Supreme Being. This is enough to begin with, without going to explain this matter any farther; for fear lest by talking too early to him of spirits, and being unseasonably forward to make him understand the incomprehensible nature of that Infinite Being, his head be either filled with false, or perplexed with unintelligible notions of Him. Let him only be told upon occasion, that God made and governs all things, hears and sees every thing, and does all manner of good to those that love and obey Him; you will find, that being told of such a God, other thoughts will be apt to rise up fast enough in his mind about Him; which, as you observe them to have any mistakes, you must set right. And I think it would be better if men generally rested in such an idea of God, without being too curious in their notions about a Being which all must acknowledge incomprehensible; whereby many, who have not strength and clearness of thought to distinguish between what they can, and what they cannot know, run themselves in superstitions or atheism, making God like themselves, or (because they cannot comprehend any thing else) none at all. And I am apt to think, the keeping children constantly morning and evening to acts of devotion to God, as to their Maker, Preserver and Benefactor, in some plain and short form of prayer,

suitable to their age and capacity, will be of much more use to them in religion, knowledge, and virtue, than to distract their thoughts with curious enquiries into His inscrutable essence and being.

137. Having by gentle degrees, as you find him capable of it, settled such an idea of God in his mind, and taught him to pray to Him, and praise Him as the Author of his being, and of all the good he does or can enjoy; forbear any discourse of other spirits, till the mention of them coming in his way, upon occasion hereafter to be set down, and his reading the scripture-history, put him upon that enquiry.

Source: John Locke, *On Politics and Education*, ed. Howard R. Penniman (New York: D. Van Nostrand Company, Inc., 1947), pp. 309-311, 318-321, 332-337.

19.2

---- ✦ ----

"ON SOVEREIGNTY,"
JEAN JACQUES ROUSSEAU

Jean Jacques Rousseau (1712-1778) was a Swiss-born political theorist who moved to Paris, and although a member of various Enlightenment social groups, remained aloof and removed from his fellow philosophes. Rousseau was critical of both the political theories that had preceded the Enlightenment as well as those philosophes whom he felt did not go far enough in promoting individual liberty.

The following is from his book The Social Contract, *which sought to reconcile the individual will with the collective needs of the state.*

---- ✦ ----

QUESTIONS

1. Compare Rousseau's discussion of personal liberty with what Locke has to say about individual intellectual freedom.
2. Is Rousseau anti-monarchy?
3. What does Rousseau mean by the general will?

CHAPTER 2
That Sovereignty is Indivisible

Just as sovereignty is inalienable, it is for the same reason indivisible; for either the will is general or it is not; either it is the will of the body of the people, or merely that of a part. In the first case, a declaration of will is an act of sovereignty and constitutes law; in the second case, it is only a declaration of a particular will or an act of administration, it is at best a mere decree.

Nevertheless, our political theorists, unable to divide the principle of sovereignty, divide it in its purpose; they divide it into power and will, divide it, that is, into executive and legislative, into the rights of levying taxation, administering justice and making war, into domestic jurisdiction and the power to deal with foreign governments. Sometimes our theorists confuse all the parts and sometimes they separate them. They make the sovereign a creature of fantasy, a patchwork of separate pieces, rather as if they were to construct a man of several bodies — one with eyes, one with legs, the other with feet and nothing else. It is said that Japanese mountebanks can cut up a child under the eyes of spectators, throw the different parts into the air, and then make the child come down, alive and all of a piece. This is more or less the trick that our political theorists perform — after dismembering the social body with a sleight of hand worthy of the fairground, they put the pieces together again anyhow.

The mistake comes from having no precise notion of what sovereign authority is, and from taking mere manifestations of authority for parts of the authority itself. For instance, the acts of declaring war and making peace have been regarded as acts of sovereignty, which they are not; for neither of these acts constitutes a *law*, but only an application of law, a particular act which determines how the law shall be interpreted — and all this will be obvious as soon as I have defined the idea which attaches to the word 'law.'...

CHAPTER 3
Whether the General Will Can Err

It follows from what I have argued that the general will is always rightful and always tends to the public good; but it does not follow that the decisions of the people are always equally right. We always want what is advantageous but we do not always discern it. The people is never corrupted, but it is often misled; and only then does it seem to will what is bad.

There is often a great difference between the will of all [what all individuals want] and the general will; the general will studies only the common interest while the will of all studies private interest, and is indeed no more than the sum of individual desires. But if we take away from these same wills, the pluses and minuses which cancel each other out, the sum of the difference is the general will.

From the deliberations of a people properly informed, and provided its members do not have any communication among themselves, the great number of small differences will always produce a general will and the decision will always be good. But if groups, sectional associations are formed at the expense of the larger association, the will of each of these groups will become general in relation to its own members and private in relation to the state; we might then say that there are no longer as many votes as there are men but only as many votes as there are groups. The differences become less numerous and yield a result less general. Finally, when one of these groups becomes so large that it can dominate the rest, the result is no longer the sum of many small differences, but one great divisive difference; then there ceases to be a general will, and the opinion which prevails is no more than a private opinion.

Thus if the general will is to be clearly expressed, it is imperative that there should be no sectional associations in the state, and that every citizen should make up his own mind for himself — such was the unique and sublime invention of the great Lycurgus. But if there are sectional associations, it is wise to multiply their number and to prevent inequality among them, as Solon, Numa and Servius did. These are the only precautions which can ensure that the general will is always enlightened and the people protected from error.

CHAPTER 4
The Limits of Sovereign Power

If the state, or nation, is nothing other than a legal person the life of which consists in the union of its members and if the most important of its cares is its own preservation, it must have a universal and compelling power to move and dispose of each part in whatever manner is beneficial to the whole. Just as nature gives each man an absolute power over all his own limbs, the social pact gives the body politic an absolute power over all its members; and it is the same power which, directed by the general will, bears, as I have said, the name of sovereignty.

However, we have to consider beside the public person those private persons who compose it, and whose life and liberty is naturally independent of it. Here we have to distinguish clearly the respective rights of the citizen and of the sovereign, and distinguish those duties which the citizens have as subjects from the natural rights which they ought to enjoy as men.

We have agreed that each man alienates by the social pact only that part of his power, his goods and his liberty which is the concern of the community; but it must also be admitted that the sovereign alone is judge of what is of such concern.

Whatever services the citizen can render the state, he owes whenever the sovereign demands them; but the sovereign, on its side, may not impose on the subjects any burden which is not necessary to the community; the sovereign cannot, indeed, even will such a thing, since according to the law of reason no less than to the law of nature nothing is without a cause.

The commitments which bind us to the social body are obligatory only because they are mutual; and their nature is such that in fulfilling them a man cannot work for others without at the same time working for himself. How should it be that the general will is always rightful and that all men constantly wish the happiness of each but for the fact that there is no one who does not take that word 'each' to pertain to himself and in voting for all think of himself? This proves that the equality of rights and the notion of justice which it produces derive from the predilection which each man has for himself and hence from human nature as such. It also proves that the general will, to be truly what it is, must be general in its purpose as well as in its nature; that it should spring from all and apply to all; and that it loses its natural rectitude when it is directed towards any particular and circumscribed object — for in judging what is foreign to us, we have no sound principle of equity to guide us....

It should nevertheless be clear from what I have so far said that the general will derives its generality less from the number of voices than from the common interest which unites them — for the general will is an institution in which each necessarily submits himself to the same conditions which he imposes on others; this admirable harmony of interest and justice gives to social deliberations a quality of equity which disappears at once from the discussion of any individual dispute precisely because in these latter cases there is no common interest to unite and identify the decision of the judge with that of the contending parties....

19.3

✤

THE *ENCYCLOPÉDIE*, JEAN LE ROND D'ALEMBERT

The Encyclopédie *of Denis Diderot and Jean le Rond d'Alembert, was published in twenty eight volumes, seventeen of text and eleven of plates. The* Encyclopédie *was one of the most ambitious and popular Enlightenment projects. It was begun in 1751, took fourteen years to complete, and involved the work of many of the important philosophers of the day. It's full title was the* Classified Dictionary of the Sciences, Arts, and Trades, *which gives some impression of the scope of human knowledge it attempted to encompass.*

The following excerpt is from an introduction which outlined the purposes and contents of the Encyclopedia, written at the beginning of the project, by d'Alembert. Like the Encyclopedia as a whole, it not only sought to record the extent of human knowledge on these subjects but also offered an opportunity for the philosophe *to critique society.*

✤

QUESTIONS

1. How does d'Alembert feel about the loss of Latin as the primary language of scholarship? Is it a bad or a good change?
2. What does d'Alembert have to say about the works of the ancients?
3. What is the principle purpose of philosophy?

B ut while intending to please, philosophy seems not to have forgotten that it is designed principally to instruct. For that reason the taste for systems — more suited to flatter the imagination than to enlighten reason — is today almost entirely banished from works of merit. One of our best philosophers seems to have delivered the death blow to it. The spirit of hypothesis and conjecture formerly was perhaps quite useful and even necessary for the renaissance of philosophy, because at that time judiciousness was less important than acquiring independence of thought. But times have changed, and a writer among us who praised systems would have come too late. The advantages now afforded by that spirit are too small to counterbalance the resulting disadvantages, and if the very small number of discoveries they once occasioned are claimed as proof of the usefulness of systems, one might just as well counsel our geometers to apply themselves to squaring the circle, because the efforts of several mathematicians to do so have given us a few theorems. The spirit of systems is in physics what metaphysics is in geometry. If it may sometimes be required in order to start us on the way, it is almost never capable by itself of leading us to truth. It can glimpse the causes of phenomena when enlightened by the observation of Nature; but it is for calculations to assure, so to speak, the existence of these causes by determining exactly the effects they can produce and by comparing these effects with those revealed to us by experience. Any hypothesis without such a support rarely acquires that degree of certitude which ought always to be sought in the natural sciences, and which is so seldom found in those frivolous conjectures honored by the name of "system." If all he could have were conjectures of that kind, the principal merit of the physicist would be, properly speaking, to have the spirit of system but never to create one. Thousands of experiments prove how dangerous the use of systems is in the other sciences.

Physics is therefore confined solely to observations and to calculations; medicine to the history of the human body, of its maladies and their remedies; natural history to the detailed description of vegetables, animals, and minerals; chemistry to the composition and experimental decomposition of bodies. In a word, all the sciences are confined, as much as possible, to facts and to consequences deduced from them, and do not concede anything to opinion except when they are forced to. I do not speak of geometry, astronomy, and mechanics, which are destined by their nature always to be perfecting themselves.

Men abuse the best things. That philosophic spirit so much in fashion today which tries to comprehend everything and to take nothing for granted extends even into belles-lettres. Some claim that it is even harmful to their progress, and indeed it is difficult to conceal that fact. Our century, which is inclined toward combination and analysis, seems to desire to introduce frigid and didactic discussion into things of sentiment. It is not that the passions and tastes do not have their own set of logic, but their logic has principles completely different from those of ordinary logic; these principles must be unraveled within us, and it must be confessed that ordinary philosophy is quite unsuited for the task. Totally immersed in the analysis of our perceptions, philosophy disentangles their nuances much more readily when the soul is in a state of tranquility than when it is in the throes of passions or of the lively sentiments which affect us. In truth, how could it possibly be easy to analyze such feelings as these with precision? We must indeed surrender ourselves to them in order to know them, even though the moment in which the soul is affected by them is the very time when it is least capable of study. It must be admitted, however, that this spirit of discussion has contributed to freeing our literature from blind admiration for the ancients; it has taught us to value in them only the beauties that we would be compelled to admire in the moderns. But it is perhaps also to the same source that we owe that species of metaphysics of the heart which has seized hold of our theaters. While we do not have to banish it entirely, still less are we obliged to let it thus hold sway. This "anatomy of the soul" has even slipped into our conversations; people make dissertations, they no longer converse; and our societies have lost their principal ornaments — warmth and gaiety.

Thus, let us not be astonished that our literary works are generally inferior to those of the preceding century. One can find the reason for this circumstance in the very efforts we make to surpass our predecessors. Taste and the art of writing make rapid progress in a short time, once the true route is open; hardly does a great genius glimpse the beautiful before he sees it in its entire extent, and imitation of *la belle Nature* seems restricted to certain limits which are reached in only a generation or two at the most, so that for the following generation imitation is all that remains. Yet this next generation is not content with this share: the riches that it has inherited authorize the desire to increase them. It strives to add to what it has received, and it misses the mark while trying to surpass it. Thus, we have at the same time more principles for good judgment, a larger fund of enlightenment, more good judges, and fewer good works. We do not say of a book that it is good, but that it is the book of a man of intelligence. In this manner did the century of Demetrius of Phalerum immediately follow that of Demosthenes, the century of Lucan and of Seneca that of Cecero and of Virgil, and our century that of Louis XIV....

The Fine Arts are not less honored in our nation. If I can believe the enlightened amateurs, our school of painting is the foremost in Europe, and several works of our sculptors would not have been disowned by the ancients. Perhaps of all these arts, music is the one which has made the most progress among us in the last fifteen years. Thanks to the labors of a manly, courageous, and fruitful genius, foreigners who could not bear our "symphonies" are beginning to enjoy them, and the French at last appear to be persuaded that Lully left much to be done in this branch of the arts. In carrying the practice of his art to such a high degree of perfection, M. Rameau has become simultaneously the model and the object of jealousy of a large number of artists, who deprecate him at the same time they are trying to imitate him. But what more specifically distinguishes him is the fact that he has very successfully pondered on the theory of music; that he has been capable of finding the principle of harmony and of melody in the chord root, that by this method he has reduced to more certain and more simple laws a science which was formerly given over to arbitrary rules, or rules dictated by blind experiment. I readily take the opportunity of celebrating this artist-philosopher in a Discourse directed principally to the praise of great men. His merit, which he has forced our century to acknowledge, will be well known only when time has made envy hold its tongue; and his name, which is dear to the most enlightened part of our nation, cannot offend anyone here. But though it might displease some alleged patrons of the arts, a philosopher would certainly be worthy of pity if even in matters of science and taste he did not permit himself to speak the truth.

Such is the wealth that we possess. What an idea of our literary treasures would result if we added to the works of so many great men those of all the scholarly associations which maintain the taste for sciences and letters and to which we owe so many excellent works! Such societies most assuredly are of great advantage in a state, if certain conditions are observed: they should not be multiplied excessively, thus facilitating the entry of an excessive number of mediocre persons; they should banish all inequalities that might exclude or discourage men who are endowed with talents that will enlighten others. Genius should be the only superiority recognized by them, and within their ranks honor should be the reward for work. Finally, a way should be found so that talents receive their due and are not deprived by intrigue of their just compensation. For let us not be mistaken: we do more harm to the progress of the mind by misplacing such rewards than in suppressing them. To the honor of letters, let us confess that even without the promise of compensation, scholars do yet increase in number. Witness England, a country to which the sciences owe so much, although their government does nothing for them. It is true that the English nation is not neglectful of the sciences, that it even respects them, and this kind of reward, superior to all others, is doubtless the surest means of making the sciences and arts flourish; because while the government distributes offices, it is the public which bestows esteem. Love of letters, a virtue among our neighbors, is still, in truth, only a fashion among ourselves, and perhaps it will never be anything else. But however dangerous might be that mode which produces a hundred proud and ignorant amateurs for every enlightened patron of the arts, perhaps we owe to it the fact that we have not returned to the barbarism into which a multitude of circumstances tends to precipitate us.

From Jean Le Rond d'Alembert, *Preliminary Disclosure to the Encyclopedia of Diderot*, trans. Richard N. Schwqb, p. 94-102. Copyright © 1963 Bobbs-Merrill Company, Inc.

19.4

---❖---

MERCANTILISM, ADAM SMITH

Adam Smith (1723-1790) was a Scottish economist who published the most influential fiscal theory of the modern era. In The Wealth of Nations, *Smith criticized the prevailing economic system of mercantilism; instead he proposed a liberal, open trade policy. Mercantilism had been the driving force of colonialism. Mercantilists were convinced that wealth was based solely on the possession of gold or silver, and that only by hoarding wealth could a state ensure its economic success. Trade was viewed as good, but only if the balance (i.e., the cost paid) remained favorable to the state. Thus when a mercantilist state traded, it did so in a limited manner, and imported fewer goods than it exported. Exportation was also limited, although as long as it brought "real" wealth (gold or silver) into a country it was good. It was most important that the state itself control all the trade, to protect that balance.*

In contrast, Smith suggested that open trade, in which people traded as much as they personally wanted without any government interference, was more beneficial to the state overall. He proposed a laissez-faire, *or free from restrictions, approach to what he called the natural economy of human interest. The following is an excerpt from* The Wealth of Nations.

---❖---

QUESTIONS

1. What benefit does open trade bring to the state?
2. Do you think Smith is views human nature in a positive or negative way?
3. What is "enlightened" about Smith's theories?

The quantity of every commodity which human industry can either purchase or produce, naturally regulates itself in every country according to the effectual demand, or according to the demand of those who are willing to pay the whole rent, labour and profits which must be paid in order to prepare and bring it to market. But no commodities regulate themselves more easily or more exactly according to this effectual demand than gold and silver; because, on account of the small bulk and great value of those metals, no commodities can be more easily transported from one place to another, from the places where they are cheap, to those where they are dear, from the places where they exceed, to those where they fall short of this effectual demand. If there were in England, for example, an effectual demand for an additional quantity of gold, a packet-boat could bring from Lisbon, or from wherever else it was to be had, fifty tons of gold, which could be coined into more than five millions of guineas. But if there were an effectual demand for grain to the same value, to import it would require, at five guineas a ton, a million of tons of shipping, or a thousand ships of a thousand tons each. The navy of England would not be sufficient.

When the quantity of gold and silver imported into any country exceeds the effectual demand, no vigilance of government can prevent their exportation. All the sanguinary laws of Spain and Portugal are not able to keep their gold and silver at home. The continual importations from Peru and Brazil exceed the effectual demand of those countries, and sink the price of those metals there below that in the neighbouring countries. If, on the contrary, in any particular country their quantity fell short of the effectual demand, so as to raise their price above that of neighbouring countries, the government would have no occasion to take any pains to import them. If it were even to take pains to prevent their importation, it would not be able to effectuate it. Those metals, when the Spartans had got wherewithal to purchase them, broke through all the barriers which the laws of Lycurgus opposed to their entrance into Lacedemon. All the sanguinary laws of the customs are not able to prevent the importation of the teas of the Dutch and Gottenburgh East India companies; because somewhat cheaper than those of the British company. A pound of tea, however, is about a hundred times the bulk of one of the highest prices, sixteen shillings, that is commonly paid for it in silver, and more than two thousand times the bulk of the same price in gold, and consequently just so many times more difficult to smuggle.

It is partly owing to the easy transportation of gold and silver from the places where they abound to those where they are wanted, that the price of those metals does not fluctuate continually like that of the greater part of other commodities, which are hindered by their bulk from shifting their situation, when the market happens to be either over or under-stocked with them. The price of those metals, indeed, is not altogether exempted from variation, but the changes to which it is liable are generally slow, gradual, and uniform. In Europe, for example, it is supposed, without much foundation, perhaps, that, during the course of the present and preceding century, they have been constantly, but gradually, sinking in their value, on account of the continual importations from the Spanish West Indies. But to make any sudden change in the price of gold and silver, so as to raise or lower at once, sensibly and remarkably, the money price of all other commodities, requires such a revolution in commerce as that occasioned by the discovery of America.

If, notwithstanding all this, gold and silver should at any time fall short in a country which has wherewithal to purchase them, there are more expedients for supplying their place, than that of almost any other commodity. If the materials of manufacture are wanted, industry must stop. If provisions are wanted, the people must starve. But if money is wanted, barter will supply its place, though with a good deal of inconveniency. Buying and selling upon credit, and the different dealers compensating their credits with one another, once a month or once a year, will supply it with less inconveniency. A well-regulated paper money will supply it, not only without any inconveniency, but, in some cases, with some advantages. Upon every account, therefore, the attention of government never was so unnecessary employed, as when directed to watch over the preservation or increase of the quantity of money in any country.

No complaint, however, is more common than that of a scarcity of money. Money, like wine, must always be scarce with those who have neither wherewithal to buy it, nor credit to borrow it. Those who have either, will seldom be in want either of the money, or of the wine which they have occasion for. This complaint, however, of the scarcity of money, is not always confined to improvident spendthrifts. It is sometimes general through a whole mercantile town, and the country in its neighbourhood. Over-trading is the common cause of it. Sober men, whose projects have been disproportioned to their capitals, are as likely to have neither wherewithal to buy money, nor credit to borrow it, as prodigals whose expense has been disproportioned to their revenue. Before their projects can be brought to bear, their stock is gone, and their credit with it. They run about everywhere to borrow money, and every body tells that they have none to lend. Even such general complaints of the scarcity of money do not always prove that the usual number of gold and silver pieces are not circulating in the country, but that many people want those pieces who have nothing to give for them. When the profits of trade happen to be greater than ordinary, over-trading becomes a general error both among great and small dealers. They do not always send more money abroad than usual, but they buy upon credit both at home and abroad, an unusual quantity of goods, which they send to some distant market, in hopes that the returns will come in before the demand for payment. The demand comes before the returns, and they have nothing at hand, with which they can either purchase money, or give solid security for borrowing. It is not any scarcity of gold and silver, but the difficulty which such people find in borrowing, and which their creditors find in getting payment, that occasions the general complaint of the scarcity of money.

It would be too ridiculous to go about seriously to prove, that wealth does not consist in money, or in gold and silver; but in what money purchases, and is valuable only for purchasing. Money, no doubt, makes always a part of the national capital; but it has already been shown that it generally makes but a small part, and always the most unprofitable part of it....

I thought it necessary, though at the hazard of being tedious, to examine at full length this popular notion that wealth consists in money, or in gold and silver. Money in common language, as I have already observed, frequently signifies wealth; and this ambiguity of expression had rendered this popular notion so familiar to us, that even they, who are convinced of its absurdity, are very apt to forget their own principles, and in the course of their reasonings to take it for granted as a certain and undeniable truth. Some of the best English writers upon commerce set out with observing, that the wealth of a country consists, not in its gold and silver only, but in its lands, houses, and consumable goods of all different kinds. In the course of their reasonings, however, the lands, houses, and consumable goods seem to slip out of their memory, and the strain of their argument frequently supposes that all wealth consists in gold and silver, and that to multiply those metals is the great object of national industry and commerce.

The two principles being established, however, that wealth consisted in gold and silver, and that those metals could be brought into a country which had no mines only by the balance of trade, or by exporting to a greater value than it imported; it necessarily became the great object of political economy to diminish as much as possible the importation of foreign goods for home consumption, and to increase as much as possible the exportation of the produce of domestic industry. Its two great engines for enriching the country, therefore, were restraints upon importation, and encouragements to exportation.

The restraints upon importation were of two kinds.

First, Restraints upon the importation of such foreign goods for home consumption as could be produced at home, from whatever country they were imported.

Secondly, Restraints upon the importation of goods of almost all kinds from those particular countries with which the balance of trade was supposed to be disadvantageous.

Those different restraints consisted sometimes in high duties, and sometimes in absolute prohibitions.

Exportation was encouraged sometimes by drawbacks, sometimes by bounties, sometimes by advantageous treaties of commerce with foreign states, and sometimes by the establishment of colonies in distant countries.

Source: Oliver J. Thatcher, ed., *The Ideas that have Influenced Civilization in the Original Documents, Volume VI* (Boston: Roberts-Manchester Publishing Co., 1901-1902), pp. 403-409.

19.5

--- ✢ ---

ON TOLERATION, VOLTAIRE

No philosophe *epitomizes the promise and the frustrations of the Enlightenment as perfectly as François-Marie Arouet, or Voltaire (1694-1778). For many, he is the Enlightenment personified. In his own time he was a lightning rod of controversy, although even his opponents admired his intellectual prowess. Perhaps it was his self-chosen role of critic-at-large that led to his many confrontations with the state (he was briefly imprisoned and ultimately exiled from France) and his disappointment with his fellow* philosophes. *Voltaire took it upon himself to criticize every aspect of European society; law, politics, religion, social mores, tradition and even intellectuals such as himself were targets. He also typifies another aspect of the French* philosophes *of the seventeenth century: a fascination with England. Many French writers were fascinated with the parliamentary traditions of England, and what they perceived as a balance of power between the monarch and parliament. Voltaire, and Montesquieu (see Source 20.3) had an idealized view of the English legal and political system.*

The French crown aside, Voltaire's favored target was undoubtedly the Catholic Church. Voltaire eventually rejected his faith (he had been educated in Jesuit schools as a child) in favor of Deism, the belief in an impersonal and distant God. Voltaire's attacks on religion and his idealism of the English state were both very influential on the subsequent French Revolution.

--- ✢ ---

QUESTIONS

1. In favoring religious toleration, is Voltaire in fact arguing against religion altogether?
2. What positive aspects of religious faith does Voltaire recognize?
3. According to Voltaire, what benefit would the government get from promoting religious toleration?

We ourselves know that in France there is a rich and populous province, where the Protestant religion prevails much more than that of the church of Rome. The University of Alsace consists almost entirely of Lutherans, and they are likewise in possession of most of the civil posts in that province; and yet the public peace has never once been disturbed by any quarrels about religion, since that province has belonged to our kings. And what is the reason? Because no one is persecuted there on account of their religion. Seek not to lay a restraint upon the mind, and you may always be sure that the mind will be yours.

I do not mean by this to insinuate that those who are of a different faith to the prince under whose government they live, should have an equal share in the places of profits and honour with those who are of the established religion of the state. In England the Roman Catholics, who are in general looked upon to be friends to the Pretender, are excluded from all civil employment and are even double taxed; but then in every other respect they enjoy the prerogatives of citizens.

Some of our bishops in France have been suspected of thinking that their honour and interest is concerned, in not suffering any Protestants within their diocese, and that this is the principal obstacle to allowing of toleration amongst us; but this I cannot believe. The Episcopal body in France is composed of persons of quality, who think and act in a manner suitable to their high birth; and as envy itself must confess that they are both generous and charitable, they therefore certainly cannot think that those whom they thus drive out of their diocese would become converts in any other country, but great honour would redound from the conversion of them at home; nor would the prelate be any loser by it in his temporals, seeing that the greater the number of the inhabitants, the greater is the value of the land.

A certain Polish bishop had a farmer, who was an Anabaptist, and a receiver of his rents who was a Socinian. Some person proposed to the bishop to prosecute the latter in the spiritual court for not believing in transubstantiation, and to turn the other out of his farm because he would not have his son christened till he was fifteen years of age; the prelate very prudently replied, that though he made no doubt of their being eternally damned in the next world, yet he found them extremely necessary to him in this.

Let us now for a while quit our own little sphere and take a survey of the rest of the globe. The grand seignior peaceable rules over subjects of twenty different religions; upwards of two hundred thousand Greeks live unmolested within the walls of Constantinople; the mufti himself nominates the Greek patriarch and presents him to the emperor; and at the same time allows of the residence of a Latin patriarch. The sultan appoints Latin bishops for some of the Greek isles; the form used on this occasion is as follows: "I command such a one to go and reside as bishop in the isle of Chios, according to the ancient custom and idle ceremonies of those people." The Ottoman empire swarms with Jacobines, Nestorians, Monothelites, Cophti, Christians of St. John, Buebres, and Banians; and the Turkish annals do not furnish us with one single instance of a rebellion occasioned by any of these different sects.

Go to India, Persia, and Tartary, and you will meet with the same toleration and the same tranquility. Peter the Great encouraged all kinds of religions throughout his vast empire: trade and agriculture have been gainers by it, and no injury every happened therefrom to the body politic.

We do not find that the Chinese government, during the course of four thousand years that it has subsisted, has ever adopted any other religion than that of the Noachides, which consists in the simple worship of one God; and yet it tolerates the superstitions of Fo, and that of a multitude of bonzes; which might be productive of dangerous consequences did not the wisdom of the tribunals keep them within proper bounds.

It is true that the great Yong-T-Chin, the most wise and magnanimous of all the emperors of China, drove the Jesuits out of his kingdom; but this was not because that prince himself was non-tolerant, but on the contrary, because the Jesuits were so. They themselves, in their letters, have given us the speech the emperor made to them on that occasion: "I know, say he, that your religion admits not of toleration; I know how you have behaved in the Manilas and at Japan; you deceived my father, but think not to deceive me in the same manner." And if we read the whole of the conversation which he deigned to hold with them, we must confess him to be the wisest and most clement of all princes. How could he, indeed, with any consistency, keep in his kingdom European philosophers who, under the pretense of teaching the use of thermometers and œolypiles, had found means to debauch a prince of the blood? But what would this emperor have said, had he read our histories, and had he been acquainted with the times of the league and the gunpowder plot?

It was sufficient for him to be informed of the outrageous and indecent disputes between those Jesuits, Dominicans, Capuchins, and secular priests, who were sent as missionaries into his dominions from one extremity of the globe to preach up truth; instead of which, they employed their time in mutually pronouncing damnation against each other. The emperor, then, did no more than send away a set of foreigners, who were disturbers of the public peace. But with what infinite goodness did he dismiss them! and with what paternal care did be provide for their accommodation in their journey, and to prevent their meeting with any insult on their way! This very act of banishment might serve as an example of toleration and humanity.

The Japanese were the most tolerant of all nations; twelve different religions were peacefully established in their empire: when the Jesuits came, they made the thirteenth; and, in a very little time after their arrival, they would not suffer any other but their own. Every one knows the consequences of these proceedings: a civil war, as calamitous as that of the league, soon spread destruction and carnage through the empire; till at length the Christian religion was itself swallowed up in the torrents of blood it had set a flowing, and the Japanese for ever shut the entrance of their country against all foreigners, looking upon us as no better than savage beasts, such as those from which the English have happily cleared their island. Colbert, the minister, who know the necessity we were in of the commodities of Japan, that wants nothing from us, laboured in vain to settle a trade with that empire; he found those people inflexible.

Thus then every thing on our Continent shows us, that we ought neither to preach up, nor to exercise non-toleration....

An Address to the Deity

No longer then do I address myself to men, but to thee, God of all beings, of all worlds, and of all ages; if it may be permitted weak creatures, lost in immensity, and imperceptible to the rest of the universe, to presume to petition thee for aught, who hast given plenty of all things and whose decrees are immutable as eternal. Deign to look with an eye of pity upon the errors annexed to our natures! let not these errors prove the sources of misery to us! Thou hast not given us hearts to hate, nor hands to kill each other; grant then that we may mutually aid and assist each other to support the burthen of this painful and transitory life! May the trifling differences in the garments that cover our frail bodies, in the mode of expressing our insignificant thoughts, in our ridiculous customs, and our imperfect laws, in our idle opinions, and in our several conditions and situations, that appear so disproportionate in our eyes, an all are equal in thine: in a word, may the slight variations that are found amongst the atoms called men, not be made use of by us as signals of mutual hatred and persecution! May those who worship thee by the light of tapers at noon-day, bear charitably with those who content themselves with the light of that glorious planet thou hast placed in the midst of the heavens! May those who dress themselves in a robe of white linen to teach their hearers that thou art to be loved and feared, not detest or revile those who teach the same doctrine in long cloaks of black wool! May it be accounted the same to adore thee in a dialect formed from an ancient or a modern language! May those, who, clothed in vestments of crimson or violet colour, rule over a little parcel of that heap of dirt called the world, and are possessed of a few round fragments of a certain metal, enjoy without pride or insolence what they call grandeur and riches, and may others look on them without envy; for thou knowest, O God, that there is nothing in all these vanities proper to inspire envy or pride.

May all men remember that they are brethren! may they alike abhor that tyranny which seeks to subject the freedom of the will, as they do the rapine which tears from the arms of industry the fruits of its peaceful labours! And if the scourge of war is not to be avoided, let us not mutually hate and destroy each other in the midst of peace; but rather make use of the few moments of our existence to join in praising, in a thousand different languages, from one extremity of the world to the other, thy goodness, O all merciful creator, to whom we are indebted for that existence.

Source: Oliver J. Thatcher, ed., *The Ideas that have Influenced Civilization in the Original Documents, Volume VI* (Boston: Roberts-Manchester Publishing Co., 1901-1902), pp. 378-391.

———— ✦ ————

QUESTIONS FOR PART 19

1. In general, do you think the Enlightenment was favorable to women?
2. How where the *philosophes* connected to the humanist movements of the Renaissance?
3. Why did the French take the lead in the Enlightenment?

PART 20

EIGHTEENTH CENTURY STATES

The Enlightenment ideas had an immediate impact on the political states of the eighteenth century. Some rulers adopted Enlightenment principles and tried to incorporate them into their legal and political systems. The results were mixed: the absolutism of the seventeenth century was transformed into Enlightened Absolutism in Austria, Prussia, and Russia. The English parliament continued to increase its powers in relation to the monarchy; the two most important statesmen in the eighteenth century were successive prime ministers Robert Walpole and William Pitt the Elder. The latter won a major victory for England when the French were driven out of Canada; it was one of several times during the century that England defeated the French. When King George III tried to augment his power by replacing Pitt the public outcry was so vociferous that reforms of Parliament and monarchy were enacted. The public knew what kinds of reforms to demand, because Enlightenment ideas had been widely publicized in magazines and newspapers. The Enlightenment's greatest success lay with the expansion of literacy and education throughout western Europe.

Other rulers and states tried to avoid Enlightenment repercussions. The most obvious attempt to turn Enlightenment ideas into reality is found in the revolutions at the end of the century, which will be discussed in a subsequent chapter.

20.1

✦

MEMOIRS, CATHERINE THE GREAT

Catherine's memoirs are an unusual document. Few monarchs of the period recorded (or publicized) such personal accounts of their rise to power. It is also unusual simply because Catherine's life was itself extraordinary. She was born in 1729, the daughter of a minor German aristocrat. Many of the ruling families of Europe were relatives; at age sixteen she was married to a distant cousin, Grand Duke Peter of Russia. Peter was incompetent and impotent; Catherine was urged by her advisors to take a lover in order to produce an heir. Her reign would forever after be filled with scandalous tales of her sexual escapades. After seventeen years of marriage Peter became Tsar; within a year he was imprisoned and murdered by his own guards at Catherine's orders. The guards then put her on the throne as Catherine II. She died in 1796.

In terms of implementing Enlightenment ideas, her reign was one of little actual success. She attempted to reform the legal system of Russia, using England as a model, but beyond drawing up a set of Instructions, *the program failed. She spoke of eradicating serfdom but feared upsetting the Russian aristocracy. She conspired with Austria and Prussia to partition Poland. At best she is remembered for the reforms she tried to implement.*

The following passage describes Catherine's memories of her early childhood.

QUESTIONS

1. Why do you think Catherine recounts the story of her childhood illness? What lessons do you think she learned from that illness that later helped her as Empress of Russia?
2. How is her childhood education an Enlightened one?
3. What do you think was the single most important lesson Catherine learned as a child?

CHAPTER 1
The First Years (1729-1739)

I was born on April 21st, 1729 (forty-two years ago) at Stettin in Pomerania. I was told later that, a son having been more desired, my arrival as the first-born had given rise to some disappointment. My father, however, showed more satisfaction at the event than all the rest of the entourage. My mother almost died in bringing me into the world and it took her nineteen irksome weeks to recover.

My wet-nurse was the wife of a Prussian soldier; she was only nineteen, gay and pretty. I was placed in the care of a lady who was the widow of a certain Herr von Hohendorf and acted as companion to my mother.

I was told that the lady showed so little sense in her treatment of me that I developed an unaccountable obstinacy. She also showed little sense regarding my mother and was soon dismissed. She was very abrupt and fond of raising her voice; she succeeded so well in her method that I never did as I was told unless the order was repeated at least three times and very loudly.

When I was two I was consigned to the care of a French refugee, Magdeleine Cardel, who had a sycophantic and obsequious disposition, and the reputation of being slightly false; she took great care that I should please my father and mother in every way and thus gain their approval of herself.

This caused me to become very secretive for my age. My father, whom I saw very seldom, considered me to be an angel, my mother did not bother much about me. She had had, eighteen months after my birth, a son whom she passionately loved, whereas I was merely tolerated and often repulsed with violence and temper, not always with justice. I was aware of all this, but not always able to understand what I really felt about it....

At the age of seven I was suddenly seized with a violent cough. It was the custom that we should kneel every night and every morning to say our prayers. One night as I knelt and prayed I began to cough so violently that the strain cause me to fall on my left side, and I had such sharp pains in my chest that they almost took my breath away. I was carried into my bed where I remained for three weeks, lying always on the left side and coughing, with a high fever and sharp pains in the chest. There was no doctor well enough versed in his science in the neighbourhood. I was given many mixtures to take, but God alone know what they were!

Finally, after much suffering, I was well enough to get up and it was discovered, as they started to put on my clothes, that I had in the meantime assumed the shape of the letter Z; my right shoulder was much higher than the left, the backbone running in a zigzag and the left side falling in. The women who attended me, also my mother's women, whom they consulted, decided to break the news to my father and my mother. The first step undertaken was to swear everybody to secrecy concerning my condition. My parents were distressed to see one of their children lame, the other a cripple. Finally after consulting several experts in strict confidence, it was decided to summon a specialist in matters of dislocation.

They searched for one in vain; they were loath to ask the only man who knew anything about it, as he was the local hangman. For a long time they hesitated. Finally, under a pledge of great secrecy, he was called in and only Babet Cardel and a housemaid were allowed into the secret. This man, after examining me, ordered that every morning at six, a girl should come to me on an empty stomach and rub my shoulder and backbone with her saliva. Then he proceeded to fabricate a sort of frame, which I never removed day or night except when changing my underclothes, and every other day he cam to examine me in the morning. Besides this he made me wear a large black ribbon which went under the neck, crossed the right shoulder round the right arm, and was fastened at the back. I do not know whether it was because of all these remedies or that I was not meant to be a cripple, but after eighteen months I began to show signs of straightening out. I was ten or eleven when I was at last allowed to discard this most cumbersome framework.

At the age of seven all my dolls and other toys were taken away, and I was told that I was now a big girl and therefore it was no longer suitable that I should have them. I had never liked dolls, and found a way of making a plaything out of anything, my hands, a handkerchief, all served that purpose. The trend of my life went on as before and this deprivation of toys must have been a mere question of etiquette, as no one interfered with me in my games.

Early in my life it was discovered that I had a good memory and I was constantly urged to learn things by heart; this was supposed to cultivate memory, but in my opinion it weakened it. Sometimes it would be fragments from the Bible, then pieces specially composed for memorizing, or La Fontaine fables, that I had to learn by heart or recite, and I was scolded when a word escaped me. I do not believe that it could be humanly possible to remember all that I had to learn by heart, nor that there was any point in doing so. I have kept to this day a German Bible, in which all the verses I knew by heart are marked in red ink.

I was given a teacher to instruct me in religion, to teach me history and geography. I learnt French and German as a matter of course. One day I asked this Lutheran priest, for that was what my teacher was, which of the Christian Churches was the most ancient. He told me that it was the Greek Church and that it was also the one closest to the teachings of the Apostles, he was convinced of that. From then onwards I have always had a great respect for the Greek Church and curiosity to learn about its doctrine and ceremonies. Now I am the head of the Church.

I remember having several wrangles with my instructor, for which I risked being flogged. The first was because I considered it unjust that Titus, Marcus Aurelius, and all the great men of antiquity, virtuous as they were, should have been damned because they did not know about the Revelation. I maintained my point with passion and determination, arguing in favour of justice, with a priest who based his opinions on passages from the Bible.

The priest complained to Babet Cardel and wanted to resort to the rod in order to convince me. Babet Cardel was not authorized to perform such operations; with great gentleness she told me that a child should not be so obstinate when arguing with a respected man of the Church and that I ought to accept his views. Babet Cardel was a Protestant and the clergyman, as I said before, a determined Lutheran.

The second argument arose about what had preceded the world. He told me that there had been chaos and I wanted to know what that chaos had been like. His replies never seemed to satisfy me, we both lost our tempers and Babet Cardel once again was summoned to our rescue.

My third quarrel with the clergyman concerned circumcision: I was determined to know what the meaning of it was and he refused to explain it to me. Babet for once exhorted me to silence. I yielded to her alone; she smiled to herself and reasoned with me so gently that I could not resist her. All my life, in fact, I preserved the inclination to yield only to gentleness and reason — and to resist all pressure.

The clergyman was bent on lowering my spirits: during one autumn he talked to me so much of the Last Judgment and of the arduous task of working out one's salvation that every night, at dusk, I would go and cry by the window. At first nobody noticed my despondency, but finally Babet Cardel became aware of it and wanted to know the reason. I was reluctant to confide in her, but did so in the end and she had the common sense to speak to the clergyman and prevent him from instilling further terror in me.

I was instructed in various womanly tasks, but took as little interest in them as I did in reading. I wanted to write and draw — but I learnt little drawing for want of a good teacher. Babet had a remarkable method for making me concentrate on my work and do anything she wanted: she loved reading: when my lessons were over, if she was satisfied with the results she would read aloud to me, if not, she read to herself. I was heartbroken when deprived of that honour....

CHAPTER 2
The School of Life (1739-1744)

I began to grow taller and the extreme ugliness with which I was afflicted was beginning to disappear when I went to visit the future King of Sweden, my uncle, then Bishop of Lübeck, in Eutin in 1739. There I met for the first time the Grand Duke, who was good-looking, well-mannered, and courteous; in fact, this boy of eleven, whose father had just died, was considered a prodigy. He was pale and looked delicate; the trouble was that his entourage tried to make this child behave as an adult and forced him to a strict discipline, thus developing in him deceitfulness and hypocrisy.

It was rumored that he already had a great inclination for drink and that his tutors had difficulty in preventing him from getting drunk at table. He was hot-tempered and rebellious, and disliked his tutors, especially Marshal Brummer, a Swede by origin. It was rumoured that Brummer, the moment he became aware of the Empress's intention to make the Grand Duke her heir, deliberately proceeded to undermine his character, just as much as before he had striven to make him worthy of the Swedish crown.

My mother, who was then very beautiful, fascinated the Grand Duke, and he danced attendance on her, but envied me my freedom. As for me, I hardly noticed him, for I was too busy frolicking around without any supervision; twice a day my mother's maids and I made a kind of milk soup which we ate between meals, which reduced my appetite at table until the sweets were served.

The hints that my uncles and aunts, also our closest intimates, dropped here and there led me to think, however, that my name and that of the Grand Duke were being coupled.

I felt no repugnance at the idea; I knew that he was one day to become King of Sweden, and the title of Queen rang sweet to my ears, child though I was. Thereafter all those who surrounded me teased me about him and gradually I got used to the thought that he was my destiny.

Two or three years went by: these ideas began to wane, others were aroused after my stay in Berlin. I often met Prince Henry of Prussia, who was attracted by me and spoke of me to his sisters, the Duchess of Brunswick and the Queen of Sweden. The latter was still unmarried. She was very fond of my mother and told her brother that I was too young for him, a mere child. In fact I was only thirteen, but taller and physically more mature than one generally is at that age. I do not know how I came to know of these negotiations, which did not displease me at all.

Source: Catherine the Great, *The Memoirs of Catherine the Great*, trans. Moura Budberg (New York: Collier Books, 1961), pp. 19-30.

20.2

---- ✤ ----

COMMON SENSE, THOMAS PAINE

Although Thomas Paine (1737-1809) was born in England he became one of the most vocal proponents of independence for the American colonies. In 1776 he published Common Sense, *a pamphlet that called for the overthrow of monarchies in favor of republics; it was a concept he wrote about often. As with many of the Enlightenment* philosophes, *Paine was a Deist and along with monarchy one of his favorite targets was traditional Christian faith.*

After the American Revolution, Paine had quite a checkered career as a diplomat for the new United States to France; he arrived there during that state's own revolution and became a delegate to the revolutionary Convention for the city of Calais. He was almost imprisoned in England for treason, was almost guillotined in France by Robespierre (who thought Paine was too sympathetic to the king), and ended up back in America. Throughout all of this he continued to write his controversial treatises.

This excerpt is from Common Sense.

---- ✤ ----

QUESTIONS

1. How does Paine refute the argument that the American colonies need the British Empire for protection?
2. What implications does Paine offer about the future relationship between America and Europe?
3. Is there any evidence of Paine's Deism in this selection?

It has lately been asserted in parliament, that the colonies have no relation to each other but through the parent country, i.e., that Pennsylvania and the Jerseys, and so on for the rest, are sister colonies by the way of England. This is certainly a very round-about way of proving relation ship, but it is the nearest and only true way of proving enemyship, if I may so call it. France and Spain never were, nor perhaps ever will be our enemies as Americans, but as our being the subjects of Great Britain.

But Britain is the parent country, say some. Then the more shame upon her conduct. Even brutes do not devour their young; nor savages make war upon their families; wherefore the assertion, if true, turns to her reproach; but it happens not to be true, or only partly so; and the phrase — parent or mother country — has been jesuitically adopted by the king and his parasites, with a low papistical design of gaining an unfair bias on the credulous weakness of our minds. Europe, and not England, is the parent country of America. This new world has been the asylum for the persecuted lovers off civil and religious liberty from every Part of Europe. Hither have they fled, not from the tender embraces of the mother, but from the cruelty of the monster; and it is so far true of England, that the same tyranny which drove the first emigrants from home pursues their descendants still.

In this extensive quarter of the globe, we forget the narrow limits of three hundred and sixty miles (the extent of England) and carry our friendship on a larger scale; we claim brotherhood with every European Christian, and triumph in the generosity of the sentiment.

It is pleasant to observe by what regular gradations we surmount the force of local prejudice, as we enlarge our acquaintance with the world. A man born in any town in England divided into parishes, will naturally associate most with his fellow parishioners, because their interests in many cases will be common, and distinguish him by the name of neighbor; if he meet him but a few miles from home, he drops the narrow idea of a street, and salutes him by the name of townsman; if he travels out of the county, and meet him in any other, he forgets the minor divisions of street and town, and calls him countryman — that is, countyman; but if in their foreign excursions they should associate in France or any other part of Europe, their local remembrance would be enlarged into that of Englishmen. And by a just parity of reasoning, all Europeans meeting in America, or any other quarter of the globe, are countrymen; for England, Holland, Germany, or Sweden, when compared with the whole, stand in the same places on the larger scale, which the divisions of street, town, and county do on the smaller ones; distinctions too limited for continental minds. Not one third of the inhabitants, even of this province, are of English descent. Wherefore, I reprobate the phrase of parent or mother country applied to England only, as being false, selfish, narrow and ungenerous.

But admitting that we were all of English descent, what does it amount to? Nothing. Britain, being now an open enemy, extinguishes every other name and title: and to say that reconciliation is our duty, is truly farcical. The first king of England, of the present line (William the Conqueror), was a Frenchman, and half the peers of England are descendants from the same country; wherefore, by the same method of reasoning, England ought to be governed by France.

Much has been said of the united strength of Britain and the colonies, that in conjunction they might bid defiance to the world. But this is mere presumption. The fate of war is uncertain; neither do the expressions mean anything; for this continent would never suffer itself to be drained of inhabitants to support the British arms in either Asia, Africa, or Europe.

I challenge the warmest advocate for reconciliation, to show a single advantage that this continent can reap by being connected with Great Britain; I repeat the challenge — not a single advantage is derived. Our corn will fetch its price in any market in Europe; and our imported goods must be paid for, buy them where you will.

Besides, what have we to do with setting the world at defiance? Our plan is commerce; and that, well attended to, will secure us the peace and friendship of all Europe; because it is the interest of all Europe to have America a free port. Her trade will always be a protection, and her barrenness of gold and silver secure her from invaders.

But the injuries and disadvantages we sustain by that connection, are without number; and our duty to mankind at large, as well as to ourselves, instructs us to renounce the alliance. Because, any submission to, or dependence on Great Britain, tends directly to involve this continent in European wars and quarrels; and sets us at variance with nations, who would otherwise seek our friendship, and against whom, we have neither anger nor complaint. As Europe is our market for trade, we ought to form no partial connection with any part of it. It is the true interest of America to steer clear of European contentions; which she never can do, while by her dependence on Britain, she is made the make-weight in the scale of British politics.

Europe is too thickly planted with kingdoms to be long at peace; and whenever a war breaks out between England and any foreign power, the trade of America goes to ruin, because of her connection with Britain. The next war may not turn out like the last, and should it not, the advocates for reconciliation now, will be wishing for separation then, because neutrality in that case would be a safer convoy than a man of war. Everything that is right or natural pleads for separation. The blood of the slain, the weeping voice of nature cries, It is time to part! Even the distance at which the Almighty has placed England and America, is a strong and natural proof, that the authority of the one, over the other, was never the design of Heaven. The time likewise at which the continent was discovered, adds weight to the argument, and the manner in which it was peopled increases the force of it. The reformation was preceded by the discovery of America; as if the Almighty graciously meant to open a sanctuary to the persecuted in future years, when home should afford neither friendship nor safety.

The authority of Great Britain over this continent is a form of government which, sooner or later, must have an end; and a serious mind can draw no true pleasure by looking forward, under the painful and positive conviction, that what he calls "the present constitution" is merely temporary. As parents, we can have no joy, knowing that this government is not sufficiently lasting to ensure any thing which we may bequeath to posterity; and by a plain method of argument, as we are running the next generation into debt, we ought to do the work of it, otherwise we use them meanly and pitifully. In order to discover the line of our duty rightly, we should take our children in our hands, and fix our station a few years farther into life; that eminence will present a prospect, which a few present fears and prejudices conceal from our sight.

Though I would carefully avoid giving unnecessary offence, yet I am inclined to believe, that all those who espouse the doctrine of reconciliation, may be included within the following descriptions. Interested men, who are not to be trusted; weak men, who cannot see; prejudiced men, who will not see; and a certain set of moderate men, who think better of the European world than it deserves; and this last class, by an ill-judged deliberation, will be the cause of more calamities to this continent than all the other three.

It is the good fortune of many to live distant from the scene of sorrow; the evil is not sufficiently brought to their doors to make them feel the precariousness with which all American property is possessed. But let our imaginations transport us for a few moments to Boston; that seat of wretchedness will teach us wisdom, and instruct us for ever to renounce a power in whom we can have no trust. The inhabitants of that unfortunate city, who but a few months ago were in ease and affluence, have now no other alternative than to stay and starve, or turn out to beg; — endangered by the fire of their friends, if they continue within the city, and plundered by the soldiery, if they leave it. In their present condition, they are prisoners without the hope of redemption; and in a general attack for their relief, they would be exposed to the fury of both armies.

Men of passive tempers look somewhat lightly over the offenses of Britain, and, still hoping for the best, are apt to call out, "Come, come, we shall be friends again for all this!" But examine the passions and feelings of mankind — bring the doctrine of reconciliation to the touchstone of nature, and then tell me, whether you can hereafter love, honor, and faithfully serve the power that has carried fire and sword into your land? If you cannot do all these, then are you only deceiving yourselves, and, by your delay, bringing ruin upon posterity. Your future connection with Britain, whom you can neither love nor honor, will be forced and unnatural; and being formed only on the plan of present convenience, will in a little time fall into a relapse more wretched than the first. But if you say, you can still pass the violations over, then I ask Hath your house been burnt? Hath your property been destroyed before your face? Are your wife and children destitute of a bed to lie on, or bread to live on? Have you lost a parent or a child by their hands, and yourself the ruined and wretched survivor? If you have not, then are you not a judge of those who have. But if you have, and can still shake hands with the murderers, then are you unworthy the name of husband, father, friend, or lover; and whatever may be your rank or title in life, you have the heart of a coward, and the spirit of a sycophant.

This is not inflaming or exaggerating matters, but trying them by those feelings and affections which nature justifies, and without which we should be incapable of discharging the social duties of life, or enjoying the felicities of it. I mean not to exhibit horror for the purpose of provoking revenge, but to awaken us from fatal and unmanly slumbers, that we may pursue determinately some fixed object. It is not in the power of Britain or of Europe to conquer America, if she do not conquer herself by delay and timidity. The present winter is worth an age if rightly employed; but if neglected, the whole continent will partake of the misfortune; and there is no punishment which that man will not deserve, be he who or what or where he will, that may be the means of sacrificing a season so precious and useful.

It is repugnant to reason, to the universal order of things, to all examples from the former ages, to suppose, that this continent can longer remain subject to any external power. The most sanguine in Britain does not think so. The utmost stretch of human wisdom cannot, at this time compass a plan short of separation, which can promise the continent even a year's security. Reconciliation is now a fallacious dream. Nature has deserted the connection, and Art cannot supply her place; for, as Milton wisely expresses it, "Never can true reconcilement grow, where wounds of deadly hate have pierced so deep."

Every quiet method for peace has been ineffectual. Our prayers have been rejected with disdain; and only tended to convince us, that nothing flatters vanity, or confirms obstinacy in kings, more than repeated petitioning — and nothing has contributed more than that very measure to make the kings of Europe absolute: Witness Denmark and Sweden. Wherefore, since nothing but blows will do, for God's sake, let us come to a final separation; and not leave the next generation to be cutting throats, under the violated unmeaning names of parent and child.

Source: Oliver J. Thatcher, ed., *The Ideas that have Influenced Civilization in the Original Documents, Volume VII (*Boston: Roberts-Manchester Publishing Co., 1901-1902), pp. 211-216.

20.3

❖

THE SPIRIT OF THE LAWS, BARON DE MONTESQUIEU

Baron Charles-Louis de Montesquieu (1689-1755) was yet another French Enlightenment philosophe *who was fascinated with England. His obsession was with the English legal system, which admittedly was one of the most advanced in Europe in the eighteenth century. Montesquieu's monumental study,* The Spirit of the Laws, *introduced three concepts to Western legal theory: one, that no political system was perfect; two, that the best governments have a separation of powers to prevent any one office of the state from becoming too powerful; and three, there should be checks and balances on the separate branches.*

QUESTIONS

1. Why does Montesquieu include so many references to classical Greece and Rome?
2. What influences did this study of law have on the United States as it developed its own law code?
3. Find an example in which Montesquieu discusses the separation of powers.

Book II
OF LAWS DIRECTLY DERIVED FROM THE NATURE OF GOVERNMENT

1. — Of the Nature of the three different Governments

There are three species of government: republican, monarchical, and despotic. In order to discover their nature, it is sufficient to recollect the common notion, which supposes three definitions, or rather three facts: that a republican government is that in which the body, or only a part of the people, is possessed of the supreme power; monarchy, that in which a single person governs by fixed and established laws; a despotic government, that in which a single person directs everything by his own will and caprice.

This is what I call the nature of each government; we must now inquire into those laws which directly conform to this nature, and consequently are the fundamental institutions....

As most citizens have sufficient ability to choose, though unqualified to be chosen, so the people, though capable of calling others to an account for their administration, are incapable of conducting the administration themselves.

The public business must be carried on with a certain motion, neither too quick nor too slow. But the motion of the people is always either too remiss or too violent. Sometimes with a hundred thousand arms they overturn all before them; and sometimes with a hundred thousand feet they creep like insects.

In a popular state the inhabitants are divided into certain classes. It is in the manner of making this division that great legislators have signalized themselves; and it is on this the duration and prosperity of democracy have ever depended.

Servius Tullius followed the spirit of aristocracy in the distribution of his classes. We find in Livy and in Dionysius Halicarnassus, in what manner he lodged the right of suffrage in the hands of the principal citizens. He had divided the people of Rome into 193 centuries, which formed six classes; and ranking the rich, who were in smaller numbers, in the first centuries, and those in middling circumstances, who were more numerous, in the next, he flung the indigent multitude into the last; and as each century had but one vote it was property rather than numbers that decided the election.

Solon divided the people of Athens into four classes. In this he was directed by the spirit of democracy, his intention not being to fix those who were to choose, but such as were eligible: therefore, leaving to every citizen the right of election, he made the judges eligible from each of those four classes;

but the magistrates he ordered to be chosen only out of the first three, consisting of persons of easy fortunes.

As the division of those who have a right of suffrage is a fundamental law in republics, so the manner of giving this suffrage is another fundamental.

The suffrage by lot is natural to democracy; as that by choice is to aristocracy.

The suffrage by lot is a method of electing that offends no one, but animates each citizen with the pleasing hope of serving his country....

In order, however, to amend the suffrage by lot, he made a rule that none but those who presented themselves should be elected; that the person elected should be examined by judges and that every one should have a right to accuse him if he were unworthy of the office: this participated at the same time of the suffrage by lot, and of that by choice. When the time of their magistracy had expired, they were obliged to submit to another judgment in regard to their conduct. Persons utterly unqualified must have been extremely backward in giving in their names to be drawn by lot.

The law which determines the manner of giving suffrage is likewise fundamental in a democracy. It is a question of some importance whether the suffrages ought to be public or secret. Cicero observes that the laws which rendered them secret towards the close of the republic were the cause of its decline. But as this is differently practised in different republics, I shall offer here my thoughts concerning this subject.

The people's suffrages ought doubtless to be public and this should be considered as a fundamental law of democracy. The lower class ought to be directed by those of higher rank, and restrained within bounds by the gravity of eminent personages. Hence, by rendering the suffrages secret in the Roman republic, all was lost; it was no longer possible to direct a populace that sought its own destruction. But when the body of the nobles are to vote in an aristocracy or in a democracy the senate as the business is then only to prevent intrigues, the suffrages cannot be too secret.

Intriguing in a senate is dangerous; it is dangerous also in a body of nobles; but not so among the people, whose nature is to act through passion. In countries where they have no share in the government, we often see them as much inflamed on account of an actor as ever they could be for the welfare of the state. The misfortune of a republic is when intrigues are at an end; which happens when the people are gained by bribery and corruption: in this case they grow indifferent to public affairs, and avarice becomes their predominant passion. Unconcerned about the government and everything belonging to it, they quietly wait for their hire.

It is likewise a fundamental law in democracies, that the people should have the sole power to enact laws....

3. — Of the Laws in relation to the Nature of Aristocracy

...It would be a very happy thing in an aristocracy if the people, in some measure, could be raised from their state of annihilation. Thus at Genoa, the bank of St. George being administered by the people gives them a certain influence in the government, whence their whole prosperity is derived.

The senators ought by no means to have the right of naming their own members; for this would be the only way to perpetuate abuses. At Rome, which in its early years was a kind of aristocracy, the senate did not fill up the vacant places in their own body; the new members were nominated by the censors....

In all magistracies, the greatness of the power must be compensated by the brevity of the duration. This most legislators have fixed to a year; a longer space would be dangerous, and a shorter would be contrary to the nature of government. For who is it that in the management even of his domestic affairs would be thus confined? At Ragusa the chief magistrate of the republic is changed every month, the other officers every week, and the governor of the castle every day. But this can take place only in a small republic environed by formidable powers, who might easily corrupt such petty and insignificant magistrates.

The best aristocracy is that in which those who have no share in the legislature are so few and inconsiderable that the governing party have no interest in oppressing them. Thus when Antipater made a law at Athens, that whosoever was not worth two thousand drachms should have no power to vote, he formed by this method the best aristocracy possible; because this was so small a sum as to exclude very few, and not one of any rank or consideration in the city.

Aristocratic families ought therefore, as much as possible, to level themselves in appearance with the people. The more an aristocracy borders on democracy, the nearer it approaches perfection: and, in proportion as it draws towards monarchy, the more is it imperfect.

But the most imperfect of all is that in which the part of the people that obeys is in a state of civil servitude to those who command, as the aristocracy of Poland, where the peasants are slaves to the nobility.

4. — Of the Relation of Laws to the Nature of Monarchical Government

The intermediate, subordinate, and dependent powers constitute the nature of monarchical government; I mean of that in which a single person governs by fundamental laws. I said the intermediate, subordinate, and dependent powers. And indeed, in monarchies the prince is the source of all power, political and civil. These fundamental laws necessarily suppose the intermediate channels through which the power flows: for if there be only the momentary and capricious will of a single person to govern the state, nothing can be fixed, and of course there is no fundamental law.

The most natural, intermediate, and subordinate power is that of the nobility. This in some measure seems to be essential to a monarchy, whose fundamental maxim is: no monarch, no nobility; no nobility, no monarch; but there may be a despotic prince.

There are men who have endeavored in some countries in Europe to suppress the jurisdiction of the nobility, not perceiving that they were driving at the very thing that was done by the parliament of England. Abolish the privileges of the lords, the clergy and cities in a monarchy, and you will soon have a popular state, or else a despotic government.

The courts of a considerable kingdom in Europe have, for many ages, been striking at the patrimonial jurisdiction of the lords and clergy. We do not pretend to censure these sage magistrates; but we leave it to the public to judge how far this may alter the constitution....

Source: Baron de Montesquieu, *The Spirit of the Laws*, trans. Thomas Nugent (New York: Hafner Publishing Company, 1949), pp. 8-18.

20.4

━━━━━ ✢ ━━━━━

GULLIVER'S TRAVELS: WHY STATES GO TO WAR,
JONATHAN SWIFT

Gulliver's Travels, written between 1721-26, is one of the best-known satires of the eighteenth century. In the following excerpt, Gulliver is asked by the fictional king of Houyhnhnms to describe the causes of war in Europe. It affords Swift an excellent opportunity to lampoon the basic nature of states and monarchy in his day.

━━━━━ ✢ ━━━━━

QUESTIONS

1. Is Swift's depiction of the warring natures of eighteenth-century states merely a satire, or does it present any positive views of those states?
2. Who ultimately does Swift seem to blame for the war-like nature of European states?
3. What is Swift's attitude toward religion in his period?

In obedience, therefore, to his Honour's commands, I related to him the Revolution under the Prince of Orange; the long war with France, entered into by the said prince, and renewed by his successor, the present queen, wherein the greatest powers of Christendom were engaged, and which still continued: I computed, at his request, that about a million of Yahoos might have been killed in the whole progress of it, and perhaps a hundred or more cities taken, and five times as many ships burnt or sunk.

He asked me what were the usual causes or motives that made one country go to war with another. I answered they were innumerable, but I should only mention a few of the chief. Sometimes the ambition of princes, who never think they have land or people enough to govern: sometimes the corruption of ministers, who engage their master in a war, in order to stifle or divert the clamour of the subjects against their evil administration. Difference in opinions has cost many millions of lives: for instance, whether *flesh* be *bread*, or *bread* be *flesh*; whether the juice of a certain *berry* be *blood* or *wine*; whether *whistling* be a vice or a virtue; whether it be better to *kiss a post*, or throw it into the fire; what is the best colour for a *coat*, whether *black*, *white*, *red*, or *grey*; and whether it should be *long* or *short*, *narrow* or *wide*, *dirty* or *clean*; with many more. Neither are any wars so furious and bloody, or of so long a continuance, as those occasioned by difference in opinion, especially if it be in things indifferent.

Sometimes the quarrel between two princes is to decide which of them shall dispossess a third of his dominions, where neither of them pretend to any right. Sometimes one prince quarrels with another for fear the other should quarrel with him. Sometimes a war is entered upon, because the enemy is too *strong*, and sometimes, because he is too *weak*. Sometimes our neighbours want the things which we *have*, or *have* the things which we *want*, and we both fight, till they take ours, or give us theirs. It is a very justifiable cause of a war, to invade a country after the people have been wasted by famine, destroyed by pestilence, or embroiled by factions among themselves. It is justifiable to enter into war against our nearest ally, when one of his towns lies convenient for us, or a territory of land, that would render our dominions round and complete. If a prince sends forces into a nation, where the people are poor and ignorant, he may lawfully put half of them to death, and make slaves of the rest, in order to civilize and reduce them from their barbarous way of living. It is a very kingly, honourable, and frequent practice, when one prince desires the assistance of another, to secure him against an invasion, that the assistant, when he has driven out the invader, should seize on the dominions himself, and kill, imprison, or banish, the prince he came to relieve. Alliance by blood, or marriage, is a frequent cause of war between princes; and the nearer the kindred is, the greater their disposition to quarrel; *poor* nations are *hungry*, and *rich* nations are *proud*; and pride and hunger will ever be at variance. For these reasons, the trade of a soldier is held the most honourable of all others; because a soldier is a Yahoo hired to kill, in cold blood, as many of his own species, who have never offended him, as possibly he can.

There is likewise a kind of beggarly princes in Europe, not able to make war by themselves, who hire out their troops to richer nations, for so much a day to each man; of which they keep three-fourths to themselves, and it is the best part of their maintenance; such are those in Germany and many northern parts of Europe.

What you have told me (said my master) upon the subject of war, does indeed discover most admirably the effects of that reason you pretend to: however, it is happy that the *shame* is greater than the *danger*; and that nature has left you utterly incapable of doing much mischief. For, your mouths lying flat with your faces, you can hardly bite each other to any purpose, unless by consent. Then as to the claws upon your feet before and behind, they are so short and tender, that one of our Yahoos would drive a dozen of yours before him. And therefore, in recounting the numbers of those who have been killed in battle, I cannot but think you have *said the thing which is not*.

I could not forbear shaking my head, and smiling a little at his ignorance. And being no stranger to the art of war, I gave him a description of cannons, culverins, muskets, carabines, pistols, bullets, powder, swords, bayonets, battles, sieges, retreats, attacks, undermines, countermines, bombardments, sea fights, ships sunk with a thousand men, twenty thousand killed on each side, dying groans, limbs flying in the air, smoke, noise, confusion, trampling to death under horses' feet, flight, pursuit, victory; fields strewed with carcasses, left for food to dogs and wolves and birds of prey; plundering, stripping, ravishing, burning, and destroying. And to set forth the valour of my own dear countrymen, I assured him, that I had seen them blow up a hundred enemies at once in a siege, and as many in a ship, and beheld the dead bodies drop down in pieces from the clouds, to the great diversion of the spectators.

Source: Jonathan Swift, *Gulliver's Travels* (New York: Bantam Books, 1962, 1976), pp. 233-234.

✦

Questions for Part 20

1. What role did Enlightenment ideas play in the development of eighteenth-century states?
2. What exactly is meant by the term Enlightened Absolutism, and do you think any of these texts reference it?
3. Compare Swift's satire of why states go to war with Thomas Paine's description of wars in Europe.

PART 21

EIGHTEENTH CENTURY SOCIETY AND CULTURE

Many aspects of European culture underwent dramatic alteration in the eighteenth century. Above all, there was the Enlightenment, whose influence cannot be overestimated. The most obvious change in European culture was the improvement in literacy rates, and the expansion of literacy to more of the populace. Whereas in past centuries reading and writing were the exclusive privilege of the aristocracy, in the eighteenth century literacy and education spread to the middle classes. Newspapers and magazines enjoyed an unprecedented popularity thanks to cheaper printing supplies and the numerous coffeehouses and clubs in which to read these papers. The *philosophes* were determined to publicize their ideas and made good use of those many periodicals. Large printing projects such as *The Encyclopédie* of Diderot in France provided more opportunities for *philosophes* to publish and for the public to read. Perhaps the best example of how wide-ranging the spread of literacy was is in the increase in education for women, although, as usual, they lagged behind men in numbers and in opportunities to use their new education.

Another statistic on the rise in the eighteenth century was population. A combination of lower death rates due to greater availability of food, the end of the bubonic plagues, and the development of medical advancements such as the forceps (which made childbirth safer for mother and infant) contributed to a continent-wide increase in population. The invention of foundling homes as an alternative to infanticide for unwanted children added slightly to population figures, although few children survived the homes and infanticide remained one of the most common methods of controlling family size.

The most notable cultural change of the century came in the gradual shift of power from the aristocracy to the middle class. The nobility still retained most of their advantages, but by the end of the century it was clear that the values and standards of the bourgeoisie were beginning to replace the Old Regime of aristocratic privilege. However, this shift was only beginning in the eighteenth century and would not be apparent until the Revolutions (American, French, and Industrial) were over.

21.1

---- ✦ ----

CLARISSA, SAMUEL RICHARDSON

The eighteenth century was the great age of the novel. The novels of the period were long, expansive affairs; typically published in two or three volumes. These novels often featured female protagonists and were incredibly popular with the newly literate female population of Europe. Because they catered to this audience, novels are an invaluable source for details about women's lives in the period. It is worth noting, however, that most of the novelists were men; it would not be until the next century that women writers became common. Novelists used this literary format as a way to explore social customs, morals, and behavior. The first true English novel, Pamela *by Samuel Richardson, was written in an epistolary form. It was such a success that Richardson followed it up with* Clarissa, *also an epistolary novel.*

In the following passage Clarissa, in a letter to a friend, tells how she has been confronted by her family and the man they wish her to marry, Solmes.

⁜

QUESTIONS

1. How is the format of this novel, written as if it was a series of letters between various characters, itself an indicator of Enlightenment influences?
2. Can you identify what class Clarissa and her family belong to from this excerpt?
3. What details about marriage customs can you discern in this passage?

A FILIAL VICTIM

Miss Clarissa Harlowe, to Miss Howe

Friday, March 3

O my dear friend, I have had a sad conflict! trial upon trial; conference upon conference! — But what law, what ceremony, can give a man a right to a heart which abhors him more than it does any of God Almighty's creatures?

I hope my mamma will be able to prevail for me. — But I will recount all, tho' I sit up the whole night to do it; for I have a vast deal to write; and will be as minute as you wish me to be.

In my last, I told you, in a fright, my apprehensions; which were grounded upon a conversation that passed between my mamma and my aunt, part of which Hannah overheard. Indeed not give you further particulars; since what I have to relate to you from different conversations that have passed between my mamma and me in the space of a very few hours, will include them all. I will begin then.

I went down this morning, when breakfast was ready, with a very uneasy heart, from what Hannah had told me yesterday afternoon; wishing for an opportunity, however, to appeal to my mamma, in hopes to engage her interest in my behalf, and purposing to try to find one, when she retired to her own apartment after breakfast: — But, unluckily, there was the odious Solmes sitting asquat between my mamma and sister, with *so much* assurance in his looks! — But you know, my dear, that those we love not, cannot do anything to please us.

Had the wretch kept his seat, it might have been well enough: But the bent and broad-shoulder'd creature must needs rise, and stalk towards a chair, which was just by that which was set for me.

I removed it at a distance, as if to make way to my own: And down I sat, abruptly I believe; what I had heard, all in my head.

But this was not enough to daunt him: The man is a very confident, he is a very bold, staring man! Indeed, my dear, the man is very confident.

He took the removed chair, and drew it so near mine, squatting in it with his ugly weight, that he press'd upon my hoop. — I was so offended (all I had heard, as I said, in my head), that I removed to another chair. I own I had too little command of myself: It gave my brother and sister too much advantage; I dare say they took it: — But I did it involuntarily, I think: I could not help it. — I knew not what I did.

I saw my papa was excessively displeased. When angry, no man's countenance ever shew'd it so much as my papa's. Clarissa Harlowe! said he, with a big voice; and there he stopp'd. — Sir! said I, and courtesy'd. — I trembled; and put my chair nearer the wretch, and sat down; my face I could feel all in a glow.

Make tea, child, said my kind mamma: Sit by me, love; and make tea.

I removed with pleasure to the seat the man had quitted; and being thus indulgently put into employment, soon recover'd myself; and in the course of the breakfasting officiously asked two or three questions of Mr. Solmes, which I would not have done, but to make up with my papa. — *Proud spirits may be brought to;* whisperingly spoke my sister to me, over her shoulder, with an air of triumph and scorn: But I did not mind her.

My mamma was all kindness and condescension. I asked her once, if she were pleased with the tea? She said, softly, and again called me *dear*, she was pleased with all I did. I was very proud of this encouraging goodness: And all blew over, as I hoped, between my papa and me; for he also spoke kindly to me two or three times.

Small incidents these, my dear, to trouble you with; only as they lead to greater; as you shall hear.

Before the usual breakfast-time was over, my papa withdrew with my mamma, telling her he wanted to speak to her. My sister, and my aunt, who was with us, next dropt away.

My brother gave himself some airs of insult, that I understood well enough; but which Mr. Solmes could make nothing of: — and at last he arose from his seat — Sister, said he, I have a curiosity to shew you: I will fetch it: And away he went; shutting the door close after him.

I saw what all this was for. I arose; the man hemming up for a speech, rising, and beginning to set his splay-feet (indeed, my dear, the man in all his ways is hateful to me) in an approaching posture. — I will save my brother the trouble of bringing to me his curiosity, said I. — I courtesy'd — Your servant, Sir — The man cry'd, Madam, Madam, twice, and look'd like a fool. — But away I went — to find my brother, to save my word. — But my brother was gone, indifferent as the weather was, to walk in the garden with my sister. A plain case, that he had left his curiosity with me, and design'd to shew me no other.

I had but just got into my own apartment, and began to think of sending Hannah to beg an audience of my mamma (the more encouraged by her condescending goodness at breakfast), when Shorey, her woman, brought me her commands to attend her in her closet.

My papa, Hannah told me, had just gone out of it with a positive, angry countenance. The I as much dreaded the audience, as I had wished for it before.

I went down, however, but, apprehending the subject, approached her trembling, and my heart in visible palpitations.

She saw my concern. Holding out her kind arms, as he sat, Come kiss me, my dear, said she, with a smile like a sun-beam breaking thro' the cloud that overshadowed her naturally benign aspect. Why flutters my jewel so?

This preparative sweetness, with the goodness just before, confirmed my apprehensions. My mamma saw the bitter pill wanting gilding.

O my mamma! was all I could say; and I clasp'd my arms round her neck, and my face sunk into her bosom.

My child! my child! restrain, said she, your powers of moving! — I dare not else trust myself with you. — And my tears trickled down her bosom, as hers bedew'd my neck.

O the words of kindness, all to be express'd in vain, that flow'd from her lips!

Lift up your sweet face, my best child, my own Clarissa Harlowe! — O my daughter, best-beloved of my heart, lift up a face so ever-amiable to me! — Why these sobs? — Is an apprehended duty so affecting a thing, that before I can speak — but I am glad, my love, you can guess at what I have to say to you. I am spared the pains of breaking to you what was a task upon me reluctantly enough undertaken to break to you.

Then rising, she drew a chair near her own, and made me sit down by her, overwhelm'd as I was with tears of apprehension of what she had to say, and of gratitude for her truly maternal goodness to me; sobs still my only language.

And drawing her chair still nearer to mine, she put her arms round my neck, and my glowing cheek, wet with my tears, close to her own: Let me talk to you, my child; since silence is your choice, hearken to me, and *be* silent.

You know, my dear, what I every day forego, and undergo, for the sake of peace: Your papa is a very good man, and means well; but he will not be controuled; nor yet persuaded. You have seem'd to pity *me* sometimes, that I am obliged to give up every point. Poor man! *his* reputation the less for it; *mine* the greater; yet would I not have this credit, if I could help it, at so dear a rate to *him* and to *myself*. You are a dutiful, a prudent, and a *wise* child, she was pleased to say (in hope, no doubt, to make me so): You would not add, I am sure, to my trouble: You would not wilfully break that peace which costs your mamma so much to preserve. Obedience is better than sacrifice. O my Clary Harlowe, rejoice my heart, by telling me I have apprehended too much! — I see your concern! I see your perplexity! I see your conflict (loosing her arm, and rising, not willing I should see how much she herself was affected). I will leave you a moment. — Answer me not (for I was essaying to speak, and had, as soon as she took her dear cheek from mine, dropt down on my knees, my hands clasped and lifted up in a supplication manner): I am not prepared for your irresistible expostulation, she was pleased to say. — I will leave you to recollection: And I charge you, on my blessing, that all this my truly maternal tenderness be not thrown away upon you.

And then she withdrew into the next apartment; wiping her eyes, as she went from me; as mine overflow'd.

Source: Arthur Quiller-Couch, ed., *The Oxford Book of English Prose* (Oxford: Clarendon Press, 1925, 1948), pp. 384-389.

21.2

---✤---

OF THE CLUB, RICHARD STEELE

Coffeehouses were popular with the middle class, who gathered there (often on a daily basis) to read newspapers and magazines, discuss politics, share Enlightenment ideas, make business deals, and enjoy the trendy new beverage. Coffee was introduced into Europe in the seventeenth century and its popularity was helped by the relatively cheap importation of sugar from the colonies. Coffeehouses were so popular that thousands were built in every major European city. In addition, there were also thousands of clubs and taverns that provided the same opportunities for different social classes (aristocratic and working classes, respectively). Women had their own clubs and teahouses to mimic the generally male-only world of the coffeehouse.

The aristocratic equivalent of the coffeehouse was the salon. *Wealthy women—the wives or mistresses of aristocratic men—would organize discussion groups and lecture series that would be attended by men and women of the noble class. Across Europe, the* salons *were the best place to hear about the latest scientific discovery or the newest philosophical debate. Running salons was the most common and acceptable way for women to participate in the Enlightenment; it was the patronage of wealthy women that ensured the movement's popularity.*

Richard Steele (1672-1729) and Joseph Addison (1672-1719) began publishing The Spectator *in 1711. In addition to describing societal values, magazines such as* The Spectator *tried to inculcate them. They encouraged education and rationalist approaches to social and intellectual problems.* The Spectator *spawned many imitators; most, like the original, did not last for very long. However, there was always another magazine or newspaper waiting to take its place. The following essay by Steele was originally published in* The Spectator, *and describes the kind of club where such a magazine might typically be read.*

---✤---

QUESTIONS

1. What clues in the text indicate that this was intended for an upper-class club rather than a middle-class coffeehouse or working-class tavern?
2. Can you find an example of the kinds of values Steele was trying to encourage amongst his readers?
3. What does Steele reveal of how men thought about women?

When he is in town, he lives in Soho-square. It is said, he keeps himself a bachelor by reason he was crossed in love by a perverse, beautiful widow of the next county to him. Before this disappointment, Sir Roger was what you call a fine gentleman, had often supped with my Lord Rochester and Sir George Etherege, fought a duel upon his first coming to town, and kicked bully Dawson in a public coffeehouse for calling him youngster. But being ill-used by the above-mentioned widow, he was very serious for a year and a half; and though, his temper being natural jovial, he at last got over it, he grew careless of himself, and never dressed afterwards. He continues to wear a coat and doublet of the same cut that were in fashion at the time of his repulse, which, in his merry humours, he tells us, has been in and out twelve times since he first wore it. It is said Sir Roger grew humble in his desires after he had forgot his cruel beauty, insomuch that it is reported he has frequently offended in point of chastity with beggars and gypsies: but this is looked upon, by his friends, rather as matter of raillery than truth. He is now in his fifty-sixth year, cheerful, gay, and hearty; keeps a good house both in town and country; a great lover of mankind; but there is such a mirthful cast in his behaviour, that he is rather beloved than esteemed. His tenants grow rich, his servants look satisfied, all the young women profess love to him, and the young men are glad of his company. When he comes into a house, he calls the servants by their names, and talks all the way up stairs to a visit. I must not omit, that Sir Roger is a justice of the quorum; that he fills the chair at a quarter-session with great abilities, and three months ago gained universal applause, by explaining a passage in the game-act....

Next to Sir Andrew in the club-room sits Captain Sentry, a gentleman of great courage, good understanding, but invincible modesty. He is one of those that deserve very well, but are very awkward at putting their talents within the observation of such as should take notice of them. He was some years a captain, and behaved himself with great gallantry in several engagements and at several sieges; but having a small estate of his own, and being next heir to Sir Roger, he has quitted a way of life in which no man can rise suitable to his merit, who is not something of a courtier as well as a soldier. I have heard him often lament, that in a profession where merit is placed in so conspicuous a view, impudence should get the better of modesty. When he has talked to this purpose, I never heard him make a sour expression, but frankly confess that he left the world, because he was not fit for it. A strict honesty, and an even regular behaviour, are in themselves obstacles to him that must press through crowds, who endeavour at the same end with himself, the favour of a commander. He will however in his way of talk excuse generals, for not disposing according to men's desert, or enquiring into it; For, says he, that great man who has a mind to help me, has as many to break through to come at me, as I have to come at him: therefore, he will conclude, that the man who would make a figure, especially in a military way, must get over all modesty, and assist his patron against the importunity of other pretenders, by a proper assurance in his own vindication. He says it is a civil cowardice to be backward in asserting what you ought to expect, as it is a military fear to be slow in attacking when it is your duty. With this candour does the gentleman speak of himself and others. The same frankness runs through all his conversation. The military part of his life has furnished him with many adventures, in the relation of which he is very agreeable to the company; for he is never overbearing, though accustomed to command men in the utmost degree below him; nor ever to obsequious, from an habit of obeying men highly above him.

But that our society may not appear a set of humorists, unacquainted with the gallantries and pleasures of the age, we have amongst us the gallant Will Honeycomb; a gentleman who, according to his years, should be in the decline of his life; but having ever been very careful of his person, and always had a very easy fortune, time has made but a very little impression, either by wrinkles on his forehead, or races on this brain. His person is well turned, and of a good height. He is very ready at that sort of discourse with which men usually entertain women. He had all his life dressed very well, and remembers habits as others do men. He can smile when one speaks to him, and laughs easily. He knows the history of every mode, and can inform you from which of the French king's wenches, or wives and daughters had their manner of curling their hair, that way of placing their hoods; whose frailty was covered by such a sort of petticoat, and whose vanity to show her foot made that part of the dress so short in such a year. In a word, all his conversation and knowledge has been in the female world. As other men of his age will take notice to you what such a minister said on such and such an occasion, he will tell you, when the duke of Monmouth danced at court, such a woman was then smitten, another was taken with him at the head of his troop in the Park. In all these important relations, he has ever about the same time received a kind glance, or a blow of a fan from some celebrated beauty, mother of the present lord Such-a-one. If you speak of a young commoner, that said a lively thing in the house, he starts up, "He has good blood in his vein; Tom Mirable begot him; the rogue cheated me in that affair; that young fellow's mother used me more like a dog than any woman I ever made advances to." This way of talking of his, very much enlivens the conversation among us of a more sedate turn, and I find there is not one of the company, but myself, who rarely speak at all, but speaks of him as that sort of man, who is usually called a well-bred fine gentleman. To conclude his character, where women are not concerned, he is an honest worthy man.

Source: J. B. Priestley, ed. *Essayists Past and Present* (New York: Books for Libraries Press, Inc., 1925, 1967), pp. 49-57.

21.3

❖

MARRIAGE OF FIGARO, BEAUMARCHIS

Marriage of Figaro *was a tremendously popular play even before its first public performance in 1784. Although written several years before, rumors of its satirical plot gave it a controversial reputation that kept it censored for years by French king Louis XVI. Once in the public domain, however, the play was a runaway hit, as was the subsequent opera based on it by Mozart. The opera premiered in 1786, and like the play, it too faced censors and controversy.*

In the first excerpt below, the Countess, her maid Suzanne, and Suzanne's fiancée Figaro (manservant to the Count), discuss what is to be done about the Count's infatuation with Suzanne. In the second excerpt, Figaro discusses the nature of fate.

❖

QUESTIONS

1. One of the more controversial aspects of this play is that it was viewed as a satirical attack on the aristocracy. Does this excerpt fit that description?
2. In what ways is the play a satire of the working classes?
3. What do these excerpts reveal about the relationships between women and men in the eighteenth century?

A CT TWO

SCENE: *A bedroom furnished with great splendour; a bed in a recess; a dais downstage of it; a door upstage right; door to a small closet downstage left; door upstage to the maid's quarters; window at the other side.*

[SUZANNE *and the* COUNTESS *enter from the right.*]

THE COUNTESS [*throwing herself into an easy-chair*]: Close the door, Suzanne, and tell me exactly what happened.

SUZANNE: I have withheld nothing from you, Madam.

THE COUNTESS: You really mean to say, Suzie, that he was endeavouring to seduce you?

SUZANNE: Not al all! His Lordship doesn't put himself to so much trouble as that with a servant: he merely wanted a financial arrangement.

THE COUNTESS: And the page was there all the time?

SUZANNE: Behind the armchair in fact. He had come to ask me to persuade you to intercede for him.

THE COUNTESS: Why didn't he come to me? Should I have refused him, Suzie?

SUZANNE: That's what I told him: but he was so distressed at leaving and particularly at parting from Your Ladyship... 'Ah! Suzie! How noble and beautiful she is! But how unapproachable!'

THE COUNTESS: Do I really seam like that, Suzie? I, who have always been his protector.

SUZANNE: He no sooner saw your ribbon which I had in my hand than he fairly leapt at it.

THE COUNTESS [*smiling*]: My ribbon! What childishness!

SUZANNE: I tried to get it back from him. He fought like a lion, Your Ladyship, His eyes flashed. 'Over my dead body!' he said in his shrill high-pitched voice.

THE COUNTESS [*lost in thought*]: And then, Suzie?

SUZANNE: And then, Madam? What can you do with such a young demon? On the one hand, respect for his godmother, on the other — 'If only I could —' And because he daren't even venture to kiss the hem of Your Ladyship's gown he wanted to embrace me, if you please!

THE COUNTESS [*still dreaming*]: A truce to these foolish things. So, my dear Suzanne, my husband ended by telling you —

SUZANNE: That if I wouldn't listen to him he would support Marceline...

THE COUNTESS [*rising and walking up and down fanning herself*]: He no longer loves me.

SUZANNE: Then why is he so jealous?

THE COUNTESS: Like all husbands, my dear — from pride — nothing more. Ah, I have loved him too dearly! I have wearied him with my solicitude and tired him with my love. That's the only offence I have been guilty of: but I don't intend to let you suffer for having rebuffed him: you shall marry your Figaro. He's the one person who can help us. Is he coming back?

SUZANNE: When he's seen the hunt move off.

THE COUNTESS [*fanning herself*]: Open the window a little. It's hot in here.

SUZANNE: Your Ladyship takes so much out of herself. [*Opens window upstage.*]

THE COUNTESS [*dreaming*]: Men are all the same....Were it not for his persistence in avoiding me...

SUZANNE: Ah, there goes His Lordship riding across the park with Pedrillo and two, three — four greyhounds.

THE COUNTESS: Then we have time still. [*Sits down.*] Was that someone knocking, Suzie?

SUZANNE [*running to open the door, saying*]: Ah! It's my Figaro! My Figaro! Do come in, my dear! Her Ladyship is anxious to see you.

FIGARO: And how about you, my dear Suzanne? There's no need for Her Ladyship to worry. What, in fact, does it amount to? A mere nothing! His Lordship finds a young woman attractive: he would like to make her his mistress. It's all very natural.

SUZANNE: Natural?

FIGARO: So he appoints me his courier and Suzie Counsellor to the Embassy....Not a bad idea at all, is it?

SUZANNE: Oh, do give up!

FIGARO: And now, because Suzanne, my fiancée, doesn't accept the honour he confers on her, he proposes to take up the cause of Marceline. What could be simpler? Somebody thwarts one's plans so one gets one's own back by upsetting theirs. Everybody does it — and it's what we are going to do too. That's all there is to it.

THE COUNTESS: Figaro! How can you treat so lightly a scheme which threatens the happiness of every one of us?

FIGARO: Who says I do so, Your Ladyship?

SUZANNE: Instead of taking our troubles to heart...

FIGARO: Isn't it sufficient that I take them in hand? No, if we are to go about things as methodically as he does, let us discourage his ardour for what is ours by giving him cause for concern for what is his.

THE COUNTESS: About me? Are you out of your mind?

FIGARO: *He* must be!

THE COUNTESS: A man so jealous as...

FIGARO: So much the better: if you are to cope with such people what you need to do is to get them annoyed. How well women understand that! Once you get a man thoroughly enraged, a little maneuvering and you can do what you like with him — lead him into the Guadalquivir if you want to. I have arranged for Bazile to receive a letter from an unseen hand warning His Lordship that a young man intends to meet you tonight at the ball.

THE COUNTESS: You'll play tricks with truth which involve a virtuous woman...

FIGARO: There are few, Madam, with whom I would have dared take the risk — lest it might prove to be true.

THE COUNTESS: I suppose I'm to be thankful for that!

FIGARO: But don't you think it's considerate of me to have arranged his little day for his so that he'll spend his time rushing round and cursing his own wife when he meant to be ingratiating himself with mine? He's already quite beside himself. He's galloping here, searching there, and worried to death! Look! There he goes – charging across country after a poor helpless hare. The time for the wedding will soon be here and he'll have done nothing to prevent it and won't dare to in Your Ladyship's presence.

SUZANNE: No, but that old blue stocking, Marceline, will.

FIGARO: Pah! A lot that worries me! You must send word to His Lordship that you'll meet him at dusk in the garden.

SUZANNE: You are still relying on that idea?

FIGARO: Oh, confound it, listen to me! Folk who won't try never get anywhere. That's my opinion.

SUZANNE: And very nice too!

THE COUNTESS: Are you going to let her go?

FIGARO: Of course not! I'll dress somebody else in Suzanne's clothes: when we surprise him at the rendezvous, how will he be able to get out of it?

SUZANNE: And who are you dressing up in my clothes?

FIGARO: Chérubin.

…

FIGARO [*gloomily walking up and down in the dark*]: Oh, woman, woman, woman, feeble creature that you are! No living thing can fail to be true to its nature. Is it yours to deceive? After stubbornly refusing when I urged her to it in the presence of her mistress — at the very moment of her plighting her word to me, in the very midst of the ceremony…and he smiled while he read it, the scoundrel! And I standing by like a blockhead! No, My Lord Count, you shan't have her, you shall not have her! Because you are a great nobleman you think you are a great genius….Nobility, fortune, rank, position! How proud they make a man feel! What have *you* done to deserve such advantages? Put yourself to the trouble of being born — nothing more! For the rest — a very ordinary man! Whereas I, lost among the obscure crowd, have had to deploy more knowledge, more calculation and skill merely to survive than has sufficed to rule all the provinces of Spain for a century! Yet you would measure yourself against me….Somebody's coming — it's she! No, it's nobody at all. The night's as dark as the very devil and here am I plying the stupid trade of husband though I'm still only half married. [*Sits down.*] Could anything be stranger than a fate like mine? Son of goodness knows whom, stolen by bandits, brought up to their way of life, I become disgusted with it and yearn for an honest profession — only to find myself repulsed everywhere. I study Chemistry, Pharmacy, Surgery, and all the prestige of a great nobleman can barely secure me the handling of a horse-doctor's probe!

From *Beaumarchis, The Barber of Seville and the Marriage of Figaro*, trans. John Wood, p. 129-132, 199. Copyright © 1967, 1985 Penguin Books, Ltd. Reprinted by permission of Penguin Books, Ltd.

21.4

ASHKENAZI JEWS OF POLAND, SOLOMON MAIMON

In addition to the dominant Christian culture of western Europe, there was also an active Jewish culture in the East. The following extract is from the autobiography of Solomon ben Joshua, (c. 1754-1800) also known as Solomon Maimon. Maimon lived through two significant events that had a tremendous impact on his life. One was the Edict of Toleration from 1791, proclaimed by Joseph II in the Holy Roman Empire. The second was the partitions of Poland in 1772, 1793, and 1795.

QUESTIONS

1. Compare this description of a typical Jewish education with the type of education common to the Christian Enlightenment.
2. Is there any evidence that the Enlightenment had an influence on the Jewish culture?
3. Maimon is recalling events from before the Edict of Toleration; how much prejudice does he face in his daily life?

SOLOMON MAIMON IN POLAND
1760-1765

I. A Polish Jewish School of the Middle Eighteenth Century

My brother Joseph and I were sent to Mirz to school. My brother, who was about twelve years old, was put to board with a schoolmaster of some repute at that time, by name Jossel. This man was the terror of all young people, "the scourge of God"; he treated those in his charge with unheard of cruelty, flogged them till the blood came, even for the slightest offense, and not infrequently tore off their ears, or beat their eyes out. [Through corporal punishment was the rule, such brutality was uncommon.] When the parents of these unfortunates came to him, and took him to task, he struck them with stones or whatever else came to hand, and drove them with his stick out of the house back to their own dwellings, without any respect of persons. All under his discipline became either blockheads or good scholars. I, who was then only seven years old, was sent to another schoolmaster…

I must now say something of the condition of the Jewish schools in general. The school is commonly a small smoky hut, and the children are scattered, some on benches, some on the bare earth. The master, in a dirty blouse, sitting on the table, holds between his knees a bowl, in which he grinds tobacco into snuff with a huge pestle like the club of Hercules, while at the same time he wields his authority. The assistant-teachers give lessons, each in his own corner, and rule those under their charge quite as despotically as the master himself. Of the breakfast, lunch, and other food sent to the school for the children, these gentlemen keep the largest share for themselves. Sometimes even the poor youngsters get nothing at all; and yet they dare not make any complaint on the subject, if they will not expose themselves to the vengeance of these tyrants. Here the children are imprisoned from morning to night, and have not an hour to themselves, except on Friday and a half-holiday at the New Moon. [The New Moon marks the beginning of a Jewish month.]

II. The Married Life of Young Maimon

I stood, however, not only under the slipper of my wife, but — what was very much worse — under the lash of my mother-in-law [Rissia]. Nothing of all that she had promised was fulfilled. Her house, which she had settled on her daughter as a dowry, was burdened with debt. Of the six years' board which she had promised me I enjoyed scarcely half a year's, and this amid constant brawls and squabbles. She even, trusting to my youth and want of spirit, ventured now and then to lay hands on me, but this I repaid not infrequently with compound interest. [He was now in his eleventh year.] Scarcely a meal passed during which we did not fling at each other's head, bowls, plates, spoons, and similar articles....

Scenes like this occurred very often. At such skirmishes of course my wife had to remain neutral, and whichever party gained the upper hand, it came home to her very closely. "Oh!" she often complained, "if only the one or the other of you had a little more patience!"

Tired of a ceaseless open war I once hit upon a stratagem which had a good effect, for a short time at least. I rose about midnight, took a large vessel of earthenware, crept with it under my mother-in-law's bed, and began to speak aloud into the vessel after the following fashion: "O Rissia, Rissia, you ungodly woman, why do you treat my beloved son so ill? If you do not mend your ways, your end is near, and you will be damned to all eternity." Then I crept out again, and began to pinch her cruelly; and after a while I slipped silently back to bed.

The following morning she got up in consternation and told my wife that my mother had appeared to her in a dream, and had threatened and pinched her on my account. In confirmation she show the blue marks on her arm. When I came from the synagogue, I did not find my mother-in-law at home, but found my wife in tears. I asked the reason, but she would tell me nothing. My mother-in-law returned with a dejected look, and eyes red with weeping. She had gone, as I afterwards learned, to the Jewish place of burial, thrown herself on my mother's grave, and begged for forgiveness of her fault. She then had the burial place measured, and ordered a wax-light, as long as its circumference, for burning in the synagogue. [Such customs were common among the Jewish and Christian masses.] She also fasted the whole day, and towards me showed herself extremely amiable.

III. *Prince Radziwill and His Jews*

Prince Radziwill [1734-1790] was, as Hettman [a general] in Poland and Voivode [a high official] in Lithuania, one of the greatest magnates, and as occupant of three inheritances in his family owned immense estates. He was not without a certain kindness of heart and good sense; but, through neglected training and a want of instruction, he became on of the most extravagant princes that ever lived....

Who can describe all the excesses he perpetrated? A few examples will, I believe, be sufficient to give the reader some idea of them. Ascertain respect for my former prince does not allow me to consider his faults as anything but faults of temperament and education, which deserve rather our pity than our hatred and contempt.

When he passed through a street, which he commonly did with the whole pomp of his court, his bands of music, and soldiers, no man, at the peril of his life, durst show himself in the street; and even in the houses people were by no means safe. The poorest, dirtiest peasant-woman, who came in his way, he would order up into his carriage beside himself.

Once he sent for a respectable Jewish barber, who, suspecting nothing but that he was wanted for some surgical operation, brought his instruments with him, and appeared before the prince. [Barbers used to perform minor surgical operations.]

"Have you brought your instruments with you?" he was asked.

"Yes, Serene Highness," he replied.

"Then," said the prince, "give me a lancet, and I will open one of your veins."

The poor barber had to submit. The prince seized the lancet; and as he did not know how to go about the operation, and beside his hand trembled as a result of his hard drinking, of course he wounded the barber in a pitiable manner. But his courtiers smiled their applause, and praised his great skill in surgery.

He went one day into a church, and being so drunk that he did not know where he was, he stood against the altar, and commenced to pollute it. All who were present became horrified. Next morning when he was sober, the clergy brought to his mind the misdeed he had committed the day before. "Eh!" said the prince, "we will soon make that good." Thereupon he issued a command to the Jews of the place, to provide at their own expense, fifty stone of wax for burning in the church. [A stone was about twenty-two pounds.] The poor Jews were therefore obliged to bring a sin-offering for the desecration of a Christian Church by an orthodox Catholic Christian....

Once he drove with the whole pomp of his court to a Jewish synagogue, and, without any one to this day knowing the reason, committed the greatest havoc, smashed windows and stoves, broke all the vessels, threw on the ground the copies of the Holy Scriptures kept in the ark, and so forth. A learned, pious Jew, who was present, ventured to lift one of these copies from the ground, and had the honor of being struck with a musket-ball by His Serene Highness' own hand. From here the train went to a second synagogue, where the same conduct was repeated, and from there they proceeded to the Jewish burial-place, where the buildings were demolished, and the monuments cast into the fire. [The desecration of synagogues and cemeteries is still common in Central and Eastern Europe.]

QUESTIONS FOR PART 21

1. Although there was an increase in literacy in the eighteenth century, one thing that has not changed is the generally public nature of reading (in clubs, coffeehouses, etc.). What does this mean for the sharing of political and philosophical ideas?
2. What was the difference between high and popular culture in the eighteenth century?
3. What roles did women play in eighteenth century culture?

PART 22

AGE OF REVOLUTIONS

The eighteenth-century revolutions (in America, Haiti, and France) were inspired by the model of the Glorious Revolution in England, 1688, and by the Enlightenment concept of personal liberty, rational government, and natural law. In a sense these revolutions were the Enlightenment put into practice. The American Revolution was the most efficient; relatively short in duration and bloodless in comparison to the chaos of the other revolutions. The relatively quick success of the American Revolution inspired imitations in the French colonies and in France. The Haitian Revolution was as much as slave revolt as a political one, and created the only free black state in the West.

The French Revolution had a less clear outcome. It began when aristocracy complained to King Louis XVI about excessively high taxation and the relentless government debt. Louis had inherited a large debt from his grandfather and father (both also named Louis); it was the price the French kings paid for absolute power and imperial ambitions. A disastrous series of continental and colonial wars (most of which France lost, usually to England) reduced the size of the French trade empire and crippled the economy. Meanwhile, Louis and his Austrian wife Marie Antoinette continued to live in excessive luxury at Versailles, which, like the wars, was paid for by taxes. In 1786 Louis proclaimed another new tax. Paris was the first element of France to refuse to pay; in 1787 the city demanded that Louis summon the Estates-General, the French equivalent of a Parliament and the only way to check his absolutism. The Estates-General only met when the King summoned it; the last time had been in 1614.

The Estates-General was divided into three bodies, one each for the three estates or orders of society (clergy, nobility, and everyone else). Usually the top two estates, clergy and nobility, voted as a bloc (each estate got one vote) and thus dominated the third estate (which in the past had been made up the peasantry). One of first crises of the French Revolution was the unexpected response of the third estate in 1789. The third estate now included educated, professional, and moneyed groups that demanded representation equal to the clergy and nobility.

Thus the Revolution progressed from an aristocratic revolt against the absolutism into a middle class uprising that demanded political, economic, and social reforms across France. The Revolution went through several more stages, creating a new body of government (the National Assembly) and a constitution. By 1792 the Assembly proclaimed the first French Republic, and Louis was soon to lose his head. In 1793 and 1794, Republican France was overrun by The Terror: show trials, executions throughout France (mostly of the middle class), and war with Austria and the Low Countries. Finally, the Revolution was taken over in 1799 by Napoleon, and France entered a new political era.

22.1

AMERICAN *DECLARATION OF INDEPENDENCE*

Thomas Jefferson, the greatest of the American philosophes, *wrote the* Declaration of Independence *in 1776. Jefferson brought the* Declaration *to the Continental Congress, which adopted it as a formal rejection of British rule and a proclamation of the American colonists' determination to establish an independent state. But the intended audience of the* Declaration *was not the British government. Jefferson instead wrote a brilliant piece of revolutionary propaganda in order to convince the colonists and the enemies of Britain that the colonists were justified in overthrowing the British Empire. The text had tremendous influence on subsequent revolutions around the world for centuries to come.*

QUESTIONS

1. What does Jefferson mean by the "laws of nature?"
2. One of the most quoted phrases of the *Declaration* is that "all men are created equal." How do you think Jefferson meant this phrase to be interpreted? What kinds of equality are there?
3. Why does the *Declaration* target all its complaints at the King, and not Parliament?

In Congress, July 4, 1776,

THE UNANIMOUS DECLARATION OF THE THIRTEEN UNITED STATES OF AMERICA,

When in the Course of human events, it becomes necessary for one people to dissolve the political bands which have connected them with another, and to assume among the powers of the earth, the separate and equal station to which the Laws of Nature and of Nature's God entitle them, a decent respect to the opinions of mankind requires that they should declare the causes which impel them to the separation.

We hold these truths to be self-evident, that all men are created equal, that they are endowed by their Creator with certain unalienable Rights, that among these are Life, Liberty and the pursuit of Happiness. That to secure these rights, Governments are instituted among Men, deriving their just powers from the consent of the governed, That whenever any Form of Government becomes destructive of these ends, it is the Right of the People to alter or to abolish it, and to institute new Government, laying its foundation on such principles and organizing its powers in such form, as to them shall seem most likely to effect their Safety and Happiness. Prudence, indeed, will dictate that Governments long established should not be changed for light and transient causes; and accordingly all experience hath shewn, that mankind are more disposed to suffer, while evils are sufferable, than to right themselves by abolishing the forms to which they are accustomed. But when a long train of abuses and usurpations, pursuing invariably the same Object evinces a design to reduce them under absolute Despotism, it is their right, it is their duty, to throw off such Government, and to provide new Guards for their future security. — Such has been the patient sufferance of these Colonies; and such is now the necessity which constrains them to alter their former Systems of Government. The history of the present King of Great Britain is a history of repeated injuries and usurpations, all having in direct object the establishment of an absolute Tyranny over these States. To prove this, let Facts be submitted to a candid world.

He has refused his Assent to Laws, the most wholesome and necessary for the public good.

He has forbidden his Governors to pass Laws of immediate and pressing importance, unless suspended in their operation till his Assent should be obtained; and when so suspended, he has utterly neglected to attend to them.

He has refused to pass other Laws for the accommodation of large districts of people, unless those people would relinquish the right of Representation in the Legislature, a right inestimable to them and formidable to tyrants only.

He has called together legislative bodies at places unusual, uncomfortable, and distant from the depository of their public Records, for the sole purpose of fatiguing them into compliance with his measures.

He has dissolved Representative Houses repeatedly, for opposing with manly firmness his invasions on the rights of the people.

He has refused for a long time, after such dissolutions, to cause others to be elected; whereby the Legislative powers, incapable of Annihilation, have returned to the People at large for their exercise; the State remaining in the mean time exposed to all the dangers of invasion from without, and convulsions within.

He has endeavoured to prevent the population of these States; for that purpose obstructing the Laws for Naturalization of Foreigners; refusing to pass others to encourage their migrations hither, and raising the conditions of new Appropriations of Lands.

He has obstructed the Administration of Justice, by refusing his Assent to Laws for establishing Judiciary powers.

He has made Judges dependent on his Will alone, for the tenure of their offices, and the amount and payment of their salaries.

He has erected a multitude of New Offices, and sent hither swarms of Officers to harass our people, and eat out their substance.

He has kept among us, in times of peace, Standing Armies without the Consent of our legislatures.

He has affected to render the Military independent of and superior to the Civil Power.

He has combined with others to subject us to a jurisdiction foreign to our constitution, and unacknowledged by our laws; giving his Assent to their Acts of pretended Legislation:

For quartering large bodies of armed troops among us:

For protecting them, by a mock Trial, from punishment for any Murders which they should commit on the Inhabitants of these States:

For cutting off our Trade with all parts of the world:

For imposing Taxes on us without our Consent:

For depriving us in many cases, of the benefits of Trial by Jury:

For transporting us beyond Seas to be tried for pretended offences

For abolishing the free System of English Laws in a neighbouring Province, establishing therein an Arbitrary government, and enlarging its Boundaries so as to render it at once an example and fit instrument for introducing the same absolute rule into these Colonies:

For taking away our Charters, abolishing our most valuable Laws, and altering fundamentally the

Forms of our Governments:

For suspending our own Legislatures, and declaring themselves invested with power to legislate for us in all cases whatsoever.

He has abdicated Government here, by declaring us out of his Protection and waging War against us.

He has plundered our seas, ravaged our Coasts, burnt our towns, and destroyed the lives of our people.

He is at this time transporting large Armies of foreign Mercenaries to compleat the works of death, desolation and tyranny, already begun with circumstances of Cruelty & perfidy scarcely paralleled in the most barbarous ages, and totally unworthy the Head of a civilized nation.

He has constrained our fellow Citizens taken Captive on the high Seas to bear Arms against their Country, to become the executioners of their friends and Brethren, or to fall themselves by their Hands.

He has excited domestic insurrections amongst us, and has endeavoured to bring on the inhabitants of our frontiers, the merciless Indian Savages, whose known rule of warfare, is an undistinguished destruction of all ages, sexes and conditions.

In every stage of these Oppressions We have Petitioned for Redress in the most humble terms: Our repeated Petitions have been answered only by repeated injury. A Prince whose character is thus marked by every act which may define a Tyrant, is unfit to be the ruler of a free people.

Nor have We been wanting in attentions to our Brittish brethren. We have warned them from time to time of attempts by their legislature to extend an unwarrantable jurisdiction over us. We have reminded them of the circumstances of our emigration and settlement here. We have appealed to their native justice and magnanimity, and we have conjured them by the ties of our common kindred to disavow these usurpations, which, would inevitably interrupt our connections and correspondence. They too have been deaf to the voice of justice and of consanguinity. We must, therefore, acquiesce in the necessity, which denounces our Separation, and hold them, as we hold the rest of mankind, Enemies in War, in Peace Friends.

We, therefore, the Representatives of the united States of America, in General Congress, Assembled, appealing to the Supreme Judge of the world for the rectitude of our intentions, do, in the Name, and by Authority of the good People of these Colonies, solemnly publish and declare, That these United Colonies are, and of Right ought to be Free and Independent States; that they are Absolved from all Allegiance to the British Crown, and that all political connection between them and the State of Great Britain, is and ought to be totally dissolved; and that as Free and Independent States, they have full Power to levy War, conclude Peace, contract Alliances, establish Commerce, and to do all other Acts and Things which Independent States may of right do. And for the support of this Declaration, with a firm reliance on the protection of divine Providence, we mutually pledge to each other our Lives, our Fortunes and our sacred Honor.

Sources: William MacDonald, ed., *Documentary Source Book of American History 1606-1898* (New York: Macmillan Company, 1908), pp. 191-194.

22.2

WHAT IS THE THIRD ESTATE? ABBE SIEYÈS

In 1789, at the first meeting of the Estates-General in one hundred and seventy five years, a member of the first estate, Abbe (Father) Sieyès wrote a description of the third estate. Sieyès (1748-1836) was a delegate for Paris. He was virtually unknown until he published a pamphlet on What is the Third Estate? *that became an immediate hit. Sieyès served the many different revolutionary governments, and was even granted a noble title by Napoleon.*

QUESTIONS

1. What is the significance of this text being authored by a member of the first estate rather than the third?
2. What does Sieyès say about the nobility?
3. How does Sieyès answer his own question: what is the third estate?

WHAT IS THE THIRD ESTATE?

What is necessary that a nation should subsist and prosper? Individual effort and public functions. All individual efforts may be included in four classes: 1. Since the earth and the waters furnish crude products for the needs of man, the first class, in logical sequence, will be that of all families which devote themselves to agricultural labor. 2. Between the first sale of the products and their consumption or use, a new manipulation, more or less repeated, adds to these products a second value more or less composite. In this manner human industry succeeds in perfecting the gifts of nature, and the crude product increases two-fold, ten-fold, one hundred-fold in value. Such are the efforts of the second class. 3. Between production and consumption, as well as between the various stages of production, a group of intermediary agents establish themselves, useful both to producers and consumers; these are the merchants and brokers; the brokers who, comparing incessantly the demands of time and place, speculate upon the profit of retention and transportation; merchants who are charged with distribution, in the last analysis, either at wholesale or at retail. This species of utility characterizes the third class. 4. Outside of these three classes of productive and useful citizens, who are occupied with real objects of consumption and use, there is also need in a society of a series of efforts and pains, whose objects are directly useful or agreeable to the individual. This fourth class embraces all those who stand between the most distinguished and liberal professions and the less esteemed services of domestics.

Such are the efforts which sustain society. Who puts them forth? The Third Estate.

Public functions may be classified equally well, in the present state of affairs, under four recognized heads; the sword, the robe, the church and the administration. It would be superfluous to take them up one by one, for the purpose of showing that everywhere the Third Estate attends to nineteen-twentieths of them, with this distinction: that it is laden with all that which is really painful, with all the burdens which the privileged classes refuse to carry. Do we give the Third Estate credit for this? That this might come about, it would be necessary that the Third Estate should refuse to fill these places, or that it should be less ready to exercise their functions. The facts are well known. Meanwhile they have dared to impose a prohibition upon the order of the Third Estate. They have said to it: "Whatever may be your services, whatever may be your abilities, you shall go thus far; you may not pass beyond!" Certain rare exceptions, properly regarded, are but a mockery, and the terms which are indulged in on such occasions, one insult the more.

If this exclusion is a social crime against the Third Estate; if it is a veritable act of hostility, could it perhaps be said that it is useful to the public weal? Alas! Who is ignorant of the effects of monopoly? If it discourages those whom it rejects, is it not well known that it tends to render less able those whom it favors? Is it not understood that every employment from which free competition is removed, becomes dearer and less effective?

In setting aside any function whatsoever to serve as an *appanage* for a distinct class among citizens, is it not to be observed that it is no longer the man alone who does the work that it is necessary to reward, but all the unemployed members of the same caste, and also the entire families of those who are employed as well as those who are not? Is it not to be remarked that since the government has become the patrimony of a particular class, it has been distended beyond all measure; places have been created, not on account of the necessities of the governed, but in the interests of the governing, etc., etc.? Has not attention been called to the fact that this order of things, which is basely and – I even presume to say – beastly respectable with us, when we find it in reading the History of Ancient Egypt or the accounts of Voyages to the Indies, is despicable, monstrous, destructive of all industry, the enemy of social progress; above all degrading to the human race in general, and particularly intolerable to Europeans, etc., etc.? But I must leave these considerations, which, if they increase the importance of the subject and throw light upon it, perhaps along with the new light, slacken our progress.

It suffices here to have made it clear that the pretended utility of a privileged order for the public service is nothing more than a chimera; that with it all that which is burdensome in this service is performed by the Third Estate; that without it the superior places would be infinitely better filled; that they naturally ought to be the lot and the recompense of ability and recognized services, and that if privileged persons have come to usurp all the lucrative and honorable posts, it is a hateful injustice to the rank and file of citizens and at the same time a treason to the public weal.

In the first place, it is not possible in the number of all the elementary parts of a nation to find a place for the caste of nobles. I know that there are individuals in great number whom infirmities, incapacity, incurable laziness, or the weight of bad habits, render strangers to the labors of society. The exception and the abuse are everywhere found beside the rule. But it will be admitted that the less there are of these abuses, the better it will be for the State. The worst possible arrangement of all would be where not alone isolated individuals, but a whole class of citizens should take pride in remaining motionless in the midst of the general movement and should consume the best part of the product without bearing any part in its production. Such a class is surely estranged to the nation by its indolence.

The noble order is not less estranged from the generality of us by its civil and political prerogatives.

What is a nation? A body of associates, living under a common law, and represented by the same legislature, etc.

Is it not evident that the noble order has privileges and expenditures which it dares to call its rights, but which are apart from the rights of the great body of citizens? It departs there from the common order, from the common law. So its civil rights make of it an isolated people in the midst of the great nation. This is truly *imperium in imperio.*

In regard to its political rights, these also it exercises apart. It has its special representatives, which are not charged with securing the interests of the people. The body of its deputies sit apart; and when it is assembled in the same hall with the deputies of simple citizens, it is none the less true that its representation is essentially distinct and separate: it is a stranger to the nation, in the first place, then by its object, which consists of defending not the general, but the particular interest.

The Third Estate embraces then all that which belongs to the nation; and all that which is not the Third Estate, cannot be regarded as being of the nation. What is the Third Estate? It is the whole.

Sources: Oliver J. Thatcher, ed., *The Ideas that have Influenced Civilization in the Original Documents, Volume VII* (Boston: Roberts-Manchester Publishing Co., 1901-1902), pp. 395-398.

22.3

---- ✢ ----

DECLARATION OF THE RIGHTS OF MAN AND THE CITIZEN

As the title clearly indicates, this Declaration *was inspired by the American Declaration written in 1776 by Thomas Jefferson. The French version was written in 1789, and was supposed to be a preamble to a constitution to be drawn up by the National Assembly, and was presented to Louis XVI to ratify. But the National Assembly became mired down in internal disputes and failed to draw up a constitution until 1791.*

The Declaration of the Rights of Man *encapsulates all of the principles upon which the French Revolution was based and is an outline of the government that was to be created by a constitution. In addition to Jefferson, it drew heavily on the language of Rousseau. Ultimately, Louis XVI refused to accept the* Declaration *and the revolution entered the next, more violent phase. In response to Louis' refusal to sign the* Declaration, *angry crowds (led primarily by women; see source 22.4) marched on Versailles and forced the king to return to Paris. Interestingly enough, as second version of this was written in 1791 by Olympe de Gouges, who entitled her version the* Declaration of the Rights of Man and Woman.

---- ✢ ----

QUESTIONS

1. Compare this to Jefferson's *Declaration*. How do they differ?
2. Does this declaration recognize a class system? Describe it and explain its purpose.
3. What does the *Declaration* say about taxes?

The representatives of the French people, organized as a national assembly, believing that the ignorance, neglect or contempt of the rights of man are the sole causes of public calamities and of the corruption of governments, have determined to set forth in a solemn declaration, the natural, inalienable and sacred rights of man, in order that this declaration, being constantly before all the members of the social body, shall remind them continually of their rights and duties; in order that the acts of the legislative power, as well as those of the executive power, may be compared at any moment with the ends of all political institutions and may thus be more respected; in order that the grievances of the citizen, based hereafter upon simple and incontestable principles, shall tend to the maintenance of the constitution and redound to the happiness of all. Hence the National Assembly recognizes and proclaims in the presence and under the auspices of the Supreme Being the following rights of man and of the citizen:

Article 1. Men are born and remain free and equal in rights. Social distinctions can only be founded upon the general good.

2.   The aim of every political association is the preservation of the natural and imprescriptible rights of man. These rights are liberty, property, security and resistance to oppression.

3.   The principle [*principe*] of all sovereignty resides essentially in the nation. No body nor individual may exercise any authority which does not proceed directly from the nation.

4.   Liberty consists in being able to do everything which injures no one else; hence the exercise of the natural rights of each man has no limits except those which assure to the other members of the society the enjoyment of the same rights. These limits can only be determined by law.

5.   Law can only prohibit such actions as are hurtful to society. Nothing may be prevented which is not forbidden by law, and no one may be forced to do anything not provided for by law.

6.   Law is the expression of the general will. Every citizen has a right to participate personally or through his representative in its formation. It must be the same for all, whether it protects or punishes. All citizens being equal in the eyes of the law are equally eligible to all dignities and to all public positions and occupations according to their abilities and without distinction except that of their virtues and talents.

7.   No person shall be accused, arrested or imprisoned except in the cases and according to the forms prescribed by law. Any one soliciting, transmitting, executing or causing to be executed any arbitrary order shall be punished. But any citizen summoned or arrested in virtue of the law shall submit without delay, as resistance constitutes an offence.

8.   The law shall provide for such punishments only as are strictly and obviously necessary, and no one shall suffer punishment except it be legally inflicted in virtue of a law passed and promulgated before the commission of the offence.

9.   All persons are held innocent until they shall have been declared guilty, if arrest shall be deemed indispensable all severity not essential to the securing of the prisoner's person shall be severely repressed by law.

10. No one shall be disquieted on account of his opinion, including his religious views, provided their manifestation does not disturb the public order established by law.

11. The free communication of ideas and opinions is one of the most precious of the rights of man. Every citizen may, accordingly, speak, write and print with freedom, being responsible, however, for such abuses of this freedom as shall be defined by law.

12. The security of the rights of man and of the citizen requires public military force. These forces are, therefore, established for the good of all and not for the personal advantage of those to whom they shall be entrusted.

13. A common contribution is essential for the maintenance of the public forces and for the cost of administration. This should be equitably distributed among all the citizens in proportion to their means.

14. All the citizens have a right to decide either personally or by their representatives as to the necessity of the public contribution, to grant this freely, to know to what uses it is put, and to fix the proportion, the mode of assessment, and of collection, and the duration of the taxes.

15. Society has the right to require of every public agent an account of his administration.

16. A society in which the observance of the law is not assured nor the separation of powers defined has no constitution at all.

17. Property being an inviolable and sacred right, no one shall be deprived thereof except where public necessity, legally determined shall clearly demand it and then only on condition that the owner shall have been previously and equitably indemnified.

Sources: Oliver J. Thatcher, ed., *The Ideas that have Influenced Civilization in the Original Documents, Volume VII* (Boston: Roberts-Manchester Publishing Co., 1901-1902), pp. 415-417.

22.4

WOMEN'S MARCH ON VERSAILLES

The French Revolutionaries were attempting to work with Louis XVI until October 1789. When Louis refused to sign the Declaration of Rights of Man and the Citizen, *and stalled on accepting other decrees from the National Assembly, a large mob from Paris marched to Versailles and forced the royal family to return to Paris. The mob was led by about seven thousand women, the wives of shopkeepers and artisans, who were also protesting high bread prices as well as the failure of the* Declaration.

The following source is a description of the march by one of the participants.

QUESTIONS

1. How much were the women of France allowed to participate in the Revolution?
2. What is the author's view of Louis?
3. Why did the women want Louis to return to Paris?

The Woman Cheret, *The Event of Paris and Versailles, by One of the Ladies Who Had the Honor to Be in the Deputation to the General Assembly* (1789)

About 8:30 in the morning, many women appeared at the city hall; some asked to speak to Messieurs Bailly and de la Fayette, to learn from them why it was so difficult to get bread and at such a high price; others wanted most absolutely for the king and queen to come to Paris and live in the Louvre where, the women said, they would be infinitely better off than at Versailles; finally, others demanded that those who had black cockades give them up immediately, that the Regiment of Flanders and the king's bodyguards be recalled, and that their majesties have no other guards than Parisian national soldiers. During this time, Messieurs de Gouvion, Major General Richard du Pin, second commandant of the volunteers of the Bastille, and Lefevre, distributor of powder, arms, and equipment, were in the greatest danger because the multitude, furious at not having found arms and ammunition, wanted to hang them, and it was only by some kind of miracle that they escaped. About noon or one o'clock, Monsieur the Marquis de la Fayette, who seemed to see nothing good in a trip to Versailles, finally came to believe that he must cede to the citizens' fervent wishes; Marie-Louise Lenoel, wife of Cheret, living in the rue Vaugirard, employed at that time in one of the most lucrative markets at Passy, abruptly leaves her virtuous mother, abandons the profits she is about to earn, mingles with the lady citizenesses going to Versailles, and flies away with them, under the supervision of sirs Hulin and Maillard, and other volunteers of the Bastille, those heroes who wanted to join to the laurels from July 14 the honor of again making the origin of the people's ills know to the National Assembly, knowledge without which great monarchs are worthless.

Arriving at daybreak, the citizenesses stopped to put themselves in order; at Sevres, the men forced shopkeepers to sell them food, paying and returning to Versailles. On the road, two or three individuals, one of whom came on the king's behalf, were arrested, saw their black cockades torn, and were forced to join the line. When the women were about to enter their majesties' residence, the bourgeoisie of Versailles, the Flanders Regiment and the dragoons (we won't speak of the officers) clapped their hands, registered their satisfaction with shouts of joy, congratulated the women on their arrival, and begged them to work for the general good. Need anyone make such a request of French-born ladies who were led by the heroes of the Bastille? A few minutes later, about 4 o'clock, our citizenesses, led by sirs Hulin and Maillard, took the road to the National Assembly, where they had great difficulty entering. What an imposing sight for them! But at the same time, their appearance must have displeased certain members of a certain order, which would never have existed had our fathers been wise enough to understand that there having been only two kinds of people when the Franks invaded the Gauls, the victors who were nobles and the vanquished who were commoners, it is the greatest foolishness to admit among the representatives of a Nation like ours, men who only enjoy goods accorded to them by blind credulity. Be that as it may and in spite of the fearfulness that our good women friends spread among the sanctimonious churchmen, several of whom cleared out, the honorable members of the National Assembly, coming to understand that the women were absolutely committed to persist until there was something definite for always, accorded to our twelve deputies (1) a new prohibition against exporting grain; (2) a promise that a tax of 24 livres would be levied on wheat, an honest price so that there can be enough bread, and bread at a price within reach of even the least comfortable citizens; (3) that meat would cost no more than 8 under the livre. At this juncture, it is said that the king's guard and the national soldiers amused themselves by firing at one another; it remains to be seen if the former distinguished themselves but the rumor is that we lost very few and that the king proved, on October 5, 1789, that he merits more than ever the title accorded him last June 17th, that of Restorer of the French Nation. Our citizenesses, clothed in glory, were returned by carriage, at his majesty's expense, to the city hall in Paris, where we welcomed them as liberators of the capital, their actions to forever ruin the present and future designs of the aristocracy.

22.5

PROCLAMATIONS, PIERRE TOUSSAINT L'OUVERTURE

Pierre Dominique Toussaint L'Ouverture (1746-1803) had been born into slavery in the French colony of Saint Domingue, in what is now Haiti. Perhaps because he was a house slave, L'Ouverture received the rare gift of an education, freedom, and eventually became an overseer on a large plantation. In 1790 he led the only slave revolt in the Americas to successfully establish a free black state in the West, although Haiti was not recognized until 1804.

In 1794 the Revolutionary Convention in Paris abolished slavery in the French colonies and offered L'Ouverture the title of general (he had become a hero to the revolutionaries in Paris) but the slaves did not stop their revolt. It now became a war between the races and economic groups. The Haitians received supplies from the Spanish, although they were also a slave-owning empire and in fact greatly feared that the Haitian example would encourage slave rebellions in their own colonies. Napoleon would attempt to restore slavery in other French colonies, and L'Ouverture would die in one Bonaparte's jails, but Haiti remained free.

QUESTIONS

1. Why do you think the Spanish were willing to help the Haitian revolt?
2. Why does L'Ouverture proclaim that "neither whites nor mulattoes have formulated" his plans?
3. The third selection is from a letter L'Ouverture wrote to a General of the Revolutionary Convention; why does L'Ouverture want the French revolutionaries to think well of him?

A. Proclamation to the Slaves of Saint Domingue (August 24, 1793)

Having been the first to champion your cause, it is my duty to continue to labor for it. I cannot permit another to rob me of the initiative. Since I have begun, I will know how to conclude. Join me and you will enjoy the rights of freemen sooner than any other way. Neither whites nor mulattoes have formulated my plans; it is to the Supreme Being alone that I owe my inspiration. We have begun, we have carried on, we will know how to reach the goal.

B. Proclamation of August 29, 1793

Brothers and Friends:

I am Toussaint L'Ouverture. My name is perhaps known to you. I have undertaken to avenge you. I want liberty and equality to reign throughout Saint Domingue. I am working towards that end. Come and join me, brothers, and combat by our side for the same cause.

C.   Letter to General Laveaux (May 18, 1794)

It is true, General, that I had been deceived by the enemies of the Republic; but what man can pride himself on avoiding all the traps of wickedness? In truth, I fell into their snares, but not without knowing the reason. You must recall the advances I had made to you before the disasters at Le Cap, in which I stated that my only goal was to unite us in the struggle against the enemies of France.

Unhappily for everyone, the means of reconciliation that I proposed – the recognition of the liberty of the blacks and a general amnesty – were rejected. My heart bled, and I shed tears over the unfortunate fate of my country, perceiving the misfortunes that must follow. I wasn't mistaken: fatal experience proved the reality of my predictions. Meanwhile, the Spanish offered their protection to me and to all those who would fight with me for the cause of their kings, and having always fought in order to have liberty I accepted their offers, seeing myself abandoned by my brothers the French. But a later experience opened my eyes to these perfidious protectors, and having understood their villainous deceit, I saw clearly that they intended to make us slaughter one another in order to diminish our numbers so as to overwhelm the survivors and reenslave them. No, they will never attain their infamous objective, and we will avenge ourselves in our turn upon these contemptible beings. Therefore, let us unite forever and, forgetting the past, occupy ourselves hereafter only with exterminating our enemies and avenging ourselves, in particular, on our perfidious neighbors.

From *The French Revolution: A Document Collection*, edited by Laura Mason and Tracey Rizzo, p. 209. Copyright © 1999 Houghton Mifflin Company. Reprinted with permission.

QUESTIONS FOR PART 22

1.   Why did the French Revolution become so violent?
2.   Did any of these Revolutions seem determined to create a class-less society?
3.   What were the roles of religion in these Revolutions?

PART 23

THE INDUSTRIAL REVOLUTION

The Industrial Revolution began in Great Britain in the eighteenth century, with a new approach to production, which was required because the accumulation of raw materials was beginning to surpass the ability to produce marketable goods. Industrialism began when Britain became overstocked with raw wool and cotton. The traditional methods of piece work, in which one woman (the traditional producer of cloth) spun thread by hand on a spindle or a wheel, and then wove the thread into cloth, could not keep up with the abundance of raw fiber. The first invention of the industrial age was the Flying Shuttle in 1733, which dramatically sped up the weaving process. This led to the need for more thread; in 1768 the first mechanized spinning device was created, the Spinning Jenny. Power for these devices was still provided by humans. In 1769 the Water Frame was invented, a water powered loom, and in 1787 the Power Loom first appeared, which used either water or animal power.

The gradual industrialization of the cloth industry, which continued to get faster as more thread was spun and woven by ever-larger machines, was the basic scenario of industrialization. The next remarkable innovation was the steam engine in 1769. Steam engines, fueled by coal, were first used to pump water out of mines, then to power machinery, then finally to move goods and people. The railroads (1830) probably produced the most conspicuous result of the Industrial Revolution. How the West understood distance and time would never be the same.

Industrialism began in Britain for several reasons. Of all the countries of Europe, Britain alone possessed more of the necessary ingredients. Britain had a ready supply of labor (although other countries had more labor, Britain had the most highly trained), pre-existing access to transportation via roads and canals (which were usually without tolls), a stable government (in a time when the rest of Europe faced Revolution and/or war), natural resources (wool, cotton, and coal), and finally, wealth and markets (from her numerous colonies).

While Industrialism may have begun in Britain, it quickly moved to the European continent and the Americas. Not all states industrialized at the same time or to the same extent as Britain, who was the world's leading industrialized power until the early twentieth century. The sources in this chapter illustrate something of the influence of the Industrial Revolution.

23.1

✤

WOMEN IN THE COAL MINES

Industrialism began with women. They might not have invented most of the machines of the industrial age, nor did they control much of the capital or markets in the eighteenth century, yet without women's labor, the industrial revolution would never have begun. The introduction to this chapter outlined the connection between industrialism and cloth production, which for centuries was dominated by the labor of women. However, as industrialization spread to other businesses, women continued to provide much of the labor. Women and children were particularly useful in the early mining industry, because their small size allowed them to fit easily down tight mine shafts.

However, in the early nineteenth century the wonderment at industrialization had turned into concerns about the ramifications of industrialization on society. The conditions in which the working class toiled and lived were recorded in several government sponsored commissions. In 1833, the English Parliament passed a series of factory and mining acts, and they included prohibitions of women and children working in mines. The following descriptions were collected by a Parliamentary commission in 1842, and reveal that the 1833 prohibition failed to keep women out of the mines.

✤

QUESTIONS

1. Why is so much attention paid to how the women dress?
2. The commission report describes what life is like in the "collier" home when horses are substituted for women in the mines. What is being said here about the proper role of women?
3. Do you think the commission was as concerned about the morality of male workers?

Scotland's Women Slaves

We consider it proper to bring into view the condition of a class in the community, intimately connected with the coal-trade, who endure a slavery scarcely tolerated in the ages of darkness and barbarism. The class alluded to is that of the women who carry coals underground, in Scotland – known by the name of Bearers.

At present, there are four modes practiced in Scotland, for transporting of coals from the wall-face to the hill. The first, most approved of, is to draw the basket of coals from the wall-face to the pit bottom by means of horses, from whence it is drawn to the hill by machinery. The next method resorted to is to draw the coals in small wheel-carriages, by men, women, or boys hired for the purpose, or by the collier himself, as practiced in the west country. In the third mode, the coals are carried by women, known by the name of Bearers, who transport them from the wall-face to the pit bottom, from whence they are drawn by machinery to the hill. The fourth and last mode is the most severe and slavish; for the women are not only employed to carry the coals from the wall-face to the pit bottom, but also to ascend with them to the hill. This latter mode is unknown in England, and is abolished in the neighbourhood of Glasgow.

Severe and laborious as this employment is, still there are young women to be found who, from early habits, have no particular aversion to the work, and who are as cheerful and light in heart as the gayest of the fair sex; and as they have it in their power to betake themselves to other work if they choose, the carrying of coals is a matter of free choice; and therefore no blame can be particularly attached to the coalmaster. Yet, still it must, even in the most favourable point of view, be looked upon as a very bad, old, and disgraceful custom. But, as married women are also as much engaged in this servitude as the young, it is in this instance that the practice is absolutely injurious and bad, even although they submit to it without repining…

In those collieries where this mode is in practice, the collier leaves his house for the pit about eleven o'clock at night, (attended by his sons, if he has any sufficiently old), when the rest of mankind are retiring to rest. Their first work is to prepare coals, by hewing them down from the wall. In about three hours after, his wife (attended by her daughters, if she has any sufficiently grown) sets out for the pit, having previously wrapped her infant child in a blanket, and left it to the care of an old woman, who, for a small gratuity, keeps three or four children at a time, and who, in their mothers' absence, feeds them with ale or whisky mixed with water. The children who are a little more advanced, are left to the care of a neighbour; and under such treatment, it is surprising that they ever grow up or thrive.

The mother, having thus disposed of her younger children, descends the pit with her older children, when each, having a basket of suitable form, lays it down, and into it the large coals are rolled; and such is the weight carried, that it frequently takes two men to life the burden upon their backs: the girls are loaded according to their strength. The mother sets out first, and in this manner they proceed to the pit bottom, and with weary steps and slow, ascend the stairs, halting occasionally to draw breath, till they arrive at the hill or pit-top, where the coals are laid down for sale; and in this manner they go for eight or ten hours almost without resting. It is no uncommon thing to see them, when ascending the pit, weeping most bitterly, from the excessive severity of the labor; but the instant they have laid down their burden on the hill, they resume their cheerfulness, and return down the pit singing.

The execution of work performed by a stout woman in that way is beyond conception. For instance, we have seen a woman, during the space of time above mentioned, take on a load of at least 170 pounds avoirdupois, travel with this 150 yards up the slope of the coal below ground, ascend a pit by stairs 117 feet, and travel upon the hill 20 yards more to where the coals are laid down. All this she will perform no less than twenty-four times as a day's work…The weight of coals thus brought to the pit top by a woman in a day amounts to 4,080 pounds, or above 36 hundredweight English, and there have been frequent instances of two tons being carried. The wages paid for this work, are eightpence per day! — a circumstance as surprising almost as the work performed…

From this view of the work performed by bearers in Scotland, some faint idea may be formed of the slavery and severity of the toil, particularly when it is considered that they are entered to this work when seven years of age, and frequently continue till they are upwards of fifty, or even sixty years old.

The collier, with his wife and children, having performed their daily task, return home, where no comfort awaits them, their clothes are frequently soaked with water and covered with mud; their shoes so very bad as scarcely to deserve the name. In this situation they are exposed to all the rigours of winter, the cold frequently freezing their clothes.

On getting home, all is cheerless and devoid of comfort; the fire is generally out, the culinary utensils dirty and unprepared, and the mother naturally seeks first after her infant child, which she nurses even before her pit clothes are thrown off…

How different is the state of matters, where horses are substituted for women, and when the wife of the collier remains at home. The husband, when he returns home from his hard labour with his sons, finds a comfortable house, a blazing fire, and his breakfast ready in an instant, which cheer his heart, and make him forget all the severities of toil; while his wife, by her industry, enables him to procure good clothes and furniture, which constitute the chief riches of this class of the community. A chest of mahogany drawers, and an eight-day clock, with a mahogany case, are the great objects of their ambition; and when the latter is brought home, all their relations and neighbours are invited upon the occasion, when a feast is given, and the whole night spent in jovial mirth...

In surveying the workings of an extensive colliery below ground, a married woman came forward, groaning under an excessive weight of coals, trembling in every nerve, and almost unable to keep her knees from sinking under her. On coming up, she said in a most plaintive and melancholy voice, 'O sir, this is sore, sore work. I wish to God the first woman who tried to bear coals had broken her back, and none would have tried it again'.

Robert Bald, civil engineer and mineral surveyor of Alloa, in *Inquiry into the condition of Women who carry Coals under Ground in Scotland, known by the name of Bearers* (Edinburgh, 1812).

'No brothel can beat it'

In England, exclusive of Wales, it is only in some of the colliery districts of Yorkshire and Lancashire that female Children of tender age and young and adult women are allowed to descend into the coal mines and regularly to perform the same kinds of underground work, and to work for the same number of hours, as boys and men; but in the East of Scotland their employment in the pits is general; and in South Wales it is not uncommon.

West Riding of Yorkshire: Southern Part, — In many of the collieries in this district, as far as relates to the underground employment, there is no distinction of sex, but the labour is distributed indifferently among both sexes, except that it is comparatively rare for the women to hew or get the coals, although there are numerous instances in which they regularly perform even this work. In great numbers of coal-pits in this district the men work in a state of perfect nakedness, and are in this state assisted in their labour by females of all ages, from girls of six years old to women of twenty-one, these females being quite naked down to the waist.

'Girls', says the Sub-commissioner [J.C. Symons], 'regularly perform all the various offices of trapping, hurrying [Yorkshire term for drawing the loaded corves], filling, riddling, tipping, and occasionally getting, just as they are performed by boys. One of the most disgusting sights I have ever seen was that of young females, dressed like boys in trousers, crawling on all fours, with belts round their waists and chains passing between their legs, at day pits at Hunshelf Bank, and in many small pits near Holmfirth and New Mills: it exists also in several other places. I visited the Hunshelf Colliery on the 18th of January: it is a day pit; that is, there is no shaft or descent; the gate or entrance is at the side of a bank, and nearly horizontal. The gate was not more than a yard high, and in same places not above 2 feet.

'When I arrived at the board or workings of the pit I found at one of the side-boards down a narrow passage a girl of fourteen years of age in boy's clothes, picking down the coal with the regular pick used by the men. She was half sitting half lying at her work, and said she found it tired her very much, and 'of course she didn't like it'. The place where she was at work was not 2 feet high. Further on were men lying on their sides and getting. No less than six girls out of eighteen men and children are employed in this pit.

'Whilst I was in the pit the Rev Mr Bruce, of Wadsley, and the Rev Mr Nelson, of Rotherham, who accompanied me, and remained outside, saw another girl of ten years of age, also dressed in boy's clothes, who was employed in hurrying, and these gentlemen saw her at work. She was a nice-looking little child, but of course as black as a tinker, and with a little necklace around her throat.

'In two other pits in the Huddersfield Union I have seen the same sight. In one near New Mills, the chain, passing high between the legs of two of these girls, had worn large holes in their trousers; and any sight more disgustingly indecent or revolting can scarcely be imagined than these girls at work – no brothel can beat it.

'On descending Messrs Hopwood's pit at Barnsley, I found assembled round a fire a group of men, boys, and girls, some of whom were of the age of puberty; the girls as well as the boys stark naked down to the waist, their hair bound up with a tight cap, and trousers supported by their hips. (At Silkstone and at Flockton they work in their shifts and trousers.) Their sex was recognizable only by their breasts, and some little difficulty occasionally arose in pointing out to me which were girls and which were boys, and which caused a good deal of laughing an joking. In the Flockton and Thornhill pits the system is even more indecent; for though the girls are clothed, at least three-fourths of the men for whom they "hurry" work *stark naked*, or with a flannel waistcoat only, and in this state they assist one another to fill the corves 18 to 20 times a day: I have seen this done myself frequently.

'When it is remembered that these girls hurry chiefly for men who are *not* their parents; that they go from 15 to 20 times a day into a dark chamber (the bank face), which is often 50 yards apart from any one, to a man working naked, or next to naked, it is not to be supposed by that where opportunity thus prevails sexual vices are of common occurrence. Add to this the free intercourse, and the rendezvous at the shaft or bullstake, where the corves are brought, and consider the language to which the young ear is habituated, the absence of religious instruction, and the early age at which contamination begins, and you will have before you, in the coal-pits where females are employed, the picture of a nursery for juvenile vice which you will go far and wide above ground to equal.'

Source: E. Royston Pike, ed., *Human Documents of the Industrial Revolution in Britain* (London: George Allen & Unwin Ltd., 1966), pp. 247-251, 253-54, 225-26.

23.2

✦

AN ORATION ON CHILD LABOR, MICHAEL SADLER

Michael Sadler was a Parliamentarian in 1832, when he gave this impassioned speech on child labor in factories. His descriptions of the dangerous working conditions led directly to the Factory Acts of 1833 that prohibited children from working in certain factories, in the mines entirely, and limited their working hours overall. The 1833 Acts are usually viewed as the first labor reform movement.

QUESTIONS

1. What does Sadler say about the parents of working children?
2. To whom does Sadler place the greatest burden in protecting children, the family or the state?
3. Sadler speaks of preserving the morals of factory children; what do you think he means?

Sadler's Impassioned Oration

The Bill which I now implore the House to sanction with its authority, has for its object the liberation of children and other young persons employed in the mills and factories of the United Kingdom, from that over-exertion and long confinement which common sense, as well as experience, has shown to be utterly inconsistent with the improvement of their minds, the preservation of their morals, and the maintenance of their health — in a word, to rescue them from a state of suffering and degradation, which it is conceived the children of the industrious classes in hardly any other country has ever endured...

I apprehend, that the strongest objections that will be offered on this occasion, will be grounded upon the pretence that the very principle of the Bill is an improper interference between the employer and the employed, and an attempt to regulate by law the market of labour. Were the market supplied by free agents, and that the children therefore ought to be regarded as such, I apprehend has but little force...

The parents who surrender their children to this infantile slavery may be separated into two classes. The first, and I trust by far the most numerous one, consists of those who are obliged, by extreme indigence, so to act, but who do it with great reluctance and bitter regret: themselves perhaps out of employment, or working at very low wages, and their families in a state of great destitution; — what can they do? The overseer refuses relief if they have children capable of working in factories whom they object to send thither. They choose therefore what they probably deem the lesser evil, and reluctantly resign their offspring to the captivity and pollution of the mill; they rouse them in the winter morning, which as a poor father says before the Lords Committee, they 'feel very sorry to do'; they receive them fatigued and exhausted, many a weary hour after the day has closed; they see them droop and sicken, and in many cases become cripples and die, before they reach their prime: and they do all this, because they must otherwise suffer unrelieved, and starve amidst their starving children. It is a mockery to contend that these parents have a choice...free agents! To suppose that parents are free agents while dooming their own flesh and blood to this fate, is to believe them monsters!

But, sir, there are such monsters; unknown indeed in the brute creation, they belong to our own kind, and are found in our own country; and they are generated by the very system which I am attacking. Dead to the instincts of nature, and reversing the order of society; instead of providing for their offspring, they make their offspring provide for them: not only for their necessities, but for their intemperance and profligacy. They purchase idleness by the toil of their infants; the price of whose happiness, health, and existence, they spend in the haunts of dissipation and vice. Thus, at the very same hour of night that the father is at his guilty orgies, the child is panting in the factory. Such wretches count upon their children as upon their cattle; — nay, to so disgusting a state of degradation does the system lead, that they make the certainty of having offspring the indispensable condition of marriage, that they may breed a generation of slaves...

But I will proceed no further with these objections. The idea of treating children, and especially the children of the poor — above all, the children of the poor imprisoned in factories — as free agents, is too absurd...The protection of poor children and young persons from these hardships and cruelties to which their age and condition have always rendered them peculiarly liable, has ever been held one of the first and most important duties of every Christian legislature. Our own has not been unmindful in this respect; and it is mainly owing to the change of circumstances that many of its humane provisions have been rendered inoperative, and that the present measure has become most necessary...

The very same opposition that has so long and so often triumphed over justice and humanity, is again organized, and actively at work...Certificates and declarations will be obtained in abundance, from divines and doctors, as to the morality and health which the present system promotes and secures...They have said that the children who were worked without any regulation, and consequently according to their employer's sole will and pleasure, were not only equally, but more, healthy, and better instructed, than those not so occupied; that night labour was in one way prejudicial, but actually preferred, that the artificial heat of the rooms was really advantageous, and quite pleasant...That so far from being fatigued with, for example, twelve hours' labour the children performed even the last hour's work with greater intent and spirit than any of the rest! What a pity the term was not lengthened! In a few more hours they would have worked in a perfect ecstasy of delight! We had been indeed informed that the women and children often cried with fatigue, but their tears were doubtless tears of rapture...

Light labour! Is the labour of holding this pen and of writing with it strenuous? And yet, ask a clerk in any of the public offices, or in any private counting house, when he has been at his employment some half-dozen hours in the day less than any of these children, whether he does not think he has had enough of this light labour — to say nothing of holidays, of which he has many, and the child none...I might appeal to the Chair, whether the lingering hours which have to be endured here, though unaccompanied with any bodily exertion whatever, are not 'weariness of the flesh'. But what would be the feelings of the youngest and most active individual amongst us, if, for example, he were compelled to pass that time, engaged in some constant and anxious employment, stunned with the noise of revolving wheels, suffocated with the heat and stench of a low, crowded, and gas-lighted apartment, bathed in sweat, and stimulated by the scourge of an inexorable taskmaster? I say, what would be his idea of the light labour of twelve or fourteen hours in such a pursuit; and when, once or twice in every week, the night also was added to such a day? And how would he feel, if long years of such light labour lay before him?

The overworking of these children occasions a weariness and lethargy which it is impossible always to resist: hence, drowsy and exhausted, the poor creatures fall too often among the machinery, which is not in many instances sufficiently sheathed; when their muscles are lacerated, their bones broken, or their limbs torn off, in which case they are constantly sent to the infirmaries to be cured, and if crippled for life, they are turned out and maintained at the public cost; or they are sometimes killed upon the spot...

Then, in order to keep the children awake, and to stimulate their exercises, means are made use of, to which I shall now advert...Sir, children are beaten with thongs prepared for the purpose. Yes, the females of this country, no matter whether children or grown up, — I hardly know which is the more disgusting outrage — are beaten upon the face, arms, and bosom — beaten in your 'free market of labour', as you term it, like slaves! These are the instruments. — (*Here the honourable member exhibited some black, heavy, leathern thongs, — one of them fixed in a sort of handle, the smack of which, when struck upon the table, resounded through the House.*) — They are quite equal to breaking an arm, but that the bones of the young are pliant. The marks, however, of the thong are long visible; and the poor wretch is flogged before its companions; flogged, I say, like a dog, by the tyrant overlooker. We speak with execration of the cart-whip of the West Indies — but let us see this night an equal feeling rise against the factory-thong of England...

I wish I could bring a group of these little ones to that bar — I am sure their silent appearance would plead more forcibly on their behalf than the loudest eloquence...At this late hours, while I am thus feebly, but earnestly, pleading the cause of these oppressed children, what numbers of them are still tethered to their toil, confined in heated rooms, bathed in perspiration, stunned with the roar of revolving wheels, poisoned with the noxious effluvia of grease and gas, till, at last, weary and exhausted, they turn out, almost naked, into the inclement air, and creep, shivering, to beds from which a relay of their young work-fellows have just risen...

Sir, I have shown the suffering — the crime — the mortality, attendant upon this system...Earnestly do I wish that I could have prevailed upon this House and his Majesty's Government to adopt the proposed measure, without the delay which will attend it further...Would that we had at once decided, as we could wish others to decide concerning our own children, under the like circumstances, or as we shall wish that we had done, when the Universal Parent shall call us to a strict account for our conduct to one of the least of these little ones! As the case, however, is otherwise...I will now move the second reading of this bill; and afterwards propose such a Committee as I hope, will assist in carrying into effect the principles of a measure so important to the prosperity, character, and happiness of the British people.

From the speech delivered by M. T. Sadler, MP. in the House of Commons, on March 16, 1832; *Memoirs of the Life and Writings of Michael Thomas Sadler* (1842), pp. 338-379.

Source: E. Royston Pike, ed., *Human Documents of the Industrial Revolution in Britain* (London: George Allen & Unwin Ltd., 1966), pp. 117-120.

23.3

LIVING CONDITIONS OF THE WORKING CLASS, EDWIN CHADWICK

In 1838, Edwin Chadwick (1800-1890), Secretary to the Poor Law Commission, began collecting reports on the living and working conditions of England's working poor. Chadwick was interested in how sanitation (or lack of it) related to the spread of diseases amongst the poor, and to their general lack of health as a class. Chadwick concluded that the unsanitary living conditions of the poor, who lived amongst refuse, open sewers, unventilated rooms, and damp surroundings, led directly to the epidemics of disease that continually plagued modern cities. Although the bubonic plague had disappeared from western Europe in the eighteenth century, it was replaced by epidemics of typhoid and cholera. In 1842 he presented his report to Parliament: Report on the Sanitary Condition of the Labouring Population of Great Britain. *After several years of debate, the Public Health Act of 1848 was passed, and for the first time in the modern age, English cities began to build new sewer lines and to pipe in clean water.*

The following two excerpts describe the living and working conditions of the poor.

---------- ✤ ----------

QUESTIONS

1. In addition to concerns about physical health, what other problems does the report reveal were caused by the overcrowded living conditions?
2. The testimonials collected in this report mostly came from local doctors; why do you think Chadwick used them rather than sending out his own investigative team?
3. Why did the working classes drink alcohol during the workday?

Mr. Thomas Brownlow, Tailor, aged 52:

It is stated that you have been a journeyman tailor, and now work for yourself. At what description of places have you worked? — I have always worked at the largest places in London; one part of my time I worked at Messrs. Allen's, of Old Bond-street, where I worked eight years; at another part of my time I worked at Messrs. Stultze's, in Clifford-street, where I worked four years. At Messrs. Allen's they had then from 80 to 100 men at work; at Messrs. Stultze's they had, when I worked there, 250 men.

'Will you describe the places of work, and the effects manifested in the health of the workmen? — The place in which we used to work at Messrs. Allen's was a room where 80 men worked together. It was a room about 16 or 18 yards long, and 7 or 8 yards wide, lighted with skylights; the men were close together, nearly knee to knee. In summer time the heat of the men and the heat of the irons made the room 20 or 30 degrees higher than the heat outside; the heat was then most suffocating, especially after the candles were lighted. I have known young men, tailors from the country, faint away in the shop from the excessive heat and closeness; persons, working-men, coming into the shop to see some of the men, used to complain of the heat, and also of the smell as intolerable; the smell occasioned by the heat of the irons and the various breaths of the men really was at times intolerable. The men sat as loosely as they possibly could, and the perspiration ran from them from the heat and the closeness. It is of frequent occurrence in such workshops that light suits of clothes are spoiled from the perspiration of the hand, and the dust and flue which arises darkening the work. I have seen 40*l.* or 50*l.* worth of work spoiled in the course of the summer season from this cause.

'In what condition are these work-places in winter? — They are more unhealthy in winter, as the heat from the candles and the closeness is much greater. Any cold currents of air which com in give annoyance to those who are sitting near the draught. There is continued squabbling as to the windows being opened; those who are near the windows, and who do not feel the heat so much as the men near the stoves, objecting to their being opened. The oldest, who had been inured to the heat, did not like the cold, and generally prevailed in keeping out the cold or the fresh air. Such has been the state of the atmosphere, that in the very coldest nights large thick tallow candles (quarter of a pound candles) have melted and fallen over from the heat.

'What was the effect of this state of the work-places upon the habits of the workmen? — It had a very depressing effect on the energies; that was the general complaint of those who came into it. Many could not stay out the hours, and went away earlier. Those who were not accustomed to the places generally lost appetite. The natural effect of the depression was, that we had recourse to drink as a stimulant. We went into the shop at six o'clock, when orders for the breakfast were called for, gin was brought in, and the common allowance was half-a-quartern. The younger hands did not begin with gin.

'Was gin the first thing taken before any solid food was taken? — Yes, and the breakfast was very light; those who took gin generally took only half-a-pint of tea and half a twopenny loaf as breakfast.

'When again was liquor brought in? — At three o'clock, when some took beer and some gin, just the same as in the morning. At five o'clock the beer and gin came in again, and was usually taken in the same quantities. At seven o'clock the shop was closed.

'After work was there any drinking? — Yes; nearly all the young men went to the public-house, and some of the others.

'What were the wages they received? — Sixpence per hour, which, at the full work, made 6s. a day, or 36s. a week.

'Did they make any reserves from this amount of wages? — No; very few had anything for themselves at the end of the week.

'How much of the habit of drinking was produced by the state of the work-place? — I should say the greater part of it; because when men work by themselves, or only two or three together, in cooler and less close places, there is scarcely any drinking between times. Nearly all this drinking proceeds from the large shops, where the men are crowded together in close rooms: it is the same in the shops in the country, as well as those in the town. In a rural place, the tailor, where he works by himself, or with only two or three together, takes very little of the fermented liquor or spirits which the men feel themselves under a sort of necessity for doing in towns. The closer the ventilation of the place of work, the worse are the habits of the men working in them.

'You referred to the practice of one large shop where you worked some time since; was that the general practice, and has there been no alteration? — It was and is now the general practice. Of late, since coffee has become cheaper, somewhat more of coffee and less of beer has been brought in; but there is as much gin now brought in between times, and sometimes more.

"What would be the effect of an alteration of the place of work — a ventilation which would give them a better atmosphere? — It would, without doubt, have an immediately beneficial effect on the habits. It might not cure those who have got into the habit of drinking; but the men would certainly drink less, and the younger ones would not be led into the habit so forcibly as they are.

'What is the general effect of this state of things upon the health of the men exposed to them? — Great numbers of them die of consumption. "A decline" is the general disease of which they die. By their own rules, a man at 50 years of age is superannuated, and is thought not to be fit to do a full day's work.

'What was the average of the ages of the men at work at such shops as those you have worked in? — Thirty-two, or thereabouts.

'In such shops were there many superannuated men, or men above 50 years of age? — Very few. Amongst the tailors employed in the shops, I should say there were not 10 men in the hundred above 50 years of age.

'When they die, what becomes of their widows and children, as they seldom make any reserve of wages? — No provision is made for the families; nothing is heard of them, and, if they cannot provide for themselves, they must go upon the parish.

'Are these habits created by the closeness of the rooms, attended by carelessness as to their mode of living elsewhere? — I think not as to their lodgings. The English and Scotch tailors are more careful as to their places of lodging, and prefer sleeping in an open place. The men, however, who take their pint of porter and their pipe of tobacco in a public-house after their hours of work, take it at a place which is sometimes as crowded as the shop. Here the single men will stay until bed-time.

'Are gin and beer the only stimulants which you conceive are taken in consequence of the want of ventilation and the state of the place of work when crowded? — No: snuff is very much taken as a stimulant; the men think snuff has a beneficial effect on the eyes. After going into these close shops from the open air, the first sensation experienced is frequently a sensation of drowsiness, then a sort of itching or uneasiness at the eye, then a dimness of the sight. Some men of the strongest sight will complain of this dimness; all eyes are affected much in a similar manner. Snuff is much used as a stimulant to awaken them up; smoking in the shops is not approved of, though it is much attempted; and the journeymen tailors of the large shops are in general great smokers at the public-houses.

'Do the tailors from villages take snuff or smoke as well as drink so much as the tailors in the large shops in the towns? — They neither take so much snuff nor tobacco, nor so much of any of the stimulants, as are taken by the workmen in the crowded shops of the towns.

'Do their eyes fail them as soon? — No, certainly not.

'With the tailors, is it the eye that fails first? — Yes; after long hours of work the first thing complained of by the tailors is that the eyes fail; the sight becomes dim, and a sort of mist comes between them and their work.

'Judging from your own practical experience, how long do you conceive that a man would work in a well-ventilated or uncrowded room, as compared with a close, crowded, ill-ventilated room? — I think it would make a difference of two hours in the day to a man. He would, for example, be able, in an uncrowded or well-ventilated room, to do his twelve hours' work in the twelve hours; whereas in the close-crowded room he would not do more than ten hours' work in the twelve.

'Of two men beginning at 20 years of age, what would be the difference in extent of labour performed by them in town shops or in the country? — A man who had begun at 20 in these crowded shops would not be so good a man at 40 as a man working to 50 in a country village; of the two, the country tailor would be in the best condition in health and strength; in point of fact he is so. The difference may be set down as a gain of 10 years' good labour. There are very few who can stand such work as the town shops 20 years.

'The eyes then become permanently injured, as well as fail during the day, in these crowded shops? — Yes, they do. After 45 years of age, the eyes begin to fail, and he cannot do a full day's work.

'Supposing a workman to work in a well-ventilated room, and to be freed from the nervous exhaustion consequent on the state of the place, might he not save at least all that he drinks in the times between his meals, or be enabled to apply it better, if he were so disposed; and, perhaps, the value of the two hours' extra work in the 12, when he is working piece-work? — Yes, certainly he might.

'Taking your account of the average loss by nervous exhaustion and bad habits to be two hours' work for 20 years, and 12 hours daily work for 10 years in addition, supposing him to be employed full time, it would be a loss of the value of 50,000 hours of productive labour (of the value at 6d. per hours, 1,250l.); or, if he were in work half a-year, at a loss of 25,000 hours; so that if he were employed the half time at the full wages, or full time at the half wages, such workmen will have lost the means of putting by a sum of not less than 600l. to maintain him in comfort when he is no longer able to work? — Yes, I think that would be found to be correct. Very few do save; but I have known some save considerable sums. I knew one man, of the name of John Hale, who saved about 600l. He was not one of the most sober men, but he was in constant employment, sometimes at Allen's and sometimes at Weston's, and he was very careful; but he died when he was about 45. I knew another man, whose name was Philip Gray, who used to prefer the smaller shops. He was a man of very good constitution, and he lived until he was about 70. He was a journeyman all his life, and he had, when he died, more than 1500l., all saved by London journeywork. He used to live in a baker's shop in Silverstreet, Golden-square.

'Was he of a penurious disposition? — He associated less with the men than others, and they knew little about him. He was dressed much the same as the rest, but he was much more clean in his person: he was remarkable for his cleanliness, and he was very neat in his person. Both he and Hale were single men.

'Can you doubt that, under favourable sanitary circumstances, such instances would become frequent? — It cannot be doubted. I have known other instances of saving, but those were not of men working on the board: they were mostly of men who had situations in the cutting-rooms.'

From *Report on the Sanitary Condition of the Labouring Population of Great Britain* by Edwin Chadwick, edited by M. W. Flinn, p. 167-170. Copyright © 1965 Edinburgh University Press. www.eup.ed.ac.uk. Reprinted with permission of Edinburgh University Press.

23.4

THE RAILROADS: NEWSPAPER ACCOUNTS OF OPENINGS AND ACCIDENTS

No innovation of the industrial has produced the same degree of awe, in the sense of both amazement and fear, as the steam locomotive. The first passenger steam engine was The Rocket, *created by George Stephenson in 1830. It carried people at the delirious speed of sixteen miles per hour from Liverpool to Manchester. By mid-century, Britain had laid over six thousand miles of tracks; by 1860 the United States had almost thirty thousand miles of tracks. The development of railroads transformed the American landscape and was fundamental in the settlement of the western half of the continent. Railroad impact was just as thorough in Europe, although less dramatic. Certainly, the cultural impact of the railroads was vast.*

The following stories about the openings of new rail lines and the inevitable accidents that occurred when people and machinery came together are taken from The Illustrated London News, *which first appeared in 1842. As an illustrated newspaper, it was perfectly poised to document the emergence and ultimate success of the railroads.*

QUESTIONS

1. What impact did the railroads have on how people thought about nature?
2. Compare the article on the railroad accident with the description of child labor accidents in factories; how was industrialization affecting the value people placed on human life?
3. Why did the nineteenth century journalists record so many technical details of train and rail specifications for their readers?

OPENING OF THE LANCASTER AND CARLISLE RAILWAY

The article continued the following week:

Leaving the summit, we enter a cutting through limestone rock, and before it approaches Shap Village, the Line runs through a circle of large boulder stones, said to be the inner circle of an ancient Druidical Temple.

The Line now proceeds on the east side of the town of Shap, along a heavy cutting through limestone rock, and passing under an elegant skew-bridge, erected at an angle of 45°.

The Line next descends along the flat portion of the Line called Shap Mines; and following the valley of the stream, the Line again runs under the turnpike-road; and thence passing Thrimby, through a thick plantation.

Here the character of the scenery is considerably altered — the bare, rugged, and sterile mountains being succeeded by fertile pastures and picturesque prospects.

The Kendal turnpike-road is crossed for the last time, by a skew-bridge at Clifton, near the entrance to Lowther Park, in which, hidden by a forest of huge oaks, stands Lowther Castle, the seat of the Earl of Lonsdale.

The scenery between Shap and Clifton is very attractive — Cross Fell, Saddleback, Skiddaw, and the other hills in the Lake District, appearing to great advantage.

We are now carried along the Lowther Embankment, and about 50 miles from Lancaster and 20 miles from Carlisle we cross the river Lowther on a magnificent viaduct, 100 feet above the stream. Its arches, six in number, are of 60 feet span each; its total length, 500 feet. It is the largest and one of the most beautiful objects of art on the Line.

A mile and a half from the Lowther Viaduct, the Line crosses the Eamont on a viaduct of great beauty, consisting of Five semi-circular arches of 50 feet span each. Its height is 70 feet, and its extreme length upwards of 300 feet.

Westmoreland is now left in the rear, and we enter "Canny Cumberland," — the two counties being divided by the stream which we have just crossed. We immediately enter a large cutting, containing 180,000 cubic yards, and the Line then runs nearly level to the town of Penrith: the Station closely adjoining ruins of the ancient Castle.

From Penrith, the Line enters the valley of the Petteril, through which it pursues almost a direct course to Carlisle, joining the Newcastle and Carlisle Railway at the London-road Station, where the line is 36 feet above the level at Morecambe Bay, and 852 feet below the Shap summit.

Besides the principal viaducts enumerated, the works on the Line comprise 15 turnpike-road bridges, 64 occupation-road bridges, 86 occupation bridges, 47 cattle creeps, and 60 level crossings.

We have abridged this outline from the *Carlisle Journal*. We add a few engineering details: —

Total quantity of gunpowder used upon the works — 4133 barrels, of 100 lbs each, or 184 tons. Coils of fuze, 61,044; length of fuze used, about 416 miles.

On the Kendal district alone (five miles) the holes drilled for blasting amount to 41 miles.

Number of nights worked, 152,147.

Horses night work, 10,500.

Rock, 844,000 cubic yards, Independent of the rock, there has been at least 400,000 cubic yards of sand requiring blasting, making the rock work nearly one-seventh of the whole excavations.

Greatest number of men employed upon the works, 9,615.

Greatest number of horses employed upon the work, 790.

The number of days' work executed on the Line is equivalent to the work of three millions of men for one day.

The excavations average nearly 100,000 yards per mile.

Making deductions for the time lost by the men, and the unusually wet country through which the Line passes, the working time in which the Line has been completed is fifteen months.

THE CONTRACTORS' DINNER

We have engraved one of the festal commemorations of the Opening of the Railway — viz., the sumptuous Dinner given by the Contractors, Messrs. Stephenson, Mackenzie, and Co. The entertainment took place in the Assembly Room of the Crown and Mitre Inn and Coffee House. This beautiful apartment was elaborately embellished for the occasion. At the upper end of the room, behind the Presidents chair, was displayed a mantle of white silk, emblazoned with the Royal arms, and arched with laurel and flowers. On each side appeared an illumination, the initials "V.A.," and surmounted by the order of the Star and Garter, within wreaths of evergreen. Against the wall, at the lower end of the room, was displayed an elegant flag, emblazoned with the incorporated arms of the towns of Lancaster and Carlisle, typical of the union of these two important towns by railway. Against the walls, on each side, were ranged silk flags bearing the titles of all the Railways for which Messrs. Stephenson, Mackenzie, and Brassey are Contractors, about a dozen in number, and constituting in the aggregate upwards of 800 miles of railway communication. In addition to these decorations, appeared a number of other devices, illuminated by Royal crowns, stars, &c.; wreaths of evergreens gemmed with roses, and inclosing loyal and other mottoes. With the luster of the illuminations, aided by the light of three chandeliers depending from the ceiling, the room presented a most brilliant appearance. The dinner, supplied by Mr. Jarman and Mrs. Wells, host and hostess of the hotel, was of the most costly description.

The dessert, wines, &c., were excellent. Mr. Scarisbrick, the celebrated organist of Kendal, presided at the pianoforte. The chair was occupied by John Stephenson, Esq.; G. Mould, Esq., officiating as Vice.

The number of guests exceeded 200, comprising not only the heads of the various departments engaged in the construction of the Railway, from the resident engineers and contractors downwards, but a considerable number of influential strangers interested in other lines, and many representatives of the trade of Carlisle, Kendal, Lancaster, Preston, &c.

At the lower end of the room was an orchestra, occupied by an instrumental band from Cobden's establishment, Cross Hall, near Chorley, and also by a party of glee singers, chiefly from Preston, conducted by Mr. Edward Scarisbrick, of Carlisle.

We regret that we have not space to report the very interesting after-dinner proceedings. After the customary loyal toasts had been duly honoured, the healths of the Chairman and Directors, the Engineers-in-Chief, the Secretary, and the Resident Engineers, of the Railway Company were drunk with great applause; and the toast of "Messrs. John Stephenson and Co." was received with immense cheering.

Mr. Stephenson's reply modestly glanced at the difficulties which he had overcome in the construction of the Railway. He concluded by observing it was consoling and satisfactory to mark the progress of science, and he trusted that the time would come, and that ere long, when passengers could travel right through to Forfar. (Cheers.) The communication by iron rails between England and Scotland would be great benefit to both countries; and, as an humble individual, he felt proud to have been the means of amalgamating both sides of the Sark by the Trunk Line, part of which had yesterday been opened. (Cheers.) He could only say he felt obliged for the kindness of the Company, in speaking of him and his partners as they had done. He only regretted he could not reply adequately to their compliments, for he would repeat that he would rather make a railway than a speech any day. (Loud cheers.)

Mr. Mould, Mr. Horn, and other speakers, in their addresses, entered into the details of the great work; so that the day's proceedings were stored with a vast amount of practical information, instead of the complimentary common-place which usually characterizes post-prandial eloquence.

GREAT RAILWAY DISASTER AT NORWICH

On the night of Thursday week, it is our painful task to state, one of the most appalling accidents that ever happened in English railway traveling occurred on the Great Eastern Railway, between Norwich and Brundall, which is a station nearly six miles from Norwich. A train carrying mails to Norwich leaves Great Yarmouth every evening at 8.46, and is joined at Reedham, twelve miles from Norwich, by another train from Lowestoft. The junction was effected that night in the ordinary course, and the combined train proceeded to Brundall, three stations further on. Here it had to wait, because the line is single, until the arrival of the evening express from Norwich to Great Yarmouth, or until permission should be given to the engine-driver to proceed. A mistaken order from Mr. T. Cooper, the night inspector at Norwich station, allowed the down express to leave Norwich, while the combined mail-train from Great Yarmouth was suffered to come on from Brundall. The consequence was that the doomed trains met at Thorpe, nearly two miles from Norwich, and ran headlong into each other. The rails were slippery from rain; there was a slight curve in the line at the fatal spot, so that the lights of neither train could be seen; there was not time to apply the brakes, and the two engines rushed at each other at full speed. The engine drawing the combined mail-train (No. 54) was one of the most approved modern construction and of great power. The engine drawing the train from Norwich was a lighter one, but had acquired, with its train, a considerable momentum. In the crash which followed the collision the funnel of engine No. 54 was carried away, and the engine from Norwich rushed on the top of its assailant, some of the carriages of each train following, until a pyramid was formed of the locomotives, the shattered carriages, and the wounded, dead, or dying passengers. Eighteen persons were killed, and four have since died.

The down train from Norwich was made up, as usual, of two portions. The larger portion, for Yarmouth, formed the first section of the train; after which came the Lowestoft carriages These two sections would be separated at Reedham, and each would then travel on its own branch line. The Yarmouth portion of the train consisted of the following carriages: 1, the engine and tender, driven by Clarke and his fireman Sewell (both killed); 2, a horse-box belonging to the Stockton and Darlington Railway Company; 3, a second-class carriage; 4, an open third-class carriage; 5, a first-class carriage; 7 and 8, composite carriages; 9 and 10, third-class carriages; 11, brake-van, containing the guard Read. Then came the Lowestoft portion of the train, in the following order: — 12, a second-class carriage; 13, a first-class carriage; 14, a third-class carriage; 15, break-van, containing the guard Black. The two guards escaped with cuts and bruises. They were in the rear part of the train, in carriages which, happily, did not leave the rails, or otherwise the whole of the Lowestoft portion of the train would have fallen into the river Yare, which is here about fifty yards wide. As it was, the Lowestoft carriages remained on the bridge, a wooden one, 69 yards long, adapted for a single line of rails, but in process of widening. Iron girders are being introduced, and there were wide chasms in the bridge. It is a wonder that no passengers were drowned in attempting to get out of these three carriages, for there was no balustrade or railing, and anybody alighting upon the planks of the bridge from the projecting step of a carriage would be likely to fall forward into the water. However, dredging in the river has produced no results. Another reason for thankfulness is that the two engines did not meet upon the bridge. Even if the bridge itself had stood firm, the foremost carriages must have been hurled into the water, and the number of deaths would have been doubled or trebled. A very slight difference in the speed of either train, or a few seconds' difference in the time of starving, would have made the calamity far more dreadful.

It will be seen that there were fourteen carriages behind the engine and tender of the down express. The following was the composition of the up mail one: — Engine and tender, Prior, driver, and Light, fireman (both killed). Then followed the Yarmouth carriages — 2, fish-truck laden with fish; 3, brake-van; 4 and 5, composite carriages; 6, third-class carriage; 7, mail-van, in which was the guard having charge of the mail-bags; 8, composite carriage. Next came the Lowestoft carriages — 9, brake-van; 10, third-class carriage; 11, first-class carriage; 12 and 13, second-class carriages; 14, third-class carriage. Thus there were thirteen carriages behind the engine of the mail, so that the two trains were pretty nearly equal in weight. It is certain, however, that the mail-train must have had a much greater momentum. Both drivers had reason for putting on increased speed, believing as they did that each train was waiting for the other; but the engine of the mail-train was heavier and more powerful than that of the express, besides which there is a slight decline all the way to Brundall. It is thought that the speed of the up mail could not have been less than from thirty to thirty-five miles an hours, while the rate at which the express was traveling would be from twenty to twenty-five miles. Imagination can only faintly conceive the fearful shock of two such bodies propelled with this velocity, each presenting exactly the same points of contact, and giving and receiving at the same instant the full force of each other's blow. It was, in fact, the meeting of two iron vans, of nearly equal size and power, urged on by steam, with an irresistible weight behind urging them on. The two engines and tenders weighted each forty-five and forty tons. This made some eighty tons of metal hurled almost through the air from opposite points, to say nothing of the dead weight of the train behind. Mathematics may calculate with this weight and velocity what was the force exerted at the point of impact. People living close by thought they heard a thunder-peal. The darkness of the night, the heavy rain that was falling, and a slight curve round which the mail-train was making its way must have prevented the two drivers from seeing each other's lights till the trains were close together. How this was in reality can never be known, as the four poor fellows who manned the two locomotives, and could alone bear witness, were killed in a moment.

Captain Tyler's official report upon the disastrous collision on the Great Eastern Railway, which occurred near Norwich on Sept. 10, has been published. He, in his conclusions, first considers the system adopted in the working of the line; then examines the immediate causes by which the accident was produced; apportions the blame between Inspector Cooper and Telegraph-clerk Robson; and, lastly, glances at the principles generally adopted in the working of single lines, and the means, by which the risk of accidents of this nature may best be provided against.

Reprinted with permission of The Illustrated London News Picture Library.

QUESTIONS FOR PART 23

1. Can you surmise why industrialization was less successful in France and Russia?
2. Why did the first inventions of the industrial age occur in the cloth business?
3. What influence did Enlightenment ideas about economy and law have on industrialization?

PART 24

THE NEW IDEOLOGIES

In the nineteenth century, Europe underwent another wave of intellectual revolutions, which rivals the Scientific Revolution and the Enlightenment in terms of impact had the Western collective psyche. Many of the ideologies of the century are familiar to the twenty-first century audience because many of them are still active today, albeit in modified forms. Another way of looking at this period is to say that the new ideologies evolved out of the work begun by those two earlier intellectual movements (the Scientific Revolution and the Enlightenment). The new ideologies were also a response to the political upheavals of the late eighteenth century, the Napoleonic Wars, and the Industrial Revolution.

This chapter presents sources illustrating the ideologies of Liberalism and Romanticism. It is important that you keep in mind that nineteenth-century definitions of these terms differ greatly from our definitions today. This is particularly true of the term "liberal," which is best defined for the nineteenth century as a belief in individual freedom from government interference (i.e., that less government was good for society as whole). Romanticism began as an artistic movement that countered the obsession with reason common to the Enlightenment; although romantic love between two people was certainly a common aspect of the movement, it was not always the central focus. Liberalism spoke of economic and political freedom; Romanticism spoke of artistic and emotional freedom.

24.1

AN ESSAY ON THE PRINCIPLE OF POPULATION, THOMAS MALTHUS

Thomas Malthus (1766-1834), an Anglican minister, is best described as an economic liberal, although his theories about population had far-reaching political and social implications. An Essay on the Principle of Population, published in 1798, was the first Western text to suggest that population growth might be bad thing. Western Europe had maintained a view of population common to the ancient world: the more people a civilization had, the more successful it was. Instead, Malthus warned that unchecked population growth would only lead to disasters: starvation, poverty, war, epidemics, and general misery. Malthus attempted to put a mathematical spin on this doomsday prophecy. According to his calculations, unchecked population growth increased geometrically, while food production increased arithmetically. The difference between the two figures is the Malthusian Principle. Malthus also described two ways in which populations are controlled (or checked). One was preventive (birth control) and the other was positive (starvation, disease, and war).

---------- ✦ ----------

QUESTIONS

1. How are Malthus' ideas "liberal" in a nineteenth-century sense of that term?
2. Malthus describes war and starvation as a positive check; what does he mean by positive?
3. Are preventive checks necessarily moral?

OF THE GENERAL CHECKS TO POPULATION, AND THE MODE OF THEIR OPERATIONS

The checks to population, which are constantly operating with more or less force in every society, and keep down the number to the level of the means of subsistence, may be classed under two general heads; the preventive and the positive checks.

The preventive check is peculiar to man, and arises from that distinctive superiority in this reasoning faculties which enables him to calculate distant consequences. Plants and animals have apparently no doubts about the future support of their offspring. The checks to their indefinite increase, therefore, are all positive. But man cannot look around him, and see distress which frequently presses upon those who have large families; he cannot contemplate his present possessions or earnings, which he now nearly consumes himself, and calculate the amount of each share, when with very little addition they must be divided, perhaps, among seven or eight, without feeling a doubt, whether if he follow the bent of his inclinations, he may be able to support the offspring which he will probably bring into the world. In a state of equality, if such can exist, this would be the simple question. In the present state of society other considerations occur. Will he not lower his rank in life, and be obliged to give up in great measure his former society? Does any mode of employment present itself by which he may reasonably hope to maintain a family? Will he not at any rate subject himself to greater difficulties, and more severe labour than in his single state? Will he not be unable to transmit to his children the same advantages of education and improvement that he had himself possessed? Does he even feel secure that, should he have a large family, his utmost exertions can save them from rags, and squalid poverty, and their consequent degradation in the community? And may he not be reduced to the grating necessity of forfeiting his independence, and of being obliged to the sparing hand of charity for support?

These considerations are calculated to prevent, and certainly do prevent, a great number of persons in all civilized nations from pursuing the dictate of nature in an early attachment to one woman.

If this restraint do not produce vice, as in many instances is the case, and very generally so among the middle and higher classes of men, it is undoubtedly the least evil that can arise from the principle of population. Considered as a restraint on an inclination, otherwise innocent, and always natural, it must be allowed to produce a certain degree of temporary unhappiness; but evidently slight, compared with the evils which result form any of the other checks to population.

When this restraint produces vice, as it does most frequently among men, and among a numerous class of females, the evils which follow are but too conspicuous. A promiscuous intercourse to such a degree as to prevent the birth of children, seems to lower in the most marked manner the dignity of human nature. It cannot be without its effect on men, and nothing can be more obvious than its tendency to degrade the female character, and to destroy all its most amiable and distinguishing characteristics. Add to which, that among those unfortunate females with which all great towns abound, more real distress and aggravated misery are, perhaps, to be found, than in any other department of human life.

When a general corruption of morals, with regard to the sex, pervades all the classes of society, its effects must necessarily be, to poison the springs of domestic happiness, to weaken conjugal and parental affection, and to lessen the united exertions and ardour of parents in the care and education of their children; effects, which cannot take place without a decided diminution of the general happiness and virtue of society; particularly, as the necessity of art in the accomplishment and conduct of intrigues, and in the concealment of their consequences, necessarily leads to many other vices.

The positive checks to population are extremely various, and include every cause, whether arising from vice or misery, which in any degree contribute to shorten the natural duration of human life. Under this head therefore may be enumerated, all unwholesome occupations, severe labour and exposure to the seasons, extreme poverty, bad nursing of children, great towns, excesses of all kinds, the whole train of common diseases and epidemic, wars, pestilence, plague, and famine.

On examining these obstacles to the increase of population which are classed under the heads of preventive and positive checks, it will appear that they are all resolvable into moral restraint, vice, and misery.

Of the preventive checks, that which is not followed by irregular gratifications, may properly be termed moral restraint.

Promiscuous intercourse, unnatural passions, violations of the marriage bed, and improper arts to conceal the consequences of irregular connections, are preventive checks that clearly come under the head of vice.

Of the positive checks, those which appear to arise unavoidably from the laws of nature, may be called exclusively misery; and those which we obviously bring upon ourselves, such as wars, excesses, and many others which it would be in our power to avoid, are of a mixed nature. They are brought upon us by vice, and their consequences are misery.

In every country, some of these checks are, with more or less force, in constant operation; yet, notwithstanding their general prevalence, there are few states in which there is not a constant effort in the population to increase beyond the means of subsistence. This constant effort as constantly tends to subject the lower classes of society to distress, and to prevent any great permanent melioration of their condition.

These effects, in the present state of society, seem to be produced in the following manner. We will suppose the means of subsistence in any country just equal to the easy support of its inhabitants. The constant effort towards population, which is found to act even in the most vicious societies, increases the number of people before the means of subsistence are increased. The food therefore which before supported eleven millions, must now be divided among eleven millions and a half. The poor consequently must live much worse, and many of them be reduced to severe distress. The number of labourers also being above the proportion of work in the market, the price of labour must tend to fall; while the price of provisions would at the same time tend to rise. The labourer therefore must do more work to earn the same as he did before. During this season of distress, the discouragements to marriage, and the difficulty of rearing a family are so great, that population is nearly at a stand. In the meantime, the cheapness of labour, the plenty of labourers, and the necessity of an increased industry among them, encourage cultivators to employ more labour upon their land; to turn up fresh soil, and to manure and improve more completely what is already in tillage; till ultimately the means of subsistence may become in the same proportion to the population as at the period from which we set out. The situation of the labourer being then again tolerably comfortable, the restraints to population are in some degree loosened; and, after a short period, the same retrograde and progressive movements, with respect to happiness, are repeated….

But without attempting to establish in all cases these progressive and retrograde movements in different countries, which would evidently require more minute histories than we possess, the following propositions are proposed to be proved:

1. Population is necessarily limited by the means of subsistence.
2. Population invariably increases, where the means of subsistence increase, unless prevented by some very powerful and obvious checks.
3. These checks, and the checks which repress the superior power of population, and keep its effects on a level with the means of subsistence, are all resolvable into moral restraint, vice, and misery.

Source: Oliver J. Thatcher, ed., *The Ideas that have Influenced Civilization in the Original Documents*, *Volume VIII* (Boston: Roberts-Manchester Publishing Co., 1901-1902), pp. 294-304.

24.2

❖

PRINCIPLES OF UTILITY, JEREMY BENTHAM

The new ideology most often associated with British writer Jeremy Bentham (1748-1832) was Utilitarianism. Bentham, who was well read in Enlightenment ideas and financially well off enough to have time to contemplate them, believed that it was natural for individuals to act in a rational manner. Left alone with their own nature, and with the least amount of government interference, Bentham thought most people would find a way to behave that brought the "greatest good" to the most people. It was the ultimate expression of nineteenth century liberalism. Bentham's understanding of how society worked was based on principles of individual behavior and self-interest. Basically Bentham believed most people acted according to their own interests, but were pragmatic enough to take the needs of the many into consideration.

Utilitarianism was passed on to his protégés, James Mill and his son John Stuart Mill (1806-1873). The younger Mill was particularly influential in the labor, prison, sanitation, and social reform movements of the nineteenth century. For instance, Mill campaigned Parliament in 1867 for women's suffrage, one of the earliest public debates on the subject.

Part of Bentham's essay On Utility *is reproduced here.*

❖

QUESTIONS

1. Do you think Bentham had a positive or negative view of humanity in general?
2. In what ways might Bentham's ideas influence the Romantic Movement?
3. How does Bentham define the interests of the community?

AN INTRODUCTION TO THE PRINCIPLES OF MORALS AND LEGISLATION.
CHAPTER I.
Of the Principle of Utility.

Nature has placed mankind under the governance to two sovereign masters, *pain* and *pleasure*. It is for them alone to point out what we ought to do, as well as to determine what we shall do. On the one hand the standard of right and wrong, on the other the chain of causes and effects, are fastened to their throne. They govern us in all we do, in all we say, in all we think: every effort we can make to throw off our subjection, will serve but to demonstrate and confirm it. In words a man may pretend to abjure their empire: but in reality he will remain subject to it all the while. The *principle of utility* recognizes this subjection, and assumes it for the foundation of that system, the object of which is to rear the fabric of felicity by the hands of reason and of law. Systems which attempt to question it, deal in sounds instead of sense, in caprice instead of reason, in darkness instead of light.

But enough of metaphor and declamation: it is not by such means that moral science is to be improved.

II.

The principle of utility is the foundation of the present work: it will be proper therefore at the outset to give an explicit and determinate account of what is meant by it. By the principle of utility is meant that principle which approves or disapproves of every action whatsoever, according to the tendency which it appears to have to augment or diminish the happiness of the party whose interest is in question: or, what is the same thing in other words, to promote or to oppose that happiness. I say of every action whatsoever; and therefore not only of every action of a private individual, but of every measure of government.

III.

By utility is meant that property in any object, whereby it tends to produce benefit, advantage, pleasure, good, or happiness (all this in the present case comes to the same thing), or (what comes again to the same thing) to prevent the happening of mischief, pain, evil, or unhappiness to the party whose interest is considered: if that party be the community in general, then the happiness of the community: if a particular individual, then the happiness of that individual.

IV.

The interest of the community is one of the most general expressions that can occur in the phraseology of morals: no wonder that the meaning of it is often lost. When it has a meaning, it is this. The community is a fictitious *body*, composed of the individual persons who are considered as constituting as it were its *members*. The interest of the community then is, what? — the sum of the interests of the several members who compose it.

V.

It is in vain to talk of the interest of the community, without understanding what is the interest of the individual. A thing is said to promote the interest, or to be *for* the interest, of an individual, when it tends to add to the sum total of his pleasures: or, what comes to the same thing, to diminish the sum total of his pains.

VI.

An action then may be said to be conformable to the principle of utility, or, for shortness sake, to utility (meaning with respect to the community at large), when the tendency it has to augment the happiness of the community is greater than any it has to diminish it.

VII.

A measure of government (which is but a particular kind of action, performed by a particular person or persons) may be said to be conformable to or dictated by the principle of utility, when in the like manner the tendency which it has to augment the happiness of the community is greater than any which it has to diminish it.

VIII.

When an action, or in particular a measure of government, is supposed by a man to be conformable to the principle of utility, it may be convenient, for the purposes of discourse, to imagine a kind of law or dictate, called a law or dictate of utility: and to speak of the action in question, as being conformable to such a law or dictate.

IX.

A man may be said to be a partizan of the principle of utility, when the approbation or disapprobation he annexes to any action, or to any measure, is determined, by and proportioned to the tendency which he conceives it to have to augment or to diminish the happiness of the community: or in other words, to its conformity or unconformity to the laws or dictates of utility.

X.

Of an action that is conformable to the principle of utility, one may always say either that it is one that ought to be done, or at least that it is not one that ought not be done. One may say also, that it is right it should be done; at least that it is not wrong it should be done: that it is a right action; at least that it is not a wrong action. When thus interpreted, the words *ought*, and *right* and *wrong*, and others of that stamp, have a meaning: when otherwise, they have none.

XI.

Has the rectitude of this principle been ever formally contested? It should seem that it had, by those who have not known what they have been meaning. Is it susceptible of any direct proof? It should seem not: for that which is used to prove every thing else, cannot itself be proved: a chain of proofs must have their commencement somewhere. To give such proof is as impossible as it is needless.

XII.

Not that there is or ever has been that human creature breathing, however stupid or perverse, who has not on many, perhaps on most occasions of his life, deferred to it. By the natural constitution of the human frame, on most occasions of their lives men in general embrace this principle, without thinking of it: if not for the ordering of their own actions, yet for the trying of their own actions, as well as of those of other men. There have been, at the same time, not many, perhaps, even of the most intelligent, who have been disposed to embrace it purely and without reserve. There are even few who have not taken some occasion or other to quarrel with it, either on account of their not understanding always how to apply it, or on account of some prejudice or other which they were afraid to examine into, or could not bear to part with. For such is the stuff that man is made of: in principle and in practice, in a right track and in a wrong one, the rarest of all human qualities is consistency.

XIII.

When a man attempts to combat the principle of utility, it is with reasons drawn, without his being aware of it, from that very principle itself. His arguments, if they prove any thing, prove not that the principle is *wrong*, but that, according to the applications he supposes to be made of it, it is *misapplied*. Is it possible for a man to move the earth? Yes; but he must first find out another earth to stand upon.

XIV.

To disprove the propriety of it by arguments is impossible; but, from the causes that have been mentioned, or from some confused or partial view of it, a man may happen to be disposed not to relish it.

Where this is the case, if he thinks the settling of his opinions on such a subject worth the trouble, let him take the following steps, and at length, perhaps, he may come to reconcile himself to it.

1.   Let him settle with himself, whether he would wish to discard this principle altogether; if so, let him consider what it is that all his reasonings (in matters of politics especially) can amount to?

2.   If he would, let him settle with himself, whether he would judge and act without any principle, or whether there is any other he would judge and act by?

3.   If there be, let him examine and satisfy himself whether the principle he things he has found is really any separate intelligible principle; or whether it be not a mere principle in words, a king of phrase, which at bottom expresses neither more nor less than the mere averment of his own unfounded sentiments; that is, what in another person he might be apt to call caprice?

4.   If he is inclined to think that his own approbation or disapprobation, annexed to the idea of an act, without any regard to its consequences, is a sufficient foundation for him to judge and act upon, let him ask himself whether his sentiment is to be a standard of right and wrong, with respect to every other man, or whether every man's sentiment has the same privilege of being a standard to itself?

5.   In the first case, let him ask himself whether his principle is not despotical, and hostile to all the rest of human race?

6.   In the second case, whether it is not anarchical, and whether at this rate there are not as many different standards of right and wrong as there are men? and whether even to the same man, the same thing, which is right to-day, may not (without the least change in its nature) be wrong to-morrow? and whether the same thing is not right and wrong in the same place at the same time? and in either case, whether all argument is not at an end? and whether, when two men have said, "I like this," and "I don't like it," they can (upon such a principle) have anything more to say?

7.   If he should have said to himself, No: for that the sentiment which he proposes as a standard must be grounded on reflection, let him say on what particulars the reflection is to turn? If on particulars having relation to the utility of the act, then let him say whether this is not deserting his own principle, and borrowing assistance from that very one in opposition to which he sets it up: or if not on those particulars, on what other particulars?

8.   If he should be for compounding the matter, and adopting his own principle in part, and the principle of utility in part, let him say how far he will adopt it?

9.   When he has settled with himself where he will stop, then let him ask himself how he justifies to himself the adopting it so far? and why he will not adopt it any farther?

10. Admitting any other principle than the principle of utility to be a right principle, a principle that is right for a man to pursue; admitting (what is not true) that the word *right* can have a meaning without reference to utility, let him say whether there is any such thing as a *motive* that a man can have to pursue the dictates of it: if there is, let him say what that motive is, and how it is to be distinguished from those which enforce the dictates of utility: if not, then lastly let him say what it is this other principle can be good for?

Source: Jeremy Bentham, *The Works of Jeremy Bentham, Volume One* (New York: Russell & Russell, Inc., 1962), pp. 1-4.

24.3

---- ✤ ----

POEMS OF WILLIAM WORDSWORTH

William Wordsworth (1770-1850) was one of the earliest of the Romantic poets, and although he led one of the quieter lifestyles (in comparison with the tumultuous lives of Byron or Shelley), he was one of the most influential of the Romantics. One of the most common themes of the Romantic Movement was a love of nature, and few expressed that love better than Wordsworth. It was more than mere sentiment, however. The Romantics deified nature (often literally) and sought to reunite the individual with his or her roots in nature. Romantic poets and writers also emphasized the sensory experience over any rational understanding of the universe.

Included here are two poems: We Are Seven, *and* Ode: Intimations of Immortality.

---- ✤ ----

QUESTIONS

1. How is Romanticism a reaction against the growing industrialization of Europe?
2. How does Wordsworth understand nature in comparison with the Enlightenment *philosophes*?
3. In what ways is Wordsworth reacting against the Classicism of previous centuries?

WE ARE SEVEN

—A simple Child,
That lightly draws its breath,
And feels its life in every limb,
What should it know of death?

I met a little cottage Girl:
She was eight years old, she said;
Her hair was thick with many a curl
That clustered round her head.

She had a rustic, woodland air,
And she was wildly clad:
Her eyes were fair, and very fair;
Her beauty made me glad.

"Sisters and brothers, little Maid,
How many may you be?"
"How many? Seven in all," she said
And wondering looked at me.

"And where are they? I pray you tell."
   She answered, "Seven are we;
And two of us at Conway dwell,
   And two are gone to sea.

"Two of us in the church-yard lie,
   My sister and my brother;
And, in the church-yard cottage, I
   Dwell near them with my mother."

"You say that two at Conway dwell,
   And two are gone to sea,
Yet ye are seven!—I pray you tell,
   Sweet Maid, how this may be."

Then did the little Maid reply,
   "Seven boys and girls are we;
Two of us in the church-yard lie,
   Beneath the church-yard tree."

"You run about, my little Maid,
   Your limbs they are alive;
If two are in the church-yard laid,
   Then ye are only five."

"Their graves are green, they may be seen,"
   The little Maid replied,
"Twelve steps or more from my mother's door,
   And they are side by side.

"My stockings there I often knit,
   My kerchief there I hem;
And there upon the ground I sit,
   And sing a song to them.

"And often after sunset, Sir,
   When it is light and fair,
I take my little porringer,
   And eat my supper there.

"The first that died was sister Jane;
   In bed she moaning lay,
Till God released her of her pain;
   And then she went away.

"So in the church-yard she was laid;
    And, when the grass was dry,
Together round her grave we played,
    My brother John and I.

"And when the ground was white with snow,
    And I could run and slide,
My brother John was forced to go,
    And he lies by her side."

"How many are you, then," said I,
    "If they two are in heaven?"
Quick was the little Maid's reply,
    "O Master! we are seven."

"But they are dead; those two are dead!
    Their spirits are in heaven!"
'Twas throwing words away; for still
The little Maid would have her will,
    And said, "Nay, we are seven!"

———————— ✣ ————————

ODE: INTIMATIONS OF IMMORTALITY

I

There was a time when meadow, grove, and stream,
The earth, and every common sight,
        To me did seem
        Apparelled in celestial light,
The glory and the freshness of a dream.
It is not now as it hath been of yore;—
        Turn wheresoe'er I may,
        By night or day,
The things which I have seen I now can see no more.

II

    The Rainbow comes and goes,
    And lovely is the Rose,
    The Moon doth with delight
Look round her when the heavens are bare.

Waters on a starry night
Are beautiful and fair;
The sunshine is a glorious birth;
But yet I know, where'er I go,
That there hath past away a glory from the earth.

III

Now, while the birds thus sing a joyous song,
And while the young lambs bound
As to the tabor's sound,
To me alone there came a thought of grief:
A timely utterance gave that thought relief,
And I again am strong:
The cataracts blow their trumpets from the steep;
No more shall grief of mine the season wrong;
I hear the Echoes through the mountains throng,
The Winds come to me from the fields of sleep,
And all the earth is gay;
Land and sea
Give themselves up to jollity,
And with the heart of May
Doth every Beast keep holiday;—
Thou Child of Joy,
Shout round me, let me hear thy shouts, thou happy
Shepherd-boy!

IV

Ye blessed Creatures, I have heard the call
Ye to each other make; I see
The heavens laugh with you in your jubilee;
My heart is at your festival,
My head hath its coronal,
The fulness of your bliss, I feel—I feel it all.
Oh evil day! if I were sullen
While Earth herself is adorning,
This sweet May-morning,
And the Children are culling
On every side,
In a thousand valleys far and wide,
Fresh flowers; while the sun shines warm,
And the Babe leaps up on his Mother's arm:—
I hear, I hear, with joy I hear!
—But there's a Tree, of many, one,

A single Field which I have looked upon,
Both of them speak of something that is gone:
    The Pansy at my feet
    Doth the same tale repeat:
Whither is fled the visionary gleam?
Where is it now, the glory and the dream?

V

Our birth is but a sleep and a forgetting:
The Soul that rises with us, our life's Star,
    Hath had elsewhere its setting,
      And cometh from afar:
    Not in entire forgetfulness,
    And not in utter nakedness,
But trailing clouds of glory do we come
    From God, who is our home:
Heaven lies about us in our infancy!
Shades of the prison-house begin to close
    Upon the growing Boy,
But He beholds the light, and whence it flows,
    He sees it in his joy;
The Youth, who daily farther from the east
    Must travel, still is Nature's Priest,
    And by the vision splendid
    Is on his way attended;
At length the Man perceives it die away,
And fade into the light of common day.

VI

Earth fills her lap with pleasures of her own;
Yearnings she hath in her own natural kind,
And, even with something of a Mother's mind,
    And no unworthy aim,
    The homely Nurse doth all she can
To make her Foster-child, her Inmate Man,
    Forget the glories he hath known,
And that imperial palace whence he came.

VII

Behold the Child among his new-born blisses,
A six years' Darling of a pigmy size!
See, where 'mid work of his own hand he lies,

Fretted by sallies of his mother's kisses,
With light upon him from his father's eyes!
See, at his feet, some little plan or chart,
Some fragment from his dream of human life,
Shaped by himself with newly-learned art;
    A wedding or a festival,
    A mourning or a funeral;
      And this hath now his heart,
    And unto this he frames his song:
      Then will he fit his tongue
To dialogues of business, love, or strife;
    But it will not be long
    Ere this be thrown aside,
    And with new joy and pride
The little Actor cons another part;
Filling from time to time his "humorous stage"
With all the Persons, down to palsied Age,
That Life brings with her in her equipage;
    As if his whole vocation
    Were endless imitation.

VIII

Thou, whose exterior semblance doth belie
    Thy Soul's immensity;
Thou best Philosopher, who yet dost keep
Thy heritage, thou Eye among the blind,
That, deaf and silent, read'st the eternal deep,
Haunted for ever by the eternal mind,—
    Mighty Prophet! Seer blest!
    On whom those truths do rest,
Which we are toiling all our lives to find,
In darkness lost, the darkness of the grave;
Thou, over whom thy Immortality
Broods like the Day, a Master o'er a Slave,
A Presence which is not to be put by;
Thou little Child, yet glorious in the might
Of heaven-born freedom on thy being's height,
Why with such earnest pains dost thou provoke
The years to bring the inevitable yoke,
Thus blindly with thy blessedness at strife?
Full soon thy Soul shall have her earthly freight,
And custom lie upon thee with a weight
Heavy as frost, and deep almost as life!

IX

O joy! that in our embers
    Is something that doth live,
    That nature yet remembers
    What was so fugitive!
The thought of our past years in me doth breed
Perpetual benediction: not indeed
For that which is most worthy to be blest—
Delight and liberty, the simple creed
Of Childhood, whether busy or at rest,
With new-fledged hope still fluttering in his breast:—
    Not for these I raise
    The song of thanks and praise;
    But for those obstinate questionings
    Of sense and outward things,
    Fallings from us, vanishings;
    Blank misgivings of a Creature
Moving about in worlds not realised,
High instincts before which our mortal Nature
Did tremble like a guilty Thing surprised:
    But for those first affections,
    Those shadowy recollections,
    Which, be they what they may,
Are yet the fountain light of all our day,
Are yet a master light of all our seeing;
    Uphold us, cherish, and have power to make
Our noisy years seem moments in the being
Of the eternal Silence: truths that wake,
    To perish never;
Which neither listlessness, nor mad endeavour,
    Nor Man nor Boy,
Nor all that is at enmity with joy,
Can utterly abolish or destroy!
    Hence in a season of calm weather
    Though inland far we be,
Our Souls have sight of that immortal sea
    Which brought us hither,
    Can in a moment travel thither,
And see the Children sport upon the shore,
And hear the mighty waters rolling evermore.

X

Then sing, ye Birds, sing, sing a joyous song!
    And let the young Lambs bound
    As to the tabor's sound!
We in thought will join your throng,
    Ye that pipe and ye that play,
    Ye that through your hearts to-day
    Feel the gladness of the May!
What though the radiance which was once so bright
Be now for ever taken from my sight,
    Though nothing can bring back the hour
Of splendour in the grass, of glory in the flower;
    We will grieve not, rather find
    Strength in what remains behind;
    In the primal sympathy
    Which having been must ever be;
    In the soothing thoughts that spring
    Out of human suffering;
    In the faith that looks through death,
In years that bring the philosophic mind.

XI

And O, ye Fountains, Meadows, Hills, and Groves,
Forebode not any severing of our loves!
Yet in my heart of hearts I feel your might;
I only have relinquished one delight
To live beneath your more habitual sway.
I love the Brooks which down their channels fret,
Even more than when I tripped lightly as they;
The innocent brightness of a new-born Day
       Is lovely yet;
The Clouds that gather round the setting sun
Do take a sober colouring from an eye
That hath kept watch o'er man's mortality;
Another race hath been, and other palms are won.
Thanks to the human heart by which we live,
Thanks to its tenderness, its joys, and fears,
To me the meanest flower that blows can give
Thoughts that do often lie too deep for tears.

Source: David Perkins, ed., English Romantic Writers (San Diego: Harcourt Brace Jovanovich, Publishers, 1967), pp. 196-97, 264, 280-82.

24.4

--- ✢ ---

SORROWS OF YOUNG WERTHER, GOETHE

Johann Wolfgang von Goethe (1749-1832) began his writing career as a Romanticist; by the time he completed his masterpiece Faust *shortly before he died, he had become a Classicist. In the* Sorrows of Young Werther, *he is still very much in his Romantic phase. The novel is written as a series of letters describing the title character's ultimately fatal attraction to genius, poetry, art, and love itself. Here Werther, in three letters, describes his tragic love for Lotte and presents his extremely romanticized view of the world.*

--- ✢ ---

QUESTIONS

1. Unrequited love, as Werther feels for Lotte, was a common theme in Romantic novels and poetry. Is there something "unromantic" about requited love?
2. According to Goethe and the Romantics, what was the relationship between humanity and nature? Where is God in that relationship?
3. Why did Goethe write this novel as a series of letters? Is there anything particularly "Romanticist" in that choice?

November 21st

She doesn't see, she doesn't feel, that she is preparing a poison that will destroy her and me, and with voluptuous delight I drink the cup she hands me to the last dregs, and to my ruination. What is the meaning of that kindly look that she so often — often?...no, not often, but sometimes gives me, the graciousness with which she sometimes accepts a chance expression of my feelings for her, the compassion for what I am enduring, that is written on her brow?

Yesterday, as I was leaving, she gave me her hand and said, "Adieu, dear Werther." Dear Werther! It was the first time she called me "dear" and I felt it to the core of me. I have repeated it to myself over and over again, and last night, when I was about to retire and was talking all sorts of things over in my mind, I suddenly said out loud, "Good night, dear Werther!" and had to laugh at myself.

November 22nd

I cannot pray: let her remain mine, yet often it seems to me that she is mine. I cannot pray: give her to me, for she belongs to another. Thus I mock my pain. Were I really to let myself go, a whole litany of antitheses would be the result.

November 24th

She knows how I suffer. Today her eyes looked deep into my heart. I found her alone. I said nothing, and she looked at me. And I no longer saw her loveliness nor the radiance of her wonderful spirit. All that had disappeared from before my eyes. Instead I had a far more glorious vision. I saw her face filled with an expression of the most intimate sympathy, the sweetest compassion.

Why couldn't I throw myself at her feet? Why couldn't I counter with an embrace and a thousand kisses? She escaped to the piano and sang to her own accompaniment in her sweet, low voice, and so melodiously. Never were her chaste lips more enchanting. It was as though they parted thirsty for the sweet tones that swelled forth from the instrument and only a furtive echo escaped them. Ah me, if only I could explain it to you! I offered no more resistance. I bowed my head and vowed that never would I presume to kiss those lips, o'er which celestial spirits hover...and yet...I want to kiss them. Ha! You see? That is what stands before my soul like a bulkhead — such bliss, and then...down, down, to atone for such a sin.... A sin?

November 30th

It seems that I am not gong to be permitted to recover, no doubt about it. Wherever I go I encounter something that upsets me utterly. Today — oh, fate, oh, humankind!

At noon I was walking along the river. I didn't feel like eating. It was a dreary day. A raw wind was blowing down from the mountains and gray rain clouds were rolling into the valley. Ahead of me, I could see a man in a shabby green coat, scrambling about among the rocks. I thought he was gathering herbs. As I drew nearer, and he, hearing me, turned around, I found myself looking into a most interesting face. Its main expression was a quiet sadness, otherwise it betrayed nothing but candor and honesty. His black hair was pinned up in two rolls; the rest hung in one thick braid down his back. Since, judging by his dress, he seemed to be a man of humble origin, I decided that he would not take offense if I chose to comment on what he was doing, so I asked him what he was looking for. With a deep sigh, he replied, "I am looking for flowers, but can find none."

"This is not the season for them," I said, smiling.

"But there are so many flowers," he replied, moving down to my level. "I have roses in my garden, and honeysuckle, two kinds. My father gave me one. They grow like weeds. I have been looking for them for two days and cannot find them. And outside there are always flowers, yellow ones, blue and red ones — and centaury has such a pretty blossom. I can't find any of them."

I could sense something mysterious, so I asked in a roundabout way, "And what does he want to do with the flowers?"

A bright, tremulous smile crossed his face. "If the gentleman won't give me away," he said, putting a finger to his lips, "I promised my sweetheart a bouquet."

"Now there's a good man!" I said.

"Oh, she has many other things," he replied. "She is rich."

"And yet she likes his nosegay," I said.

"Oh," he countered, "she has jewels and a crown."

"What is her name?"

"If the Netherlands would only pay me," he said, "it would make a changed man of me. Yes, yes, there was a time when I was very well off. Now that's all over and done with. Now I am…" He turned his moist eyes skyward to express the rest.

"So he was once a happy man?" I asked.

"Ah, if only I could be like that again," he replied. "How happy I used to feel in those days — so merry, like a fish in water."

"Henry!" cried an old woman who now came up the path. "Henry, where are you? We've been looking for you everywhere. Come and eat."

"Is that your son?" I asked, stepping forward.

"Indeed he is my poor son," she said. "God has given me a heavy cross to bear."

"How long has be been that way?" I asked.

"Quiet like that," she said, "he has been only for the past six months. God be thanked that he is as he is now. The year before, he was a raving maniac and they had to keep him chained in the madhouse. Now he does no harm, but he is always troubled, has kings and emperors on his mind. He was such a good, quiet lad who helped toward my support and could write a pretty hand, but suddenly he became despondent and fell into a violent fever, and from that into raving madness, and now he is as you see him. If I were to tell you, sir —"

I interrupted her flood of words with the question, "What sort of time was it that he praises so highly, when he was so happy, so content?"

"The fool," she cried, with a pitying smile. "He means the time he was deranged, the time spent in the madhouse, when he didn't know what was going on around him — that's the time he is forever praising so highly."

It struck me like a thunderbolt. I pressed a coin to her hand and hurried away.

"So that was when you were happy!" I cried aloud, as I hastened back to town. "When you felt like a fish in water!" Oh dear God in heaven, hast Thou made it man's fate that he cannot be happy until he has found his reason and lost it again? Poor wretch! Yet how I envy him his dim mind, envy him pining away in his confusion. He goes out hopefully in the winter to pick flowers for his queen and grieves when he finds none and can't grasp when he finds none…and I? I go out without hope in my heart, with no purpose, and return home as I went. He can see the man he would be if only the Netherlands would pay him. Fortunate fellow! He can ascribe his lack of bliss to an earthly hindrance. He doesn't feel, he doesn't even know, that his misery lies in his destroyed heart, in his disordered mind — a fate from which all the kings on earth cannot save him!

The miserable wretch should perish who dares to mock a sick man journeying to a far-off healing spring that will only make his sickness worse and the rest of his days more painful; and so should he who looks down arrogantly on a man with a sorely afflicted heart who, to rid himself of his guilty conscience and cast off the sufferings of his soul, and with every day of his journey endured, his heart rests lightened of many anxieties. And you dare to call it madness, you sophists on your downy cushions? Madness? O God, Thou dost see my tears. Why didst Thou, Who made man poor, have to give him brothers who would rob him even of the little he has, of the little faith he has in Thee, Thou all-loving God? For what is faith in a healing root or in the tears of the grapevine but faith in Thee, in that Thou hast imbued all that surrounds us with the powers of salvation and the forces that ease pain, of which we stand in hourly need. Father Whom I know not, Father Who once filled my whole soul but has turned his face from me now — call me unto Thee. Be silent no longer. Thy silence will not deter this thirsting soul. Could any man — could any father — be angry with a son who comes back unexpectedly and throws his arms around his neck, crying, "Here I am, returned to thee, my father. Be not angry that I interrupted my wanderings, which according to Thy will, I should have endured longer. The world is the same everywhere — in effort and work, in reward and joy — but what concern is it of mine? Only where Thou art can I be content. There I will suffer and rejoice." Wouldst Thou, dear heavenly Father, cast out such a man?

December 1st

William! The fellow I wrote to you about, that fortunate unfortunate man, was once secretary to Lotte's father, and his passionate love for her — which he nurtured, concealed, but finally disclosed, and because of which he was dismissed — drove him mad. Try to feel, as you read these dry words, with what derangement they filled me when Albert mentioned it to me just as casually as you read about it now.

Source: Johann Wolfgang von Goethe, *Sorrows of Young Werther*, trans. by Catherine Hutter (New York: Signet Classic, 1962), pp. 95-98.

———— ✢ ————

QUESTIONS FOR PART 24

1. In what ways is secularization a feature of Utilitarianism and Romanticism?
2. What is the role of education in both of these new ideologies?
3. What do the Liberals and the Romantics have in common?

PART 25

NATIONALISM AND REALISM

This chapter takes a look at two more of the new ideologies of the nineteenth century, Nationalism and Realism. As with Liberalism and Romanticism from the last chapter, the first (Nationalism) was a political theory while the second (Realism) was an artistic movement.

No other political movement of the nineteenth century had as much affect on Western history than that of Nationalism. Furthermore, Nationalism was exported out of Europe to her colonies and became a worldwide phenomenon in the nineteenth and twentieth centuries. Nationalism is the belief that national identity is based on shared language, traditions, ethnicity, common customs, and so forth. National identity, according to this theory, is not based on dynastic association or political boundaries, although these definitions of national identity may overlap. Many nationalists come to believe that their national identities are self-evident. It is worth noting that many of the new ideologies of the nineteenth century can be combined with one another, and with other theoretical concepts. Nationalism, for instance, often intertwined with Romanticism or with Liberalism, to produce Romantic Nationalism or Liberal Nationalism, although no such combination was inevitable.

In culture, Realism soon supplanted Romanticism as the most popular literary form. As social reform gained in popularity, Realist art (literature and the visual) became a vehicle for examination, reflection, and protest. The novels of Henri Balzac, Nikolai Gogol, Emile Zola, and Gustave Flaubert were filled with minute observations of everyday life and human behavior. Playwrights such as Henrik Ibsen and George Bernard Shaw wrote piercing observations on the human condition for the stage. In general, most Realist art focused on the unsatisfied and unfulfilled nature of nineteenth century life.

25.1

--- ✢ ---

PROCLAMATION TO THE PEOPLE OF VENEZUELA, SIMÓN BOLÍVAR

Simón Bolívar (1783-1839) led the second wave of American revolutions for independence. In 1807 Napoleon had deposed the Bourbon king of Spain; in 1814 the Bourbons had been restored to the throne. However, the restoration was not popular with the Spanish, who saw the Bourbons, a dynasty of French ancestry, as a foreign power. A revolt broke out, and in 1822 another French army invaded Spain, to once again restore the Bourbons.

During these several years of invasion and internal chaos, Spain neglected its colonial empire. Colonies in South America took advantage of this to declare their independence. The first "liberator" of South America was Bolívar; in 1819 he led Columbia to freedom, and in 1821 did the same for Venezuela. In 1824, in Peru, the Spanish army made its last stand in South America, only to be defeated by Bolívar and José de San Martín. Naturally Bolívar and San Martín were drawing upon lessons learned in the American, Haitian, and French revolutions. But they were also inspired by the new ideologies of nationalism and liberalism.

---- ✤ ----

QUESTIONS

1. Was Bolívar a South American nationalist or a Spanish nationalist?
2. Who does Bolívar mean when he speaks of the "American?"
3. Compare this with Thomas Jefferson's *Declaration of Independence*; does freedom mean the same thing to both of these men?

PROCLAMATION TO THE PEOPLE OF VENEZUELA

Trujillo, June 15, 1813.

S imón Bolívar, Liberator of Venezuela, Brigadier of the Union, General in Chief of the Northern Army

To his fellow-countrymen:

Venezuelans: an army of your brothers, sent by the Sovereign Congress of New Granada, has come to liberate you. Having expelled the oppressors from the provinces of Mérida and Trujillo, it is now among you.

We are sent to destroy the Spaniards, to protect the Americans, and to reëstablish the republican governments that once formed the Confederation of Venezuela. The states defended by our arms are again governed by their former constitutions and tribunals, in full enjoyment of their liberty and independence, for our mission is signed only to break the chains of servitude which still shackle some of our towns, and not to impose laws or exercise acts of dominion to which the rules of war might entitle us.

Moved by your misfortunes, we have been unable to observe with indifference the afflictions you were forced to experience by the barbarous Spaniards, who have ravished you, plundered you, and brought you death and destruction. They have violated the sacred rights of nations. They have broken the most solemn agreements and treaties. In fact, they have committed every manner of crime, reducing the Republic of Venezuela to the most frightful desolation. Justice therefore demands vengeance, and necessity compels us to exact it. Let the monsters who infest Colombian soil, who have drenched it in blood, be cast out forever; may their punishment be equal to the enormity of their perfidy, so that we may eradicate the stain of our ignominy and demonstrate to the nations of the world that the sons of America cannot be offended with impunity.

Despite our just resentment toward the iniquitous Spaniards, our magnanimous heart still commands us to open to them for the last time a path to reconciliation and friendship; they are invited to live peacefully among us, if they will abjure their crimes, honestly change their ways, and coöperate with us in destroying the intruding Spanish government and in the reëstablishment of the Republic of Venezuela.

Any Spaniard who does not, by every active and effective means, work against tyranny in behalf of this just cause, will be considered an enemy and punished; as a traitor to the nation, he will inevitably be shot by a firing squad. On the other hand, a general and absolute amnesty is granted to those who come over to our army with or without their arms, as well as to those who render aid to the good citizens who are endeavoring to throw off the yoke of tyranny. Army officers and civil magistrates who proclaim the government of Venezuela and join with us shall retain their posts and position; in a word, those Spaniards who render outstanding service to the State shall be regarded and treated as Americans.

And you Americans who, by error or treachery, have been lured from the paths of justice, are informed that your brothers, deeply regretting the error of your ways, have pardoned you as we are profoundly convinced that you cannot be truly to blame, for only the blindness and ignorance in which you have been kept up to now by those responsible for your crimes could have induced you to commit them. Fear not the sword that comes to avenge you and to sever the ignoble ties with which your executioners have bound you to their own fate. You are hereby assured, with absolute impunity, of your honor, lives, and property. The single title, "Americans," shall be your safeguard and guarantee. Our arms have come to protect you, and they shall never be raised against a single one of you, our brothers.

This amnesty is extended even to the very traitors who most recently have committed felonious acts, and it shall be so religiously applied that no reason, cause, or pretext will be sufficient to oblige us to violate our offer, however extraordinary and extreme the occasion you may give to provoke our wrath.

Spaniards and Canary Islanders, you will die, though you be neutral, unless you actively espouse the cause of America's liberation. Americans, you will live, even if you have trespassed.

General Headquarters, Trujillo, June 15, 1813. The 3d [year].

Simón Bolívar

Source: Vicente Lecuna and Harold A. Bierck, Jr., eds., *Selected Writings of Bolívar, Volume One* (New York: The Colonial Press, Inc., 1951), pp. 31-32.

25.2

———— ✢ ————

COMMUNIST MANIFESTO, MARX AND ENGELS

Karl Marx (1818-1883) and Friedrich Engels (1820-1895) were German writers who were both familiar with the industrialization of Britain. Marx had studied the phenomena as a journalist and historian, while Engels had managed a family factory in Manchester. They first met in 1842 and shared a mutual passion for radical labor reform. In 1848 they published their Communist Manifesto. *The failure of all the liberal attempts at revolution in that year led them both to exile themselves to Britain full time, to continue their research and writing.*

Marx and Engels were convinced that the working class of Europe had undergone a process of proletarianization, which had reduced them from independent artisans to hourly wage slaves. They were also convinced as proletarianization increased, as workers become more disaffected, they would inevitably rise up and seize power. The Marx / Engels ideal state was one in which there was no class, no property, and no competition. They both believed that the worker revolution coming soon, and that it would be a violent upheaval. This was Marx's understanding of history via Hegel (1770-1831). Hegel's theory of the dialectic, of history as shaped by opposing and clashing forces, is at the heart of Marx and Engels' understanding of class development. Their ideas are second only to nationalism in the duration of its influence.

---- ✤ ----

QUESTIONS

1. How is Communism an anti-nationalist movement?
2. Do Marx and Engels oppose all forms of private property?
3. What function does the family have in the Communist state?

MANIFESTO OF THE COMMUNIST PARTY

A specter is haunting Europe — the specter of communism. All the powers of old Europe have entered into a holy alliance to exorcise this specter: Pope and Czar, Metternich and Guizot, French radicals and German police spies.

Where is the party in opposition that has not been decried as communistic by its opponents in power? Where is the opposition that has not hurled back the branding reproach of communism, against the more advanced opposition parties, as well as against its reactionary adversaries?

Two things result from this fact:

I. Communism is already acknowledged by all European powers to be itself a power.

II. It is high time that communists should openly, in the face of the whole world, publish their views, their aims, their tendencies, and meet this nursery tale of the specter of communism with a Manifesto of the party itself.

To this end, communists of various nationalities have assembled in London and sketched the following manifesto, to be published in the English, French, German, Italian, Flemish and Danish languages.

I. BOURGEOIS AND PROLETARIANS

The history of all hitherto existing society is the history of class struggles.

Freeman and slave, patrician and plebeian, lord and serf, guild-master and journeyman, in a word, oppressor and oppressed, stood in constant opposition to one another, carried on an uninterrupted, now hidden, now open fight, a fight that each time ended, either in a revolutionary reconstitution of society at large, or in the common ruin of the contending classes....

II. PROLETARIANS AND COMMUNISTS

In what relation do the communists stand to the proletarians as a whole?

The communists do not form a separate party opposed to the other working-class parties.

They have no interests separate and apart from those of the proletariat as a whole.

They do not set up any sectarian principles of their own, by which to shape and mould the proletarian movement.

The communists are distinguished from the other working-class parties by this only: 1. In the national struggles of the proletarians of the different countries, they point out and bring to the front the common interests of the entire proletariat, independently of all nationality. 2. In the various stages of development which the struggle of the working class against the bourgeoisie has to pass through, they always and everywhere represent the interests of the movement as a whole.

The communists, therefore, are on the one hand, practically, the most advanced and resolute section of the working-class parties of every country, that section which pushes forward all others; on the other hand, theoretically, they have over the great mass of the proletariat the advantage of clearly understanding the lines of march, the conditions, and the ultimate general results of the proletarian movement.

The immediate aim of the communists is the same as that of all other proletarian parties: formation of the proletariat into a class, overthrow of the bourgeois supremacy, conquest of political power by the proletariat....

Abolition of the family! Even the most radical flare up at this infamous proposal of the communists.

On what foundation is the present family, the bourgeois family, based? On capital, on private gain. In its completely developed form, this family exists only among the bourgeoisie. But this state of things finds its complement in the practical absence of the family among the proletarians, and in public prostitution.

The bourgeois family will vanish as a matter of course when its complement vanishes, and both will vanish with the vanishing of capital.

Do you charge us with wanting to stop the exploitation of children by their parents? To this crime we plead guilty.

But, you say, we destroy the most hallowed of relations, when we replace home education by social.

And your education! Is not that also social, and determined by the social conditions under which you educate, by the intervention direct or indirect, of society, by means of schools, etc.? The communists have not invented the intervention of society in education; they do but seek to alter the character of that intervention, and to rescue education from the influence of the ruling class.

The bourgeois claptrap about the family and education, about the hallowed co-relation of parents and child, becomes all the more disgusting, the more, by the action of modern Industry, all the family ties among the proletarians are torn asunder, and their children transformed into simple articles of commerce and instruments of labor.

But you communists would introduce community of women, screams the bourgeoisie in chorus.

The bourgeois sees his wife a mere instrument of production. He hears that the instruments of production are to be exploited in common, and, naturally, can come to no other conclusion that the lot of being common to all will likewise fall to the women.

He has not even a suspicion that the real point aimed at is to do away with the status of women as mere instruments of production.

For the rest, nothing is more ridiculous than the virtuous indignation of our bourgeois at the community of women which, they pretend, is to be openly and officially established by the communists. The communists have no need to introduce community of women; it has existed almost from time immemorial.

Our bourgeois, not content with having wives and daughters of their proletarians at their disposal, not to speak of common prostitutes, take the greatest pleasure in seducing each other's wives.

Bourgeois marriage is, in reality, a system of wives in common and thus, at the most, what the communists might possibly be reproached with is that they desire to introduce, in substitution for a hypocritically concealed, an openly legalized community of women. For the rest, it is self-evident that the abolition of the present system of production must bring with it the abolition of the community of women springing from that system, i.e., of prostitution both public and private.

The communists are further reproached with desiring to abolish countries and nationality.

The working men have no country. We cannot take from them what they have not got. Since the proletariat must first of all acquire political supremacy, must rise to be the leading class of the nation, must constitute itself *the* nation, it is so far, itself national, though not in the bourgeois sense of the word.

National differences and antagonism between peoples are daily more and more vanishing, owing to the development of the bourgeoisie, to freedom of commerce, to the world market, to uniformity in the mode of production and in the conditions of life corresponding thereto.

The supremacy of the proletariat will cause them to vanish still faster. United action, of the leading civilized countries at least, is one of the first conditions for the emancipation of the proletariat.

In short, the communists everywhere support every revolutionary movement against the existing social and political order of things.

In all these movements, they bring to the front, as the leading question in each, the property question, no matter what its degree of development at the time.

Finally, they labor everywhere for the union and agreement of the democratic parties of all countries.

The communists disdain to conceal their views and aims. They openly declare that their ends can be attained only by the forcible overthrow of all existing social conditions. Let the ruling classes tremble at a communistic revolution. The proletarians have nothing to lose but their chains. They have a world to win.

WORKERS OF ALL COUNTRIES, UNITE!

Source: Karl Marx and Friedrich Engels, *Basic Writings on Politics and Philosophy*, ed. Lewis S. Feuer (New York: Anchor Books, 1959), pp. 6-7, 20-29, 41.

25.3

✧

CATHOLIC RIGHTS IN IRELAND, DANIEL O'CONNELL

There were six centers of nationalist unrest in the second half of the nineteenth century; all were places that tried and failed to achieve some sort of political recognition for their nationalist identity in the wars and treaties of the first half of the century. These six were: Poland (which would not exist again as a state until 1919), Germany, Italy, the Austrian Empire, the Balkans, and Ireland. There were other pockets of nationalist tensions, but these were the most problematic.

The Irish Question — whether Ireland should be freed from British control — remained unsettled until after the First World War. But it was an issue as early as the Act of Union in 1800, in which Ireland became a full member in Great Britain. The Irish Question is also an example of how ideologies can overlap. When Daniel O'Connell (1775-1847) pushed for equal rights for Irish Catholics, he was speaking as both a liberal (for legal equality and religious toleration for Catholics) and as a nationalist (for traditional Irish Catholic nationhood). O'Connell had been elected to Parliament, but as a Catholic could not legally take his seat. The Catholic Emancipation Act was passed in 1829 and for the first time since 1673 allowed Catholics (Irish and English) to sit in Parliament. It was a liberal victory and also the first step in achieving Irish Home Rule.

O'Connell gave the following speech in 1814.

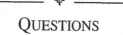

QUESTIONS

1. How does religion become part of a nationalist identity? Is it necessarily a part of that identity?
2. In what ways does O'Connell make religious toleration an issue of reason?
3. O'Connell speaks of the independence of the Catholic Church; can you find any evidence that he also wants political independence for Ireland?

CATHOLIC RIGHTS IN IRELAND
Daniel O'Connell
Dublin: 23 February 1814

I wish to submit to this meeting a resolution, calling on the different countries and cities in Ireland to petition for unqualified emancipation. It is a resolution which has been already and frequently adopted; and when we persevered in our petitions, even at periods when we despaired of success; it becomes our pleasing duty to present them now that the symptoms of the times seemed so powerfully to promise an approaching relief.

Truth, reason and justice are our advocates; and evening England let me tell you that those powerful advocates have some authority. They are, it is true, more frequently resisted there than in most other countries; but yet they have some sway among the English at all times. Passion may confound and prejudice darken the English understanding; and interested passion and hired prejudice have been successfully employed against us at former periods; but the present season appears singularly well calculated to aid the progress of our cause, and to advance the attainment of our important objects.

I do not make the assertion lightly. I speak after deliberate investigation, and from solemn conviction, my clear opinion that we shall, during the present session of Parliament, obtain a portion at least, if not the entire, of our emancipation. We cannot fail, unless we are disturbed in our course by those who graciously style themselves our friends, or are betrayed by the treacherous machinations of part of our own body.

Yes, everything, except false friendship and domestic treachery, forebodes success. The cause of man is in its great advance. Humanity has been rescued from much of it thraldom. In the states of

Europe, where the iron despotism of the feudal system so long classed men into two species — the hereditary masters and the perpetual slaves; when rank supplied the place of merit, and to be humbly born operated as a perpetual exclusion: — in many parts of Europe man is reassuming his natural station, and artificial distinctions have vanished before the force of truth and the necessities of governors....

The cause of liberty has made, and is making, great progress in states heretofore despotic. In all the countries in Europe, in which any portion of freedom prevails, the liberty of conscience is complete. England alone, of all the states pretending to be free, leaves shackles upon the human mind; England alone, amongst free states, exhibits the absurd claim of regulating belief by law, and forcing opinion by statute. Is it possible to conceive that this gross, this glaring, this iniquitous absurdity can continue? Is it possible, too, to conceive that it can continue to operate, not against a small and powerless sect, but against the millions, comprising the best strength, the most affluent energy of the empire? — a strength and an energy daily increasing, and hourly appreciating their own importance. The present system, disavowed by liberalized Europe, disclaimed by sound reason, abhorred by genuine religion, must soon and for ever be abolished.

Let it not be said that the princes of the Continent were forced by necessity to give privileges to their subjects, and that England has escaped from a similar fate. I admit that the necessity of procuring the support of the people was the mainspring of royal patriotism on the Continent; but I totally deny that the ministers of England can dispense with a similar support. The burdens of the war are permanent; the distresses occasioned by the peace are pressing; the financial system tottering, and to be supported in profound peace only by a war taxation. In the meantime, the resources of corruption are mightily diminished. Ministerial influence is necessarily diminished by one-half of the effective force of indirect bribery; full two-thirds must be disbanded. Peculation and corruption must be put upon half pay, and no allowances. The ministry lose not only al those active partisans; those outrageous loyalists, who fattened on the public plunder during the seasons of immense expenditure; but those very men will themselves swell the ranks of the malcontents, and probably be the most violent in their opposition. They have no sweet consciousness to reward them in their present privation; and therefore they are likely to exhaust the bitterness of their sols on their late employers. Every cause conspires to render this the period in which the ministry should have least inclination, least interest, least power, to oppose the restoration of our rights and liberties....

There is further encouragement at this particular crisis. Dissension has ceased in the Catholic body. Those who paralysed our efforts, and gave our conduct the appearance and reality of weakness, and wavering, and inconsistency, have all retired. Those who were ready to place the entire of the Catholic feelings and dignity, and some of the Catholic religion too, under the feet of every man who pleased to call himself our friend, and to prove himself our friend, by praising on every occasion, and upon no occasion, the oppressors of the Catholics, and by abusing the Catholics themselves; the men who would like the Catholic cause to this patron and to that, and sacrifice it at one time to the minister, and at another to the opposition, and make it this day the tool of one party, and the next the instrument of another party; the men, in fine, who hoped to traffic upon our country and our religion — who would buy honours, and titles, and places, and pensions, at the price of purity, and dignity, and safety of the Catholic Church in Ireland; all those men have, thank God, quitted us, I hope for ever. They have returned into silence and secession, or have frankly or covertly gone over to our enemies. I regret deeply and bitterly that they have carried with them some few who, like my Lord Fingal, entertain no other motives than those of purity and integrity, and who, like that noble lord, are merely mistaken.

But I rejoice at this separation — I rejoice that they have left the single-hearted, and the disinterested, and the indefatigable, and the independent, and the numerous, and the sincere Catholics to work out their emancipation unclogged, unshackled, and undismayed. They have bestowed on us another bounty also — they have proclaimed the causes of their secession — they have placed out of doubt the cause of the diversions. It is not intemperance, for that we abandoned; it is not the introduction of extraneous topics, for those we disclaimed; it is simply and purely, veto or no veto — restriction or no restriction — no other words; it is religion and principle that have divided us; thanks, many thanks to the tardy and remote candour of the seceders, that has at length written in large letters *the cause of their secession — it is the Catholic Church of Ireland — it is whether that Church shall continue independent of a Protestant ministry or not. We are for its independence* — the seceders are for its dependence.

Whatever shall be the fate of our emancipation question, thank God we are divided for ever from those who would wish that our Church should crouch to the partisans of the Orange system. Thank God, secession has displayed its cloven foot, and avowed itself to be synonymous with vetoism.

Those are our present prospects of success. First, man is elevated from slavery almost everywhere, and human nature has become more dignified, and, I may say, more valuable. Secondly, England wants our cordial support, and knows that she has only to secede to us justice in order to obtain our affectionate assistance. Thirdly, this is the season of successful petition, and the very fashion of the times entitles our petition to succeed. Fourthly, the Catholic cause is disencumbered of hollow friends and interested speculators. Add to all these the native and inherent strength of the principle of religious freedom and the inert and accumulating weight of our wealth, our religion, and our numbers, and where is the sluggard that shall dare to doubt our approaching success?

Besides, even our enemies must concede to us that we act form principle, and from principle only. We prove our sincerity when we refuse to make our emancipation a subject of traffic and barter, and ask for relief only upon those grounds which, if once established, would give to every other sect the right to the same political immunity. All we ask is "a clear stage and no favour." We think the Catholic religion the most rationally consistent with the divine scheme of Christianity, and, therefore, all we ask is that everybody should be left to his unbiased reason and judgment. If Protestants are equally sincere, why do they call the law, and the bribe, and the place, and the pension, in support of their doctrines? Why do they fortify themselves behind pains, and penalties, and exclusions, and forfeitures? Ought not our opponents to feel that they degrade the sanctity of their religion when they call in the profane aid of temporal rewards and punishments, and that they proclaim the superiority of our creed when they thus admit themselves unable to content against it upon terms of equality, and by the weapons of reason and argument, and persevere in refusing us all we ask — "a clear stage and no favour."

Yes, Mr. Chairman, our enemies, in words and by action, admit and proclaim our superiority. It remains to our friends alone, and to that misguided and ill-advised portion of the Catholics who have shrunk into secession — it remains for those friends and seceders alone to undervalue our exertions, and underrate our conscientious opinions.

Great and good God, in what a cruel situation are the Catholics of Ireland placed! If they have the manliness to talk of their oppressors as the paltry bigots deserve — if they have the honesty to express, evening measured language, a small portion of the sentiments of abhorrence which peculating bigotry ought naturally to inspire — if they condemn the principle which established the Inquisition in Spain and Orange lodges in Ireland, they are assailed by the combined clamour of those parliamentary friends and title-seeking, place-hunting seceders. The war-whoop of "*intemperance*" is sounded, and a persecution is instituted by our advocates and our seceders — against the Catholic who dares to be honest and fearless, and independent!

But I tell you what they easily forgive — nay, what our friends, sweet souls, would vindicate to-morrow in parliament, if the subject arose there. Here it is — here is the *Dublin Journal* of the 21st of

February, printed just two days ago. In the administration of Lord Whitworth, and the secretaryship of Mr. Peel, there is a government newspaper — a paper supported solely by the money of the people; for its circulation is little, and its private advertisements less. Here is a paper continued in existence like a wounded reptile — only whilst in the rays of the sun, by the heat and warmth communicated to it by the Irish administration. Let me read two passages for you. The first calls *"Popery the deadly enemy of pure religion and rational liberty."* Such is the *temperate* description the writer gives of the Catholic faith. With respect to the purity of religion I shall not quarrel with him. I only differ with him in point of taste; but I should be glad to know what this creature calls rational liberty. I suppose such as existed at Lacedæmon — the dominion of Spartans over Helots – the despotism of masters over slaves, that is his rational liberty. We will readily pass so much by. but attend to this: —

"I will," says this moderate and temperate gentleman, *"lay before the reader such specimens of the* POPISH SUPERSTITION *as will convince him that the treasonable combinations cemented by oaths, and the* NOCTURNAL ROBBERY AND ASSASSINATION *which have prevailed for many years past in Ireland, and still exist in many parts of it, are produced as a necessary consequence by its intolerant and sanguinary principles."*...

I close with conjuring the Catholics to persevere in their present course.

Let us never tolerate the slightest inroad on the discipline of our ancient, our holy Church. Let us never consent that she should be made the hireling of the ministry. *Our forefathers would have died, nay, they perished in hopeless slavery rather than consent to such degradation.*

Let us rest upon the barrier where they expired, *or go back into slavery rather than forward into irreligion and disgrace!* Let *us* also advocate our cause on the two great principles — first, that of an eternal separation in the spirituals between our Church and the State; secondly, that of *the eternal right to freedom of conscience* — a right which, I repeat it with pride and pleasure, would exterminate the Inquisition in Spain and bury in oblivion the bloody orange flag of dissension in Ireland!

Source: *British Orations from Ethelbert to Churchill* (New York: E. P. Dutton, 1915, 1960), pp. 203-214.

25.4

--- ✦ ---

MADAME BOVARY, GUSTAVE FLAUBERT

Flaubert's Madame Bovary *was written in 1857, and with its minute details of everyday life in mid-nineteenth century France, is the epitome of the Realist novel. The title character is a tragic figure of failed hope and romantic dreams; at once an indictment of Romantic ideals as well as a recognition of the attraction Romanticism had. Here, at the end of the novel, faced with financial ruin, Emma Bovary turns to a spurned suitor one last time for help. When he fails her, again, she chooses the ultimate escape from her problems.*

QUESTIONS

1. *Madame Bovary* is usually described as a Realist novel. What is "realistic" in this excerpt? How does that differ from Romanticism, the literary opposite of Realism?
2. In what ways is Emma Bovary "middle class?"
3. Why does Emma say to Rodolphe that she pities him?

She entered, as she always had, by the little park gate, and then came to the main courtyard, planted round with a double row of thick-crowned lindens, their long branches rustling and swaying. All the dogs in the kennel barked, but though their outcry echoed and re-echoed, no one came.

She climbed the wide, straight, wooden-banistered stairs that led up to the hall with its paving of dusty flagstones. A row of doors opened onto it, as in a monastery or an inn. His room was at the far end, the last on the left. When her fingers touched the latch her strength suddenly left her: she was afraid that he would not be there — she almost wished that he wouldn't be, and yet he was her only hope, her last chance of salvation. For a minute she collected her thoughts; then, steeling her courage to the present necessity, she entered.

He was smoking a pipe before the fire, his feet against the mantelpiece.

"Oh, it's you! he said, rising quickly.

"Yes, here I am…. Rodolphe, I want…I need some advice…"

Despite her best efforts she couldn't go on.

"You haven't changed — you're as charming as ever!"

"Oh my charms!" she answered bitterly. "They can't amount to much, since you scorned them."

He launched into apology, justifying his conduct in terms that were vague but the best he could muster.

She let herself be taken in — not so much by what he said, as by the sound of his voice and the very sight of him; and she pretended to believe — or perhaps she actually did believe — the reason he gave for their break. It was a secret, he said, involving the honor — the life, even — of a third person.

She looked at him sadly. "Whatever it was," she said, "I suffered a great deal."

He answered philosophically:

"That's how life is!"

"Has it been kind to you, at least," asked Emma, "since we parted?"

"Oh, neither kind nor unkind, particularly."

"Perhaps it would have been better had we stayed together."

"Yes…perhaps!"

"Do you really think so?" she said, coming closer.

And she sighed:

"Oh Rodolphe! If you knew! I loved you very much!"

She took his hand; and for a few moments their fingers were intertwined — like that first day, at the Agricultural Show! Pride made him struggle against giving in to his feelings. But she leaned heavily against him, and said:

"How did you ever think that I could live without you? Happiness is a habit that's hard to break! I was desperate! I thought I'd die! I'll tell you all about it. And you…you stayed away from me…!"

It was true: for the past three years he had carefully avoided her, out of the natural cowardice that characterizes the stronger sex; and now Emma went on, twisting and turning her head in coaxing little movements that were loving and catlike.

"You have other women — admit it. Oh, I sympathize with them: I don't blame them. You seduced them, the way you seduced me. You're a man! You have everything to make us love you. But you and I'll begin all over again, won't we? We'll love each other! Look — I'm laughing, I'm happy! Speak to me!"

And indeed she was ravishing to see, with a tear trembling in her eye like a raindrop in a blue flower-cup after a storm.

He drew her onto his lap, and with the back of his hand caressed her sleek hair: in the twilight a last sunbeam was gleaming on it like a golden arrow. She lowered her head, and soon he was kissing her on the eyelids, very gently, just brushing them with his lips.

"But you've been crying!" he said. "Why?"

She burst into sobs: Rodolphe thought it was from the violence of her love; when she didn't answer him he interpreted her silence as the ultimate refuge of her womanly modesty, and exclaimed:

"Ah! Forgive me! You're the only one I really care about! I've been stupid and heartless! I love you — I'll always love you....What is it? Tell me!"

He was on his knees.

"Well, then...I'm ruined, Rodolphe! You've got to lend me three thousand francs!"

"But...but...?" he said, slowly rising, a worried expression coming over his face.

"You know," she went on quickly, "my husband gave his money to a notary to invest, and the notary absconded. We've borrowed, patients haven't paid.... The estate isn't settled yet: we'll be getting something later. But today — just for three thousand francs — they're going to sell us out: now, this very instant. I counted on your friendship. I came to you."

"Ah," thought Rodolphe, suddenly pale. "So that's why she came!"

And after a moment he said, calmly:

"I haven't got it, dear lady."

He wasn't lying. If he had had it he would probably have given it to her, unpleasant though it usually is to make such generous gifts: of all the icy blasts that blow on love, a request for money is the most chilling and havoc-wreaking.

For a long moment she stared at him. Then:

"You haven't got it!"

She said it again, several times:

"You haven't got it! I might have spared myself this final humiliation. You never loved me! You're no better than the rest!"

She was giving herself away; she no longer knew what she was saying.

Rodolphe broke in, assuring her that he was "hard up" himself.

"Ah, I pity you!" said Emma. "How I pity you!"

And as her eyes fell on a damascened rifle that glittered in a trophy on the wall:

"When you're as poor as all that you don't put silver on the stock of your gun! You don't buy things with tortoise-shell inlay!" she went on, pointing to the Boulle clock. "Or silver-gilt whistles for your whip!" — she touched them — "or charms for your watch chain! Oh, he has everything! Even a liqueur case in his bedroom! You pamper yourself, you live well, you have a chateau, farms, woods; you hunt, you make trips to Paris.... Why, even things like this," she cried, snatching up his cuff links from the mantelpiece, "the tiniest trifles, you can raise money on...! Oh, I don't want them! Keep them."

And she hurled the two buttons so violently that their gold chain snapped as they struck the wall.

"But I — I'd have given you everything, I'd have sold everything, worked my fingers to the bone, begged in the streets, just for a smile from you, for a look, just to hear you say 'Thank you.' And you sit there calmly in your chair, as though you hadn't made me suffer enough already! If it hadn't been for you I could have been happy! What made you do it? Was it a bet? You loved me, though: you used to say so.... And you said so again just now. Ah, you'd have done better to throw me out! My hands are still hot from your kisses; and right there on the rug you swore on your knees that you'd love me forever. You made me believe it: for two years you led me on in a wonderful, marvelous dream.... Our plans for going away — you remember? Oh! That letter you wrote me! It tore my heart in two! And now when I come back to him — and find him rich and happy and free — to implore him for help that anybody would give me — come in distress, bringing him all my love — he refuses me, because it would cost him three thousand francs!"

"I haven't got it," answered Rodolphe, with the perfect calm that resigned anger employs as a shield.

She walked out. The walls were quaking, the ceiling was threatening to crush her; and she went back down the long avenue of trees, stumbling against piles of dead leaves that were scattering in the wind. At last she reached the ditch before the gate: she broke her nails on the latch, so frantically did she open it. Then, a hundred yards further on, out of breath, ready to drop, she paused. She turned: and once again she saw the impassive chateau, with its park, its gardens, its three courtyards, its many-windowed façade.

From *Madame Bouvary* by Gustave Flaubert, translated by Francis Steegmulller, p. 351-355. Copyright © 1957 by Francis Steegmuller. Used by permission of Random House, Inc.

QUESTIONS FOR PART 25

1. How does Realism differ from Romanticism?
2. Is Nationalism also always a form of Liberalism?
3. Although we normally associate Nationalism with the nineteenth century, it has antecedents. Can you think of any event prior to this period when Nationalist ideas were expressed?

PART 26

AGE OF PROGRESS

The concept of an Age of Progress is difficult for many students to grasp. When used in relation to the late-nineteenth century, it refers to three developments. One was the attempt by various western European countries to reform, usually through some version of labor or economic reform. Second, was the fruition of the bourgeois revolution of culture, and the creation of a society that brought education, improved living conditions, and more entertainment opportunities to the working classes. The third development was the creation of nation-states, such as the dual monarchy of Austria-Hungary (1867), the German Empire (1871), and France's Third Republic (1875). The model of the progressive state was Great Britain, which issued the Great Reform Act of 1832 (expanding the franchise), Factory Act of 1833 (labor reform), and the Reform Act of 1867 (further extension of the franchise). Above all else, the Age of Progress refers to Europe's firm conviction that progress, i.e., improvement, is not only possible, but, in fact, guaranteed.

The Age of Progress was the stepchild of the Industrial Revolution. Many aspects of it were unexpected results of industrialism. As more factories, mines, and railroads were built, it became apparent to the middle class that the working class needed reforms. This led the middle class to explore its values. Increased industrialism also provided the raw materials that made progress possible. Railroads brought fast access to holiday centers such as the beaches (Nice, Bath); factories and trade provided money for education, luxury goods, and material wealth (which became *the* dominant standard of the age); and the success of the first Industrial Revolution encouraged a second one that brought even more of the populace (such as women) into the Industrial Age. Although many of these reforms would benefit the working class, it is important to keep in mind that each was actually designed to benefit and protect the middle class.

26.1

---- ✤ ----

SPEECH ON LABOR REFORM, OTTO VON BISMARCK

Count Otto von Bismarck (1815-1898) was the architect of the modern German state. As Chancellor to Prussian King William I (1861-1888), Bismarck led the Prussian kingdom to victory against Denmark (1864), Austria (1866), and France (1870-71) in the wars of German Unification. Each victory brought more land under Prussia's control; Bismarck was especially interested in land that was populated with

German speaking peoples, marking nationalism as at least one of his motivations. The result was the proclamation in 1871, at Versailles, of the German Empire. King William I then became Kaiser William I.

Bismarck was as well known for his conservative politics as for his military victories. A man of junker (noble in Prussia) lineage, he generally sought to protect aristocratic privileges whenever possible. But Bismarck was also a master of Realpolitik, *a nineteenth century theory of power that favored the pragmatic over emotional. Bismarck had his romantic side (he was known as the "mad junker" for his emotionalism) but he was very much a realist about power. His decision to create the "little" German Empire and exclude Austria (whose emperor might compete with William I), in spite of his dream of "big" Germany," is an example of his pragmatism.*

Bismarck's conservatism was also evident in his rejection of all things socialist or communist. He did create a Reichstag (legislative house) *chosen by universal male suffrage, but he also knew that most Prussian men would vote as conservatively as he wanted them to. His primary goal was to protect the state and the army (which were inseparable under Bismarck). The following excerpt is from a speech Bismarck gave before the Reichstag in 1881, in response to accusations that his labor reforms were too conservative. The speech was entitled "Practical Christianity."*

QUESTIONS

1. What is Bismarck's position on the duties of a state toward its citizens who cannot take care of themselves?
2. Find and discuss an example of Bismarck's aristocratic background.
3. Is Bismarck making any claims about the religious beliefs (or lack thereof) of the Socialists?

Our present poor laws keep the injured laboring man from starvation. According to law, at least, nobody need starve. Whether in reality this never happens I do not know. But this is not enough in order to let the men look contentedly into the future and to their own old age. The present bill intends to keep the sense of human dignity alive which even the poorest German should enjoy, if I have my way. He should feel that he is no mere eleemosynary, but that he possesses a fund which is his very own. No one shall have the right to dispose of it, or to take it from him, however poor he may be. This fund will open for him many a door, which otherwise will remain closed to him and it will secure for him better treatment in the house where he has been received, because when he leaves he can take away with him whatever contributions he has been making to the household expenses.

If you have ever personally investigated the conditions of the poor in our large cities, or of the village paupers in the country, you have been able to observe the wretched treatment which the poor occasionally receive even in the best managed communities, especially if they are physically weak or crippled. This happens in the houses of their stepmothers, or relatives of any kind, yes also in those of their nearest of kin. Knowing this, are you not obliged to confess that every healthy laboring man, who sees such things, must say to himself: "Is it not terrible that a man is thus degraded in the house which he used to inhabit as master and that his neighbor's dog is not worse off than he?" Such things do happen. What protection is there for a poor cripple, who is pushed into a corner, and is not given enough to eat? There is none. But if he has as little as 100 or 200 marks of his own, the people will think twice before they oppress him. We have been in a position to observe this in the case of the military invalids. Although only five or six dollars are paid every month, this actual cash amounts to something in the household where the poor are boarded, and the thrifty housewife is careful not to offend or to lose the boarder who pays cash.

I, therefore, assure you that we felt the need of insisting by this law on a treatment of the poor which should be worthy of humanity. Next year I shall be able fully to satisfy Mr. Richter in regard to the amount of the extent of attention which the State will give to a better and more adequate care of all the unemployed. This will come as a natural consequence, whether or no the present bill is passed. Today this bill is a test, as it were. We are sounding to see how deep the waters are, financially, into which we are asking the State and the country to enter. You cannot guard yourselves against such problems by delivering elegant and sonorous speeches, in which you recommend the improvement of our laws of liability, without in the least indicating how this can be done. In this way you cannot settle these questions, for you are acting like the ostrich, who hides his head lest he see his danger. The Government has seen its duty and is facing, calmly and without fear, the dangers which we heard described here a few days ago most eloquently and of which we were given convincing proofs.

We should, however, also remove, as much as possible, the causes which are used to excite the people, and which alone render them susceptible to criminal doctrines. It is immaterial to me whether or no you will call this Socialism. If you call it Socialism, you must have the remarkable wish of placing the Imperial Government, in so far as this bill of the allied governments is concerned, in the range of the very critique which Mr. von Puttkamer passed here on the endeavors of the Socialists. It would then almost seem that with this bill only a very small distance separated us from the murderous band of Hasselmann, the incendiary writings of Most, and the revolutionary conspiracies of the Congress of Wyden; and that even this distance would soon disappear. Well, gentlemen, this is, of course, the very opposite of true. Those who fight with such oratorical and meaningless niceties are counting on the many meanings of the word "socialism." As a result of the kind of programs which the Socialists have issued, this term is, in our public opinion today, almost synonymous with "criminal." If the government endeavors to treat the injured workingmen better in the future, and especially more becomingly, and not to offer to their as yet vigorous brethren the spectacle, as it were, of an old man on the dump heap slowly starving to death, this cannot be called socialistic in the sense in which that murderous band was painted to us the other day. People are playing a cheap game with the shadow on the wall when they call our endeavors socialistic.

If the representative Mr. Bamberger, who took no offense at the word "Christian," wishes to give a name to our endeavors which I could cheerfully accept, let it be: "Practical Christianity," but *sans phrase*, for we shall not pay the people with words and speeches, but with actual improvements. Yet, death alone is had for the asking. If you refuse to reach into your pocketbook, or that of the State, you will not accomplish anything. If you should place the whole burden on the industries, I do not know whether they could bear it. Some might be able to do it, but not all. Those who could do it are the industries where the wages are but a small fraction of the total cost of production. Among such I mention the chemical factories, and the mills which with twenty mill hands can do an annual business of several million marks. The great mass of laborers, however, does not work in such establishments, which I am tempted to call aristocratic — without wishing to excite any class-hatred. They are in industries where the wages amount to 80 or 90 per cent of the cost of production. Whether the latter can bear the additional burden I do not know.

It is, moreover, perfectly immaterial whether the assessment is made on the employer or on the employee. In either case the industry will have to bear it, for the contribution of the laborer will eventually, and of necessity, be added to the expenses of the industry. There is a general complaint that the average wages of the laborers make the saving of a surplus impossible. If you wish, therefore, to add a burden to the laborers whose present wages are no more than sufficient, the employers will have to increase the wages, or the laborers will leave them for other occupations....

Alms constitute the first step of Christian charity, such as must exist in France, for instance, to a great extent. There are no poor-laws in France, and every poor man has the right to starve to death if charitable people do not prevent him from doing so. Charity is the first duty, and the second is, the assistance given by districts and according to law. A State, however, which is composed very largely of Christians — even if you are horrified at hearing it called a Christian state, — should let itself be permeated with the principles which it confesses, and especially with those which have to do with the help of our neighbors, and the sympathy one feels for the lot which threatens the old and the sick.

Source: Edmund von Mach, trans., Kuno Francke, ed., *The German Classics: Masterpieces of German Literature, Volume X* (New York: The German Publication Society, 1914), pp. 228-31. 236.

26.2

❖

PROTEST AGAINST STATE REGULATION OF VICE, JOSEPHINE BUTLER

Many of the progressive reforms of the late nineteenth century were aimed specifically at women of the working class. Some of the most impressive reforms came in the field of education, which opened up to women more than ever before. Compulsory education laws were passed in Austria (1869), France (1882), and Britain (1880 and 1902) that required boys and girls to have at least an elementary education, if only to provide skilled labor for industry. Boys and girls were not always learning the same skills in these schools, but they were learning. Higher education also opened up to women, as many universities allowed women in as degree-seeking students for the first time.

However, as with many of the period's reforms in general, those aimed at working-class women were really devised to protect the middle class (men and women) in some way, or to force middle-class values and standards upon the working class. An example of a progressive reform that was meant to "help" working class women was Britain's Contagious Diseases Acts of 1864-1886. These were designed to halt the alarming spread of venereal disease in large cities. The Acts allowed the police to seize women suspected of prostitution, confine them to "lock hospitals, examine them, and if they were found to be infected, they remained locked up until cured." The prostitutes (or suspected prostitutes) were also taught about morals and virtues.

Middle-class women successfully protested the laws, noting that the laws punish only women. The male clients of these prostitutes were not charged under the Acts, and the idea of men infecting other men with venereal disease was not addressed in the law.

Leading the opposition to these "vice regulations" was Josephine Butler. Here is an excerpt from her Personal Reminiscences of a Great Crusade.

⁘

QUESTIONS

1. What does Josephine imply by calling her campaign a "crusade?"
2. In addition to opposing the Contagious Diseases Acts, did Butler also argue for the legalization of prostitution ("vice")?
3. What authority does Florence Nightingale bring to the Parliament discussion of the Acts?

There were four Acts; the first, tentative, in 1864. This was repealed when the Act of 1866 was passed, and this, after verbal amendment in 1868, was still further extended by the Act of 1869. This last Act was not allowed much peace, for it was in the autumn of the same year that the opposition arose; in fact, a powerful protest had been raised shortly before the passing of this complete Act. Mrs. Harriet Martineau, with all the shrewdness and enlightenment of a true woman and an able politician, had seen the tendency of a certain busy medical and military clique in this direction. The then editor of the *Daily News*, who was favourable to our views, asked Mrs. Martineau to write a series of letters in his paper. This she did, and her letters are extremely weighty, and wonderful to read at this day, when we have an immense accumulation of evidence to support her and our views, which she, of course, did not possess. Her advice on this matter concerning our army is admirable. Speaking of our poor soldiers, she says: — "But while favouring the element of brutality in him (the soldier), we had not need go further and assume in practice that his animalism is a necessity which must be provided for. This is the fatal step which it is now hoped that the English Parliament and the English people may be induced to take. If the soldier is more immoral than his contemporaries of the working class, it must be because the standard of morality is lower in the army than out of it. Shall we then raise it to what we clearly see it might be, or degrade it further by a practical avowal that vice is in the soldier's case a necessity to be provided for, like his need of food and clothing? This admission of the necessity of vice is the point on which the whole argument turns, and on which irretrievable consequences depend. Once admitted, the necessity of a long series of fearful evils follow of course. There can be no resistance to seduction, procuration, disease, regulation, *when once the original necessity is granted.* Further, the admission involves civil as well as military society, and starts them together on the road which leads down to what moralists of all ages and nations have called the lowest hell….It is a national disgrace that our people should have even been asked to regard and treat their soldiers and sailors as pre-destined fornicators." And in another of her letters to the *Daily News* Mrs. Martineau, writing of her experience of Continental cities, said: "There is evidence accessible to all that the Regulation System creates horrors worse than those which it is supposed to restrain. Vice once stimulated by such a system imagines and dares all unutterable things. And such things perplex with misery the lives of parents of missing children in Continental cities, and daunt the courage of rulers, and madden the moral sense, and gnaw the conscience of whole orders of sinners and sufferers, of whom we can form no conception here. We shall have entered upon our national decline whenever we agree to the introduction of such a system."

We, the women of England, were not the first to arise in opposition of this iniquity. For at least fifteen years before our call to the work, warning lights had been held out from time to time by persons or societies who thoroughly knew the system, and dreaded the disastrous effects for our country of its establishment in our midst.

A group of Baptist and other Nonconformist Ministers, in which my relative, the late Charles Birrell, took a leading part, early went to the Government, conveying an earnest warning and protest on the subject. I cannot fix the exact date of this event; but I have a vivid recollection of the account of it given to me by Mr. Birrell. I believe it was during the Administration of Lord John Russell.

In 1860 a Committee of the House of Lords sat to consider the question of introducing the Acts for the regulation of vice into India, or establishing a more complete form of the Acts already existing there. The majority of the witnesses examined by that Committee were wholly opposed to the system. Miss Florence Nightingale was one of those witnesses. Her recorded evidence and expression of opinion are lengthy, and exactly what we might expect from a true-hearted and an experienced woman. Lord Frederick Fitz-Clarence, Commander-in-Chief of the forces in India, said that "after giving the whole subject his best attention, he concurred with his predecessors in command of the army in believing that police measures of the kind in question could not be carried on without involving the certain degradation and oppression of many innocent women, and occasioning other evils which, in his opinion, would be very much greater than that which it was their object to remedy."

A third strong protest was that of the officers of the Rescue Society in London. They made a series of very strong efforts against the threatened introduction of the regulation system....

"At this crisis we learned that the *Women* of England are taking this question in hand. We were rejoiced beyond measure when we saw the announcement of your Ladies' National Association.

"I tell you candidly I had felt an almost utter despair in seeing that, after putting forth our pamphlet, and writing thousands of letters, imploring our legislators, clergy, principal public men and philanthropists to look into the question, such a stoical indifference remained. We felt, on hearing of your Association, that Providence had well chosen the means for the defeat of these wicked Acts. The ladies of England will save the country from this fearful curse; for I fully believe that through them it has even now had its death blow. The men who charge the ladies foremost in the struggle with indelicacy are not worthy the name of men. As to our Members of Parliament, pray do not excuse their ignorance; do not try to palliate their error by saying the Act was passed at the fag end of the session. The papers placed in their hands by ourselves, the letters of warning we addressed to them, leave them no excuse. Knowing, as none but ourselves can know, what was done to arouse them, I cannot but conclude that, with a few honourable exceptions, our Members of Parliament cared nothing about the matter until public opinion forced them to look into it. But for the Ladies' National Association we should have had no discussion, and the Acts would by this date have probably been extended throughout the country. I say this solemnly, and from an intimate knowledge of all the plans of the Association formed to extend these Acts. Go on; give the country no rest till this law is abolished. — Yours truly, Daniel Cooper."...

On the 1st January, 1870, was published the famous Women's Protest, as follows:

"We, the undersigned, enter our solemn protest against these Acts.

"1st. — Because, involving as they do such a momentous change in the legal safeguards hitherto enjoyed by women in common with men, they have been passed, not only without the knowledge of the country, but unknown, in a great measure, to Parliament itself; and we hold that neither the Representatives of the People, nor the Press, fulfil the duties which are expected of them, when they allow such legislation to take place without the fullest discussion.

"2nd. — Because, so far as women are concerned, they remove every guarantee of personal security which the law has established and held sacred, and put their reputation, their freedom, and their persons absolutely in the power of the police.

"3rd. — Because the law is bound, in any country professing to give civil liberty to its subjects, to define clearly an offence which it punishes.

"4th. — Because it is unjust to punish the sex who are the victims of a vice, and leave unpunished the sex who are the main cause, both of the vice and its dreaded consequences; and we consider that liability to arrest, forced medical treatment, and (where this is resisted) imprisonment with hard labour, to which these Acts subject women, are punishments of the most degrading kind.

"5th. — Because, by such a system, the path of evil is made more easy to our sons, and to the whole of the youth of England; inasmuch as a moral restraint is withdrawn the moment the State recognizes, and provides convenience for, the practice of a vice which it thereby declares to be necessary and venial.

"6th. — Because these measures are cruel to the women who come under their action — violating the feelings of those whose sense of shame is not wholly lost, and further brutalising even the most abandoned.

"7th. — Because the disease which these Acts seek to remove has never been removed by any such legislation. The advocates of the system have utterly failed to show, by statistics or otherwise, that these regulations have in any case, after several years' trial, and when applied to one sex only, diminished disease, reclaimed the fallen, or improved the general morality of the country. We have, on the contrary, the strongest evidence to show that in Paris and other Continental cities where women have long been outraged by this system, the public health and morals are worse than at home.

"8th. — Because the conditions of this disease, in the first instance, are moral, not physical. The moral evil through which the disease makes its way separates the case entirely from that of the plague, or other scourges, which have been placed under police control or sanitary care. We hold that we are bound, before rushing into experiments of legalizing a revolting vice, to try to deal with the *causes* of the evil, and we dare to believe that with wiser teaching and more capable legislation, those causes would not be beyond control."

Sources: Josephine E. Butler, *Personal Reminiscences of a Great Crusade* (Connecticut: Hyperion Books, Inc., 1976), pp. 1-10.

26.3

❖

MILITANT SUFFRAGISTS, EMMELINE PANKHURST

Once they had access to education, and had proven themselves capable of political activism, the next reform middle-class women sought was to change the franchise systems of the West. Suffragettes (or Suffragists; their name comes from the word suffrage, or right to vote) from across Europe and America took varied approaches to promoting their quest for the vote. All, however, believed that getting the vote would allow them to obtain more reforms later on. Some, such as Millicent Fawcett in Britain or Hubertine Auclert in France, took the route piloted by Butler, in petitioning their governments for suffrage, while others (mostly in Britain) tried a more dramatic way of publicizing their movement. These were the "militant suffragists" who chained themselves to Parliament in London, went on hunger strikes, vandalized, and even committed public suicide were all attempts used by various militant suffragists. Women did finally get the vote, but not until after World War I.

In Britain, the most famous militant suffragists were members of one family: the Pankhursts. Emmeline (1858-1929) and her daughters Christabel (1880-1958) and Sylvia (1882-1960) founded the Women's Social and Political Union in 1903. In 1913 Emmeline gave the following speech in Connecticut.

--- ✛ ---

QUESTIONS

1. In what ways does Pankhurst tailor her speech to the interests of her American audience?
2. How does Pankhurst define "government?"
3. What dangers do you see in using the language of war and violence to advocate political change?

I do not come here as an advocate, because whatever position the suffrage movement may occupy in the United States of America, in England it has passed beyond the realm of advocacy and it has entered into the sphere of practical politics. It has become the subject of revolution and civil war, and so to-night I am not here to advocate woman suffrage. American suffragists can do that very well for themselves. I am here as a soldier who has temporarily left the field of battle in order to explain — it seems strange it should have to be explained — what civil war is like when civil war is waged by women. I am not only here as a soldier temporarily absent from the field of battle; I am here — and that, I think, is the strangest part of my coming — I am here as a person who, according to the law courts of my country, it has been decided, is of no value to the community at all; and I am adjudged because of my life to be a dangerous person. So you see there is some special interest in hearing so unusual a person address you. I dare say, in the minds of many of you — you will perhaps forgive me this personal touch — that I do not look either very like a soldier or very like a convict, and yet I am both.

It would take too long to trace the course of militant methods as adopted by women, because it is about eight years since the word militant was first used to describe what we were doing; it is about eight years since the first militant action was taken by women. It was not militant at all, except that it provoked militancy on the part of those who were opposed to it. When women asked questions in political meetings and failed to get answers, they were not doing anything militant. To ask questions at political meetings is an acknowledged right of all people who attend public meetings; certainly in my country, men have always done it, and I hope they do it in America, because it seems to me that if you allow people to enter your legislatures without asking them any questions as to what they are going to do when they get there you are not exercising your citizen rights and your citizen duties as you ought. At any rate in Great Britain it is a custom, a time-honored one, to ask questions of candidates for Parliament and ask questions of members of the government. No man was ever put out of a public meeting for asking a question until Votes for Women came onto the political horizon. The first people who were put out of a political meeting for asking questions, were women; they were brutally ill-used; they found themselves in jail before twenty-four hours had expired. But instead of the newspapers, which are largely inspired by the politicians, putting militancy and the reproach of militancy, if reproach there is, on the people who had assaulted the women, they actually said it was the women who were militant and very much to blame.

It was not the speakers on the platform who would not answer them, who were to blame, or the ushers at the meeting; it was the poor women who had had their bruises and their knocks and scratches, and who were put into prison for doing precisely nothing but holding a protest meeting in the street after it was all over. However, we were called militant for doing that, and we were quite willing to accept the name, because militancy for us is time-honored; you have the church militant and in the sense of spiritual militancy we were very militant indeed. We were determined to press this question of the enfranchisement of the women to the point where we were no longer to be ignored by the politicians as had been the case for about fifty years, during which time women had patiently used every means open to them to win their political enfranchisement.

Enough of Sympathy

Experience will show you that if you really want to get anything done, it is not so much a matter of whether you alienate sympathy; sympathy is a very unsatisfactory thing if it is not practical sympathy. It does not matter to the practical suffragist whether she alienates sympathy that was never of any use to her. What she wants is to get something practical done, and whether it is done out of sympathy or whether it is done out of fear, or whether it is done because you want to be comfortable again and not be worried in this way, doesn't particularly matter so long as you get it. We had enough of sympathy for fifty years; it never brought us anything; and we would rather have an angry man going to the government and saying, my business is interfered with and I won't submit to its being interfered with any longer because you won't give women the vote, than to have a gentleman come onto our platforms year in and year out and talk about his ardent sympathy with woman suffrage.

"Put them is prison," they said; 'that will stop it." But it didn't stop it. They put women in prison for long terms of imprisonment, for making a nuisance of themselves — that was the expression when they took petitions in their hands to the door of the House of Commons; and they thought that by sending them to prison, giving them a day's imprisonment, would cause them to all settle down again and there would be no further trouble. But it didn't happen so at all: instead of the women giving it up, more women did it, and more and more and more women did it until there were three hundred women at a time, who had not broken a single law, only "made a nuisance of themselves" as the politicians say.

The whole argument with the anti-suffragists, or even the critical suffragist man, is this: that you can govern human beings without their consent. They have said to us, "Government rests upon force; the women haven't force, so they must submit." Well, we are showing them that government does not rest upon force at all; it rests upon consent. As long as women consent to be unjustly governed, they can be; but directly women say: "We withhold our consent, we will not be governed any longer so long as that government is unjust," not by the forces of civil war can you govern the very weakest woman. You can kill that woman, but she escapes you then; you cannot govern her. And that is, I think, a most valuable demonstration we have been making to the world.

Death or the Vote

Now, I want to say to you who think women cannot succeed, we have brought the government of England to this position, that it has to face this alternative; either women are to be killed or women are to have the vote. I ask American men in this meeting, what would you say if in your State you were faced with that alternative, that you must either kill them or give them their citizenship — women, many of whom you respect, women whom you know have lived useful lives, women whom you know, even if you do not know them personally, are animated with the highest motives, women who are in pursuit of liberty and the power to do useful public service? Well, there is only one answer to that alternative; there is only one way out of it, unless you are prepared to put back civilization two or three generations; you must give those women the vote. Now that is the outcome of our civil war.

You won your freedom in American when you had the Revolution, by bloodshed, by sacrificing human life. You won the Civil War by the sacrifice of human life when you decided to emancipate the negro. You have left it to the women in your land, the men of all civilized countries have left it to women, the work out their own salvation. That is the way in which we women of England are doing. Human life for us is sacred, but we say if any life is to be sacrificed it shall be ours; we won't do it ourselves, but we will put the enemy in the position where they will have to choose between giving us freedom or giving us death.

Sources: Jennifer A. Hurley, ed., *Women's Rights: Great Speeches in History* (San Diego: Greenhaven Press, Inc., 2002), pp. 96-100.

26.4

✤

THE JEWISH QUESTION AND ZIONISM, THEODORE HERZL

The Zionist movement is a combination of liberal ideas (the right of every individual Jew to personal liberty and religious toleration), nationalism (the creation of a nation-state for Jews as a people), and a progressive movement (it was modeled on the democratic reform movements, such as those that enfranchised all male citizens in Britain and Prussia). The founder of the World Zionist Organization was Theodore Herzl (1860-1904), an Austrian Jew who recognized a tragic reality in the Age of Progress: anti-Semitism was on the rise and Jews were no longer safe anywhere in Europe. In 1896 he published a pamphlet on the Jewish State.

✤

QUESTIONS

1. Does Herzl seriously consider putting a Jewish state in Argentine rather than Palestine?
2. Compare this text to the speech by Emmeline Pankhurst. What is dangerous about taking such extreme positions as militancy and self-exile to ensure personal liberty?
3. From this selection, can you tell if Herzl was an observant or secular Jew? Does it matter?

II. — The Jewish Question

No one can deny the gravity of the situation of the Jews. Wherever they live in perceptible numbers, they are more or less persecuted. Their equality before the law, granted by statute, has become practically a dead letter. They are debarred from filling even moderately high positions, either in the army, or in any public or private capacity. And attempts are made to thrust them out of business also: "Don't buy from Jews!"

Attacks in Parliaments, in assemblies, in the press, in the pulpit, in the street, on journeys — for example, their exclusion from certain hotels — even in places of recreation, become daily more numerous. The forms of persecution varying according to the countries and social circles in which they occur. In Russia, imposts are levied on Jewish villages; in Rumania, a few persons are put to death; in Germany, they get a good beating occasionally; in Austria, Anti-Semites exercise terrorism over all public life; in Algeria, there are traveling agitators; in Paris, the Jews are shut out of the so-called best social circles and excluded from clubs. Shades of anti-Jewish feeling are innumerable. But this is not to be an attempt to make out a doleful category of Jewish hardships.

I do not intend to arouse sympathetic emotions on our behalf. That would be foolish, futile, and undignified proceeding. I shall content myself with putting the following questions to the Jews: Is it not true that, in countries where we live in perceptible numbers, the position of Jewish lawyers, doctors, technicians, teachers, and employees of all descriptions becomes daily more intolerable? Is it not true, that the Jewish middle classes are seriously threatened? Is it not true, that the passions of the mob are incited against our wealthy people? Is it not true, that our poor endure greater sufferings than any other proletariat? I think that this external pressure makes itself felt everywhere. In our economically upper classes it causes discomfort, in our middle classes continual and grave anxieties, in our lower classes absolute despair.

Everything tends, in fact, to one and the same conclusion, which is clearly enunciated in that classic Berlin phrase: *"Juden Raus!"* (Out with the Jews!)

I shall now put the Question in the briefest possible form: Are we to "get out" now and where to? Or, may we yet remain? And, how long?...

PREVIOUS ATTEMPTS AT A SOLUTION

The artificial means heretofore employed to overcome the troubles of Jews have been either too petty — such as attempts at colonization — or attempts to convert the Jews into peasants in their present homes. What is achieved by transporting a few thousand Jews to another country? Either they come to grief at once, or prosper, and then their prosperity creates Anti-Semitism. We have already discussed these attempts to divert poor Jews to fresh districts. This diversion is clearly inadequate and futile, if it does not actually defeat its own ends; for it merely protracts and postpones a solution, and perhaps even aggravates difficulties....

EFFECTS OF ANTI-SEMITISM

The oppression we endure does not improve us, for we are not a whit better than ordinary people. It is true that we do not love our enemies; but he alone who can conquer himself dare reproach us with that fault. Oppression naturally creates hostility against oppressors, and our hostility aggravates the pressure. It is impossible to escape from this eternal circle....

I referred previously to our "assimilation". I do not for a moment wish to imply that I desire such an end. Our national character is too historically famous, and, in spite of every degradation, too fine to make its annihilation desirable. We might perhaps be able to merge ourselves entirely into surrounding races, if these were to leave us in peace for a period of two generations. But they will not leave us in peace. For a little period they manage to tolerate us, and then their hostility breaks out again and again. The world is provoked somehow by our prosperity, because it has for many centuries been accustomed to consider us as the most contemptible among the poverty-stricken. In its ignorance and narrowness of heart, it fails to observe that prosperity weakens our Judaism and extinguishes our peculiarities. It is only pressure that forces us back to the parent stem; it is only hatred encompassing us that makes us strangers once more. Thus, whether we like it or not, we are now, and shall henceforth remain, a historic group with unmistakable characteristics common to us all.

We are one people — our enemies have made us one without our consent, as repeatedly happens in history. Distress binds us together, and, thus united, we suddenly discover our strength. Yes, we are strong enough to form a State, and, indeed, a model State. We possess all human and material resources necessary for the purpose....

THE PLAN

The whole plan is in its essence perfectly simple, as it must necessarily be if it is to come within the comprehension of all.

Let the sovereignty be granted us over a portion of the globe large enough to satisfy the rightful requirements of a nation; the rest we shall manage for ourselves.

The creation of a new State is neither ridiculous nor impossible. We have in our day witnessed the process in connection with nations which were not largely members of the middle class, but poorer, less educated, and consequently weaker than ourselves. The Governments of all countries scourged by Anti-Semitism will be keenly interested in assisting us to obtain the sovereignty we want.

The plan, simple in design, but complicated in execution, will be carried out by two agencies: The Society of Jews and the Jewish Company.

The Society of Jews will do the preparatory work in the domains of science and politics, which the Jewish Company will afterwards apply practically.

The Jewish Company will be the liquidating agent of the business interests of departing Jews, and will organize commerce and trade in the new country.

We must not imagine the departure of the Jews to be a sudden one. It will be gradual, continuous, and will cover many decades. The poorest will go first to cultivate the soil. In accordance with a preconceived plan, they will construct roads, bridges, railways and telegraph installations; regulate rivers; and build their own dwellings; their labor will create trade, trade will create markets and markets will attract new settlers, for every man will go voluntarily, at his own expense and his own risk. The labor expended on the land will enhance its value, and the Jews will soon perceive that a new and permanent sphere of operation is opening here for that spirit of enterprise which has heretofore met only with hatred and obloquy....

The emigrants standing lowest in the economic scale will be slowly followed by those of a higher grade. Those who at this moment are living in despair will go first. They will be led by the mediocre intellects which we produce so superabundantly and which are persecuted everywhere.

This pamphlet will open a general discussion on the Jewish Question, but that does not mean that there will be any voting on it. Such a result would ruin the cause from the outset, and dissidents must remember that allegiance or opposition is entirely voluntary. He who will not come with us should remain behind.

Let all who are willing to join us, fall in behind our banner and fight for our cause with voice and pen and deed....

PALESTINE OR ARGENTINE?

Shall we choose Palestine or Argentine? We shall take what is given us, and what is selected by Jewish public opinion. The Society will determine both these points.

Argentine is one of the most fertile countries in the world, extends over a vast area, has a sparse population and a mild climate. The Argentine Republic would derive considerable profit from the cession of a portion of its territory to us. The present infiltration of Jews has certainly produced some discontent, and it would be necessary to enlighten the Republic on the intrinsic difference of our new movement.

Palestine is our ever-memorable historic home. The very name of Palestine would attract our people with a force of marvelous potency. If His Majesty the Sultan were to give us Palestine, we could in return undertake to regulate the whole finances of Turkey. We should there form a portion of a rampart of Europe against Asia, an outpost of civilization as opposed to barbarism. We should as a neutral State remain in contact with all Europe, which would have to guarantee our existence. The sanctuaries of Christendom would be safeguarded by assigning to them an extra-territorial status such as is well-known to the law of nations. We should form a guard of honor about these sanctuaries, answering for the fulfillment of this duty with our existence. This guard of honor would be the great symbol of the solution of the Jewish question after eighteen centuries of Jewish suffering.

Sources: Theodore Herzl, *The Jewish State* (New York: American Zionists Emergency Council, 1946), pp. 85-96.

--- ✢ ---

QUESTIONS FOR PART 26

1. From just the sources you read, what "progress" or improvement was actually achieved and for whom?
2. Why were middle-class women so active in political movements? Is there precedent for their behavior?
3. What role does economics play in the possibility of having progressive reforms?

PART 27

WESTERN ANXIETY

Just as Europe reached its peak of confidence in the Age of Progress, a few men near the end of the nineteenth century introduced the Western collective psyche to new philosophical insecurities. Charles Darwin, Sigmund Freud, and Friedrich Nietzsche worked in very different disciplines, yet contributed to the same general ethos of uncertainty. Most Europeans continued to think in terms of progress, but a few began to question the potential of human beings to truly improve. All three of these men questioned the singularity of the human creation; each of the three was at some point in his career accused of rejecting the idea of creation altogether, and although European culture was more secular than ever, it was also by and large not ready to take the final step away from faith.

At the same time these three men worked out their unsettling ideas, Pope Pius IX was attempted to hold off change. He systematically rejected modern philosophies and ideas in the *Syllabus of Errors* in 1864, which is the last source in this chapter.

27.1

NATURAL SELECTION, T. H. HUXLEY

The contribution of Charles Darwin (1809-1882) to Western thought is well known and need not be recounted in detail here. The response to Darwin's basic theory of evolution as a continual process of competition and change was as fascinating as the theory itself. Darwin was well aware that his ideas were going to be controversial, which is why he delayed the publication of his groundbreaking The Origin of Species *until 1859. He only published it then because another theorist (Alfred Russell Wallace) had also reached the same conclusions about evolution as he. Thus Darwin was not alone in thinking of an evolutionary model, which reveals the complexity of the nineteenth-century intellectual community. For everyone who rejected evolution out of hand, there was an equal number of persons who recognized the value of his idea. Darwin was controversial but he was not entirely unwelcome.*

However, by 1859 Darwin was also old, far too weak to travel around defending his theories. Instead, Darwin stayed at home and worked on his even more contentious work, The Descent of Man *(1871). Darwin found an able champion in one of his early supporters, a biologist named T. H. Huxley (1825-1895). He publicly debated Darwin's theory at scientific meetings across England, and earned the nickname "Darwin's Bulldog" for his tenacity.*

QUESTIONS

1. Why is it significant that Darwin's theory of natural selection is "simple and comprehensible?"
2. Why do you think that Huxley's discussion of the "struggle for existence" was so unsettling for his audience?
3. Does Huxley seem to believe in a divine cause (i.e., God) at work in nature?

SELECTION UNDER DOMESTICATION; NATURAL SELECTION

The Baker Street Bazaar has just been exhibiting its familiar annual spectacle. Straight-backed, small-headed, big-barrelled oxen, as dissimilar from any wild species as can well be imagined, contended for attention and praise with sheep of half-a-dozen different breeds and styles of bloated preposterous pigs, no more like a wild boar or sow than a city alderman is like an ourangoutang. The cattle show has been, and perhaps may again be, succeeded by a poultry show, of whose crowing and clucking prodigies it can only be certainly predicated that they will be very unlike the aboriginal *Phasianus gallus*. If the seeker after animal anomalies is not satisfied, a turn or two in Seven Dials will convince him that the breeds of pigeons are quite as extraordinary and unlike one another and their parent stock, while the Horticultural Society will provide him with any number of corresponding vegetable aberrations from nature's types...

On careful inquiry it is found that all these, and the many other artificial breeds or races of animals and plants, have been produced by one method. The breeder — and a skilful one must be a person of much sagacity and natural or acquired perceptive faculty — notes some slight difference, arising he knows not how, in some individuals of his stock. If he wish to perpetuate the difference, to form a breed with the peculiarity in question strongly marked, he selects such male and female individuals as exhibit the desired character, and breeds from them. Their offspring are then carefully examined, and those which exhibit the peculiarity the most distinctly are selected for breeding; and this operation is repeated until the desired amount of divergence from the primitive stock is reached. It is then found that by continuing the process of selection — always breeding, that is, from well-marked forms, and allowing no impure crosses to interfere — a race may be formed, the tendency of which to reproduce itself is exceedingly strong; nor is the limit to the amount of divergence which may be thus produced known; but one thing is certain, that, if certain breeds of dogs, or of pigeons, or of horses, were known only in a fossil state, no naturalist would hesitate in regarding them as distinct species.

But in all these cases we have human interference. Without the breeder there would be no selection, and without the selection no race. Before admitting the possibility of natural species having originated in any similar way, it must be proved that there is in Nature some power which takes the place of man, and performs a selection *sua sponte*. It is the claim of Mr Darwin that he professes to have discovered the existence and the *modus operandi*, of this 'natural selection', as he terms it; and, if he be right, the process is perfectly simple and comprehensible, and irresistibly deducible from very familiar but well nigh forgotten facts.

Who, for instance, has duly reflected upon all the consequences of the marvelous struggle for existence which is daily and hourly going on among living beings? Not only does every animal live at the expense of some other animal or plant, but the very plants are at war. The ground is full of seeds that cannot rise into seedlings; the seedlings rob one another of air, light and water, the strongest robber winning the day, and extinguishing his competitors. Year after year, the wild animals with which man never interferes are, on the average, neither more nor less numerous than they were; and yet we know that the annual produce of every pair is from one to perhaps a million young; so that it is mathematically certain that, on the average, as many are killed by natural causes as are born every year, and those only escape which happen to be a little better fitted to resist destruction than those which die. The individuals of a species are like the crew of a foundered ship, and none but good swimmers have a chance of reaching the land.

Such being unquestionably the necessary conditions under which living creatures exist, Mr Darwin discovers in them the instrument of natural selection. Suppose that in the midst of this incessant competition some individuals of a species (A) present accidental variations which happen to fit them a little better than their fellows for the struggle in which they are engaged, then the chances are in favour, not only of these individuals being better nourished than the others, but of their predominating over their fellows in other ways, and of having a better chance of leaving offspring, which will of course tend to reproduce the peculiarities of their parents. Their offspring will, by a parity of reasoning, tend to predominate over their contemporaries, and there being (suppose) no room for more than one species such as A, the weaker variety will eventually be destroyed by the new destructive influence which is thrown into the scale, and the stronger will take its place. Surrounding conditions remaining unchanged, the new variety (which we may call B) — supposed, for argument's sake, to be the best adapted for these conditions which can be got out of the original stock — will remain unchanged, all accidental deviations from the type becoming at once extinguished, as less fit for their post than B itself. The tendency of B to persist will grow with its persistence through successive generations, and it will acquire all the characters of a new species.

But, on the other hand, if the conditions of life change in any degree, however slight, B may no longer be that form which is best adapted to withstand their destructive, and profit by their sustaining, influence; in which case if it should give rise to a more competent variety (C), this will take its place and become a new species; and thus, by natural selection, the species B and C will be successively derived from A.

That this most ingenious hypothesis enables us to give a reason for many apparent anomalies in the distribution of living beings in time and space, and that it is not contradicted by the main phenomena of life and organization appear to us to be unquestionable; and, so far, it must be admitted to have an immense advantage over any of its predecessors. But it is quite another matter to affirm absolutely either the truth or falsehood of Mr Darwin's views at the present stage of the inquiry. Goethe has an excellent aphorism defining that state of mind which he calls 'Thätige Skepsis' — active doubt. It is doubt which so loves truth that it neither dares rest in doubting nor extinguish itself by unjustified belief; and we commend this state of mind to students of species, with respect to Mr Darwin's or any other hypothesis, as to their origin. The combined investigations of another twenty years may, perhaps, enable naturalists to say whether the modifying causes and the selective power, which Mr Darwin has satisfactorily shown to exist in Nature, are competent to produce al the effects he ascribes to them; or whether, on the other hand, he has been led to over-estimate the value of the principle of natural selection, as greatly as Lamarck over-estimated his *vera causa* of modification by exercise.

But there is, at all events, one advantage possessed by the more recent writer over his predecessor. Mr Darwin abhors mere speculation as nature abhors a vacuum. He is as greedy of cases and precedents as any constitutional lawyer, and all the principles he lays down are capable of being brought to the test of observation and experiment. The path he bids us follow professes to be, not a mere airy track, fabricated of ideal cobwebs, but a solid and broad bridge of facts. If it be so, it will carry us safely over many a chasm in our knowledge, and lead us to a region free from the snares of those fascinating but barren virgins, the Final Causes, against whom a high authority has so justly warned us. 'My sons, dig in the vineyard,' were the last words of the old man in the fable: and, though the sons found no treasure, they made their fortunes by the grapes.

(The Darwinian Hypothesis, 1859)

Source: T. H. Huxley, *The Essence of T. H. Huxley*, ed. Cyril Bibby (New York: St. Martin's Press, 1967) pp. 165-168.

27.2

---- ✤ ----

"A DREAM IS A FULFILLMENT OF A WISH," SIGMUND FREUD

Sigmund Freud (1856-1939) addressed the issues of human behavior and motivation, and created the modern science of psychology. His principle contribution to Western thought in general and to the anxiety of the late nineteenth century in particular was the theory of the unconscious. It is an understanding of behavior that goes beyond the act itself to the impulse that caused it, which is often hidden and seems unrelated to the act itself. Freud's theories were also disturbing because he believed that most actions relate in some way to sexuality, often to the conflict between social repressions and sexual drives, particularly as children. The unconscious is shaped by this conflict and behavior is only an outward external expression of these internal conflicts. Even though many of his particular theories have been rejected, his overall understanding of behavior and motivation is still widely accepted. This was not always so; the very idea that children had sexuality offended many of Freud's contemporaries, just as Darwin's suggestion that man and animal were one and the same offended them.

The Interpretation of Dreams was Freud's first published work (1900); this selection deals with the concept of wish fulfillment.

---- ✤ ----

QUESTIONS

1. What do Freud and Darwin's theories have in common?
2. One area in which Freud is still controversial today is in his theories about women. How does he characterize women in this selection?
3. Before Freud, what did people think dreams were?

I t is easy to prove that dreams often reveal themselves without any disguise as fulfilments of wishes; so that it may seem surprising that the language of dreams was not understood long ago. For instance, there is a dream that I can produce in myself as often as I like — experimentally, as it were. If I eat anchovies or olives or any other highly salted food in the evening, I develop thirst during the night which wakes me up. But my waking is preceded by a dream; and this always has the same content, namely, that I am drinking. I dream I am swallowing down water in great gulps, and it has the delicious taste that nothing can equal but a cool drink when one is parched with thirst. Then I wake up and have to have a real drink. This simple dream is occasioned by the thirst which I become aware of when I wake. The thirst gives rise to a wish to drink, and the dream shows me that wish fulfilled. In doing so it is performing a function — which it was easy to divine. I am a good sleeper and not accustomed to be woken by any physical need. If I can succeed in appeasing my thirst by *dreaming* that I am drinking, then I need not wake up in order to quench it. This, then, is a dream of convenience. Dreaming has taken the place of action, as it often does elsewhere in life. Unluckily my need for water to quench my thirst cannot be satisfied by a dream in the same way as my thirst for revenge against my friend Otto and Dr. M.; but the good intention is there in both cases. Not long ago this same dream of mine showed some modification. I had felt thirsty even before I fell asleep, and I had emptied a glass of water that stood on the table beside my bed. A few hours later during the night I had a fresh attack of thirst, and this had inconvenient results. In order to provide myself with some water I should have had to get up and fetch the glass standing on the table by my wife's bed. I therefore had an appropriate dream that my wife was giving me a drink out of a vase; this vase was an Etruscan cinerary urn which I had brought back from a journey to Italy and had since given away. But the water in it tasted so salty (evidently because of the ashes in the urn) that I woke up. It will be noticed how conveniently everything was arranged in this dream. Since its only purpose was to fulfil a wish, it could be completely egoistical. A love of comfort and convenience is not really compatible with consideration for other people. The introduction of the cinerary urn was probably yet another wish-fulfilment. I was sorry that the vase was no longer in my possession — just as the glass of water on my wife's table was out of my reach. The urn with its ashes fitted in, too, with the salty taste in my mouth which had now grown stronger and which I knew was bound to wake me....

Here is another dream in which once again the stimulus produced its effect during actual sleep. One of my women patients, who had been obliged to undergo an operation on her jaw which had taken an unfavourable course, was ordered by her doctors to wear a cooling apparatus on the side of her face day and night. But as soon as she fell asleep she used to throw it off. One day, after she had once more thrown the apparatus on the floor, I was asked to speak to her seriously about it. 'This time I really couldn't help it,' she answered. 'It was because of a dream I had in the night. I dreamt I was in a box at the opera and very much enjoying the performance. But Herr Karl Meyer was in the nursing-home and complaining bitterly of pains in his jaw. So I told myself that as I hadn't any pain I didn't need the apparatus; and I threw it away.' The dream of this poor sufferer seems almost like a concrete representati0n of a phrase that sometimes forces its way on to people's lips in unpleasant situations: 'I must say I could think of something more agreeable than this.' The dream gives a picture of this more agreeable thing. The Herr Karl Meyer on to whom the dreamer transplanted her pains was the most indifferent young man of her acquaintance that she could call to mind.

The wish-fulfilment can be detected equally easily in some other dreams which I have collected from normal people. A friend of mine, who knows my theory of dreams and has told his wife of it, said to me one day: 'My wife has asked me to tell you that she had a dream yesterday that she was having her period. You can guess what that means.' I could indeed guess it. The fact that this young married woman dreamt that she was having her period meant that she had missed her period. I could well believe that she would have been glad to go on enjoying her freedom a little longer before shouldering the burden of motherhood. It was a neat way of announcing her first pregnancy. Another friend of mine wrote and told me that, not long before, his wife had dreamt that she had noticed some milk stains on the front of her vest. This too was an announcement of pregnancy, but not of a first one. The young mother was wishing that she might have more nourishment to give her second child than she had had for her first....

These examples will perhaps be enough to show that dreams which can only be understood as fulfilments of wishes and which bear their meaning upon their faces without disguise are to be found under the most frequent and various conditions. They are mostly short and simple dreams, which afford a pleasant contrast to the confused and exuberant compositions that have in the main attracted the attention of the authorities. Nevertheless, it will repay us to pause for a moment over these simple dreams. We may expect to find the very simplest forms of dreams in *children*, since there can be no doubt that their psychical productions are less complicated than those of adults. Child psychology, in my opinion, is destined to perform the same useful services for adult psychology that the investigation of the structure or development of the lower animals has performed for research into the structure of the higher classes of animals. Few deliberate efforts have hitherto been made to make use of child psychology for this purpose.

The dreams of young children are frequently pure wish-fulfilments and are in that case quite uninteresting compared with the dreams of adults. They raise not problems for solution; but on the other hand they are of inestimable importance in proving that, in their essential nature, dreams represent fulfilments of wishes. I have been able to collect a few instances of such dreams from material provided by my own children.

I have to thank an excursion which we made to the lovely village of Hallstatt in the summer of 1896 for two dreams: one of these was dreamt by my daughter, who was then eight and a half, and the other by her brother of five and a quarter. I must explain by way of preamble that we had been spending the summer on a hillside near Aussee, from which, in fine weather, we enjoyed a splendid view of the Dachstein. The Simony Hütte could be clearly distinguished through a telescope. The children made repeated attempts at seeing it through the telescope — I cannot say with what success. Before our excursion I had told the children that Hallstatt lay at the foot of the Dachstein. They very much looked forward to the day. From Hallstatt we walked up the Echerntal, which delighted the children with its succession of changing landscapes. One of them, however, the five-year-old boy, gradually became fretful. Each time a new mountain came into view he asked if that was the Dachstein and I had to say, 'No, only one of the foothills.' After he had asked the question several times, he fell completely silent; and he refused point-blank to come with us up the steep path to the waterfall. I thought he was tired. But next morning he came to me with a radiant face and said: 'Last night I dreamt we were at Simony Hütte.' I understood him then. When I had spoken about the Dachstein, he had expected to climb the mountain in the course of our excursion to Hallstatt and to find himself at close quarters with the hut which there had been so much talk about in connection with the telescope. But when he found that he was being fobbed off with foothills and a waterfall, he felt disappointed and out of spirits. The dream was a compensation. I tried to discover its details, but they were scanty: 'You have to climb up steps for six hours' — which was what he had been told....

A friend of mine has reported a dream to me which was very much like my son's. The dreamer was an eight-year-old girl. Her father had started off with several children on a walk to Dornbach, with the idea of visiting the Rohrer Hütte. As it was getting late, however, he had turned back, promising the children to make up for the disappointment another time. On their way home they had passed the signpost that marks the path up to the Hameau. The children had then asked to be taken up to the Hameau; but once again for the same reason they had to be consoled with the promise of another day. Next morning the eight-year-old girl came to her father and said in satisfied tones: 'Daddy, I dreamt last night that you went with us to the Rohrer Hütte and the Hameau.' In her impatience she has anticipated the fulfilment of her father's promises.

Here is an equally straightforward dream, provoked by the beauty of the scenery at Aussee in another of my daughters, who was at that time three and a quarter. She had crossed the lake for the first time, and the crossing had been to short for her: when we reached the landing-stage she had not wanted to leave the boat and had wept bitterly. Next morning she said: 'Last night I went on the lake.' Let us hope that her dram-crossing had been of a more satisfying length.

My eldest boy, then eight years old, already had dreams of his phantasies coming true: he dreamt that he was driving in a chariot with Achilles and that Diomede was the charioteer. As may be guessed, he had been excited the day before by a book on the legends of Greece which had been given to his elder sister.

If I may include words spoken by children in their sleep under the heading of dreams, I can at this point quote one of the most youthful drams in my whole collection. My youngest daughter, then nineteen months old, had had an attack of vomiting one morning and consequently been kept without food all day. During the night after this day of starvation she was heard calling out excitedly in her sleep: 'Anna Fweud, stwawbewwies, wild stwawbewwies, omblet, pudden!' At that time she was in the habit of using her own name to express the idea of taking possession of something. The menu included pretty well everything that must have seemed to her to make up a desirable meal. The fact that strawberries appeared in it in two varieties was a demonstration against the domestic health regulations. It was based upon the circumstance, which she had no doubt observed, that her nurse had attributed her indisposition to a surfeit of strawberries. She was thus retaliating in her dream against this unwelcome verdict.

Source: Sigmund Freud, *The Interpretation of Dreams*, trans. James Strachey (New York: Avon Books, 1965), pp. 155-167.

27.3

The Antichrist, Friedrich Nietzsche

Friedrich Nietzsche (1844-1900) was and is much misunderstood in the twentieth and the twentieth-first century. He was idealized (and misquoted) by Hitler and the Nazi propaganda machine, which will use Nietzsche's idea of an ubermensch *or "superman" to defend the destruction of lesser races (such as the Jews and Slavs) and the rise of the pure, Aryan race. In reality, Nietzsche was not really important for what he said as much as what he questioned. He drew into question everything accepted and assumed certain by the traditional, middle class, European culture of his day. He questioned democratic systems, nationalism, Christianity, rationalism, morality, science, etc. For Nietzsche all of these only limited human intellect, making one weak, excessively humble and meek. Instead, he praised a return to classical Greek heroic values; striving for personal glory rather than submitting to the democratic or nationalistic principle. Nietzsche is the glorification of the individual.*

QUESTIONS

1. How does Nietzsche challenge the Newtonian view of a mechanical universe?
2. In reference to God and faith, would you describe Nietzsche as a skeptic, atheist, or agnostic?
3. Why does Nietzsche blame Christianity most for what he sees as the weakness of Europe?

What is god? Everything that heightens the feeling of power in a man, the will to power, power itself.

What is bad? Everything that is born of weakness.

What is happiness? The feeling that power is *growing*, that resistance is overcome.

Not contentedness but more power; not peace but war; not virtue but fitness (Renaissance virtue, *virtù*, virtue that is moraline-free).

The weak and the failures shall perish: first principle of *our* love of man. And they shall even be given every possible assistance.

What is more harmful than any vice? Active pity for all the failures and all the weak: Christianity....

Mankind does *not* represent a development toward something better or stronger or higher in the sense accepted today. "Progress" is merely a modern idea, that is, a false idea. The European of today is vastly inferior in value to the European of the Renaissance: further development is altogether *not* according to any necessity in the direction of elevation, enhancement, or strength.

In another sense, success in individual cases is constantly encountered in the most widely different places and cultures: here we really do find a *higher type*, which is, in relation to mankind as a whole, a kind of overman. Such fortunate accidents of great success have always been possible and will perhaps always be possible. And even whole families, tribes, or peoples may occasionally represent such a *bull's eye*....

Whatever a theologian feels to be true *must* be false: this is almost a criterion of truth. His most basic instinct of self-preservation forbids him to respect reality at any point or even to let it get a word in. Wherever the theologians' instinct extends, *value judgments* have been stood on their heads and the concepts of "true" and "false" are of necessity reversed: whatever is most harmful to life is called "true"; whatever elevates it, enhances, affirms, justifies it, and makes it triumphant, is called "false." When theologians reach out for *power* through the "conscience" of princes (*or* of peoples), we need never doubt what really happens at bottom: the will to the end, the nihilistic will, wants power....

Let us not underestimate this: *we ourselves*, we free spirits, are nothing less than "revaluation of all values," an *incarnate* declaration of "true" and "untrue." The most valuable insights are discovered last; but the most valuable insights are the *methods*. All the methods, *all* the presuppositions of our current scientific outlook, were opposed for thousands of years with the most profound contempt. For their sake, men were excluded from the company of "decent" people and considered "enemies of God," despisers of the truth, and "possessed." Anyone with a scientific bent was a Chandala.

We have had the whole pathos of mankind against us — their conception of what truth *ought* to be: every "thou shalt" has hitherto been aimed against us. Our objectives, our practice, our quiet, cautious, mistrustful manner — all these were considered utterly unworthy and contemptible.

In the end one might well ask whether it was not really an *aesthetic* taste that kept mankind in blindness for so long: a picturesque effect was demanded of the truth, and the lover of knowledge was expected to make a strong impression on the senses. Our *modesty* offended men's taste longest of all. How well they divined that, these turkeycocks of God!...

In Christianity neither morality nor religion has even a single point of contact with reality. Nothing but imaginary *causes* ("God," "soul," "ego," "spirit," "free will" — for that matter, "unfree will"), nothing but imaginary *effects* ("sin," "redemption," "grace," "punishment," "forgiveness of sins"). Intercourse between imaginary *beings* ("God," "spirits," "souls"); an imaginary *natural* science (anthropocentric, no trace of any concept of natural causes); an imaginary *psychology* (nothing but self-misunderstandings, interpretations of agreeable or disagreeable general feelings — for example, of the states of the *nervus sympathicus* — with the aid of the sign language of the religio-moral idiosyncrasy: "repentance," "pangs of conscience," "temptation by the devil," "the presence of God"); an imaginary *teleology* ("the kingdom of God," "the Last Judgment," "eternal life").

This *world of pure fiction* is vastly inferior to the world of dreams insofar as the latter *mirrors* reality, whereas the former falsifies, devalues, and negates reality. Once the concept of "nature" had been invented as the opposite of "God," "natural" had become a synonym of "reprehensible": this whole world of fiction is rooted in *hatred* of the natural (of reality!); it is the expression of a profound vexation at the sight of reality.

But this explains everything. Who alone has good reason to lie his way out of reality? He who suffers from it. But to suffer from reality is to be a piece of reality that has come to grief. The preponderance of feelings of displeasure over feelings of pleasure is the cause of this fictitious morality and religion; but such a preponderance provides the very formula for decadence.

A critique of the *Christian conception of God* forces us to the same conclusion. A people that still believes in itself retains its own god. In him it reveres the conditions which let it prevail, its virtues: it projects its pleasure in itself, its feeling of power, into a being to whom one may offer thanks. Whoever is rich wants to give of his riches; a proud people needs a god: it wants to *sacrifice*. Under such conditions, religion is a form of thankfulness. Being thankful for himself, man needs a god. Such a god must be able to help and to harm, to be friend and enemy — he is admired whether good or destructive. The *anti-natural* castration of a god, to make him a god of the good alone, would here be contrary to everything desirable. The evil god is needed no less than the good god: after all, we do not owe our own existence to tolerance and humanitarianism.

What would be the point of a god who knew nothing of wrath, revenge, envy, scorn, cunning, and violence? who had perhaps never experienced the delightful *ardeurs* of victory and annihilation? No one would understand such a god: why have him then?

To be sure, when a people is perishing, when it feels how its faith in the future and its hope of freedom are waning irrevocably, when submission begins to appear to it as the prime necessity and it becomes aware of the virtues of the subjugated as the conditions of self-preservation, then its god *has to* change too. Now he becomes a sneak, timid and modest; he counsels "peace of soul," hate-no-more, forbearance, even "love" of friend and enemy. He moralizes constantly, he crawls into the cave of every private virtue, he becomes god for everyman, he becomes a private person, a cosmopolitan.

Formerly, he represented a people, the strength of a people, everything aggressive and power-thirsty in the soul of a people; now he is merely the good god.

Indeed, there is no other alternative for gods: *either* they are the will to power, and they remain a people's gods, *or* the incapacity for power, and then they necessarily become *good*.

Source: Friedrich Nietzsche, *The Portable Nietzsche*, trans. Walter Kaufmann (New York: Penguin Books, 1954, 1982), pp. 570-71, 576-585.

27.4

✢

SYLLABUS OF ERRORS, POPE PIUS IX

Cardinal Giovanni Maria Mastai-Ferretti became Pope Pius IX in 1846. He began his pontificate as a moderate willing to try liberal reforms, but after the revolution of 1848 (during which Pius was forced to flee Rome for two years of exile), he became increasingly conservative. In fact, he was so conservative as to be a vocal reactionary. He preached against nationalism, liberalism, and progress, and when Italy was unified in 1871 he refused to recognize the new king Victor Emmanuel II. During the same period, Pius re-energized the Catholic Church by increasing missionary activities, founding religious houses and restoring bishoprics in Britain and the Netherlands. He issued the Syllabus of Errors *in 1864, a condemnation of modern scientific and philosophical theories, and religious propositions. He also convened the first Vatican Council and had the doctrines of the Immaculate Conception and Papal Infallibility proclaimed. Pius ensured that the papacy would survive any of the rapidly changing ideologies of the modern era, yet in such a way that he antagonized both Catholics and Protestants in the West.*

✢

QUESTIONS

1. In the *Encyclical*, Pius speaks of the "greatest loss of soul." How does he equate that to the new ideas of the nineteenth century?
2. Why does Pius single out socialism and communism for particular condemnation?
3. Is Pius opposed to all education?

QUANTA CURA
Encyclical of Pope Pius IX Condemning Current Errors
December 8, 1864
63

To Our Venerable Brethren, all Patriarchs, Primates, Archbishops, and Bishops having favor and Communion of the Holy See.
    Venerable Brethren, Health and Apostolic Benediction.

With how great care and pastoral vigilance the Roman Pontiffs, our predecessors, fulfilling the duty and office committed to them by the Lord Christ Himself in the person of most Blessed Peter, Prince of the Apostles, of feeding the lambs and the sheep, have never ceased sedulously to nourish the Lord's whole flock with words of faith and with salutary doctrine, and to guard it from poisoned pastures, is thoroughly known to all, and especially to you, Venerable Brethren. And truly the same, Our Predecessors, asserters of justice, being especially anxious for the salvation of souls, had nothing ever more at heart than by their most wise Letters and Constitutions to unveil and condemn all those heresies and errors which, being adverse to our Divine Faith, to the doctrine of the Catholic Church, to purity of morals, and to the eternal salvation of men, have frequently excited violent tempests, and have miserably afflicted both Church and State. For which cause the same Our Predecessors, have, with Apostolic fortitude, constantly resisted the nefarious enterprises of wicked men, who, like raging waves of the sea foaming out their own confusion, and promising liberty whereas they are the slaves of corruption, have striven by their deceptive opinions and most pernicious writings to raze the foundations of the Catholic religion and of civil society, to remove from among men all virtue and justice, to deprave persons, and especially inexperienced youth, to lead it into the snares of error, and at length to tear it from the bosom of the Catholic Church....

3. But, although we have not omitted often to proscribe and reprobate the chief errors as from a fountain. Which false and perverse opinions are on that ground the more to be detested, because they chiefly tend to this, that that salutary influence be impeded and (even) removed, which the Catholic Church, according to the institution and command of her Divine Author, should freely exercise even to the end of the world — not only over private individuals, but over nations, peoples, and their sovereign princes; and (tend also) to take away that mutual fellowship and concord of counsels between Church and State which has ever proved itself propitious and salutary, both for religious and civil interests. For you well know, venerable brethren, that at this time men are found not a few who, applying to civil society the impious and absurd principle of *naturalism*, as they call it, dare to teach that "the best constitution of public society and (also) civil progress altogether require that human society be conducted and governed without regard being had to religion any more than if it did not exist; or, at least, without any distinction being made between the true religion and false ones." And, against the doctrine of Scripture, of the Church, and of the Holy Fathers, they do not hesitate to assert that "that is the best condition of civil society, in which no duty is recognized, as attached to the civil power, of restraining by enacted penalties, offenders against the Catholic religion, except so far as public peace may require." From which totally false idea of social government they do not fear to foster that erroneous opinion, most fatal in its effects on the Catholic Church and the salvation of souls, called by Our Predecessor, Gregory XVI, *an insanity*, viz., that "liberty of conscience and worship is each man's personal right, which ought to be legally proclaimed and asserted in every rightly constituted society; and that a right resides in the citizens to an absolute liberty, which should be restrained by no authority whether ecclesiastical or civil, whereby they may be able openly and publicly to manifest and declare any of their ideas whatever, either by word of mouth, by the press, or in any other way." But, while they rashly affirm this, they do not think and consider that they are preaching *liberty of perdition*; and that "if human arguments are always allowed free room for discussion, there will never be wanting men who will dare to resist truth, and to trust in the flowing speech of human wisdom; whereas we know, from the very teaching of our Lord Jesus Christ, how carefully Christian faith and wisdom should avoid this most injurious babbling."

4. And, since where religion has been removed from civil society, and the doctrine and authority of divine revelation repudiated, the genuine notion itself of justice and human right is darkened and lost, and the place of true justice and legitimate right is supplied by material force, thence it appears why it is

that some, utterly neglecting and disregarding the surest principles of sound reason, dare to proclaim that "the people's will, manifested by what is called public opinion or in some other way, constitutes a supreme law, free from all divine and human control; and that in the political order accomplished facts, from the very circumstance that they are accomplished, have the force of right." But who does not see and clearly perceive that human society, when set loose from the bonds of religion and true justice, can have, in truth, no other end than the purpose of obtaining and amassing wealth, and that (society under such circumstances) follows no other law in its actions, except the unchastened desire of ministering to its own pleasure and interests? For this reason, men of the kind pursue with bitter hatred the Religious Orders, although these have deserved extremely well of Christendom, civilization and literature, and cry out that the same have no legitimate reason for being permitted to exist; and thus (these evil men) applaud the calumnies of heretics. For, as Pius VI, Our Predecessor, taught most wisely, "the abolition of regulars is injurious to that state in which the Evangelical counsels are openly professed; it is injurious to a method of life praised in the Church as agreeable to Apostolic doctrine; it is injurious to the illustrious founders, themselves, whom we venerate on our altars, who did not establish these societies but by God's inspiration. And (these wretches) also impiously declare that permission should be refused to citizens and to the Church, 'whereby they may openly give alms for the sake of Christian charity"; and that the law should be abrogated "whereby on certain fixed days servile works are prohibited because of God's worship;" and on the most deceptive pretext that the said permission and law are opposed to the principles of the best public economy. Moreover, not content with removing religion from public society, they wish to banish it also from private families. For, teaching and professing the most fatal error of *Communism and Socialism*, they assert that "domestic society or the family derives the whole principle of its existence from the civil law alone; and, consequently, that on civil law alone depend all rights of parents over their children, and especially that of providing for education." By which impious opinions and machinations these most deceitful men chiefly aim at this result, viz., that the salutary teaching and influence of the Catholic Church may be entirely banished from the instruction and education of youth, and that the tender and flexible minds of young men may be infected and depraved by every most pernicious error and vice. For all who have endeavored to throw into confusion things both sacred and secular, and to subvert the right order of society, and to abolish all rights, human and divine, have always (as we above hinted) devoted all their nefarious schemes, devices and efforts, to deceiving and depraving incautious youth and have placed all their hope in its corruption. For which reason they never cease by every wicked method to assail the clergy, both secular and regular, from whom (as the surest monuments of history conspicuously attest), so many great advantages have abundantly flowed to Christianity, civilization and literature, and to proclaim that "the clergy, as being hostile to the true and beneficial advance of science and civilization, should be removed from the whole charge and duty of instructing and educating youth."

5. Others meanwhile, reviving the wicked and so often condemned inventions of innovators, dare with signal impudence to subject to the will of the civil authority the supreme authority of the Church and of this Apostolic See given to her by Christ Himself, and to deny all those rights of the same Church and See which concern matters of the external order. For they are not ashamed of affirming "that the Church's laws do not bind in conscience unless when they are promulgated by the civil power; that acts and decrees of the Roman Pontiffs, referring to religion and the Church, need the civil power's sanction and approbation, or at least its consent; that the Apostolic Constitutions, whereby secret societies are condemned (whether an oath of secrecy be or be not required in such societies), and whereby their frequenters and favourers are smitten with anathema — have no force in those regions of the world wherein associations of the kind are tolerated by the civil government; that the excommunication

pronounced by the Council of Trent and by Roman Pontiffs against those who assail and usurp the Church's right and possessions, rests on a confusion between the spiritual and temporal orders, and (is directed) to the pursuit of a purely secular good; that the Church can decree nothing which binds the conscience of the faithful in regard to their use of temporal things; that the church has no right of restraining by temporal punishments those who violate her laws; that it is conformable to the principles of sacred theology and public law to assert and claim for the civil government a right of property in those goods which are possessed by the Church, by the Religious Orders, and by other pious establishments." Nor do they blush openly and publicly to profess the maxim and principle of heretics from which arise so many perverse opinions and errors. For they repeat that the "ecclesiastical power is not by divine right distinct from , and independent of, the civil power, and that such distinction and independence cannot be preserved without the civil power's essential rights being assailed and usurped by the Church." Nor can we pass over in silence the audacity of those who, not enduring sound doctrine, contend that "without sin and without any sacrifice of the Catholic profession assent and obedience may be refused to those judgments and decrees of the Apostolic See, whose object is declared to concern the Church's general good and her rights and discipline, so only it does not touch the dogmata of faith and morals." But no one can be found not clearly and distinctly to see and understand how grievously this is opposed to the Catholic dogma of the full power given from God by Christ our Lord Himself to the Roman Pontiff of feeding, ruling and guiding the Universal Church....

7. And besides these things, you know very well, Venerable Brethren, that in these times the haters of truth and justice and most bitter enemies of our religion, deceiving the people and maliciously lying, disseminate sundry and other impious doctrines by means of pestilential books, pamphlets and newspapers dispersed over the whole world. Nor are you ignorant also, that in this our age some men are found who, moved and excited by the spirit of Satan, have reached to that degree of impiety as not to shrink from denying our Ruler and Lord Jesus Christ, and from impugning His Divinity with wicked pertinacity. Here, however, we cannot but extol you, venerable brethren, with great and deserved praise, for not having failed to raise with all zeal your episcopal voice against impiety so great.

8. Therefore, in this our letter, we again most lovingly address you, who, having been called unto a part of our solicitude, are to us, among our grievous distresses, the greatest solace, joy and consolation, because of the admirable religion and piety wherein you excel, and because of that marvelous love, fidelity, and dutifulness, whereby, bound as you are to us, and to this Apostolic See in most harmonious affection, you strive strenuously and sedulously to fulfill your most weighty episcopal ministry. For from your signal pastoral zeal we expect that, taking up the sword of the spirit which is the word of God, and strengthened by the grace of our Lord Jesus Christ, you will, with redoubled care, each day more anxiously provide that the faithful entrusted to your charge "abstain from noxious verbiage, which Jesus Christ does not cultivate because it is not His Father's plantation." Never cease also to inculcate on the said faithful that all true felicity flows abundantly upon man from our august religion and its doctrine and practice; and that happy is the people whose God is their Lord. Teach that "kingdoms rest on the foundation of the Catholic Faith; and that nothing is so deadly, so hastening to a fall, so exposed to all danger, (as that which exists) if, believing this alone to be sufficient for us that we receive free will at our birth, we seek nothing further from the Lord; that is, if forgetting our Creator we abjure his power that we may display our freedom. And again do not fail to teach "that the royal power was given not only for the governance of the world, but most of all for the protection of the Church; and that there is nothing which can be of grater advantage and glory to Princes and Kings than if, as another most wise and courageous Predecessor of ours, St. Felix, instructed the Emperor Zeno, they "permit the Catholic Church to practice her laws, and allow no one to oppose her liberty. For it is certain that this mode of

conduct is beneficial to their interests, viz., that where there is question concerning the causes of God, they study, according to His appointment, to subject the royal will to Christ's Priests, not to raise it above theirs."

Source: Claudia Carlen, ed., *The Papal Encyclicals: 1740-1878* (Raleigh: Pierian Press, 1990), pp. 381-85.

✢

Questions for Part 27

1. Of the three new systems of thought — Darwin, Freud, and Nietzsche — which do you think was the most damaging to the confidence of Western culture?
2. Were there any similarities between how Pope Pius IX viewed Europe and how Nietzsche viewed it?
3. Is there a way to interpret the ideas expressed in these sources to incorporate them into progressive theories?

PART 28

WORLD WAR I

Most of the twentieth century viewed the first World War, or the Great War as it was called until 1939 offered another "great" war, as a noble failure. It was described as a clash between the human body and machinery, a clash between man and the industrialization of the Age of Progress. The war has taken on a tragic romantic glow, in which the individual soldier, reduced to cannon fodder, has become a martyr to the industrial age.

The reality of the war was both more and less noble that hindsight tells us. In 1914 Archduke Ferdinand, heir to the Austrian throne, was assassinated by Gavrilo Princip, a Serb nationalist. There are no heroes here; Princip was at best a bumbling terrorist who got lucky (he literally ran into Ferdinand by accident) while the Archduke was universally disliked. Austria had to declare war on Serbia, however, because the empire was facing several tricky nationalist movements, and to let Serbia get away with this would have been fatal to the empire. That one declaration of war by Austria led to the first truly world war. A complicated system of alliances, some going back to the end of the Napoleonic Wars, brought most of Europe into the war, as well as European colonies and international allies. Most went into the war happily; nations got to display their new technological might and individual soldiers got to be heroes.

However, few realized how devastating the new technology was, and that the military strategists behind the technology were not as innovative as their machinery. Old ways of fighting met new ways to kill. In four years, millions would die while approximately five miles were gained by both sides. The true tragedy of the Great War was the next great war that it created. The sources in this chapter reveal the personal side of the war and give a glimpse of the problems the war created for the future.

28.1

---✢---

POEMS OF WILFRED OWEN

Wilfred Owen (1893-1918), like many of his fellow soldiers, was at first eager to go to war. He enlisted in September 1915. Owen was already an accomplished poet when he went to war and used his poetry to record his experiences and impressions of the war. In 1917 Owen was sent to a hospital in Scotland to recover from shell shock, then returned to active duty. He died in November 1918. It was seven days before the armistice was signed. Owen was twenty-five years old.

Here are three war poems by Owen, including his celebrated "Dulce et Decorum Est."

QUESTIONS

1. The poem *"Dulce et Decorum Est"* is usually interpreted as an anti-war poem. Yet does it also romanticize war?
2. What does the poem "The Show" tell us about life in the trenches?
3. In "Anthem for Doomed Youth," Owen compares the soldiers to cattle; what is he saying about the nature of modern warfare?

ANTHEM FOR DOOMED YOUTH

What passing-bells for these who die as cattle?
    Only the monstrous anger of the guns.
Only the stuttering rifles' rapid rattle
Can patter out their hasty orisons.
No mockeries now for them; no prayers nor bells;
Nor any voice of mourning save the choirs,-
The shrill, demented choirs of wailing shells;
And bugles calling for them from sad shires.

What candles may be held to speed them all?
Not in the hands of boys, but in their eyes
Shall shine the holy glimmers of goodbyes.
The pallor of girls' brows shall be their pall;
Their flowers the tenderness of patient minds,
And each slow dusk a drawing-down of blinds.

DULCE ET DECORUM EST

Bent double, like old beggars under sacks,
    Knock-kneed, coughing like hags, we cursed through sludge,
Till on the haunting flares we turned our backs,
And towards our distant rest began to trudge,
Men marched asleep. Many had lost their boots,
But limped on, blood-shod. All went lame, all blind;
Drunk with fatigue; deaf even to the hoots
Of gas-shells dropping softly behind.

Gas! Gas! Quick boys! — An ecstasy of fumbling,
Fitting the clumsy helmets just in time,
But someone still was yelling out and stumbling
And floundering like a man in fire or lime,
Dim through the misty panes and thick green light,
As under a green sea, I saw him drowning.

In all my dreams before my helpless sight
He plunges at me, guttering, choking, drowning,

If in some smothering dreams, you too could pace
Behind the wagon that we flung him in,
And watch the white eyes writhing in his face,
His hanging face, like a devil's sick of sin;
If you could hear, at every jolt, the blood
Come gargling from the froth-corrupted lungs,
Bitter as the cud

Of vile, incurable sores on innocent tongues,--
My friend, you would not tell with such high zest
To children ardent for some desperate glory,
The old Lie: *Dulce et decorum est*
Pro patria mori.

THE SHOW

> *We have fallen in the dreams the ever-living*
> *Breathe on the tarnished mirror of the world,*
> *And then smooth out with ivory hands and sigh*
> — W. B. Yeats

My soul looked down from a vague height with Death,
As unremembering how I rose or why,
And saw a sad land, weak with sweats of dearth,
Gray, cratered like the moon with hollow woe,
And fitted with great pocks and scabs of plaques.

Across its beard, that horror of harsh wire,
There moved thin caterpillars, slowly uncoiled.
It seemed they pushed themselves to be as plugs
Of ditches, where they writhed and shrivelled, killed.

By them had slimy paths been trailed and scraped
Round myriad warts that might be little hills.

From gloom's last dregs these long-strung creatures crept,
And vanished out of dawn down hidden holes.

(And smell came up from those foul openings
As out of mouths, or deep wounds deepening.)

On dithering feet upgathered, more and more,
Brown strings towards strings of gray, with bristling spines,
All migrants from green fields, intent on mire.

Those that were gray, of more abundant spawns,
Ramped on the rest and ate them and were eaten.

I saw their bitten backs curve, loop, and straighten,
I watched those agonies curl, lift, and flatten.

Whereat, in terror what that sight might mean,
I reeled and shivered earthward like a feather.

And Death fell with me, like a deepening moan.
And He, picking a manner of worm, which half had hid
Its bruises in the earth, but crawled no further,
Showed me its feet, the feet of many men,
And the fresh-severed head of it, my head.

Source: Oscar Williams, ed., *The War Poets* (New York: The John Day Company, 1945), pp. 36-38, 40-41.

28.2

✢

POEMS OF SIEGFRIED SASSOON

Siegfried Sassoon (1886-1967) was even more enthusiastic about the war than Wilfred Owen. Sassoon enlisted in 1914, a few days before Britain declared war on Germany. His brother also enlisted and was killed at Gallipoli in 1915. Sassoon responded by becoming even more aggressive, volunteering for dangerous missions. In spite of this, Sassoon survived the war, although he suffered from trench fever and German measles, at different times.

In 1917 he wrote an official declaration of pacifism, which earned him a diagnosis of shell shock and a brief convalescence before being returned to the army. He was finally relieved of duty in 1918 after a head-wound.

✢

QUESTIONS

1. Compare Sassoon's "The Dug-Out" with Owen's "The Show"; what do both men say about the futility of the trenches?
2. Is "Does it Matter?" an anti-war poem?
3. Pretend you know nothing about the kinds of weapons used in the first World War; try to describe them from the poem "The Rear-Guard."

THE REAR-GUARD

Groping along the tunnel step by step,
He winked his prying torch with patching glare
From side to side, and sniffed the unwholesome air.
Tins, bottles, boxes, shapes too vague to know,-
A mirror smashed, the mattress from a bed;
And he, exploring, fifty feet below
The rose gloom of battle overhead
Tripping, he grabbed the wall; saw some one lie
Humped and asleep, half-hidden by a rug;
And stooped to give the sleeper's arm a tug.
"I'm looking for Headquarters."
No reply....
"God blast your neck" (for days *he'd* had no sleep),
"Get up and guide me through this stinking place."
Then, with a savage kick at the silent heap,
He flashed his beam across a livid face
Horribly glaring up; and the eyes yet wore
Agony dying hard ten days before;
And twisted fingers clutched a blackening wound.
Alone, he staggered on until he found
Dawn's ghost, that filtered down a shafted stair
To the dazed, muttering creatures underground,
Who hear the boom of shells in muffled sound.
At last, with sweat of horror in his hair,
He climbed through darkness to the twilight air,
Unloading hell behind him, step by step.

DOES IT MATTER?

Does it matter? — losing your leg?...
For people will always be kind,
      And you need not show that you mind
When the others come in after hunting
To gobble their muffins and eggs.
Does it matter ? — losing your sight?...
There's such splendid work for the blind;
And people will always be kind,
As you sit on the terrace remembering
And turning your face to the light.
Do they matter? — those dreams from the pit?...
You can drink and forget and be glad,
And people won't say that you're mad;
For they'll know you've fought for your country
And no one will worry a bit.

THE DUG-OUT

Why do you lie with your legs ungainly huddled,
    And one arm bent across your sullen, cold,
Exhausted face? It hurts my heart to watch you,
Deep-shadowed from the candle's guttering gold;
And you wonder why I shake you by the shoulder;
Drowsy, you mumble and sigh and turn your head....
You are too young to fall asleep for ever;
And when you sleep you remind me of the dead.

AFTERMATH

Have you forgotten yet?...
    For the world's events have rumbled on since those gagged days,
Like traffic checked while at the crossing of city-ways:
And the haunted gap in your mind has filled with thoughts that flow
Like clouds in the lit heaven of life; and you're a man reprieved to go,
Taking your peaceful share of Time, with joy to spare.
But the past is just the same--and War's a bloody game...
Have you forgotten yet?...
Look down, and swear by the slain of the War that you'll never forget.

Do you remember the dark months you held the sector at Mametz —
The nights you watched and wired and dug and piled sandbags on parapets?
Do you remember the rats; and the stench
Of corpses rotting in front of the front-line trench —
And dawn coming, dirty-white, and chill with a hopeless rain?
Do you ever stop and ask, "Is it all going to happen again?"

Do you remember that hour of din before the attack —
And the anger, the blind compassion that seized and shook you then
As you peered at the doomed and haggard faces of your men?
Do you remember the stretcher-cases lurching back
With dying eyes and lolling heads--those ashen-grey
Masks of the lads who once were keen and kind and gay?

Have you forgotten yet?...
Look up, and swear by the green of the spring that you'll never forget!

Source: Oscar Williams, ed., *The War Poets* (New York: The John Day Company, 1945), pp. 73, 75-76.

28.3

⸎

THE FOURTEEN POINTS, WOODROW WILSON

Of all the participants in the peace process following the Great War, American President Woodrow Wilson (1856-1924) was the most idealistic. He had been reluctant to send American troops to the war until the sinking of the Lusitania in 1915 (one hundred and twenty eight Americans drowned with the ship); even then he delayed until 1917. The role of the U.S. in the fighting has been largely exaggerated; however, it is impossible to downplay the role Wilson played in shaping the peace talks, even if the final treaty of Versailles was not what Wilson hoped it would be. Most of The Fourteen Points *were lost, or so mutated as to be unrecognizable, but without Wilson's proposal, the peace negotiations might have been delayed even longer. The war ended when Germany sued for peace according to Wilson's* Fourteen Points *plan.*

The Fourteen Points, which he presented in the following speech to the U.S. Congress in 1918, promised self-determination for nationalities, freedom of the seas (no more unrestricted submarine warfare or blockades), open diplomacy, and above all, the formation of an international body to ensure peace and establish common policies. Called the League of Nations, with its own court, it was the model for the United Nations at the end of the second World War.

⸎

QUESTIONS

1. What ultimately does Wilson hope this war will have accomplished?
2. Point III speaks of removing economic barriers; is this Wilson being greedy for more American trade?
3. In the actual Versailles Treaty, which of Wilson's points were omitted?

I t will be our wish and purpose that the processes of peace, when they are begun, shall be absolutely open and that they shall involve and permit henceforth no secret understandings of any kind. The day of conquest and aggrandizement is gone by; so is also the day of secret covenants entered into in the interest of particular governments and likely at some unlooked-for moment to upset the peace of the world. It is this happy fact, now clear to the view of every public man whose thoughts do not still linger in an age that is dead and gone, which makes it possible for every nation whose purposes are consistent with justice and the peace of the world to avow nor or at any other time the objects it has in view.

We entered this war because violations of right had occurred which touched us to the quick and made the life of our own people impossible unless they were corrected and the world secure once for all against their recurrence. What we demand in this war, therefore, is nothing peculiar to ourselves. It is that the world be made fit and safe to live in; and particularly that it be made safe for every peace-loving nation which, like our own, wishes to live its own life, determine its own institutions, be assured of justice and fair dealing by the other peoples of the world as against force and selfish aggression. All the peoples of the world are in effect partners in this interest, and for our own part we see very clearly that unless justice be done to others it will not be done to us. The program of the world's peace, therefore, is our program; and that program, the only possible program, as we see it, is this:

I.   Open covenants of peace, openly arrived at, after which there shall be no private international understandings of any kind but diplomacy shall proceed always frankly and in the public view.

II.   Absolute freedom of navigation upon the seas, outside territorial waters, alike in peace and in war, except as the seas may be closed in whole or in part by international action for the enforcement of international covenants.

III.   The removal, so far as possible, of all economic barriers and the establishment of an equality of trade conditions among all the nations consenting to the peace and associating themselves for its maintenance.

IV.   Adequate guarantees given and taken that national armaments will be reduced to the lowest point consistent with domestic safety.

V.   A free, open-minded, and absolutely impartial adjustment of all colonial claims, based upon a strict observance of the principle that in determining all such questions of sovereignty the interests of the populations concerned must have equal weight with the equitable claims of the government whose title is to be determined.

VI.   The evacuation of all Russian territory and such a settlement of all questions affecting Russia as will secure the best and freest cooperation of the other nations of the world in obtaining for her an unhampered and unembarrassed opportunity for the independent determination of her own political development and national policy and assure her of a sincere welcome into the society of free nations under institutions of her own choosing; and, more than a welcome, assistance also of every kind that she may need and may herself desire. The treatment accorded Russia by her sister nations in the months to come will be the acid test of their good will, of their comprehension of her needs as distinguished from their own interests, and of their intelligent and unselfish sympathy.

VII.   Belgium, the whole world will agree, must be evacuated and restored, without any attempt to limit the sovereignty which she enjoys in common with all other free nations. No other single act will serve as this will serve to restore confidence among the nations in the laws which they have themselves set and determined for the government of their relations with one another. Without this healing act the whole structure and validity of international law is forever impaired.

VIII. All French territory should be freed and the invaded portions restored, and the wrong done to France by Prussia in 1871 in the matter of Alsace-Lorraine, which has unsettled the peace of the world for nearly fifty years, should be righted, in order that peace may once more be made secure in the interest of all.

IX.   A readjustment of the frontiers of Italy should be effected along clearly recognizable lines of nationality.

X.   The peoples of Austria-Hungary, whose place among the nations we wish to see safeguarded and assured, should be accorded the freest opportunity to autonomous development.

XI.   Rumania, Serbia, and Montenegro should be evacuated; occupied territories restored; Serbia accorded free and secure access to the sea; and the relations of the several Balkan states to one another determined by friendly counsel along historically established lines of allegiance and nationality; and international guarantees of the political and economic independence and territorial integrity of the several Balkan states should be entered into.

XII.   The Turkish portions of the present Ottoman Empire should be assured a secure sovereignty, but the other nationalities which are now under Turkish rule should be assured an undoubted security of life and an absolutely unmolested opportunity of autonomous development, and the Dardanelles should be permanently opened as a free passage to the ships and commerce of all nations under international guarantees.

XIII.   An independent Polish state should be erected which should include the territories inhabited by indisputably Polish populations, which should be assured a free and secure access to the sea, and whose political and economic independence and territorial integrity should be guaranteed by international covenant.

XIV.   A general association of nations must be formed under specific covenants for the purpose of affording mutual guarantees of political independence and territorial integrity to great and small states alike.

In regard to these essential rectifications of wrong and assertions of right we feel ourselves to be intimate partners of all the governments and peoples associated together against the Imperialists. We cannot be separated in interest or divided in purpose. We stand together until the end.

For such arrangements and covenants we are willing to fight and to continue to fight until they are achieved; but only because we wish the right to prevail and desire a just and stable peace such as can be secured only by removing the chief provocations to war, which this program does remove. We have no jealousy of German greatness, and there is nothing in this program that impairs it. We grudge her no achievement or distinction of learning or of pacific enterprise such as have made her record very bright and very enviable. We do not wish to injure her or to block in any way her legitimate influence or power. We do not wish to fight her either with arms or with hostile arrangements of trade if she is willing to associate herself with us and the other peace-loving nations of the world in covenants of justice and law and fair dealing. We wish her only to accept a place of equality among the peoples of the world, — the new world in which we now live, — instead of a place of mastery.

Neither do we presume to suggest to her any alteration or modification of her institutions. But it is necessary, we must frankly say, and necessary as a preliminary to any intelligent dealings with her on our part, that we should know whom her spokesmen speak for when they speak to us, whether for the Reichstag majority or for the military party and the men whose creed is imperial domination.

We have spoken now, surely, in terms too concrete to admit of any further doubt or question. An evident principle runs through the whole program I have outlined. It is the principle of justice to all peoples and nationalities, and their right to live on equal terms of liberty and safety with one another, whether they be strong or weak. Unless this principle be made its foundation no part of the structure of international justice can stand. The people of the United States could act upon no other principle; and to the vindication of this principle they are ready to devote their lives, their honor, and everything they possess. The moral climax of this the culminating and final war for human liberty has come, and they are ready to put their own strength, their own highest purpose, their own integrity and devotion to the test.

Source: Woodrow Wilson, *The Papers of Woodrow Wilson, Volume 45*, ed. Arthur S. Link (Princeton: Princeton University Press, 1984), pp. 534-39.

28.4

---- ✤ ----

VERSAILLES TREATY: PART VIII REPARATION

When historians trace the rise of Nazism back to the Versailles Treaty, they usually cite the disarmament, reparations, and guilt clauses. The articles collected here list some of the numerous reparations clauses of the Treaty.

---- ✤ ----

QUESTIONS

1. One can reconstruct the devastation of the war from the reparations clauses. Using these Articles, list some of the material losses of the war.
2. What is the overall tone of the treaty when listing Germany's obligations to military and civilian victims of the war?
3. Why does Germany have to provide the French and Belgian governments with actual livestock rather than just the monetary equivalent?

ARTICLE 235

In order to enable the Allied and Associated Powers to proceed at once to the restoration of their industrial and economic life, pending the full determination of their claims, Germany shall pay in such installments and in such manner (whether in gold, commodities, ships, securities or otherwise) as the Reparation Commission may fix, during 1919, 1920 and the first four months Of 1921 , the equivalent of 20,000,000,000 gold marks. Out of this sum the expenses of the armies of occupation subsequent to the Armistice of November 11, 1918, shall first be met, and such supplies of food and raw materials as may be judged by the Governments of the Principal Allied and Associated Powers to be essential to enable Germany to meet her obligations for reparation may also, with the approval of the said Governments, be paid for out of the above sum. The balance shall be reckoned towards liquidation of the amounts due for reparation. Germany shall further deposit bonds as prescribed in paragraph 12 (c) Of Annex II hereto.

ARTICLE 236

Germany further agrees to the direct application of her economic resources to reparation as specified in Annexes, III, IV, V, and VI, relating respectively to merchant shipping, to physical restoration, to coal and derivatives of coal, and to dyestuffs and other chemical products; provided always that the value of the property transferred and any services rendered by her under these Annexes, assessed in the manner therein prescribed shall be credited to her towards liquidation of her obligations under the above Articles....

ANNEX I

Compensation may be claimed from Germany under Article 232 above in respect of the total damage under the following categories:

(1) Damage to injured persons and to surviving dependents by personal injury to or death of civilians caused by acts of war, including bombardments or other attacks on land, on sea, or from the air, and all the direct consequences thereof, and of all operations of war by the two groups of belligerents wherever arising.

(2) Damage caused by Germany or her allies to civilian victims of acts of cruelty, violence or maltreatment (including injuries to life or health as a consequence of imprisonment, deportation, internment or evacuation, of exposure at sea or of being forced to labour), wherever arising, and to the surviving dependents of such victims.

(3) Damage caused by Germany or her allies in their own territory or in occupied or invaded territory to civilian victims of all acts injurious to health or capacity to work, or to honour, as well as to the surviving dependents of such victims.

(4) Damage caused by any kind of maltreatment of prisoners of war.

(5) As damage caused to the peoples of the Allied and Associated Powers, all pensions and compensation in the nature of pensions to naval and military victims of war (including members of the air force), whether mutilated, wounded, sick or invalided, and to the dependents of such victims, the amount due to the Allied and Associated Governments being calculated for each of them as being the capitalised cost of such pensions and compensation at the date of the coming into force of the present Treaty on the basis of the scales in force in France at such date.

(6) The cost of assistance by the Government of the Allied and Associated Powers to prisoners of war and to their families and dependents.

(7) Allowances by the Governments of the Allied and Associated Powers to the families and dependents of mobilised persons or persons serving with the forces, the amount due to them for each calendar year in which hostilities occurred being calculated for each Government on the basis of the average scale for such payments in force in France during that year.

(8) Damage caused to civilians by being forced by Germany or her allies to labour without just remuneration.

(9) Damage in respect of all property wherever situated belonging to any of the Allied or Associated States or their nationals, with the exception of naval and military works or materials, which has been carried off, seized, injured or destroyed by the acts of Germany or her allies on land, on sea or from the air, or damage directly in consequence of hostilities or of any operations of war.

(10) Damage in the form of levies, fines and other similar exactions imposed by Germany or her allies upon the civilian population....

ANNEX IV

...

6

As an immediate advance on account of the animals referred to in paragraph 2 (a) above, Germany undertakes to deliver in equal monthly installments in the three months following the coming into force of the present Treaty the following quantities of live stock:

(1) To the French Government.

500 stallions (3 to 7 years);
30,000 fillies and mares (18 months to 7 years), type: Ardennais, Boulonnais or Belgian;
2,000 bulls (18 months to 3 years);
90,000 milch cows (2 to 6 years);
1,000 rams;
100,000 sheep;
10,000 goats.

(2) To the Belgian Government.

200 stallions (3 to 7 years), large Belgian type;
5,000 mares (3 to 7 years), large Belgian type;
5,000 fillies (18 months to 3 years), large Belgian type;
2,000 bulls (18 months to 3 years);
50,000 milch cows (2 to 6 years);
40,000 heifers;
200 rams;
20,000 Sheep;
15,000 sows.

The animals delivered shall be of average health and condition.

To the extent that animals so delivered cannot be identified as animals taken away or seized, the value of such animals shall be credited against the reparation obligations of Germany in accordance with paragraph 5 of this Annex....

ARTICLE 246

Within six months from the coming into force of the present Treaty, Germany will restore to His Majesty the King of the Hedjaz the original Koran of the Caliph Othman, which was removed from Medina by the Turkish authorities and is stated to have been presented to the ex-Emperor William II.

Within the same period Germany will hand over to His Britannic Majesty's Government the skull of the Sultan Mkwawa which was removed from the Protectorate of German East Africa and taken to Germany.

The delivery of the articles above referred to will be effected in such place and in such conditions as may be laid down by the Governments to which they are to be restored.

ARTICLE 247

Germany undertakes to furnish to the University of Louvain, within three months after a request made by it and transmitted through the intervention of the Reparation Commission, manuscripts, incunabula, printed books, maps and objects of collection corresponding in number and value to those destroyed in the burning by Germany of the Library of Louvain. All details regarding such replacement will be determined by the Reparation Commission.

Germany undertakes to deliver to Belgium, through the Reparation Commission, within six months of the coming into force of the present Treaty, in order to enable Belgium to reconstitute two great artistic works:

(1) The leaves of the triptych of the Mystic Lamb painted by the Van Eyck brothers, formerly in the Church of St. Bavon at Ghent, now in the Berlin Museum;

(2) The leaves of the triptych of the Last Supper, painted by Dierick Bouts, formerly in the Church of St. Peter at Louvain, two of which are now in the Berlin Museum and two in the Old Pinakothek at Munich.

Source: Philip Mason Burnett, ed., *Reparation at the Paris Peace Conference: From the Standpoint of the American Delegation* (New York: Octagon Books, Inc., 1965), pp. 217-18, 220-22, 225-26, 235. 241-42.

28.5

---- ✢ ----

A GREAT BEGINNING, LENIN

Vladimir Illich Ulyanov (1870-1924), better known as Lenin, had been active in Russian politics since 1887. Lenin was from a middle-class background and had legal training, which he used to organize a revolutionary Marxist group in 1894. He was arrested, and after several years in Siberia, he was sent into exile in Switzerland. Lenin continued to organize revolutionary groups in Russia, as well as establishing contacts with Marxists in other countries. In 1903, from exile, he split the Russian Social Democratic Party into two groups, taking control of the majority group, the Bolsheviks, and seeking the support of Russian peasants and workers.

By 1917 the Russian war effort was faltering; soldiers were refusing to fight, food was scarce and weapons even more so. Yet, Tsar Nicholas II (1894-1917) refused to surrender. The Germans decided to encourage Nicholas to withdraw from the war (leaving Germany with only one front) by smuggling Lenin into Russia. The trick worked. Lenin and the Bolshevik Party used the dissatisfaction of the Russian populace with the war, the Romanovs, and the lack of food to stage the first Communist revolution and then sued Germany for peace.

In the following speech, Lenin discusses the work that must still be done to turn Russia into a successful Communist state.

---- ✢ ----

QUESTIONS

1. What must still be done to abolish all social classes?
2. Lenin was dedicated to promoting Communism; yet how is he using rhetoric here to placate the Russian people?
3. What are Lenin's feelings about women and their role in the successful Communist state?

A nd what does the "abolition of classes" mean? All those who call themselves socialists recognise this as the ultimate goal of socialism, but by no means all give thought to its significance. Classes are large groups of people differing from each other by the place they occupy in a historically determined system of social production, by their relation (in most cases fixed and formulated in law) to the means of production, by their role in the social organisation of labour, and, consequently, by the dimensions of the share of social wealth of which they dispose and the mode of acquiring it. Classes are groups of people one of which can appropriate the labour of another owing to the different places they occupy in a definite system of social economy.

Clearly, in order to abolish classes completely, it is not enough to overthrow the exploiters, the landowners and capitalists, not enough to abolish *their* rights of ownership; it is necessary also to abolish *all* private ownership of the means of production, it is necessary to abolish the distinction between town and country, as well as the distinction between manual workers and brain workers. This requires a very long period of time. In order to achieve this an enormous step forward must be taken in developing the productive forces; it is necessary to overcome the resistance (frequently passive, which is particularly stubborn and particularly difficult to overcome) of the numerous survivals of small-scale production; it is necessary to overcome the enormous force of habit and conservatism which are connected with these survivals.

The assumption that all "working people" are equally capable of doing this work would be on empty phrase, or the illusion of an antediluvian, pre-Marxist socialist; for this ability does not come of itself, but grows historically, and grows *only* out of the material conditions of large-scale capitalist production. This ability, at the beginning of the road from capitalism to socialism, is possessed by the proletariat *alone*. It is capable of fulfilling the gigantic task that confronts it, first, because it is the strongest and most advanced class in civilised societies; secondly, because in the most developed countries it constitutes the majority of the population, and thirdly, because in backward capitalist countries, like Russia, the majority of the population consists of semi-proletarians, i.e., of people who regularly live in a proletarian way part of the year, who regularly earn a part of their means of subsistence as wage-workers in capitalist enterprises....

In order to achieve victory, in order to build and consolidate socialism, the proletariat must fulfil a twofold or dual task: first, it must, by its supreme heroism in the revolutionary struggle against capital, win over the entire mass of the working and exploited people; it must win them over, organise them and lead them in the struggle to overthrow the bourgeoisie and utterly suppress their resistance. Secondly, it must lead the whole mass of the working and exploited people, as well as all the petty-bourgeois groups, on to the road of new economic development, towards the creation of a new social bond, a new labour discipline, a new organisation of labour, which will combine the last word in science and capitalist technology with the mass association of class-conscious workers creating large-scale socialist industry.

The second task is more difficult than the first, for it cannot possibly be fulfilled by single acts of heroic fervour; it requires the most prolonged, most persistent and most difficult mass heroism in *plain, everyday* work. But this task is more essential than the first, because, in the last analysis, the deepest source of strength for victories over the bourgeoisie and the sole guarantee of the durability and permanence of these victories can only be a new and higher mode of social production, the substitution of large-scale socialist production for capitalist and petty-bourgeois production....

If we get down to brass tacks, however, has it ever happened in history that a new mode of production has taken root immediately, without a long succession of setbacks, blunders and relapses? Half a century after the abolition of serfdom there were still quite a number of survivals of serfdom in the Russian countryside. Half a century after the abolition of slavery in America the position of the Negroes was still very often one of semi-slavery. The bourgeois intellectuals, including the Mensheviks and Socialist-Revolutionaries, are true to themselves in serving capital and in continuing to use absolutely false arguments — before the proletarian revolution they accused us of being utopian; after the revolution they demand that we wipe out all traces of the past with fantastic rapidity!

We are not utopians, however, and we know the real value of bourgeois "arguments"; we also know that for some time after the revolution traces of the old ethics will inevitably predominate over the young shoots of the new. When the new has just been born the old always remains stronger than it for some time, this is always the case in nature and in social life. Jeering at the feebleness of the young shoots of the new order, cheap scepticism of the intellectuals and the like — these are, essentially, methods of bourgeois class struggle against the proletariat, a defence of capitalism against socialism. We must carefully study the feeble new shoots, we must devote the greatest attention to them, do everything to promote their growth and "nurse" them. Some of them will inevitably perish. We cannot vouch that precisely the "communist *subbotniks*" will play a particularly important role. But that is not the point. The point is to foster each and every shoot of the new; and life will select the most viable. If the Japanese scientist, in order to help mankind vanquish syphilis, had the patience to test six hundred and five preparations before he developed a six hundred and sixth which met definite requirements then those who want to solve a more difficult problem, namely, to vanquish capitalism, must have the perseverance to try hundreds and thousands of new methods, means and weapons of struggle in order to elaborate the most suitable of them.

The "communist *subbotniks*" are so important because they were initiated by workers who were by no means placed in exceptionally good conditions, by workers of various specialities, and some with no speciality at all, just unskilled labourers, who are living under *ordinary*, i.e., *exceedingly hard*, conditions. We all know very well the main cause of the decline in the productivity of labour that is to be observed not only in Russia, but all over the world; it is ruin and impoverishment, embitterment and weariness caused by the imperialist war, sickness and malnutrition. The latter is first in importance. Starvation — that is the cause. And in order to do away with starvation, productivity of labour must be raised in agriculture, in transport and in industry. So, we get a sort of vicious circle: in order to raise productivity of labour we must save ourselves from starvation, and in order to save ourselves from starvation we must raise productivity of labour.

We know that in practice such contradictions are solved by breaking the vicious circle, by bringing about a radical change in the temper of the people, by the heroic initiative of the individual groups which often plays a decisive role against the background of such a radical change. The unskilled labourers and railway workers of Moscow (of course, we have in mind the majority of them, and not a handful of profiteers, officials and other whiteguards) are working people who are living in desperately hard conditions. They are constantly underfed, and now, before the new harvest is gathered, with the general worsening of the food situation, they are actually starving. And yet these starving workers, surrounded by the malicious counter-revolutionary agitation of the bourgeoisie, the Mensheviks and the Socialist-Revolutionaries, are organising "communist *subbotniks*," working overtime *without any pay*, and achieving *an enormous increase in the productivity of labour* in spite of the fact that they are weary, tormented, and exhausted by malnutrition. Is this not supreme heroism? Is this not the beginning of a change of momentous significance?...

Communism is the higher productivity of labour — compared with that existing under capitalism — of voluntary, class-conscious and united workers employing advanced techniques. Communist *subbotniks* are extraordinarily valuable as the *actual* beginning of *communism* ; and this is a very rare thing, because we are in a stage when "only the *first steps* in the transition from capitalism to communism are being taken" (as our Party Programme quite rightly says).

Communism begins when the *rank-and-file workers* display an enthusiastic concern that is undaunted by arduous toil to increase the productivity of labour, husband *every* pood *of grain, coal, iron* and other products, which do not accrue to the workers personally or to their "close" kith and kin, but to their "distant" kith and kin, i. e., to society as a whole, to tens and hundreds of millions of people united first in one socialist state, and then in a union of Soviet republics.

In *Capital*, Karl Marx ridicules the pompous and grandiloquent bourgeois-democratic great charter of liberty and the rights of man, ridicules all this phrase-mongering about liberty, equality and fraternity *in general*, which dazzles the petty bourgeois and philistines of all countries, including the present despicable heroes of the despicable Berne International. Marx contrasts these pompous declarations of rights to the plain, modest, practical, simple manner in which the question is presented by the proletariat — the legislative enactment of a shorter working day is a typical example of such treatment. The aptness and profundity of Marx's observation become the clearer and more obvious to us the more the content of the proletarian revolution unfolds. The "formulas" of genuine communism differ from the pompous, intricate, and solemn phraseology of the Kautskys, the Mensheviks and the Socialist-Revolutionaries and their beloved "brethren" of Berne in that they reduce every thing to the *conditions of labour*. Less chatter about "labour democracy," about "liberty, equality and fraternity," about "government by the people," and all such stuff; the class conscious workers and peasants of our day see through these pompous phrases of the bourgeois intellectual and discern the trickery as easily as a person of ordinary common sense and experience, when glancing at the irreproachably "polished" features and immaculate appearance of the "fain fellow, dontcher know," immediately and unerringly puts him down as "in all probability, a scoundrel."...

Take the position of women. In this field, not a single democratic party in the world, not even in the most advanced bourgeois republic, has done in decades so much as a hundredth part of what we did in our very first year in power. We really razed to the ground the infamous laws placing women in a position of inequality, restricting divorce and surrounding it with disgusting formalities, denying recognition to children born out of wedlock, enforcing a search for their fathers, etc., laws numerous survivals of which, to the shame of the bourgeoisie and of capitalism, are to be found in all civilised countries. We have a thousand times the right to be proud of what we have done in this field. But the more *thoroughly* we have cleared the ground of the lumber of the old, bourgeois laws and institutions, the clearer it is to us that we have only cleared the ground to build on but are not yet building.

Notwithstanding all the laws emancipating woman, she continues to be a *domestic slave*, because *petty housework* crushes, strangles, stultifies and degrades her, chains her to the kitchen and the nursery, and she wastes her labour on barbarously unproductive, petty, nerve-racking, stultifying and crushing drudgery. The real *emancipation of women*, real communism, will begin only where and when an all-out struggle begins (led by the proletariat wielding the state power) against this petty housekeeping, or rather when its *wholesale transformation* into a large-scale socialist economy begins.

Do we in practice pay sufficient attention to this question, which in theory every Communist considers indisputable? Of course not. Do we take proper care of the *shoots* of communism which already exist in this sphere? Again the answer is *no*. Public catering establishments, nurseries, kindergartens — here we have examples of these shoots, here we have the simple, everyday means, involving nothing pompous, grandiloquent or ceremonial, which can *really emancipate women*, really lessen and abolish their inequality with men as regards their role in social production and public life. These means are not new, they (like all the material prerequisites for socialism) were created by large-scale capitalism. But under capitalism they remained, first, a rarity, and secondly — which is particularly important — either *profit-making* enterprises, with all the worst features of speculation, profiteering, cheating and fraud, or "acrobatics of bourgeois charity," which the best workers rightly hated and despised.

There is no doubt that the number of these institutions in our country has increased enormously and that they are *beginning* to change in character. There is no doubt that we have far more *organising talent* among the working and peasant women than we are aware of, that we have far more people than we know of who can organise practical work, with the co-operation of large numbers of workers and of still larger numbers of consumers, without that abundance of talk, fuss, squabbling and chatter about plans, systems, etc., with which our big-headed "intellectuals" or half-baked "Communists" are "affected." But we *do not nurse* these shoots of the new as we should....

That great beginning, the "communist *subbotnik*," must also be utilised for another purpose, namely, to *purge* the Party. In the early period following the revolution, when the mass of "honest" and philistine-minded people was particularly timorous, and when the bourgeois intellectuals to a man, including, of course, the Mensheviks and Socialist-Revolutionaries, played the lackey to the bourgeoisie and carried on sabotage, it was absolutely inevitable that adventurers and other pernicious elements should hitch themselves to the ruling party. There never has been, and there never can be, a revolution without that. The whole point is that the ruling party should be able, relying on a sound and strong advanced class, to purge *its* ranks.

We started this work long ago. It must be continued steadily and untiringly. The mobilisation of Communists for the war helped us in this respect: the cowards and scoundrels fled from the Party's ranks. Good riddance! *Such* a reduction in the Party's membership means an *enormous increase* in its strength and weight. We must continue the purge, and that new beginning, the "communist *subbotnik*," must be utilised for this purpose: members should be accepted into the Party only after six months', say, "trial," or "probation," at "working in a revolutionary way." A similar test should be demanded of *all* members of the Party who joined after October 25, 1917, and who have not proved by some special work or service that they are absolutely reliable, loyal and capable of being Communists.

The purging of the Party, through the steadily *increasing demands* it makes in regard to working in a genuinely communist way, will improve the state *apparatus* and will bring much nearer the *final transition* of the peasants to the side of the revolutionary proletariat.

Source: Lenin, *The Lenin Anthology,* Robert C. Tucker, ed., (New York: W. W. Norton & Company, Inc., 1975), pp. 478-488.

✤

QUESTIONS FOR PART 28

1. How might the success of the Bolshevik revolution have encouraged the negotiators at Versailles to deal so harshly with Germany? Could they blame Germany for the Russian Revolution?
2. Compare the Versailles reparations clauses with Wilson's *Fourteen Points*. Do they seem to be addressing the same war?
3. How did Europe so misjudge this war before it started?

PART 29

EUROPE BETWEEN THE WARS

The inter-war years of the 1920s and 1930s were some of the most unsettled in modern Western history. Europe came out of World War I with tremendous debts and vastly reduced manpower, which hampered the rebuilding of the continent. Yet the greatest loss was the loss of confidence. The Age of Progress no longer seemed quite so assured. The United States had earned the respect of Europe, playing her first major role in international politics, but chose to retreat into relative isolation after the war was over and the treaties were signed. The economic catastrophe of the Great Depression, which began in 1929 (although the seeds of the crisis were in place in the mid-1920s) only served to deepen the sense of angst in the West.

In addition to the continuing problems faced by the West, the inter-war period was also unstable because there was no consensus, by either people or states, on how best to deal with the new reality of life, the lack of faith in progress. The inter-war period was a time of experimentation in all levels of society, bar one: politics. The Great War had revealed that even progressive, liberal states were not proof against disaster. Instead, one by one Western states (for this includes the United States, which could no longer be omitted from any discussion of the West) looked for political stability by turning into anti-democratic, conservative, authoritarian states. Above all else, these states were reactionary, and the most common targets were Jews and Bolsheviks.

Diversity was apparent, however, in the arts and culture. Hemlines got higher, music faster, women of all classes went to work, and art became less narrative, more imaginative. The sources of this section highlight the cultural and political responses between the wars.

29.1

SURREALISM AND DADAISM: RENE MAGRITTE AND MAN RAY

Surrealism was an artistic and literary movement that emphasized an unrestrained imagination, and attempted to recreate dream experiences. As one might expect, it was heavily influenced by the theories of Freud. The movement began in France in the early 1920s. It is sometimes related to Dadaism, another artistic and literary movement popular in Europe during the first World War. Dadaism used the absurd, the extreme, and the irrational to convey the experience of absurdity. Both Dadaism and Surrealism were attempts to break away from traditional realistic or rational art forms, not by denying that reality exists, but by denying that reality had any meaning.

The first source in this section is an essay by Rene Magritte (1898-1967) on why he became a Surrealist. The second source is a statement on Dada by Man Ray (1890-1976). Ray was a photographer, sculptor, painter, and writer who worked in both Dadaism and Surrealism.

———————— ✧ ————————

QUESTIONS

1. How is the statement by Man Ray both a statement *about* Dadaism and a statement *of* Dadaism?
2. According to Magritte, what do his surrealist paintings have in common with Marxism?
3. Why does Magritte paint every day objects out of their original context?

LIFELINE

In my childhood I used to play with a little girl in the old crumbling cemetery of an out-of-the-way provincial town, where I always spent my vacations. We would lift the iron grates and descend to the underground passageways. Climbing back up to the light one day I happened upon a painter from the Capital, who amidst those scattered dead leaves and broken stone columns seemed to me to be up to something magical.

When, about 1915, I myself began to paint, the memory of that enchanting encounter with the painter bent by first steps in a direction having little to do with common sense. A singular fate willed that someone, probably to have some fun at my expense, should send me the illustrated catalogue of an exposition of futurist paintings. As a result of that joke I came to know of a new way of painting. In a state of intoxication I set about creating busy scenes of stations, festivities, or cities, in which the little girl bound up with my discovery of the world of painting lived out an exceptional adventure. I cannot doubt that a pure and powerful sentiment, namely, eroticism, saved me from slipping into the traditional chase after formal perfection. My interest lay entirely in provoking an emotional shock.

This painting as search for pleasure was followed next by a curious experience. Thinking it possible to possess the world I loved at my own good pleasure, once I should succeed in fixing its essence upon canvas, I undertook to find out what its plastic equivalents were.

The result was a series a highly evocative but abstract and inert images that were, in the last analysis, interesting only to the intelligence of the eye. This experience made it possible for me to view the world of the real in the same abstract manner. Despite the shifting richness of natural detail and shade, I grew able to look at a landscape as though it were but a curtain hanging in front of me. I had become skeptical of the dimension in depth of a countryside scene, of the remoteness of the line of the horizon.

In 1925 I made up my mind to break with so passive an attitude. This decision was the outcome of an intolerable interval of contemplation I went through in a working-class Brussels beerhall: I found the door moldings endowed with a mysterious life and I remained a long time in contact with their reality. A feeling bordering upon terror was the point of departure for a will to action upon the real, for a transformation of life itself.

When moreover, I found that same will allied to a superior method and doctrine in the works of Karl Marx and Frederick Engels, and became acquainted about that time with the Surrealists, who were then violently demonstrating their loathing for all the bourgeois values, social and ideological, that have kept the world in its present ignoble state, — it was then that I became convinced that I must thenceforward live with danger, that life and the world might thereby come up in some measure to the level of thought and the affections.

I painted pictures in which objects were represented with the appearance they have in reality, in a style objective enough to ensure that their upsetting effect — which they would reveal themselves capable of provoking owing to certain means utilized — would be experienced in the real world whence the objects had been borrowed. This by a perfectly natural transposition.

In my pictures I showed objects situated where we never find them. *They represented the realization of the real if unconscious desire existing in most people.*

The lizards we usually see in our houses and on our faces, I found more eloquent in the sky habitat. Turned wood table legs lost the innocent existence ordinarily lent to them, when they appeared to dominate a forest. A woman's body floating above a city was an initiation for me into some of love's secrets. I found it very instructive to show the Virgin Mary as an undressed lover. The iron bells hanging from the necks of our splendid horses I caused to sprout like dangerous plants from the edge of a chasm.

The creation of new objects, the transformation of known objects, the change of matter for certain other objects, the association of words with images, the putting to work of ideas suggested by friends, the utilization of certain scenes from half-waking or dream states, were other means employed with a view to establishing contact between consciousness and the external world. The titles of the pictures were chosen in such a way as to inspire a justifiable mistrust of any tendency the spectator might have to over-read self-assurance.

One night in 1936, I awoke in a room where a cage and the bird sleeping in it had been placed. A magnificent visual aberration caused me to see an egg, instead of the bird, in the cage. I had just fastened upon a new and astonishing poetic secret, for the shock experienced had been provoked by the affinity of two objects: cage and egg, *whereas before, I had provoked this shock by bringing together two unrelated objects.* From the moment of that revelation I sought to find out whether other objects besides the cage might not likewise show — by bringing to light some element that was characteristic and to which they had been rigorously predestined — the same evident poetry as the egg and cage had produced by their coming together. In the course of my investigations I came to a conviction that I had always known beforehand that element to be discovered, that certain thing above all others attached obscurely to each object; only, this knowledge had always lain as though hidden in the more inaccessible zones of my mind. Since this research could yield only one exact "tag" for each object, my investigations came to be a search *for the solution of a problem for which I had three data: the object, the thing attached to it in the shadow of my consciousness, and the light under which that thing would become apparent.*

The problem of the door called for an opening through which one could pass. I showed, in by *Réponse Imprévue*, a closed door in a room; in the door an irregular shaped opening reveals the night.

Woman was responsible for *Le Viol (The Rape)*. In that picture a woman's face is made up of the essential details of her body. Her breasts have become eyes, he nose is represented by her navel, and the mouth is replaced by the sexual zone.

The problem of the window led to *La Condition humaine*. In front of a window, as seen from the interior of a room, I placed a picture that represented precisely the portion of landscape blotted out by the picture. For instance, the tree represented in the picture displaced the tree situated behind it, outside the room. For the spectator it was simultaneously inside the room; in the picture the outside the room. For the spectator it was simultaneously inside the room; in the picture the outside, in the real landscape, in thought. Which is how we see the world, namely, outside of us, though having only one representation of it within us. Similarly, we sometimes situate in the past something going on in the present. Time and space then lose that unrefined meaning in which daily experience alone takes stock.

A problem to the solution of which I applied myself, over a long period, was that of the horse. In the course of my research I again had occasion to find that my unconscious knew beforehand the thing that had to be brought to light. In fact, the first glimmer of an idea was that of the final solution, however vaguely adumbrated. It was the idea of a horse carrying three shapeless masses. Their significance became clear only after a long series of trials and experiments. First I painted an object consisting of a jar and a label bearing the image of horse, with the following printed letters: *HORSE PRESERVE (CONFITURE DE CHEVAL)*. I next thought of a horse whose head was replaced by a hand, with its index finger pointing in the direction: "Forward." But I realized that this was merely the equivalent of a unicorn.

I lingered long over an intriguing combination. In a black room, I placed a horsewoman seated near a table; with her head resting on her hand, she was dreamily gazing at a landscape whose limits were the silhouette of a horse. The animal's lower body and forelegs were earthen-colored, while upward from a horizontal line at the level of the horsewoman's eyes, the horse's coat was painted in different sky and cloud hues. What finally put me on the right track was a horseman in the position assumed while riding a galloping horse. From the sleeve of the arm thrust forward emerged the head of a noble charger, and the other arm, thrown back, held a riding whip. Beside this horseman I placed an American Indian in an identical posture, and I suddenly divined the meaning of the three shapeless masses I had placed on the horse at the beginning of my experiment.

I knew that they were horsemen and I then put the finishing touches to *La Chaîne sans fin.* In a setting of desert land and dark sky, a plunging horse is mounted by a modern horseman, a knight of the dying Middle Ages, and a horseman of antiquity.

Nietzche is of the opinion that without a burning sexual system Raphael could not have painted such a throng of Madonnas. This is at striking variance with motives usually attributed to that venerated painter: priestly influences, ardent Christian piety, esthetic ideals, search for pure beauty, etc., etc.... But Nietzsche's view of the matter makes possible a more sane interpretation of pictorial phenomena, and the violence with which that opinion is expressed is directly proportionate to the clarity of the thought underlying it.

Only the same mental freedom can make possible a salutary renewal in all the domains of human activity.

This disorderly world which is our world, swarming with contradictions, still hangs more or less together through explanations, by turns complex and ingenious, but apparently justifying it and excusing those who meanly take advantage of it. Such explanations are based on a certain experience, true.

But it is to be remarked that what is invoked is "ready-made" experience, and that if it does give rise to brilliant analysis, such experience is not itself an outcome of an analysis of its own real conditions.

Future society will develop an experience which will be the fruit of a profound analysis whose perspectives are being outlined under our very eyes. And it is under the favor of such a rigorous preliminary analysis that pictorial experience such as I understand it may be instituted.

That pictorial experience which puts the real world on trial inspired in me belief in an infinity of possibles now unknown to life. I know I am not alone in affirming that their conquest is the only valid end and reason for the existence of man.

DADAMADE

Who made Dada? Nobody and everybody. I made Dada when I was a baby and I was roundly spanked by my mother. Now everyone claims to be the author of Dada. For the past thirty years. In Zurich, in Cologne, in Paris, in London, in Tokyo, in San Francisco, in New York. I might claim to be the author of Dada in New York. In 1912 before Dada. In 1919, with the permission and with the approval of other Dadaists I legalized Dada in New York. Just once. That was enough. The times did not deserve more. That was a Dadadate. The one issue of New York Dada did not even bear the names of the authors. How unusual for Dada. Of course, there were a certain number of collaborators. Both willing and unwilling. Both trusting and suspicious. What did it matter? Only one issue. Forgotten — not even seen by most Dadaists or anti-Dadaists. Now we're are trying to revive Dada. Why? Who cares? Who does not care? Dada is dead. Or is Dada still alive?

We cannot revive something that is alive just as we cannot revive anything that is dead.

Is Dadadead? Is Dadalive? Dada is. Dadaism.

Source: "Lifeline," Rene Magritte and "Dadamade," Man Ray, from *Surrealist Painters and Poets: An Anthology*, Mary Ann Caws, ed. (Cambridge: The MIT Press, 2001), pp. 33-39, 43-44.

29.2

+

PROFESSIONS FOR WOMEN, VIRGINIA WOOLF

Virginia Woolf (1882-1941) lived in a world of writers from her earliest childhood. Her father was a critic and writer, and frequently brought writers home. In 1904, with both her parents dead, Virginia and her siblings moved to Bloomsbury, which became a home to a revolving list of writers and artists known as the Bloomsbury Circle. She married Leonard Woolf in 1912; eventually the couple would open up their own press. In spite of this joint venture, Virginia was a vehement proponent of women's financial independence. She believed that it was the only way women would achieve artistic and personal independence.

Virginia wrote numerous novels and several collections of essays, including the following one on women.

+

QUESTIONS

1. Why does Woolf have to kill the "Angel in the House?"
2. When Woolf asks "…the room is your own, but is it still bare?" of whom is she speaking?
3. Why is this essay called *Professions for Women*?

PROFESSIONS FOR WOMEN

When your secretary invited me to come here, she told me that your Society is concerned with the employment of women and she suggested that I might tell you something about my own professional experiences. It is true I am a woman; it is true I am employed; but what professional experiences have I had? It is difficult to say. My profession is literature; and in that profession there are fewer experiences for women than in any other, with the exception of the stage — fewer, I mean, that are peculiar to women. For the road was cut many years ago — by Fanny Burney, by Aphra Behn, by Harriet Martineau, by Jane Austen, by George Eliot — many famous women, and many more unknown and forgotten, have been before me, making the path smooth, and regulating my steps. Thus, when I came to write, there were very few material obstacles in my way. Writing was a reputable and harmless occupation. The family peace was not broken by the scratching of a pen. No demand was made upon the family purse. For ten and sixpence one can buy paper enough to write all the plays of Shakespeare — if one has a mind that way. Pianos and models, Paris, Vienna, and Berlin, masters and mistresses, are not needed by a writer. The cheapness of writing paper is, of course, the reason why women have succeeded as writers before they have succeeded in the other professions.

But to tell you my story — it is a simple one. You have only got to figure to yourselves a girl in a bedroom with a pen in her hand. She had only to move that pen from left to right — from ten o'clock to one. Then it occurred to her to do what is simple and cheap enough after all — to slip a few of those pages into an envelope, fix a penny stamp in the corner, and drop the envelope into the red box at the corner. It was thus that I became a journalist; and my effort was rewarded on the first day of the following month — a very glorious day it was for me — by a letter from an editor containing a cheque for one pound ten shillings and sixpence. But to show you how little I deserve to be called a professional woman, how little I know of the struggles and difficulties of such lives, I have to admit that instead of spending that sum upon bread and butter, rent, shoes and stockings, or butcher's bills. I went out and bought a cat — a beautiful cat, a Persian cat, which very soon involved me in bitter disputes with my neighbors.

What could be easier than to write articles and to buy Persian cats with; the profits? But wait a moment. Articles have to be about something. Mine, I seem to remember, was about a novel by a famous man. And while I was writing this review, I discovered that if I were going to review books I should need to do battle with a certain phantom. And the phantom was a woman, and when I came to know her better I called her after the heroine of a famous poem. The Angel in the House. It was she who used to come between me and my paper when I was writing reviews. It was she who bothered me and wasted my time and so tormented me that at last I killed her. You who come of a younger and happier generation may not have heard of her — you may not know what I mean by The Angel in the House. I will describe her as shortly as I can. She was intensely sympathetic. She was immensely charming. She was utterly unselfish. She excelled in the difficult arts of family life. She sacrificed herself daily. If there was chicken, she took the leg; if there was a draught she sat in it — in short she was so consitituted that she never had a mind or a wish of her own, but preferred to sympathize always with the minds and wishes of others. Above all — I need not say it — she was pure. Her purity was supposed to be her chief beauty — her blushes, her great grace. In those days — the last of Queen Victoria — every house had its Angel. And when I came to write I encountered her with the very first words. The shadow of her wings fell on my page; I heard the rustling of her skirts in the room. Directly, that is to say, I took my pen in my hand to review that novel by a famous man, she slipped behind me and whispered: "My dear, you are a young woman. You are writing about a book that has been written by a man. Be sympathetic; be tender; flatter; deceive; use all the arts and wiles of our sex. Never let anybody guess that you have a mind of your own. Above all, be pure." And she made as if to guide my pen. I now record the one act for which I take some credit to myself, though the credit rightly belongs to some excellent ancestors of mine who left me a certain sum of money — shall we say five hundred pounds a year? — so that it was not necessary for me to depend solely on charm for my living. I turned upon her and caught her by the throat. I did my best to kill her. My excuse if I were to be had up at a court of law, would be that I acted in self-defence. Had I not killed her she would have killed me. She would have plucked the heart out of my writing. For as I found directly I put pen to paper, you cannot review even a novel without having a mind of your own, without expressing what you think to be the truth about human relations, morality, sex. And all these questions, according to the Angel of the House cannot be dealt with freely and openly by women; they must charm, they must conciliate, they must — to put it bluntly — tell lies if they are to succeed. Thus, whenever I felt the shadow of her wing or the radiance of her halo upon my page, I took up the inkpot and flung it at her. She died hard. Her fictitious nature was of great assistance to her. It is far harder to kill a phantom than a reality. She was always creeping back when I thought I had despatched her. Though I flatter myself that I killed her in the end, the struggle was severe; it took much time that had better have been spent upon learning Greek grammar; or in roaming the world in search of adventures. But it was a real experience; it was an experience that was bound to befall all women writers at that time. Killing the Angel in the House was part of the occupation of a woman writer.

But to continue my story. The Angel was dead; what then remained? You may say that what remained was a simple and common object — a young woman in a bedroom with an inkpot. In other words, now that she had rid herself of falsehood, that young woman had only to be herself. Ah, but what is "herself?" I mean, what is a woman? I assure you, I do not know. I do not believe that you know. I do not believe that anybody can know until she has expressed herself in all the arts and professions open to human skill. That indeed is one of the reasons why I have come here — out of respect for you, who are in process of showing us by your experiments what a woman is, who are in process of providing us, by your failures and successes, with that extremely important piece of information.

But to continue the story of my professional experiences. I made one pound s ten and six by my first review; and I bought a Persian cat with the proceeds. Then I grew ambitious. A Persian cat is all very well, I said; but a Persian cat is not enough. I must have a motor-car. And it was thus that I became a novelist — for it is a very strange thing that people will give you a motor-car if you will tell them a story. It is a still stranger thing that there is nothing so delightful in the world as telling stories. It is far pleasanter than writing reviews of famous novels. And yet, if I am to obey your secretary and tell you my professional experiences as a novelist, I must tell you about a very strange experience that befell me as a novelist. And to understand it you must try first to imagine a novelist's state of mind. I hope I am not giving away professional secrets if I say that a novelist's chief desire is to be as unconscious as possible. He has to induce in himself a state of perpetual lethargy. He wants life to proceed with the utmost quiet and regularity. He wants to see the same faces, to read the same books, to do the same things day after day, month after month, while he is writing, so that nothing may break the illusion in which he is living — so that nothing may disturb or disquiet the mysterious nosings about, feelings round, darts, dashes, and sudden discoveries of that very shy and illusive spirit, the imagination. I suspect that this state is the same both for men and women. Be that as it may, I want you to imagine me writing a novel in a state of trance. I want you to figure to yourselves a girl sitting with a pen in her hand, which for minutes, and indeed for hours, she never dips into the inkpot. The image that comes to my mind when I think of this girl is the image of a fisherman lying sunk in dreams on the verge of a deep lake with a rod held out over the water. She was letting her imagination sweep unchecked round every rock and cranny of the world that lies submerged in the depths of our unconscious being. Now came the experience that I believe to be far commoner with women writers than with men. The line raced through the girl's fingers. Her imagination had rushed away. It had sought the pools, the depths, the dark places where the largest fish slumber. And then there was a smash. There was an explosion. There was foam and confusion. The imagination had dashed itself against something hard. The girl was roused from her dream. She was indeed in a state of the most acute and difficult distress. To speak without figure, she had thought of something, something about the body, about the passion, which it was unfitting for her as a woman to say. Men, her reason told her, would be shocked. The consciousness of what men will say of a woman who speaks the truth about her passions had roused her from her artist's state of unconsciousness. She could write no more. The trance was over. Her imagination could work no longer. This I believe to be a very common experience with women writers — they are impeded by the extreme conventionality of the other sex. For though men sensibly allow themselves great freedom in these respects, I doubt that they realize or can control the extreme severity with which they condemn such freedom in women.

These then were two very genuine experiences of my own. These were two of the adventures of my professional life. The first — killing the Angel in the House — I think I solved. She died. But the second, telling the truth about my own experiences as a body, I do not think I solved. I doubt that any woman has solved it yet. The obstacles against her are still immensely powerful — and yet they are very difficult to define. Outwardly, what is simpler than to write books? Outwardly, what obstacles are there for a woman rather than for a man? Inwardly, I think, the case is very different; she has still many ghosts to fight, many prejudices to overcome. Indeed it will be a long time still, I think, before a woman can sit down to write a book without finding a phantom to be slain, a rock to be dashed against. And if this is so in literature, the freest of all professions for women, how is it in the new professions which you are now for the first time entering?

Those are the questions that I should like, had I time, to ask you. And indeed, if I have laid stress upon these professional experiences of mine, it is because I believe that they are, though in different forms, yours also. Even when the path is nominally open — when there is nothing to prevent a woman from being a doctor, a lawyer, a civil servant — there are many phantoms and obstacles, as I believe, looming in her way. To discuss and define them is I think of great value and importance; for thus only can the labour be shared, the difficulties be solved. But besides this, it is necessary also to discuss the ends and the aims for which we are fighting, for which we are doing battle with these formidable obstacles. Those aims cannot be taken for granted; they must be perpetually questioned and examined. The whole position, as I see it — here in this hall surrounded by women practising for the first time in history I know not how many different professions — is one of extraordinary interest and importance. You have won rooms of your own in the house hitherto exclusively owned by men. You are able, though not without great labour and effort, to pay the rent. You are earning your five hundred pounds a year. But this freedom is only a beginning; the room is your own, but it is still bare. It has to be furnished; it has to be decorated; it has to be shared. How are you going to furnish it, how are you going to decorate it? With whom are you going to share it, and upon what terms? These, I think are questions of the utmost importance and interest. For the first time in history you are able to ask them; for the first time you are able to decide for yourselves what the answers should be. Willingly would I stay and discuss those questions and answers — but not tonight. My time is up; and I must cease.

1931

From *The Death of the Mother and Other Essays*, © 1942 Harcourt Brace Jonavich, Inc., renewed 1970 by Marjorie T. Parsons. Executrix.

29.3

--- ✤ ---

THUS WE TOOK ROME, BENITO MUSSOLINI

Before he became dictator of Italy in 1922, Benito Mussolini (1883-1945) was already quite well known for his journalism, particularly for his work in Popolo d'Italia *(People of Italy), a Fascist newspaper. Fascism was an invention of Mussolini's. The name comes from* Fascio de Combattimento *(League of Combat), the political party he created for the 1919 parliamentary elections. Although the Fascists failed then, they won in 1921, partly because they frequently targeted the communists and socialists and gained the support of Italy's middle class. Many of Mussolini's Fascist ideas would spread to Germany and Japan.*

Mussolini's style of journalism was typical of the newspapers of the inter-war period. He was unabashedly partisan (in favor of the Fascists) and flamboyant in his style. Mussolini did not, as we might expect of journalists today, make any pretense of being unbiased. His skill with writing and propaganda served him well when he seized power and during the second World War. His autobiography, from which the following account of his march on Rome in 1922 comes, is a masterpiece of propaganda. The march itself was a propaganda moment, staged as if it were a military triumph when in fact the king allowed the march to happen by appointing Mussolini Prime Minister.

--- ✤ ---

QUESTIONS

1. When Mussolini speaks of the national party of the right, what political party does he mean?
2. After winning the coup, why does Mussolini allow the king to keep his title?
3. What effect does marching in Rome, as a victor, have on him?

We selected as general concentration headquarters the town of Perugia, capital of Umbria, where many roads flow to a centre and from which it is easy to reach Rome. In case of military and political failure we could, by crossing the Appennine range, retire to the Valley of the Po. In any revolutionary movement of history that zone has always been properly considered the keystone of any situation. There our domination was absolute and undisputed. We selected the watchword; we fixed the details of the action. Everything had to be reported to me — in the offices of the *Popolo d'Italia*. Trusted Fascist messengers wove webs like scurrying spiders. I wrote the proclamation which was to be addressed to the country on the eve of action. We knew from very faithful unforgettable friends that the army, unless exceptional circumstances arose, would maintain itself on a ground of amiable neutrality....

But suddenly, when I knew that everything was ready, I issued from Milan, through the *Popolo d'Italia*, by means of independent publications, and through the correspondents of all the Italian newspapers, my proclamation of revolution. It had been signed by the quadrumvirate. Here is the text of the memorable document:

"Fascisti! Italians!

"The time for determined battle has come! Four years ago at this season the national army loosed the final offensive which brought it to Victory. To-day the army of the black shirts again takes possession of the Victory, which has been mutilated, and, going directly to Rome, brings Victory again to the glory of that Capitol. From now on 'principi' and 'triari' are mobilized. The martial law of Fascism now becomes a fact. By order of the Duce all the military, political and administrative functions of the party management are taken over by a secret Quadrumvirate of Action with dictatorial powers.

"The army, the reserve and safeguard of the Nation, must not take part in this struggle. Fascism renews its highest homage given to the Army of Vittorio Veneto. Fascism, furthermore, does not march against the police, but against a political class both cowardly and imbecile, which in four long years has not been able to give a Government to the Nation. Those who form the productive class must know that Fascism wants to impose nothing more than order and discipline upon the Nation and to help to raise the strength which will renew progress and prosperity. The people who work in the fields and in the factories, those who work in the railroads or in the offices, have nothing to fear from the Fascist Government. Their just rights will be protected. We will even be generous with unarmed adversaries.

"Fascism draws its sword to cut the multiple Gordian knots which tie and burden Italian life. We call God and the spirit of our five hundred thousand dead to witness that only one impulse sends us on, that only one passion burns within us — the impulse and the passion to contribute to the safety and greatness of our Country.

"Fascisti of all Italy!

"Stretch forth like Romans your spirits and your sinews! We must win. We will.

"Long live Italy! Long live Fascism!

"The Quadrumvirate."

At night there reached me the first news of bloody clashes in Cremona, Alessandri and Bologna, and of the assaults on munition factories and upon military barracks. I had composed my proclamation in a very short and resounding form; it had impressed the whole of the Italian people. Our life was suddenly brought into an ardent atmosphere of revolution. News of the struggles that were taking place in the various cities, sometimes exaggerated by the imaginations of reporters, gave a dramatic touch to the revolution. Responsible elements of the country asserted that as a result of this movement there would at last be a government able to rule and to command respect. The great mass of the population, however, looked out astonished, as it were from their windows....

The Sovereign understood that the revolution of the black shirts was the conclusion of three years of struggle and of fighting; he understood that only with the victory of one party could we reach pacification and that order and progress in civil life which are essential to the harmony of the Italian people.

Out of respect for the most orthodox constitutional forms, the King allowed Facta to follow the rules of the Constitution. We had then resignations, designations, consultations, communications, charges, and so and so on. At this moment came a sinister maneuver that impressed me as being ominous. The National party of the right, which had a great similarity of outlook with the Fascisti, although it had not the same system of campaign, advanced some singular claims by means of emissaries.

The National right asserted in fact that it was the keystone of the situation. Salandra, who was the most typical representative of the group, was disposed to sacrifice himself and to take upon his back the cross of power. This was to be understood as an aid for the Fascisti. I protested energetically against such a solution, which would have perpetuated compromise and error. Fascism was under arms, it was dominating the centres of national life, it had a very well-defined aim, it had followed deliberately an extra-parliamentary path and it could not allow its victory to be mutilated or adulterated in such a manner. That was my exact answer to the mediators of the union between the National right and Fascism. No compromise!…

In Rome an indescribable welcome awaited me. I did not want any delay. Even before making contacts with my political friends I motored to the Quirinal. I wore a black shirt. I was introduced without formalities into the presence of His Majesty the King. The Stefani agency and the great newspapers of the world gave stilted or speculative details about this interview. I will limit myself, for obvious reasons of reserve, to declare that the conference was characterized by great cordiality. I concealed no plans, nor did I fail to make plain my ideas of how to rule Italy. I obtained the Sovereign's approbation. I took up lodgings at the Savoy Hotel and began work. First I made arrangements with the general command of the army to bring militia to Rome and to have them defile in proper formation in a review before the King. I gave detailed and precise orders. One hundred thousand black shirts paraded in perfect order before the Sovereign. They brought to him the homage of Fascist Italy!

I was then triumphant and in Rome! I killed at once all unnecessary demonstrations in my honor. I gave orders that not a single parade should take place without the permission of the General Fascist Command. It was necessary to give to everybody from the first moment a stern and rigid sense of discipline in line with the régime that I had conceived.

I discouraged every manifestation on the part of army officers who wanted to bring me their plaudits. I have always considered the army outside and above every kind of politics. The army must, in my opinion, be inspired by absolute and conscientious discipline; it must devote itself, with the deepest will, only to the defense of frontiers and of historical rights. The army is an institution which must be preserved inviolate. It must not suffer the slightest loss in its integrity and in its high dedication.

But other and more complex problems surged about me at that moment. I was in Rome not only with the duty of composing a new ministry; I had also firmly decided to renew and rebuild from the very bottom the life of the Italian people. I vowed to myself that I would impel it toward higher and more brilliant aims.

Rome sharpened my sense of dedication. The Eternal City, "caput mundi," has two Courts and two Diplomacies. It has seen in the course of centuries imperial armies defeated under its walls. It has witnessed the decay of the strong, and the rise of universal waves of civilization and of thought. Rome, the coveted goal of princes and leaders, the universal city, heir to the old Empire and the power of Christianity! Rome welcomed me as leader of national legions, as a representative, not of a party or a group, but of a great faith and of an entire people.

Source: Benito Mussolini, *My Rise and Fall* (New York: Da Capo Press, 1998), pp.175-189.

29.4

MEIN KAMPF, ADOLF HITLER

In 1923, Adolf Hitler (1889-1945) led an unsuccessful coup against the Weimar Republic. Sixteen of his paramilitary SA (Sturmabteilung, the Storm Troops) were killed, and Hitler and his personal aide

Rudolf Hess (1894-1987) were arrested. Hitler was sentenced to five years in prison; he served less than a year. While incarcerated, he wrote Mein Kampf, *or* My Struggle. *The book is part autobiography, part self-mythologizing, and part manifesto. In this excerpt, Hitler explains how the "pure" German races have been corrupted and presents his views on the Jews. Upon his release from prison, Hitler led the Nazi Party on a fairly fast rise to power; by 1933 Hitler was named Chancellor of Germany.*

It is quite clear from this early date that the Jews are already his primary target.

———————— ✤ ————————

QUESTIONS

1. How does Hitler use scientific language to "prove" his racial theories?
2. Does Hitler find anything admirable about Jews?
3. What does Hitler have to say about the first World War?

The great civilizations of the past have all been destroyed simply because the originally creative race died out through blood-poisoning.

In every case the original cause of the downfall has been the failure to remember that all civilization depends on men, and not vice-versa — that in order to preserve a particular civilization the man who created it must also be preserved. But his preservation is dependent on the iron-clad law that it is necessary and just for the best and strongest man to be victor.

He who would live, then, must fight, and he who will not do battle in this world of eternal struggle does not deserve to live.

Even though this were harsh, it simply is so. But certainly by far the harshest fate is that which befalls the man who believes he can conquer Nature, and yet fundamentally is but mocking her. Distress, misfortune and disease are Nature's reply.

The man who mistakes and ignores race laws is really cheating himself of the happiness which is fated to be his. He blocks the triumphant advance of the best race, and thus the *sine qua non* of all human progress. Burdened with human sensitivity he is entering the sphere of the helpless beast.

It is futile to argue over what race or races were the original sustainers of human civilization and thus the real founders of everything we include in the word *humanity*. It is simpler to ask ourselves this question about the present, and here the answer is plain and easy. The human culture, the results of art, science and invention which we see before us are almost exclusively the creative product of an Aryan. But this very fact permits the not unfounded deduction that he alone was the creator of a higher human life, and thus is the prototype of what we today mean by the word *man*. He is the Prometheus of humanity, from whose radiant brow the divine spark of genius has always sprung, ever lighting anew the fire which, in the form of knowledge, has illuminated the night of speechless mysteries, and thus sent man up the road to lordship over the other creatures of this earth. Take him away, and perhaps within a few thousand years profound darkness will descend again upon earth, human civilization will vanish, and the world become a desert.

If we were to divide humanity into three classes, the founders, sustainers and destroyers of civilization, probably the Aryan would be the only possible representative of the first class. He laid the foundation and built the walls of all human creations, and only the outward form and color are determined by the particular characteristics of the individual peoples. He furnishes the great building-stones and plans for all human progress, and only the execution depends on the character of the various races. Within a few decades the whole of Eastern Asia, for example, will call a culture its own whose ultimate foundation is Hellenic spirit and Germanic technology, just as in our own case. Only the *outward* form will — at least in part — shows traits of Asiatic character. It is not true, as many people suppose, that Japan is superimposing European technical progress on her own civilization; European science and technology are being garnished with Japanese style. The basis of real life is no longer a specially Japanese civilization, although that does set the color of life (which owing to the inner difference, is more outwardly conspicuous to the European), but the tremendous scientific and technical work of Europe and America, that is of Aryan peoples. Only on the basis of these achievements can the East follow general human progress. It is the basis of the struggle for daily bread; it forges the weapons and tools. Only the outward dress is gradually accommodated to the Japanese character.

If, starting today, all further Aryan influence on Japan were to cease, supposing Europe and America to be destroyed, Japan's present advance in science and technology might continue for a while; but within a few years the well would run dry, the Japanese individuality would gain, but the present civilization would ossify, and would sink back into the sleep from which it was awakened seven decades ago by the wave a Aryan civilization. And just as the present Japanese development owes its life to an Aryan source, so once in the dim past an alien influence and an alien spirit must have awakened the Japanese culture of the time. The best proof of this is the fact of the later hardening and complete rigidity. This can happen to a people only if the originally creative racial core has been lost, or if the outside influence is lacking which furnished the impulse and the materials for the first cultural development. But if it is known that a people receives and digests the essential substance of a civilization from alien races, and grows rigid each time the external influence ceases, the race may indeed be called a "sustainer" of civilization, but never a "creator."…

The most extreme contrast to the Aryan is the Jew. In scarcely any of the world's peoples is the self-preservation instinct more strongly developed than in the so-called Chosen. The best proof of this is the mere fact of the race's existence. Where is the people that have undergone so few changes of inner proclivity, of character, etc., in the last two thousand years as the Jewish? And what people has gone through greater upheavals — and yet always come through the most tremendous catastrophes of humanity still the same? What an infinitely tenacious will to live, to preserve the species becomes evident in these facts!

The intellectual qualities of the Jew have been trained in the course of thousands of years. He is considered "clever" today, and in a certain sense has always been so. But his understanding is not the product of his own development, but of object-lessons from others. Even the human mind cannot scale heights without steps; for every upward stride it needs the foundation of the past, and this in the inclusive sense which can reveal itself only in civilization in general. Any thinking rests to but a small degree on one's own perception, and preponderantly on the experiences of previous times. The general level of civilization provides the individual (mostly without his noticing it) with such a wealth of knowledge that he is more easily able, thus armed, to take further steps of his own. The boy of today, for instance, grows up amidst a veritable host of technical achievements of past centuries, so that he takes for granted, without noticing much which only a hundred years ago was a mystery to the greatest minds, although it is of decisive importance to him in following and understanding our progress in the field in question. If even a genius of the twenties of the last century were suddenly to return from the grave today, his mere intellectual adjustment alone to the present time would be more difficult than it is for a modern fifteen-year-old boy of ordinary gifts. He would lack all the endless preliminary knowledge which our contemporary of today absorbs unconsciously, so to speak, as he grows up amid the scenes of his particular general civilization.

Since the Jew, for reasons which will immediately appear, has never possessed a culture of his own, the basis for his mental processes has always been furnished by others.

In every age his intellect has developed by means of the civilization surrounding him. The reverse of the process has never taken place.

For even though the self-preservation instinct of the Jewish people is not less but greater than that of other peoples, even if its intellectual powers often give the impression of being equal to the mental gifts of other races, it yet totally lacks the all-important requirement of a civilized people, the spirit of idealism.

The Jewish people's self-sacrifice does not go beyond the native instinct of individual self-preservation. Its apparently strong feeling of affinity is based upon a very primitive herd instinct, such as occurs in many other forms of life in this world. Here the fact is worthy of remark that herd instinct leads to mutual support only so long as a common danger makes it seem useful or unavoidable. The same pack of wolves which a moment before was united in falling on its prey back up, as hunger is satisfied, into its component animals. The same is true of horses, which try to defend themselves in unison against attack, and scatter again when danger is past.

The same thing holds for the Jew. His will to self-sacrifice is only apparent. It exists only so long as the life of each individual makes it absolutely necessary. The moment the common enemy is defeated, the common danger averted, or the plunder secured, the apparent harmony of Jews among themselves comes to an end, giving way once more to their original proclivities. The Jews are agreed only when a common danger forces them or common prey tempts them; if neither is the case, the qualities of crassest egoism come into their own, and in a turn of the hand the united people becomes a swarm of rats carrying on bloody battle among themselves.

If the Jews were alone in the world, they would smother in filth and offal, and would try mutually to overreach and exterminate one another in embittered battle, except as the lack of any willingness for self-sacrifice, expressing it all in their cowardice, turned even this battle into a sham....

To what extent the Jew's adoption of alien culture is but an echo, or rather a corruption, may be seen from the fact that he is found most often in the art which seems least dependent on personal originality, acting.

But even here he is really only the "mummer," or rather an ape, for even here he lacks the final touch of real greatness; even here he is not the brilliant creator, but the superficial imitator, and all his little tricks and dodges cannot hide the inner lifelessness. But here the Jewish press lends loving aid, raising such hosannas over every bungler, no matter how mediocre, so long as he be a Jew, that the rest of the world ends by believing it actually has an artist before it, whereas in truth the man is a mere wretched comedian.

No, the Jew possesses no civilization-building power; he has not and never did have the idealism without which there can be no upward development of man. Consequently his intellect is never constructive, but destructive — in very rare cases perhaps at best provocative, and then as the very archetype of the "power whose will is always evil and whose issue always good." It is not through him that any progress of humanity takes place, but despite him....

Thus the Jew in all ages has lived in the states of other peoples, and has formed there his own state, although it has usually sailed under the colors of the designation "religious community" so long as outward circumstances did not make a complete unveiling of his nature seem indicated. But if he thought himself strong enough to do without the protective covering, he always dropped the veil, and suddenly was what so many had refused to see and to believe — the Jew.

The Jew's life as a parasite within the body of other nations and states is the origin of a peculiarity which caused Schopenhauer to make the above-mentioned pronouncement, that the Jew is the "great master of the lie." Existence drives the Jew to lie, and indeed to lie continually, as it forces warm clothes upon the Northerner.

His life within other peoples can in the end endure only if he succeeds in creating the impression that his is not a matter of a people, but only of a "religious community," even though a special one. But this itself is the first great lie....

Jewry has always been a people with definite racial characteristics, and never a religion; only the matter of its advancement caused it early to seek a means to distract inconvenient attention from its members. And what indeed could have been more fitting and at the same time more innocent than the insinuation of the borrowed idea of a religious community? For even here everything is borrowed, or rather stolen, the Jew can derive no religious institution from his own original nature because he lacks idealism in any form, and the belief in a Hereafter is therefore absolutely foreign to him. But according to the Aryan concept no religion is imaginable which lacks a belief in some form of survival after death. And in fact the Talmud is a book to prepare not for the Hereafter but for a practical and prosperous life in this world.

The Jewish religious teaching is primarily a rule to keep the blood of Jewry pure and to regulate the intercourse of Jews among themselves, and still more with the rest of the world — with the non-Jews. But even here it is a matter not of ethical problems but of extremely elementary economic ones. Of the moral value of Jewish religious instruction there are and have long been quite detailed studies (not of Jewish authorship; the creeds of the Jews themselves, of course, are made to suit the purpose) which to Aryan eyes make this sort of religion seem absolutely monstrous. But the best indication is the product of this religious education, the Jew himself. His life is of this world alone, and his spirit is inwardly as foreign to true Christianity as his nature was two thousand years ago to the great Founder of the new teaching Himself. He, it is true, made no secret of His disposition toward the Jewish people, and even resorted to the whip if necessary to drive out from the Lord's temple this adversary of any real humanity, who then as always saw in religion only a means for a business livelihood. But of course Christ was nailed to the cross for this, while our present party Christianity lowers itself in elections to beg for Jewish votes, and afterward tries to hatch political skullduggery with atheistical Jewish parties — and against its own nationality, at that....

To stand up under the defeats on the battlefield in August of 1918 would have been child's-play. They bore no relation to the victory of our people. It was not they that overthrew us; we were overthrown by the power which prepared for these defeats by decades of systematic work in robbing our people of the political and moral instincts and forces which alone enable and thus entitle peoples to survive.

By passing heedlessly over the question of preserving the racial foundations of our nationality, the old Empire also neglected the sole right which can give life in this world. Peoples which become or allow themselves to be bastardized sin against the will of Eternal Providence, and their downfall at the hands of one stronger is not an injustice done them, but merely the restoration of justice. If a people no longer respects the characteristics given it by Nature and rooted in its blood, it has no further right to complain of the loss of its earthly existence.

Everything in the world is to be improved. Every defeat may father a later victory. Every lost war may be the cause of a later revival, every distress may crucify human energy, and from every oppression may come the forces for a new spiritual rebirth so long as the blood is kept pure.

Sources: Adolf Hitler, *Mein Kampf* (New York: Stackpole Sons Publishers, 1939), pp. 279-319.

———— ✣ ————

QUESTIONS FOR PART 29

1. How are these writers, individually or in common, responding to the first World War?
2. Compare the use of language in Mussolini's and Hitler's texts.
3. Are the artistic and political responses of the inter-war period only about reacting to things?

PART 30

WORLD WAR II

The First World War had been the war to end all wars, yet within twenty years it would be completely overshadowed by the Second World War. Between 1939-1945, between thirty-five and fifty-five million people had been killed across the world. The war was one of racism (against Jews, against the Japanese, against Slavs) and anti-Western hatred (by Japan). It was simultaneously a war of imperialism and of anti-imperialism (Germany, Russia, and Japan began the war to build empires, as well as to destroy the old empires of Britain, France, and China). The War involved the use of technology to cause an unprecedented level of destruction. The War also revealed the infinite capacity of human beings in general and of Western civilization in particular to survive. It was a war of unparalleled acts of heroism, as well as of hatred.

Many of the major players in the Second World War had one thing in common: they were impassioned and unparalleled public speakers. It was the great age of oratory, even if many of the speeches were orations of hate. You can sense something of the greatness of these speakers in two of the selections — speeches by Winston Churchill and Adolf Hitler — although the performance of the speeches is lost on paper.

The remaining two sources indicate the extent of the war's impact on Western civilization, on the diplomatic and public side as well as the personal.

30.1

APPEASEMENT: CONVERSATION BETWEEN CHAMBERLAIN AND HITLER

On September 20, 1938, British Prime Minister Neville Chamberlain (1869-1940) and German Chancellor Adolf Hitler (1889-1945) met in Munich to discuss Germany's plans concerning Czechoslovakia. Five days before this meeting, the Nazis had demanded that the Sudetenland in Czechoslovakia be handed over to Germany, claiming the right of nationalist interest in re-uniting the Germans of Czechoslovakia with greater Germany. The Czechoslovakian state was one of the multi-ethnic creations of the Versailles Treaty, and Hitler claimed its existence violated the right of self-determination by the Germans of the Sudetenland. The Munich Conference included Chamberlain, Hitler, and representatives from France and Germany. Czechoslovakia was not at the meeting.

However, Chamberlain was not only in Munich to discuss this recent crisis. He used the meeting as a chance to determine if Hitler's nationalist goals had been fulfilled or if the Fuhrer had plans for further invasions in Europe, as recorded in this private meeting between the two men.

---- ✦ ----

QUESTIONS

1. Chamberlain asks Hitler if he will refrain from bombing Prague or killing women and children from the air if the Czechs resist; can you think of a particular event prior to this that Chamberlain might be remembering?
2. On September 1, 1939, Hitler's army invaded Poland. Is there any indication in this conversation that he had that plan in mind?
3. Why does Chamberlain bring up the subject of trade?

Prime Minister: He warmly appreciated Herr Hitler's words, but there was now something he wished to say to him by way of an appeal. He had been told that Herr Hitler intended, if the Czechs accepted the proposals, to treat them very generously. This was what he (the Prime Minister) would have expected from Herr Hitler, but he was obliged to consider the possibility that the Czech Government might be mad enough to refuse the terms and attempt resistance. In such an eventuality he wanted to ask Herr Hitler to make sure that nothing should be done which would diminish the high opinion of him which would be held throughout the world in consequence of yesterday's proceedings. In particular, he trusted that there would be no bombardment of Prague or killing of women and children by attacks from the air.

Herr Hitler: Before answering that specific question, he would like to say something on a point of principle. Years ago he made proposals for the restriction of the use of the air arm. He himself fought in the Great War and has a personal knowledge of what air bombardment means. It had been his intention, if he had to use force, to limit air action to front line zones as a matter of principle, but even if the Czechs were mad enough to reject the terms and he had consequently to take forcible action, he would always try to spare the civilian population and to confine himself to military objectives. He hated the thought of little babies being killed by gas bombs.

The Prime Minister: He thanked Herr Hitler for these assurances and would now turn to another matter. He wished to report to him a conversation which he had had the previous evening with Signor Mussolini on the subject of Spain. He had suggested to the Duce the possibility that the Four Great Powers might call upon the two sides in Spain to establish an armistice and that they might offer their services in assisting them to arrive at a settlement of their differences. The Duce had said, in reply, that he was tired of Spain. (Here Herr Hitler laughed heartily.) He had lost 50,000 men there; Franco had time and again thrown away his opportunities of securing a victory. He, Mussolini, was no longer afraid of Bolshevistic domination. He had never had any territorial aims in Spain, and it was his intention shortly to withdraw a considerable body of Italians. As to the suggestion, the Duce had expressed his intention of thinking it over. Had the Führer anything to say upon this subject?

Herr Hitler: First of all he desired to repeat what he had many times said before, that Germany had no territorial ambitions in Spain, and that all these rumours about her desiring to occupy Morocco or any other territory were pure invention. He had only supported Franco against bolshevism, of which they had had experience in Munich. He did not know whether it was true that the danger of communism in Spain was over (here the Prime Minister interjected: 'The Duce says so'), and he did not know how it would be possible to induce the two parties to agree to a truce, but he agreed with Mussolini that the end of the Spanish conflict would be welcome, and he would be delighted to withdraw the few German volunteers who were there as soon as ever the others were willing to do the same. If Spain were to become Communist, he feared that the infection would spread to France, from France to Belgium, from Belgium to Holland, and one did not know where it would stop.

The Prime Minister: He too did not know how a truce could be secured, but he had thought that if the two sides received a call from the Four Great Powers they might well be induced to listen and that, once the truce had been called, the Powers might be able to help in getting a settlement. However, he only now wished to report to the Führer what had passed between himself and Mussolini on this subject and he hoped that the Führer to would give it his personal attention.

Herr Hitler assented.

The Prime Minister: Whenever they began to talk about future Anglo-German relations, no doubt the Führer would have some requests to make and he would not be surprised if, in turn, the Prime Minister asked something from him. (Here the Führer smiled broadly.) He was oppressed by the thought of the increasing burden which was being imposed upon all countries by the expenditure upon armaments, which was eating up the capital which ought to be employed on building houses, on better food and on improving the health of the people. Accordingly he had listened with sympathy to Herr Hitler's views on the restriction of air action, but it seemed to him that the difficulty was in inducing people to believe that agreements to abstain from air bombardment would in fact be carried out in practice. They could see to-day both in Spain and China how women and children and civilians were being blown to pieces by aerial bombing, but whenever a protest was made to those responsible for this bombing they replied always that they had been aiming at military objectives and that the civilians had suffered because of their proximity to them.

Several efforts had been made in the past to bring about disarmament, but only one of them had been at all effective, namely, that which began as the Washington Treaty and was continued in London, in which the tonnage of warships and the caliber of their guns was [sic] limited. Basing his views on this experience, he concluded that the qualitative method of restricting armaments was the one which had the most practical results and, moreover, had the additional advantage that it was more easy to control. It was much more possible to see that a country was not constructing bigger weapons than it had agreed to than it was to make sure that it was not constructing more such weapons.

Bombing from the air had now become a highly specialised affair for which machines with specialised devices and instruments had been developed, and it was no longer possible to maintain that it was of no use to abolish the bombing machine because bombs could still be dropped from civilian machines. It was true that bombs could be dropped from any machine in the air, but to make an effective military use of them it was nowadays necessary to use the highly specialised instrument which had been devised for this purpose. Therefore the abolition of bombing aircraft seemed to him to be the practical thing to agree upon.

He knew what the Führer would say in reply to this proposal. He would say that it would be all very well if he were dealing only with him or with France and Italy, but there was Russia and Russia would not agree. Nevertheless, bearing in mind the perfection which had been reached by the modern fighter machine and also the pitch of efficiency to which Herr Hitler had brought his anti-aircraft defences, and bearing also in mind that in future he need no longer regard Czechoslovakia as a starting-off place for Russian aggression, could he not feel that Russia could be left out of account?

Herr Hitler: The situation about air disarmament is just the same as it is in the case of the naval situation. If a single nation refuses to agree, all the others have to follow her example. One sees what has happened in the case of the Naval Treaty. When Japan refused to agree, all the other nations had to give up their restriction. It would be just the same if one tried to abolish bombing aircraft. It could only be accepted if all did the same. He himself had proposed years ago —
1. The abolition of bombing aircraft;
2. If '1' could not be accepted, the abolition of bombing outside a zone of 15 to 20 kilom. from the front line; and
3. If neither '1' or '2' were accepted, the limitation of bombing to a zone which could be reached by heavy artillery.

He himself was particularly attached to '1', which was, in his view, in line with the Geneva Agreement providing for the exemption of non-combatants from the effects of warfare. The development of bombing from the air extends the horrors of war to the non-combatant population and is therefore a barbarism.

Modern bombers have a range from 6,000 to 8,000 kilom. Unlike Germany, whose ideology is confined to herself, Russia's ideology is an article for export. Poland intervenes geographically between Germany and Russia, but he had no very clear idea of her powers of resistance. The same is the case with Roumania. As to Czechoslovakia, he did not know whether the Czechs had changed their mind, but they had only got to prepare a few landing grounds and it would be possible for Russia to land from 2,000 to 4,000 machines in a space of from two or three hours. One ought not to overestimate the effectiveness of anti-aircraft defences and devices, especially in the case of Germany, where her vulnerable industrial establishments were so close to the frontier that they could be destroyed before the anti-aircraft defences had adequate warning to put themselves into operation. To give practical effect to the Prime Minister's suggestion, it would be necessary to effect an all-around international agreement.

The Prime Minister: Then it is understood that Herr Hitler does not exclude the participation of Germany in such an agreement by the nations which, to be universal, would, of course, mean the assent of Russia and in turn of Japan.

Herr Hitler: The most universal measure ever taken for the limitation of armaments was the Red Cross agreement when the Powers decided that they would not revert to actions which used to be, at one time, general, such as the killing of prisoners, &c. It was only possible because the whole world agreed to it.

The Prime Minister: He would now leave this question and turn to another, namely, the relations between Germany and South-Eastern Europe. He had read expressions of German opinion indicating a suspicion that England desired not a military but an economic encirclement of Germany. This was a suspicion which, if entertained, was without foundation. He, however, desired to see an improvement in international trade. Yesterday's proceedings would certainly ease the political tension, but something more positive was required in the economic sphere and he would particularly like to see a relaxation in the restrictions on international trade which now existed. Had the Führer any suggestions to make on this subject?

Herr Hitler: In South-Eastern Europe German relations were economic, but there were no political ties. These economic relations were quite natural because Germany is a great producer of industrial articles and a large consumer of raw materials and foodstuffs. The Balkan States are the other way round. They produce the primary products and consume industrial articles. The greatest difficulties which Germany had experienced with the United States were because Germany was willing to import raw materials and food from the United States, but the United States could not accept payment in the only form which was possible to Germany, namely, the export of industrial goods, because the United States was herself and immense producer of these goods and at the time had 12,000,000 unemployed. That was why Germany had been unable to settle her difficulties with the United States.

One day, but not now when there was so little time, he would like very much to have a full discussion with the Prime Minister on these economic problems. His own idea for the reconstruction of world economy was that it should not be on an artificial basis, but that it should be founded on national exchanges between primary producers and producers of industrial goods. International trade could not be permanently improved by artificial means such as tariffs or loans. He wanted a continuous flow of the exchange production of raw materials against industrial products, and that his theory was not wrong was shown by the fact that there was in Germany a considerable internal prosperity, and this was due to the fact that he had organized this exchange on the lines he had indicated.

The Prime Minister: It certainly would be interesting some day to have a talk upon this profoundly important problem, and he would only say now that it seemed to him that there was a considerable difference between the internal conditions in Germany, which were under a strict central control, and the regulation of the relations between different countries where there was no such control. Moreover, he would have thought that, even if Herr Hitler's theories were not only correct but capable of being put into practice, there would still be required loans to facilitate this flow into the two directions mentioned by Herr Hitler.

Now, he would not keep Herr Hitler any longer, but he wished to say that he thought it would be a pity if this meeting passed off with nothing more than the settlement of the Czech question, which had been agreed upon yesterday. What he had in mind was to suggest to Herr Hitler that it would be helpful to both countries and to the world in general if they could issue some statement which showed the agreement between them on the desirability of better Anglo-German relations, leading to a greater European stability. Accordingly, he had ventured to draft a short statement which he would now ask Herr Hitler to read and to consider whether he would be disposed to issue such a statement over the signatures of himself and the Prime Minister to the public. As the observations were translated to Herr Hitler he ejaculated at intervals 'Ja! Ja!' and when it was finished he said he would certainly agree to sign this document. When did the Prime Minister wish to do so?

The Prime Minister: Immediately.

Herr Hitler: Then let us sign.

Appendix to No. 1228

We, the German Führer and Chancellor and the British Prime Minster, have had a further meeting to-day and are agreed in recognizing that the question of Anglo-German relations is of the first importance for the two countries and for Europe.

We regard the agreement signed last night and the Angle-German Naval Agreement as symbolic of the desire of our two peoples never to go to war with one another again.

We are resolved that the method of consultation shall be the method adopted to deal with any other questions that may concern our two countries, and we are determined to continue our efforts to remove possible sources of difference and thus to contribute to assure the peace of Europe.

(Signed) A. Hitler.
(Signed) Neville Chamberlain.

September 30, 1938.

Source: E. L. Woodward, Rohan Butler, and Margaret Lambert, eds., *Documents on British Foreign Policy 1919-1939* (London: His Majesty's Stationery Office, 1949), pp. 635-640.

30.2

✢

NEVER IN THE FIELD OF HUMAN CONFLICT, WINSTON CHURCHILL

Winston Churchill (1874-1965), Prime Minister of Great Britain, delivered this speech on August 18, 1940 a few weeks into the Battle of Britain. The Battle of Britain was a series of aerial bombings throughout August and September, 1940. The first targets had been industrial and military centers, as well as ports and harbors. In September, the Luftwaffe *(German Air Force) began to bomb civilian centers.*

In the speech, given shortly before civilians became targets, Churchill briefly summarized what had already passed in the war and predicted that Nazi Germany will ultimately be defeated.

✢

QUESTIONS

1. Why does Churchill seem positive about the fact that 92,000 British civilians are dead, wounded, or missing in this, the first year of the war?
2. What does Churchill see as the relationship between the two world wars?
3. How is this a "new kind of war?"

Almost a year has passed since the war began, and it is natural for us, I think, to pause on our journey at this milestone and survey the dark, wide field. It is also useful to compare the first year of this second war against German aggression with its forerunner a quarter of a century ago. Although this war is in fact only a continuation of the last, very great differences in its character are apparent. In the last war millions of men fought by hurling enormous masses of steel at one another. "Men and shells" was the cry, and prodigious slaughter was the consequence. In this war nothing of this kind has yet appeared. It is a conflict of strategy, of organization, of technical apparatus, of science, mechanics and morale. The British casualties in the first 12 months of the Great War amounted to 365,000. In this war, I am thankful to say, British killed, wounded, prisoners and missing, including civilians, do not exceed 92,000, and of these a large proportion are alive as prisoners of war. Looking more widely around, one may say that throughout all Europe, for one man killed or wounded in the first year perhaps five were killed or wounded in 1914-15.

The slaughter is only a small fraction, but the consequences to the belligerents have been even more deadly. We have seen great countries with powerful armies dashed out of coherent existence in a few weeks. We have seen the French Republic and the renowned French Army beaten into complete and total submission with less than the casualties which they suffered in any one of half a dozen of the battles of 1914-18. The entire body — it might almost seem at times the soul — of France has succumbed to physical effects incomparably less terrible than those which were sustained with fortitude and undaunted will power 25 years ago. Although up to the present the loss of life has been mercifully diminished, the decisions reached in the course of the struggle are even more profound upon the fate of nations than anything that has ever happened since barbaric times. Moves are made upon the scientific and strategic boards, advantages are gained by mechanical means, as a result of which scores of millions of men become incapable of further resistance, or judge themselves incapable of further resistance, and a fearful game of chess proceeds from check to mate by which the unhappy players seem to be inexorably bound.

There is another more obvious difference from 1914. The whole of the warring nations are engaged, not only soldiers, but the entire population, men, women and children. The fronts are everywhere. The trenches are dug in the towns and streets. Every village is fortified. Every road is barred. The front line runs through the factories. The workmen are soldiers with different weapons but the same courage. These are great and distinctive changes from what many of us saw in the struggle of a quarter of a century ago. There seems to be every reason to believe that this new kind of war is well suited to the genius and the resources of the British nation and the British Empire; and that, once we get properly equipped and properly started, a war of this kind will be more favorable to us than the somber mass slaughters of the Somme and Passchendaele. If it is a case of the whole nation fighting and suffering together, that ought to suit us, because we are the most united of all the nations, because we entered the war upon the national will and with our eyes open, and because we have been nurtured in freedom and individual responsibility and are the products, not of totalitarian uniformity, but of tolerance and variety....

Hitler is now sprawled over Europe. Our offensive springs are being slowly compressed, and we must resolutely and methodically prepare ourselves for the campaigns of 1941 and 1942. Two or three years are not a long time, even in our short, precarious lives. They are nothing in the history of the nation, and when we are doing the finest thing in the world, and have the honor to be the sole champion of the liberties of all Europe, we must not grudge these years or weary as we toil and struggle through them. It does not follow that our energies in future years will be exclusively confined to defending ourselves and our possessions. Many opportunities may lie open to amphibious power, and we must be ready to take advantage of them. One of the ways to bring this war to a speedy end is to convince the enemy, not by words, but by deeds, that we have both the will and the means, not only to go on indefinitely, but to strike heavy and unexpected blows. The road to victory may not be so long as we expect. But we have no right to count upon this. Be it long or short, rough or smooth, we mean to reach our journey's end....

Rather more than a quarter of a year has passed since the new Government came into power in this country. What a cataract of disaster has poured out upon us since then! The trustful Dutch overwhelmed; their beloved and respected Sovereign driven into exile; the peaceful city of Rotterdam the scene of a massacre as hideous and brutal as anything in the Thirty Years' War; Belgium invaded and beaten down; our own fine Expeditionary Force, which King Leopold called to his rescue, cut off and almost captured, escaping as it seemed only by a miracle and with the loss of all its equipment; our Ally, France, out; Italy in against us; all France in the power of the enemy, all its arsenals and vast masses of military material converted or convertible to the enemy's use; a puppet Government set up at Vichy which may at any moment be forced to become our foe; the whole western seaboard of Europe from the North Cape to the Spanish frontier in German hands; all the ports, all the airfields on this immense front employed against us as potential springboards of invasion. Moreover, the German air power, numerically so far outstripping ours, has been brought so close to our Island that what we used to dread greatly has come to pass and the hostile bombers not only reach our shores in a few minutes and from many directions, but can be escorted by their fighting aircraft. Why, Sir, if we had been confronted at the beginning of May with such a prospect, it would have seemed incredible that at the end of a period of horror and disaster, or at this point in a period of horror and disaster, we should stand erect, sure of ourselves, masters of our fate and with the conviction of final victory burning unquenchable in our hearts. Few would have believed we could survive; none would have believed that we should today not only feel stronger but should actually be stronger than we have ever been before.

Let us see what has happened on the other side of the scales. The British nation and the British Empire, finding themselves alone, stood undismayed against disaster. No one flinched or wavered; nay, some who formerly thought of peace, now think only of war. Our people are united and resolved, as they have never been before. Death and ruin have become small things compared with the shame of defeat or failure in duty. We cannot tell what lies ahead. It may be that even greater ordeals lie before us. We shall face whatever is coming to us. We are sure of ourselves and of our cause, and that is the supreme fact which has emerged in these months of trial....

Why do I say all this? Not, assuredly, to boast; not, assuredly, to give the slightest countenance to complacency. The dangers we face are still enormous, but so are our advantages and resources. I recount them because the people have a right to know that there are solid grounds for the confidence which we feel, and that we have good reason to believe ourselves capable, as I said in a very dark hour two months ago, of continuing the war "if necessary alone, if necessary for years." I say it also because the fact that the British Empire stands invincible, and that Nazidom is still being resisted, will kindle again the spark of hope in the breasts of hundreds of millions of down-trodden or despairing men and women throughout Europe, and far beyond its bounds, and that from these sparks there will presently come cleansing and devouring flame.

The great air battle which has been in progress over this Island for the last few weeks has recently attained a high intensity. It is too soon to attempt to assign limits either to its scale or to its duration. We must certainly expect that greater efforts will be made by the enemy than any he has so far put forth. Hostile air fields are still being developed in France and the Low Countries, and the movement of squadrons and material for attacking us is still proceeding. It is quite plain that Herr Hitler could not admit defeat in his air attack on Great Britain without sustaining most serious injury. If after all his boastings and bloodcurdling threats and lurid accounts trumpeted round the world of the damage he has inflicted, of the vast numbers of our Air Force he has shot down, so he says, with so little loss to himself; if after tales of the panic-stricken British crushed in their holes cursing the plutocratic Parliament which has led them to such a plight — if after all this his whole air onslaught were forced after a while tamely to peter out, the Fuhrer's reputation for veracity of statement might be seriously impugned. We may be sure, therefore, that he will continue as long as he has the strength to do so, and as long as any preoccupations he may have in respect of the Russian Air Force allow him to do so....

The gratitude of every home in our Island, in our Empire, and indeed throughout the world, except in the abodes of the guilty, goes out to the British airmen who, undaunted by odds, unwearied in their constant challenge and mortal danger, are turning the tide of the World War by their prowess and b~ their devotion. Never in the field of human conflict was so much owed by so many to so few. All hearts go out to the fighter pilots, whose brilliant actions we see with our own eyes day after day; but we must never forget that all the time, night after night, month after month, our bomber squadrons travel far into Germany, find their targets in the darkness by the highest navigational skill, aim their attacks, often under the heaviest fire, often with serious loss, with deliberate careful discrimination, and inflict shattering blows upon the whole of the technical and war-making structure of the Nazi power. On no part of the Royal Air Force does the weight of the war fall more heavily than on the daylight bombers, who will play an invaluable part in the case of invasion and whose unflinching zeal it has been necessary in the meanwhile on numerous occasions to restrain....

A good many people have written to me to ask me to make on this occasion a fuller statement of our war aims, and of the kind of peace we wish to make after the war, than is contained in the very considerable declaration which was made early in the autumn. Since then we have made common cause with Norway, Holland and Belgium. We have recognized the Czech Government of Dr. Benes, and we have told General de Gaulle that our success will carry with it the restoration of France. I do not think it would be wise at this moment, while the battle rages and the war is still perhaps only in its earlier stage, to embark upon elaborate speculations about the future shape which should be given to Europe or the new securities which must be arranged to spare mankind the miseries of a third World War. The ground is not new, it has been frequently traversed and explored, and many ideas are held about it in common by all good men, and all free men. But before we can undertake the task of rebuilding we have not only to be convinced ourselves, but we have to convince all other countries that the Nazi tyranny is going to be finally broken. The right to guide the course of world history is the noblest prize of victory. We are still toiling up the hill; we have not yet reached the crest-line of it; we cannot survey the landscape or even imagine what its condition will be when that longed-for morning comes. The task which lies before us immediately is at once more practical, more simple and more stern. I hope — indeed, I pray — that we shall not be found unworthy of our victory if after toil and tribulation it is granted to us. For the rest, we have to gain the victory. That is our task....

Source: *British Orations from Ethelbert to Churchill* (New York: E. P. Dutton, 1915, 1960), pp. 364-369.

30.3

TWO SPEECHES, HITLER

One of Hitler's greatest assets as a politician had always been his exceptional skill at oratory. This is clearly on display in these two speeches. The first outlines his plans for Europe; he delivered this speech on August 22, 1939 to a meeting of his military commanders. It is a very frank and revealing talk.

Nine days later Germany invaded Poland.

Hitler delivered the second speech near the end of the war, on January 30, 1945. Determined to rally the Germany citizens, even though the German army was officially in retreat, Hitler gave this radio address.

On April 30, 1945, Hitler committed suicide; on May 7, 1945, Germany surrendered.

QUESTIONS

1. Compare the two speeches. Does Hitler's confidence in German victory still seem as high in 1945 as it had been in 1939?
2. In the first speech, does Hitler seem concerned about anyone being able to stop the German conquests?
3. What relationship does Hitler see between Jews and the Bolsheviks?

August 22, 1939

The decision to attack Poland was arrived at in spring. Originally there was fear that because of the political constellation we would have to strike at the same time against England, France, Russia and Poland. This risk too we should have had to take. [German field marshal Hermann] Goring had demonstrated to us that his Four Year Plan is a failure and that we are at the end of our strength, if we do not achieve victory in a coming war.

Since the autumn of 1938 and since I have realized that Japan will not go with us unconditionally and that [Italian dictator Benito] Mussolini is endangered by that nitwit of a King and the treacherous scoundrel of a Crown Prince, I decided to go with [Russian leader Joseph] Stalin. After all there are only three great statesmen in the world, Stalin, I, and Mussolini. Mussolini is the weakest, for he has been able to break the power neither of the crown nor of the [Roman Catholic] Church. Stalin and I are the only ones who visualize the future. So in a few weeks hence I shall stretch out my hand to Stalin at the common German-Russian frontier and with him undertake to re-distribute the world.

Our strength lies in our quickness and in our brutality; [Mongol leader] Genghis Khan has sent millions of women and children into death knowingly and with a light heart. History sees in him only the great founder of States. As to what the weak Western European civilisation asserts about me, that is of no account. I have given the command and I shall shoot everyone who utters one word of criticism, for the goal to be obtained in the war is not that of reaching certain lines but of physically demolishing the opponent. And so for the present only in the East I have put my death-head formations in place with the command relentlessly and without compassion to send into death many women and children of Polish origin and language. Only thus we can gain the living space that we need. Who after all is today speaking about the destruction of the Armenians?

Colonel-General [Walther] von Brauchitsch has promised me to bring the war against Poland to a close within a few weeks. Had he reported to me that he needs two years or even only one year, I should not have given the command to march and should have allied myself temporarily with England instead of Russia for we cannot conduct a long war. To be sure a new situation has arisen. I experienced those poor worms [French premier Êdouard] Daladier and [British prime minister Neville] Chamberlain in Munich. They will be too cowardly to attack. They won't go beyond a blockade. Against that we have our autarchy and the Russian raw materials.

Poland will be depopulated and settled with Germans. My pact with the Poles was merely conceived of as a gaining of time. As for the rest, gentlemen, the fate of Russia will be exactly the same as I am now going through with in the case of Poland. After Stalin's death — he is a very sick man — we will break the Soviet Union. Then there will begin the dawn of the German rule of the earth.

The little States cannot scare me. After [President Kemal Atatürk's] death Turkey is governed by cretins and half idiots. [King] Carol of Roumania is through and through the corrupt slave of his sexual instincts. The King of Belgium and the Nordic kings are soft jumping jacks who are dependent upon the good digestions of their over-eating and tired peoples.

We shall have to take into the bargain the defection of Japan. I save Japan a full year's time. The Emperor is a counterpart to the last Czar — weak, cowardly, undecided. May he become a victim of the revolution. My going together with Japan never was popular. We shall continue to create disturbances in the Far East and in Arabia. Let us think as "gentlemen" and let us see in these peoples at best lacquered half maniacs who are anxious to experience the whip.

The opportunity is as favourable as never before. I have but one worry, namely that Chamberlain or some other such pig of a fellow will come at the last moment with proposals or with ratting. He will fly down the stairs, even if I shall personally have to trample on his belly in the eyes of the photographers.

No, it is too late for this. The attack upon and the destruction of Poland begins Saturday early. I shall let few companies in Polish uniform attach in Upper Silesia or in the Protectorate. Whether the world believes it is quite indifferent. The world believes only in success.

For you, gentlemen, fame and honour are beginning as they have not since centuries. Be hard, be without mercy, act more quickly and brutally than the others. The citizens of Western Europe must tremble with horror. That is the most human way of conducting a war. For it scares the others off.

The new method of conducting war corresponds to the new drawing of the frontiers. A war extending from [the Polish cities of] Reval, Lublin, Kaschau to the mouth of the Danube. The rest will be given to the Russians. [Foreign Minister Joachim von] Ribbentrop has orders to make every offer and to accept every demand. In the West I reserve to myself the right to determine the strategically best line. Here one will be able to work with Protectorate regions, such as Holland, Belgium and French Lorraine.

And now, on to the enemy, in Warsaw we will celebrate our reunion.

January 30, 1945

THE FIGHT AGAINST BOLSHEVISM

B ut if this is possible at all, it is only because a change has taken place in the German people since 1933. If Germany today were the Germany envisaged by the Versailles Treaty, Europe would long since have been swept away by the hurricane from Central Asia. It is hardly necessary to argue with those eternal blockheads who maintain that an unarmed Germany would, owing to its impotence, not have become the victim of this Jewish international world plot. Such reasoning would amount to a reversal of all laws of nature.

When was a helpless goose ever not eaten by the fox because she was constitutionally incapable of harboring aggressive designs? And when was a wolf ever reformed and become a pacifist because sheep do not wear armor? If there are still bourgeois states who earnestly believe this, that only proves how necessary it was to do away with an era that by its educational system managed to cultivate and maintain such notions, nay, even granted them political influence.

The fight against this Jewish Asiatic bolshevism had been raging long before National Socialism came into power. The only reason why it had not already overrun Europe during the years 1919-20 was that it was then itself too weak and too poorly armed.

Its attempt to eliminate Poland was not abandoned because of its compassion for the Poland of that time but only because of the lost battle before Warsaw. Its intention to annihilate Hungary was not discarded because they changed their minds, but because Bolshevist power could not be maintained militarily. Nor was the attempt to smash Germany given up because this achievement was not desired but because it proved impossible to overcome the natural resistance [and] stamina of our people....

God the Almighty has made our nation. By defending its existence we are defending His work. The fact that this defense is fraught with incalculable misery, suffering and hardships makes us even more attached to this nation. But it also gives us that hard will needed to fulfill our duty even in the most critical struggle; that is, not only to fulfill our duty toward the decent, noble Germans, but also our duty toward those few infamous ones who turn their backs on their people.

In this fateful battle there is therefore for us but one command: He who fights honorably can thus save his own life and the lives of his loved ones. But he who, because of cowardice or lack of character, turns his back on the nation shall inexorably die an ignominious death.

That National Socialism succeeded in awakening and strengthening this spirit in our German people is a great achievement. Only when this mighty world drama will have died away and the bells of peace are ringing will realization come of what the German people owes to this spiritual renaissance: No less than its existence in this world....

I herewith repeat my prophecy: England will not only not be in a position to control bolshevism but her development will unavoidably evolve more and more toward the symptoms of this destructive disease.

The democracies are unable to rid themselves now of the forces they summoned from the steppes of Asia.

All the small European nations who capitulated, confident of Allied assurances, are facing complete annihilation. It is entirely uninteresting whether this fate will befall them a little earlier or later; what counts is its implacability. The Kremlin Jews are motivated only by tactical considerations; whether in one case they act with immediate brutality or, in another case, with some reticence, the result will always be the same.

Germany, however, shall never suffer this fate. The guarantor thereof is the victory achieved twelve years ago within our country. Whatever our enemies may plot, whatever sufferings they may inflict on our German cities, on German landscapes and, above all, on our people, all that cannot bear any comparison with the irreparable misery, the tragedy that would befall us if the plutocratic-Bolshevistic conspiracy were victorious.

Therefore, it is all the more necessary on this twelfth anniversary of the rise to power to strengthen the heart more than ever before and to steel ourselves with yet a greater, harder spirit of resistance, until we can again — as we did before — put on the graves of the dead of this enormous struggle a wreath inscribed with the words: "and yet you were victorious."

Therefore I expect every German to do his duty to the last and that he be willing to take upon himself every sacrifice he will be asked to make; I expect every able-bodied German to fight with the complete disregard for his personal safety; I expect the sick and the weak or those otherwise unavailable for military duty to work with their last strength; I expect city dwellers to forge the weapons for this struggle and I expect the farmer to supply the bread for the soldiers and workers of this struggle by imposing restrictions upon himself; I expect all women and girls to continue supporting this struggle with utmost fanaticism.

In this appeal I particularly address myself to German youth. In vowing ourselves to one another, we are entitled to stand before the Almighty and ask Him for His grace and His blessing. No people can do more than that everybody who can fight, fights, and that everybody who can work, works, and that they all sacrifice in common, filled with but one thought: to safeguard freedom and national honor and thus the future of life.

However grave the crisis may be at the moment, it will, despite everything, finally be mastered by our unalterable will, by our readiness for sacrifice and by our abilities. We shall overcome this calamity, too, and this fight, too, will not be won by central Asia but by Europe; and at its head will be the nation that has represented Europe against the East for 1,500 years and shall represent it for all times: our Greater German Reich, the German nation.

Source: Thomas Streissguth, ed. *World War II: Great Speeches in History* (San Diego: Greenhaven Press, 2003), pp. 52-54, 115-121.

30.4

❖

HOLOCAUST SURVIVOR ACCOUNT

Today the Holocaust looms large in the popular understanding of the Second World War. Yet the full extent of the Holocaust was not realized until several years after the war. Europe and the United States were aware that Nazi Germany was segregating Jews and reducing their legal rights as early as the Nuremberg Laws of 1935, but as there were anti-Semitic laws and movements across the West, no one either realized or acknowledged the extent of Hitler's determination to annihilate the Jews. Although Hitler had those plans in place before the war began, he was careful to keep them within his circle of top advisors. There were rumors about the deportations, and of the "disappearance" of Jews, but the existence of extermination camps was not known. As Allied armies moved across Germany and Nazi-held Poland in 1945, soldiers first discovered and liberated the camps. By then almost six million Jews had been killed, nearly the entire Jewish populations of Germany and Poland. Approximately eight million non-Jews—Polish, Russians, Gypsies, homosexuals, political dissidents—were killed in labor and prisoner of war camps by the Nazi Empire.

The following source is an account of Aranka Siegal and her family during the war. It is a story of legal marginalization, confinement to the ghettos, deportation, and finally incarceration in the Bergen-Belsen concentration camp.

—————— ✦ ——————

QUESTIONS

1. Before the segregationist laws were put into effect, did Siegal's family feel threatened by their Christian neighbors?
2. How does being a child during the Holocaust affect how Aranka remembers it?
3. Aranka speaks of seeing factory smokestacks running when she first arrives at the camp; what is she really seeing and when does she realize it?

Curfews were imposed, which meant we reached the market when there was nothing left to buy. We could only obtain food from the few Jewish-owned stores. Soon the next decree put an end to even that; it declared that Jews could no longer own stores, but would have to hand over their businesses to the Christians. Jews, however, might remain as clerks in their own stores. With that decree, the black market, which had started with food rationing, took off in earnest. Prices for a kilo of sugar or butter skyrocketed. The whole mood of the city changed; frustration, anger, greed, jealousy, and secrecy were fueled by the effects of the constant propaganda in newspapers, radio, posters and the ever-constant drum of the town crier. Long established relationships between Christian and Jewish neighbors became estranged, awkward, and uncertain....

I arrived at school one day to find another student in my seat. Before I could think of anything to say, I looked for my teacher and realized that there were some other confused students standing near her at the blackboard. Mrs. Szabo, a usually composed, sympathetic, and fair teacher, motioned for me to come and stand with the cluster of girls. Her face was flushed, and she wrung her hands as she turned to face the six of us, saying, "I'm sorry to inform you girls that, as of today, Jewish children are not allowed to attend public school."

I felt more humiliated than I had ever felt before, and was certain that I would never be able to pick my head up and look in the faces of my friends again. The six of us turned toward the door and walked out without a word of comment, never to return to the schoolhouse that had been so much a part of our lives for the past six years....

It had been bad enough when my father was drafted into a *Munka Tabor* (an army work camp for Jews). But at least we had received post cards from him once in a great while. From Lilli and Lajos we heard nothing.

Soon after their deportation I overheard a conversation between my mother and Mrs. Gerber. Mother was quoting her mother's words of warning: "You are fooling yourself. You are living among gentiles and you think they are your friends. I just hope you never have to depend on them. They are neighborly, but there is a difference between neighborly, and your own. Only your own can feel your pain."

"She was right," said Mother, "I should have listened to her. Not one of them came to express their sympathy. And surely the whole street must have witnessed the tragedy of two Hungarian policemen walking a young Hungarian soldier in uniform, handcuffed. If they only knew how proud Lajos was of that uniform...." That's when Mother started to be bitter, resentful, and mistrusting of our Christian neighbors....

I heard voices and, turning to the porch, I saw that our yard had been invaded. Military and police uniforms mingled. Strange male voices spoke, asked questions, and gave orders. Mother came out, holding Joli in her arms and Sandor by the hand. She was surrounded by hostile men. One of the men stood reading the names of our whole family, which the census taker had posted on our porch. They had come to take us away.

I ran for Iboya, who was out at work, and together we raced back to Gyar Street. The policeman with the notebook drew a thick black line through each of our names as he pronounced it. We climbed into the wagon, carrying a few bundles of belongings. My mother wanted to lock the house, but the policeman told her there was no need. "Take a good look, woman," he said, as he motioned the driver to start. "I doubt you'll ever see it again."...

I was filled with burning questions. Why has the world turned against us? Could no one stop this madness? Where is God? I wanted to ask my mother, but I couldn't even look at her. She had tied a kerchief on her head before the march, knotting it in the front, with her face drawn deep inside. She responded to no one except the two little ones.

The line kept slowing down, stopping and starting to move again. We inched along. An exodus of families marched through weeds, toward the waiting cattle cars. The sun had no mercy, it burned through the layers of our clothing and made us sweat. My mouth was parched and I wished someone would come along with a water bucket, but we passed no houses. No civilization, no humanity. Only the robot guards and some of the white arm banded youths. One of them approached my mother and said "Mrs. Davidowics, I want to ask you something, since your German is better than mine. I overheard two trainmen talking, and they mentioned the word 'Auschwitz.' Do you know what it means?"

"No," she answered.

We were less than two meters away, when we became aware of why the lines stopped so often. We heard shrieks and cries from ahead of us. Mother, Mrs. Gerber, Judy and I stepped out of our line to investigate. We witnessed people being searched by German soldiers before being ordered up into the cattle cars. They were reaching in and under their clothing. When we got to where the soldiers were standing by the train, one of them grabbed Judy and put his hand under her blouse. Mother pushed back her scarf and suddenly became responsive. She put Joli down and clutched Iboya and me to her side.

"*Nein!* You will not touch my daughters!" she declared in German, her voice filled with anger and fear. They laughed at her, and as we got to the head of the line, Iboya, Mother, and I were pulled apart by three of the leering guards. The back of my neck was suddenly in an iron grip, and a coarse, rough hand brushed down my chest and over my breasts, bursting the buttons of my blouse. Bending over me so close that I could smell the sausage on his breath and see the tobacco stains on his teeth, the soldier reached into my panties and felt inside my private parts. I couldn't tell if my eyes stung more from hurt or shame. He shoved me on.

I believed, naively, that the search, and our next two days and two nights imprisoned in the indescribably inhumane conditions of the cattle car, were as cruel and unbearable an experience as life could ever bring. I did not realize that the moment the cattle car door was shut behind us, our former life and everything in it was lost forever. As a child I had heard my Babi use the Jewish expression, "It is for the best that man does not know his destiny." If I had known what lay ahead, I would have spent my time in the cattle car differently, and saved myself regrets in the future....

By the second day, conditions in our cattle car — hunger, thirst, exhaustion from lack of sleep, only two buckets for toilet facilities, and air too foul to breathe, and the foreboding of the unknown had made the morale of the hardiest among us sink to despair. All we wanted was to "get there," where ever that might be, and to have the doors thrust open, to breathe fresh air before we suffocated.

When the train stopped, all of us except the very sick stood up. Mother called Iboya and me so we would exit together. Some emaciated prisoners in striped uniforms entered our car to help carry off the sick. One of the prisoners came over to me and asked in Yiddish "How old are you?" I exaggerated and said, "I'm fourteen." "No, no, you must remember to say you're sixteen." Pointing to Iboya, I said, "My sister is sixteen." Turning to her, he said, "You're seventeen."...

The air was pungent with the smell of burning rubber and smoke. Low buildings with tall chimneys stood in the near distance. "Factories," I thought. Large flakes of ash like black butterflies, floated in the air. Old men and women hugged, kissed and cried as they were being separated. The lines kept moving. The German soldiers were using their whips, dogs were barking, and children were crying.

Soon the line in front of us disappeared and we were facing four SS men. One of them was holding an officer's baton. Another asked Iboya and me our age. When I heard Iboya say "seventeen," I remembered to say, "sixteen." The one holding the baton let it fall between Mother and the two little ones, pushing them away from her to the right. Mother stood petrified, while seconds passed. Then a decision registered. Turning from Iboya and me, she picked up Joli and took Sandor by the hand. "They need me more," she said. Her eyes murky with tears, she turned to us and said, "Be brave and look after each other. Stay together." It was her last act as our mother. She walked off to the right with the two little ones.

An hour later we passed by the arrival area on our way to the barracks. We had been changed from civilians to prisoners. Our hair had been clipped to the roots, our clothing confiscated in exchange for a one-piece gray garment and wooden shoes. Iboya looked right at me and didn't recognize me. We all looked alike, stripped of our individuality and human dignity. We looked like a herd of sheep. We were also drugged with some tranquilizer disguised in a drink. When we walked past the railroad tracks, the cattle cars were gone, the platform lay silent and void of all human presence, as if our whole experience was just a bad dream.

The factories, it seemed, were running — their chimneys were spouting endless black smoke and red flames. The black butterflies multiplied. One of them landed on my arm. I tried to brush it away. It left a black grimy smudge. But we were still ignorant of our hellish surroundings, or the meaning of the "selection" of Mother and the two little ones....

When the Gestapo inspectors finally arrived, belted and buckled in full uniform and black shiny boots, our *blokova* gave them the Nazi salute and made her report in careful German without a trace of Yiddish. They stayed a long time, counting us over and over, as they walked up and down the line. We stood terrified, holding our breath, like robots. They never looked at us. We were just numbers....

In January of 1945, with the Russians approaching, the Germans decided to evacuate the camp and send us on a death march. It was the most bitter cold winter. We walked in the snow, sleet, wind, ice, and rain. The sun was rarely visible. Our clothing was soaked. There was no way to dry it. When some people fell and couldn't keep up with the lines, the German guards shot them without mercy and left the bodies on the side of the road.

By the second week, I could not put one foot in front of the other. I felt chilled to the bone and feverish and I had lost the will to live. I told Iboya that I was just going to sit down and let them shoot me like the others. "Why keep on suffering, when I know for sure that I can never reach our destination, wherever that may be?" I was so frozen that I had even convinced myself that if I were shot, my blood would warm me up....

By the time we reached Bergen-Belsen in early March, we had lost more than half of our women, and of those left half had death written all over them. We learned to recognize the signs: their eyes hollow, with water bags like large blisters under them; protruding bellies; swollen ankles and their walk — bodies leaning forward as if they were about to fall on their faces any second, which is just what would happen. What was so amazing is that some undetermined inner strength drove them on. Life was seeping out of their bodies, and yet they kept walking. After a while I couldn't look at them. Whenever we chanced to be near a house with a window, I would try to catch my image and examine it for those signs. None of those women lasted to witness liberation.

From all we had seen we had become conditioned to accept a lot of horror, but when we arrived at Bergen-Belsen we immediately wished that we were back in Christianstadt. Bodies so wasted that their skin was transparent and their skeletons visible through it were more than even we could bear. And there were piles of bodies five to six feet high. Men in scarcely better shape had to make the rounds each morning with wheelbarrows, collecting these wasted corpses. One held the wrists while another held the ankles of the limbs as thin as ropes, and they swung the cadaver to the top of the pile, knowing too well that soon they could become part of those decomposing corpses. The bitter cold of the winter had kept the corpses frozen, but now the March wind and the thawing ground made the stench unbearable.

Iboya and I, through some unexplainable miracle, and several close call, lived long enough, if barely, to greet the British army, our liberators, on 15 April 1945. I had developed a case of dysentery, from which so many had already died and continued to die even after liberation. But Iboya dragged me out of the barrack, ran after a medic, and cried, "My sister is dying. You must help her." She held on to his arm and wouldn't let go until he had me put on a stretcher and marked my forehead with a red cross, an indication for the ambulance that I could be saved by immediate attention.

From *The Holocaust Personal Accounts*, edited by David Scrase and Wolfgang Meider, p. 125-130, 133-138, 140-142. Copyright © 2001 The Center for Holocaust Studies at the University of Vermont. Reprinted with permission.

30.5

YEAR OF DECISIONS (WHY WE DROPPED THE BOMB), HARRY TRUMAN

Harry S. Truman (1884-1972) became President of the United States on April 12, 1945, when Franklyn D. Roosevelt died. At the time, America was still at war with Germany and Japan, and although victory in Europe now seemed certain, the outcome of the Pacific War was a bit less positive. One of the most controversial decisions any American President of the twenty century has had to make is the one that faced Truman in August 1945: whether to use the atomic bomb on Japan or not.

In this excerpt from Truman's Memoirs, he discusses why he decided to drop the bomb on Hiroshima on August 6, 1945, which resulted in the death of 140,000 people.

---- ✢ ----

QUESTIONS

1. Truman claims that Stalin "showed no special interest" when told that the U.S. had an atomic weapon. Do you believe that claim?
2. What do you think was the most persuasive reason for using the bomb?
3. Why is Truman so emphatic that it was his decision alone, in the end, to use the bomb?

The historic message of the first explosion of an atomic bomb was flashed to me in a message from Secretary of War Stimson on the morning of July 16. The most secret and the most daring enterprise of the war had succeeded. We were now in possession of a weapon that would not only revolutionize war but could alter the course of history and civilization. This news reached me at Potsdam the day after I had arrived for the conference of the Big Three.

Stimson flew to Potsdam the next day to see me and brought with him at once details of the test. I received him at once and called in Secretary of State Byrnes, Admiral Leahy, General Marshall, General Arnold, and Admiral King to join us at my office at the Little White House. We reviewed our military strategy in the light of this revolutionary development. We were not ready to make use of this weapon against the Japanese, although we did not know as yet what effect the new weapon might have, physically or psychologically, when used against the enemy. For that reason the military advised that we go ahead with the existing military plans for the invasion of the Japanese home islands.

At Potsdam, as elsewhere, the secret of the atomic bomb was kept closely guarded. We did not extend the very small circle of Americans who knew about it. Churchill naturally knew about the atomic bomb project from its very beginning, because it had involved the pooling of British and American technical skill.

On July 24 I casually mentioned to Stalin that we had a new weapon of unusual destructive force. The Russian Premier showed no special interest. All he said was that he was glad to hear it and hoped we would make "good use of it against the Japanese."

A month before the test explosion of the atomic bomb the service Secretaries and the Joint Chiefs of Staff had laid their detailed plans for the defeat of Japan before me for approval. There had apparently been some differences of opinion as to the best route to be followed, but these had evidently been reconciled, for when General Marshall had presented his plan for a two-phase invasion of Japan, Admiral King and General Arnold had supported the proposal heartily.

The Army plan envisaged an amphibious landing in the fall of 1945 on the island of Kyushu, the southernmost of the Japanese home islands. This would be accomplished by our Sixth Army, under the command of General Walter Krueger. The first landing would then be followed approximately four months later by a second great invasion, which would be carried out by our Eighth and Tenth Armies, followed by the First Army transferred from Europe, all of which would go ashore in the Kanto plains area near Tokyo. In all, it had been estimated that it would require until the late fall of 1946 to bring Japan to her knees.

This was a formidable conception, and all of us realized fully that the fighting would be fierce and the losses heavy. But it was hoped that some of Japan's forces would continue to be preoccupied in China and others would be prevented from reinforcing the home islands if Russia were to enter the war.

There was, of course, always the possibility that the Japanese might choose to surrender sooner. Our air and fleet units had begun to inflict heavy damage on industrial and urban sites in Japan proper. Except in China, the armies of the Mikado had been pushed back everywhere in relentless successions of defeats.

Acting Secretary of State Grew had spoken to me in late May about issuing a proclamation that would urge the Japanese to surrender but would assure them that we would permit the Emperor to remain as head of the state. Grew backed this with arguments taken from his ten years' experience as our Ambassador in Japan, and I told him that I had already given thought to this matter myself and that it seemed to me a sound idea....

It was my decision then that the proclamation to Japan should be issued from the forthcoming conference at Potsdam. This, I believed, would clearly demonstrate to Japan and to the world that the Allies were united in their purpose. By that time, also, we might know more about two matters of significance for our future effort: the participation of the Soviet Union and the atomic bomb. We knew that the bomb would receive its first test in mid-July. If the test of the bomb was successful, I wanted to afford Japan a clear chance to end the fighting before we made use of this newly gained power. If the test should fail, then it would be even more important to us to bring about a surrender before we had to make a physical conquest of Japan. General Marshall told me that it might cost half a million American lives to force the enemy's surrender on his home grounds.

But the test was now successful. The entire development of the atomic bomb had been dictated by military considerations. The idea of the atomic bomb had been suggested to President Roosevelt by the famous and brilliant Dr. Albert Einstein, and its development turned out to be a vast undertaking. It was the achievement of the combined efforts of science, industry, labor, and the military, and it had no parallel in history. The men in charge and their staffs worked under extremely high pressure, and the whole enormous task required the services of more than one hundred thousand men and immense quantities of material. It required over two and a half years and necessitated the expenditure of two and a half billions of dollars.

Only a handful of the thousands of men who worked in these plants knew what they were producing. So strict was the secrecy imposed that even some of the highest-ranking officials in Washington had not the slightest idea of what was going on. I did not. Before 1939 it had been generally agreed among scientists that it was theoretically possible to release energy from the atom. In 1940 we had begun to pool with Great Britain all scientific knowledge useful to war, although Britain was at war at that time and we were not. Following this — in 1942 — we learned that the Germans were at work on a method to harness atomic energy for use as a weapon of war. This, we understood, was to be added to the V-1 and V-2 rockets with which they hoped to conquer the world. They failed, of course, and for this we can thank Providence. But now a race was on to make the atomic bomb — a race that became "the battle of the laboratories."...

We could hope for a miracle, but the daily tragedy of a bitter war crowded in on us. We labored to construct a weapon of such overpowering force that the enemy could be forced to yield swiftly once we could resort to it. This was the primary aim of our secret and vast effort. But we also had to carry out the enormous effort of our basic and traditional military plans....

My own knowledge of these developments had come about only after I became president, when Secretary Stimson had given me the full story. He had told me at that time that the project was nearing completion and that a bomb could be expected within another four months. It was at his suggestion, too, that I had then set up a committee of top men and had asked them to study with great care the implications the new weapon might have for us....

It was their recommendation that the bomb be used against the enemy as soon as it could be done. They recommended further that it should be used without specific warning and against a target that would clearly show its devastating strength. I had realized, of course, that an atomic bomb explosion would inflict damage and casualties beyond imagination. On the other hand, the scientific advisers of the committee reported, "We can propose no technical demonstration likely to bring an end to the war; we see no acceptable alternative to direct military use." It was their conclusion that no technical demonstration they might propose, such as over a deserted island, would be likely to bring the war to an end. It had to be used against an enemy target.

The final decision of where and when to use the atomic bomb was up to me. Let there be no mistake about it. I regarded the bomb as a military weapon and never had any doubt that it should be used. The top military advisers to the President recommended its use, and when I talked to Churchill he unhesitatingly told me that he favored the use of the atomic bomb if it might aid to end the war.

In deciding to use this bomb I wanted to make sure that it would be used as a weapon of war in the manner prescribed by the laws of war. That meant that I wanted it dropped on a military target. I had told Stimson that the bomb should be dropped as nearly as possibly upon a war production center of prime military importance.

Stimson's staff had prepared a list of cities in Japan that might serve as targets. Kyoto, though favored by General Arnold as a center of military activity, was eliminated when Secretary Stimson pointed out that it was cultural and religious shrine of the Japanese.

Four cities were finally recommended as targets: Hiroshima, Kokura, Niigata, and Nagasaki. They were listed in that order as targets for the first attack. The order of selection was in accordance with the military importance of these cities, but allowance would be given for weather conditions at the time of the bombing. Before the selected targets were approved as proper for military purposes, I personally went over them in detail with Stimson, Marshall, and Arnold, and we discussed the matter of timing and the final choice of the first target.

General Spaatz, who commanded the Strategic Air Forces, which would deliver the bomb on the target, was given some latitude as to when and on which of the four targets the bomb would be dropped. That was necessary because of weather and other operational considerations. In order to get preparations under way, the War Department was given orders to instruct General Spaatz that the first bomb would be dropped as soon after August 3 as weather would permit. The order to General Spaatz read as follows:

To: General Carl Spaatz
    Commanding General
    United States Army Strategic Air Forces

1.   The 509 Composite Group, 20th Air force will deliver its first special bomb as soon as weather will permit visual bombing after 2 August 1945 on one of the targets: Hiroshima, Kokura, Niigata and Nagasaki. To carry military and civilian scientific personnel from the War Department to observe and record the effects of the explosion of the bomb, additional aircraft will accompany the airplane carrying the bomb. The observing planes will stay several miles distant from the point of impact of the bomb.

2.   Additional bombs will be delivered on the above targets as soon as made ready by the project staff. Further instructions will be issued concerning targets other than those listed above.

3. Dissemination of any and all information concerning the use of the weapon against Japan is reserved to the Secretary of War and the President of the United States. No communiqué on the subject or release of information will be issued by Commanders in the field without specific prior authority. Any news stories will be sent to the War Department for special clearance.

4. The foregoing directive is issued to you by direction and with the approval of the Secretary of War and the Chief of Staff, U.S.A. It is desired that you personally deliver one copy of this directive to General MacArthur and one copy to Admiral Nimitz for their information.

/s/ Thos. T. Handy
General, GSC
Acting Chief of Staff

With this order the wheels were set in motion for the first use of an atomic weapon against a military target. I had made the decision. I also instructed Stimson that the order would stand unless I notified him that the Japanese reply to our ultimatum was acceptable.

A specialized B-29 unit, known as the 509th Composite Group, had been selected for the task, and seven of the modified B-29's, with pilots and crews, were ready and waiting for orders. Meanwhile ships and planes were rushing the materials for the bomb and specialists to assemble them to the Pacific island of Tinian in the Marianas.

On July 28, Radio Tokyo announced that the Japanese government would continue to fight. There was no formal reply to the joint ultimatum of the United States, the United Kingdom, and China. There was no alternative now. The bomb was scheduled to be dropped after August 3 unless Japan surrendered before that day.

On August 6, the fourth day of the journey home from Potsdam, came the historic news that shook the world. I was eating lunch with members of the *Augusta's* crew when Captain Frank Graham, White House Map Room watch officer, handed me the following message:

TO THE PRESIDENT
FROM THE SECRETARY OF WAR

Big bomb dropped on Hiroshima August 5 at 7:15 P.M. Washington time. First reports indicate complete success which was even more conspicuous than earlier test.

Harry S. Truman, from *Memoirs, Vol. 1: Year of Decision* (Garden City: Doubleday and Co., 1955), p. 415-421. Copyright © 1955 Time, Inc. Reprinted by permission of Margaret Truman Daniel.

QUESTIONS FOR PART 30

1. Using the sources here, who do you think is the most effective speaker?
2. Compare the account of Chamberlain's visit with Hitler and Truman's discussion of how he informed the other Allies about the bomb. What role did diplomacy play in the war?
3. In what ways technology determining policy in the first half of the twentieth century?

PART 31

COLD WAR

The post World War II period, from 1945-1970, was a period of rapid economic recovery and a new political conflict. The harsh reality of four devastating years of warfare had to be dealt with; the physical rebuilding of Europe was itself an arduous challenge. Complicating the rebuilding and recovery was the developing Cold War. All was not peaceful between the victors. The tensions between the Allied powers were obvious even before the war ended; after 1945 the potential for the West to obliterate itself and indeed all life — through nuclear weapons only — exacerbated those tensions. Further unsettling to Europe was the fact that the dominant states were new to the political stage; they were not new states, but never before had the United States or Russia (Soviet Union) had so much power over so many people. This was the age of superpowers.

The period after World War II is also comparable to the period after World War I; between 1945-1989 (the Cold War era) the West was in the same sort of cultural angst that she had been in between 1919-1939. The most significant difference between the two periods was the degree of economic prosperity and materialism in the West. Even in the communist nations materialism was a common theme; in the West materialism meant consumerism, in eastern Europe it meant weapons proliferation. The Cold War, as with the inter-war period, was also a time of dramatic cultural and social changes. The Civil Rights movement in the United States, the decline of industry in Britain, economic recession, the sexual revolution, and the feminist movement forever altered how people of the West lived, and how the West thought of itself and the world.

31.1

--- ✦ ---

ON THE MARSHALL PLAN, GEORGE C. MARSHALL

George C. Marshall gave this speech at Harvard University in 1947. In it, he proposes rebuilding Europe economically as a way of shaping Europe politically. All of the Allies, although relieved at victory, were nonetheless concerned that if Europe were not rebuilt, and rebuilt quickly, communism would spread and a new war might potentially occur. The United States was also hoping that the Plan would lead to more markets for American manufactured goods and thus ultimately benefit the country economically. Marshall was Secretary of State to President Truman when he offered this Plan, which was enacted in 1948.

Marshall's speech sums up the entire policy of the United States after the war: rebuild and prevent another war. Marshall's plan, coupled with Harry Truman's policy of "containing" communism (the Truman Doctrine), are the two most important pieces of post-war strategy.

---- ✤ ----

QUESTIONS

1. In what ways is the Marshall Plan aimed at preventing the spread of communism?
2. Why does the Plan include giving money to Germany, after the United States has spent so much money and effort in her defeat?
3. What role does Marshall envision for European leaders in shaping the Plan?

I need not tell you, gentlemen, that the world situation is very serious. That must be apparent to all intelligent people. I think one difficulty is that the problem is one of such enormous complexity that the very mass of facts presented to the public by press and radio make it exceedingly difficult for the man in the street to reach a clear appraisement of the situation. Furthermore, the people of this country are distant from the troubled areas of the earth and it is hard for them to comprehend the plight and consequent reaction of the long-suffering peoples, and the effect of those reactions on their governments in connection with our efforts to promote peace in the world.

In considering the requirements for the rehabilitation of Europe the physical loss of life, the visible destruction of cities, factories, mines, and railroads was correctly estimated, but it has become obvious during recent months that this visible destruction was probably less serious than the dislocation of the entire fabric of European economy. For the past 10 years conditions have been highly abnormal. The feverish maintenance of the war effort engulfed all aspects of national economics. Machinery has fallen into disrepair or is entirely obsolete. Under the arbitrary and destructive Nazi rule, virtually every possible enterprise was geared into the German war machine. Long-standing commercial ties, private institutions, banks, insurance companies and shipping companies disappeared, through the loss of capital, absorption through nationalization or by simple destruction. In many countries, confidence in the local currency has been severely shaken. The breakdown of the business structure of Europe during the war was complete. Recovery has been seriously retarded by the fact that two years after the close of hostilities a peace settlement with Germany and Austria has not been agreed upon. But even given a more prompt solution of these difficult problems, the rehabilitation of the economic structure of Europe quite evidently will require a much longer time and greater effort than had been foreseen.

There is a phase of this matter which is both interesting and serious. The farmer has always produced the foodstuffs to exchange with the city dweller for the other necessities of life. This division of labor is the basis of modern civilization. At the present time it is threatened with breakdown. The town and city industries are not producing adequate goods to exchange with the food-producing farmer. Raw materials and fuel are in short supply. Machinery is lacking or worn out. The farmer or the peasant cannot find the goods for sale which he desires to purchase. So the sale of his farm produce for money which he cannot use seems to him unprofitable transaction. He, therefore, has withdrawn many fields from crop cultivation and is using them for grazing. He feeds more grain to stock and finds for himself and his family an ample supply of food, however short he may be on clothing and the other ordinary gadgets of civilization. Meanwhile people in the cities are short of food and fuel. So the governments are forced to use their foreign money and credits to procure these necessities abroad. This process exhausts funds which are urgently needed for reconstruction. Thus a very serious situation is rapidly developing which bodes no good for the world. The modern system of the division of labor upon which the exchange of products is based is in danger of breaking down.

The truth of the matter is that Europe's requirements for the next three or four years of foreign food and other essential products — principally from America — are so much greater than her present ability to pay that she must have substantial additional help, or face economic, social, and political deterioration of a very grave character.

The remedy lies in breaking the vicious circle and restoring the confidence of the European people in the economic future of their own countries and of Europe as a whole. The manufacturer and the farmer throughout wide areas must be able and willing to exchange their products for currencies the continuing value of which is not open to question.

Aside from the demoralizing effect on the world at large and the possibilities of disturbances arising as a result of the desperation of the people concerned, the consequences to the economy of the United States should be apparent to all. It is logical that the United States should do whatever it is able to do to assist in the return of normal economic health in the world, without which there can be no political stability and no assured peace. Our policy is directed not against any country or doctrine but against hunger, poverty, desperation, and chaos. Its purpose should be the revival of working economy in the world so as to permit the emergence of political and social conditions in which free institutions can exist. Such assistance, I am convinced, must not be on a piecemeal basis as various crises develop. Any assistance that this Government may render in the future should provide a cure rather than a mere palliative. Any government that is willing to assist in the task of recovery will find full cooperation, I am sure, on the part of the United States Government. Any government which maneuvers to block the recovery of other countries cannot expect help from us. Furthermore, governments, political parties, or groups which seek to perpetuate human misery in order to profit therefrom politically or otherwise will encounter the opposition of the United States.

It is already evident that, before the United States Government can proceed much further in its efforts to alleviate the situation and help start the European world on its way to recovery, there must be some agreement among the countries of Europe as to the requirements of the situation and the part those countries themselves will take in order to give proper effect to whatever action might be undertaken by this Government. It would be neither fitting nor efficacious for this Government to undertake to draw up unilaterally a program designed to place Europe on its feet economically. This is the business of the Europeans. The initiative, I think, must come from Europe. The role of this country should consist of friendly aid in the drafting of a European program so far as it may be practical for us to do so. The program should be a joint one, agreed to by a number, if not all European nations.

An essential part of any successful action on the part of the United States is an understanding on the part of the people of America of the character of the problem and the remedies to be applied. Political passion and prejudice should have no part. With foresight, and a willingness on the part of our people to face up to the vast responsibilities which history has clearly placed upon our country, the difficulties I have outlined can and will be overcome.

Source: Allan M. Winkler, ed., *The Cold War: A History in Documents* (Oxford: University Press, 2000), pp. 163-165.

31.2

❖

"SINEWS OF PEACE" (IRON CURTAIN), WINSTON CHURCHILL

Winston Churchill continued to give influential speeches that helped shape world policy long after the second World War had ended and he left office. One of his most famous speeches is the "Sinews of Peace" commencement address for Westminster College. This speech, which appears here, is famous for coining the phrase "iron curtain." It was also a pessimistic portrait of life in Europe after the war, as divided as it ever was, although now the enemies were capitalism and communism. This speech is the battle cry of the Cold War.

❖

QUESTIONS

1. How does Churchill characterize the United States in this speech? Is this merely flattery?
2. Why does Churchill want to arm the United Nations Organization?
3. Compare this speech to Marshall's. Do the two men envision the same international role for the United States in European politics?

The United States stands at this time at the pinnacle of world power. It is a solemn moment for the American Democracy. For with primacy in power is also joined an awe inspiring accountability to the future. If you look around you, you must feel not only the sense of duty done but also you must feel anxiety lest you fall below the level of achievement. Opportunity is here now, clear and shining for both our countries. To reject it or ignore it or fritter it away will bring upon us all the long reproaches of the after-time. It is necessary that constancy of mind, persistency of purpose, and the grand simplicity of decision shall guide and rule the conduct of the English-speaking peoples in peace as they did in war. We must, and I believe we shall, prove ourselves equal to this severe requirement....

When I stand here this quiet afternoon I shudder to visualise what is actually happening to millions now and what is going to happen in this period when famine stalks the earth. None can compute what has been called "the unestimated sum of human pain." Our supreme task and duty is to guard the homes of the common people from the horrors and miseries of another war. We are all agreed on that.

Our American military colleagues, after having proclaimed their "over-all strategic concept" and computed available resources, always proceed to the next step — namely, the method. Here again there is widespread agreement. A world organisation has already been erected for the prime purpose of preventing war, UNO, the successor of the League of Nations, with the decisive addition of the United States and all that that means, is already at work. We must make sure that its work is fruitful, that it is a reality and not a sham, that it is a force for action, and not merely a frothing of words, that it is a true temple of peace in which the shields of many nations can some day be hung up, and not merely a cockpit in a Tower of Babel. Before we cast away the solid assurances of national armaments for self-preservation we must be certain that our temple is built, not upon shifting sands or quagmires, but upon the rock. Anyone can see with his eyes open that our path will be difficult and also long, but if we persevere together as we did in the two world wars — though not, alas, in the interval between them — I cannot doubt that we shall achieve our common purpose in the end.

I have, however, a definite and practical proposal to make for action. Courts and magistrates may be set up but they cannot function without sheriffs and constables. The United Nations Organisation must immediately begin to be equipped with an international armed force. In such a matter we can only go step by step, but we must begin now. I propose that each of the Powers and States should be invited to delegate a certain number of air squadrons to the service of the world organisation. These squadrons would be trained and prepared in their own countries, but would move around in rotation from one country to another. They would wear the uniform of their own countries but with different badges. They would not be required to act against their own nation, but in other respects they would be directed by the world organisation. This might be started on a modest scale and would grow as confidence grew. I wished to see this done after the First World War, and I devoutly trust it may be done forthwith.

It would nevertheless be wrong and imprudent to entrust the secret knowledge or experience of the atomic bomb, which the United States, Great Britain, and Canada now share, to the world organisation, while it is still in its infancy. It would be criminal madness to cast it adrift in this still agitated and un-united world. No one in any country has slept less well in their beds because this knowledge and the method and the raw materials to apply it, are at present largely retained in American hands. I do not believe we should all have slept so soundly had the positions been reversed and if some Communist or neo-Fascist State monopolised for the time being these dread agencies. The fear of them alone might easily have been used to enforce totalitarian systems upon the free democratic world, with consequences appalling to human imagination. God has willed that this shall not be and we have at least a breathing space to set our house in order before this peril has to be encountered: and even then, if no effort is spared, we should still possess so formidable a superiority as to impose effective deterrents upon its employment, or threat of employment, by others. Ultimately, when the essential brotherhood of man is truly embodied and expressed in a world organisation with all the necessary practical safeguards to make it effective, these powers would naturally be confided to that world organisation....

All this means that the people of any country have the right, and should have the power by constitutional action, by free unfettered elections, with secret ballot, to choose or change the character or form of government under which they dwell; that freedom of speech and thought should reign; that courts of justice, independent of the executive, unbiased by any party, should administer laws which have received the broad assent of large majorities or are consecrated by time and custom. Here are the title deeds of freedom which should lie in every cottage home. Here is the message of the British and American peoples to mankind. Let us preach what we practise — let us practise what we preach.

I have now stated the two great dangers which menace the homes of the people: War and Tyranny. I have not yet spoken of poverty and privation which are in many cases the prevailing anxiety. But if the dangers of war and tyranny are removed, there is no doubt that science and co-operation can bring in the next few years to the world, certainly in the next few decades newly taught in the sharpening school of war, an expansion of material well-being beyond anything that has yet occurred in human experience. Now, at this sad and breathless moment, we are plunged in the hunger and distress which are the aftermath of our stupendous struggle; but this will pass and may pass quickly, and there is no reason except human folly or sub-human crime which should deny to all the nations the inauguration and enjoyment of an age of plenty. I have often used words which I learned fifty years ago from a great Irish-American orator, a friend of mine, Mr. Bourke Cockran. "There is enough for all. The earth is a generous mother; she will provide in plentiful abundance food for all her children if they will but cultivate her soil in justice and in peace." So far I feel that we are in full agreement....

A shadow has fallen upon the scenes so lately lighted by the Allied victory. Nobody knows what Soviet Russia and its Communist international organisation intends to do in the immediate future, or what are the limits, if any, to their expansive and proselytising tendencies. I have a strong admiration and regard for the valiant Russian people and for my wartime comrade, Marshal Stalin. There is deep sympathy and goodwill in Britain — and I doubt not here also — towards the peoples of all the Russias and a resolve to persevere through many differences and rebuffs in establishing lasting friendships. We understand the Russian need to be secure on her western frontiers by the removal of all possibility of German aggression. We welcome Russia to her rightful place among the leading nations of the world. We welcome her flag upon the seas. Above all, we welcome constant, frequent and growing contacts between the Russian people and our own people on both sides of the Atlantic. It is my duty however, for I am sure you would wish me to state the facts as I see them to you, to place before you certain facts about the present position in Europe.

From Stettin in the Baltic to Trieste in the Adriatic, an iron curtain has descended across the Continent. Behind that line lie all the capitals of the ancient states of Central and Eastern Europe. Warsaw, Berlin, Prague, Vienna, Budapest, Belgrade, Bucharest and Sofia, all these famous cities and the populations around them lie in what I must call the Soviet sphere, and all are subject in one form or another, not only to Soviet influence but to a very high and, in many cases, increasing measure of control from Moscow. Athens alone — Greece with its immortal glories — is free to decide its future at an election under British, American and French observation. The Russian-dominated Polish Government has been encouraged to make enormous and wrongful inroads upon Germany, and mass expulsions of millions of Germans on a scale grievous and undreamed-of are now taking place. The Communist parties, which were very small in all these Eastern States of Europe, have been raised to pre-eminence and power far beyond their numbers and are seeking everywhere to obtain totalitarian control. Police governments are prevailing in nearly every case, and so far, except in Czechoslovakia, there is no true democracy.

Turkey and Persia are both profoundly alarmed and disturbed at the claims which are being made upon them and at the pressure being exerted by the Moscow Government. An attempt is being made by the Russians in Berlin to build up a quasi-Communist party in their zone of Occupied Germany by showing special favours to groups of left-wing German leaders. At the end of the fighting last June, the American and British Armies withdrew westwards, in accordance with an earlier agreement, to a depth at some points of 150 miles upon a front of nearly four hundred miles, in order to allow our Russian allies to occupy this vast expanse of territory which the Western Democracies had conquered....

The safety of the world requires a new unity in Europe, from which no nation should be permanently outcast. It is from the quarrels of the strong parent races in Europe that the world wars we have witnessed, or which occurred in former times, have sprung. Twice in our own lifetime we have seen the United States, against their wishes and their traditions, against arguments, the force of which it is impossible not to comprehend, drawn by irresistible forces, into these wars in time to secure the victory of the good cause, but only after frightful slaughter and devastation had occurred. Twice the United States has had to send several millions of its young men across the Atlantic to find the war; but now war can find any nation, wherever it may dwell between dusk and dawn. Surely we should work with conscious purpose for a grand pacification of Europe, within the structure of the United Nations and in accordance with its Charter. That I feel is an open cause of policy of very great importance.

In front of the iron curtain which lies across Europe are other causes for anxiety. In Italy the Communist Party is seriously hampered by having to Support the Communist-trained Marshal Tito's claims to former Italian territory at the head of the Adriatic. Nevertheless the future of Italy hangs in the balance. Again one cannot imagine a regenerated Europe without a strong France. All my public life I have worked for a Strong France and I never lost faith in her destiny, even in the darkest hours. I will not lose faith now. However, in a great number of countries, far from the Russian frontiers and throughout the world, Communist fifth columns are established and work in complete unity and absolute obedience to the directions they receive from the Communist centre. Except in the British Commonwealth and in the United States where Communism is in its infancy, the Communist parties or fifth columns constitute a growing challenge and peril to Christian civilisation. These are sombre facts for anyone to have to recite on the morrow of a victory gained by so much splendid comradeship in arms and in the cause of freedom and democracy; but we should be most unwise not to face them squarely while time remains.

The outlook is also anxious in the Far East and especially in Manchuria. The Agreement which was made at Yalta, to which I was a party, was extremely favourable to Soviet Russia, but it was made at a time when no one could say that the German war might not extend all through the summer and autumn of 1945 and when the Japanese war was expected to last for a further 18 months from the end of the German war. In this country you are all so well-informed about the Far East, and such devoted friends of China, that I do not need to expatiate on the situation there....

On the other hand I repulse the idea that a new war is inevitable; still more that it is imminent. It is because I am sure that our fortunes are still in our own hands and that we hold the power to save the future, that I feel the duty to speak out now that I have the occasion and the opportunity to do so. I do not believe that Soviet Russia desires war. What they desire is the fruits of war and the indefinite expansion of their power and doctrines. But what we have to consider here to-day while time remains, is the permanent prevention of war and the establishment of conditions of freedom and democracy as rapidly as possible in all countries. Our difficulties and dangers will not be removed by closing our eyes to them. They will not be removed by mere waiting to see what happens; nor will they be removed by a policy of appeasement. What is needed is a settlement, and the longer this is delayed, the more difficult it will be and the greater our dangers will become.

From what I have seen of our Russian friends and Allies during the war, I am convinced that there is nothing they admire so much as strength, and there is nothing for which they have less respect than for weakness, especially military weakness. For that reason the old doctrine of a balance of power is unsound. We cannot afford, if we can help it, to work on narrow margins, offering temptations to a trial of strength. If the Western Democracies stand together in strict adherence to the principles of the United Nations Charter, their influence for furthering those principles will be immense and no one is likely to molest them. If however they become divided or falter in their duty and if these all-important years are allowed to slip away then indeed catastrophe may overwhelm us all.

Last time I saw it all coming and cried aloud to my own fellow-countrymen and to the world, but no one paid any attention. Up till the year 1933 or even 1935, Germany might have been saved from the awful fate which has overtaken her and we might all have been spared the miseries Hitler let loose upon mankind. There never was a war in all history easier to prevent by timely action than the one which has just desolated such great areas of the globe. It could have been prevented in my belief without the firing of a single shot, and Germany might be powerful, prosperous and honoured to-day; but no one would listen and one by one we were all sucked into the awful whirlpool. We surely must not let that happen again. This can only be achieved by reaching now, in 1946, a good understanding on all points with Russia under the general authority of the United Nations Organisation and by the maintenance of that good understanding through many peaceful years, by the world instrument, supported by the whole strength of the English-speaking world and all its connections. There is the solution which I respectfully offer to you in this Address to which I have given the title "The Sinews of Peace."

Source: Winston Churchill, *Winston S. Churchill: His Complete Speeches 1897-1963*, Robert Rhodes James, ed. (New York: Chelsea House Publishers, 1974), pp. 7285-7293.

31.3

❖

IN THE YEAR 2525, DENNY ZAGER AND RICHARD EVANS

Although usually dismissed as a novelty hit for songwriting and performing duo Denny Zager and Richard Evans, the song "In the Year 2525" does convey some of the popular attitudes toward the Cold War, the increasing dominance of technology in people's lives, and the threat of nuclear destruction.

❖

QUESTIONS

1. Compare this song with Churchill's discussion of the "gleaming wings of science." Does this song say anything positive about technology?
2. How is this song a protest about the Cold War?
3. What is meant by the phrase "Man has cried a billion tears / For what he never knew"?

IN THE YEAR 2525
(EXORDIUM & TERMINUS)

In the year 2525
If man is still alive
If woman can survive
They may find......

In the year 3535
Ain't gonna need to tell the truth, tell no lies
Everything you think, do and say
Is in the pill you took today

In the year 4545
Ain't gonna need your teeth, won't need your eyes
You won't find a thing to chew
Nobody's gonna look at you

In the year 5555
Your arms hanging limp at your sides
Your legs got nothing to do
Some machine doing that for you

In the year 6565
Ain't gonna need no husband, won't need no wife
You'll pick your son, pick your daughter too
From the bottom of a long glass tube

In the year 7510
If God's a-comin, he oughta make it by then
Maybe he'll look around himself and say
"Guess it's time for the Judgment day."

In the year 8510
God's gonna shake his mighty head
He'll either say "I'm pleased where man has been"
Or tear it down and start again

In the year 9595
I'm kinda wondering if man's gonna be alive
He's taken everything this old earth can give
And he ain't put back nothing…

Now it's been ten 10,000 years
Man has cried a billion tears
For what he never knew
Now man's reign is through

But through eternal night
The twinkling of starlight
So very far away
Maybe it's only yesterday…

In the year 2525
If man is still alive
If woman can survive
They may find……

Source: Denny Zager and Richard Evans, *In the Year 2525*, 1969.

31.4

❖

OHIO, NEIL YOUNG

In 1970 members of the Ohio National Guard killed four college students at Kent State University. Students at the university were protesting American involvement in the Vietnam War and the draft, although three of those killed were not involved in the protest. Kent State was the latest in a series of college campus protests against the war that began in the early 1960s. The shootings at Kent State sparked public outrage against the National Guard and sympathy for protesters across the country. Neil Young wrote this song, Ohio, as an expression of that public outrage. It is also a clear example of how powerfully popular culture was used in the twentieth century as a medium for protest.

❖

QUESTIONS

1. What does Young mean by the phrase "Should have been done long ago?"
2. Who are the "tin soldiers?"
3. How effective is the use of simple lyrics and a few repetitive phrases in creating a protest song?

OHIO

Tin soldiers and Nixon coming,
We're finally on our own.
This summer I hear the drumming,
Four dead in Ohio.

Gotta get down to it
Soldiers are gunning us down
Should have been done long ago.
What if you knew her
And found her dead on the ground
How can you run when you know?

Gotta get down to it
Soldiers are gunning us down
Should have been done long ago.
What if you knew her
And found her dead on the ground
How can you run when you know?

Tin soldiers and Nixon coming,
We're finally on our own.
This summer I hear the drumming,
Four dead in Ohio.

Sources: Neil Young, *Ohio*, from *4 Way Street*, Crosby, Stills, Nash, and Young. Atlantic Records, 1971.

QUESTIONS FOR PART 31

1. What role did popular culture have in affecting political policy in the 1960s? How is this role new?
2. How had the position of Europe in global politics changed because of the Cold War?
3. Did Churchill's speech describe or create the Cold War?

PART 32

THE WEST SINCE 1970

It is always difficult to assess the development of a time period that is in progress. History is a tricky lens with which to view the present. It is possible to point out the trends and themes that seem important now, but of course impossible to predict what will still seem to be important when the current age becomes a period people look back upon. One of the problems in evaluating an era in process is that it all looks important. Trying to understand the contemporary world of the last few decades is particularly problematic given the rapidity with which things – cultural, political, social, economic, military – have changed. Furthermore, the West is still changing and it is the speed of change that makes the post-Cold War era so difficult to read. Globalization was a gradual development when it first began in the sixteenth century; today globalization is a fact of life, although relationships between the West and the rest of the world are ever evolving. Nowhere is globalization more apparent than through popular culture.

Throughout the events of the twentieth century, and into the twenty-first, it became clear that the original term "West" no longer has the same meaning. It is no longer limited to Europe (the United States has in many ways come to dominate the West), and it is no longer so certain that the term "West" has any significance beyond a point on the compass. The documents of this section try to highlight a few of the significant trends of Western history since 1970. They all have in common a critical tone. One unifying theme of all of Western history has been the general sense of confidence the West has had in itself. The integration of world cultures and politics, and the crisis of identity, has led a gradual erosion of Western feelings of self-importance, and criticism of the West (internally and externally) has become increasingly vocal.

32.1

✦

SPEECH AT THE 10TH CONGRESS OF THE POLISH UNITED WORKERS' PARTY, MIKHAIL GORBACHEV

The Cold War ended in a series of extraordinary events between 1989 and 1991. Peaceful revolutions by people — demanding democratic freedoms, ethnic independence, and economic diversity — swept aside one communist government after another in eastern Europe. It was as much a victory for capitalism as for democracy. Eventually the revolutions reached Moscow itself and the Soviet Union ceased to exist in 1991. Overseeing all of this was Mikhail Gorbachev, Party secretary in 1985 and ruler of the Soviet Empire since 1985. Gorbachev was in theory committed to communism but in reality accepted the need for the Soviet Union to reform itself economically. This in turn necessitated political reforms. The economic and political transformations were gradual. The cultural reforms that followed; the opening up of the Communist Party to closer scrutiny by the people, the introduction of Western style music and luxury goods, was probably an unintended result of Gorbachev's initial reforms. This approach to state reform was known as glasnost, *or "openness."*

On June 30, 1986, five years before the end of the Soviet Union, Gorbachev gave this speech in Poland in which he speaks prophetically of what increased Western influence through glasnost *will do to communist states.*

---------- ✛ ----------

QUESTIONS

1. Why is Gorbachev so determined to convince the Polish communists that Moscow will not abandon them?
2. What one Western cultural trait does Gorbachev seem to fear will do the most damage to the communist states?
3. What reason do you think most motivated Gorbachev to end the Cold War?

Comrades, the 10th Congress of the Polish United Workers' Party is, for understandable reasons, attracting the special attention of all Communists, of broad political circles all over the world. The Polish crisis of the end of the 1970s and early 1980s reflected the contradictions of your society. But it also absorbed the complexity of the current contention of the two systems and brought out in sharp form the problems that socialism encounters at this highly complicated state, this turning point, in its development. That is why the lessons of the Polish crisis are important for all Communists, not only the Polish.

The first of these lessons, and probably the most substantial, as we see it, is that those events have, despite their complexity and ambiguity, shown clearly that socialism has sunk deep roots and that the working people in our countries cannot conceive living without it. And this means the socialist gains are irreversible. As Comrade Jaruzelski put it so aptly in this report, Marxist-Leninist ideas have become part of the "national bloodstream" and socialist values and standards are indissoluble components of the social mentality.

It showed, too, that now socialism is an international reality, an alliance of states brought close together by common political, economic, cultural and defensive interests. To raise one's hand against the socialist system, to try subverting it from outside, to try prying away any country from the socialist community — all this encroaches on the will of the people, and, indeed, on the postwar arrangements, and, in the final analysis, on peace.

Another important conclusion we can draw refers to what may be described as the live nerve of socialist society — the place and role of the working class and of its Party, and the significance of the enduring organic link between them.

We know the basic points of the relevant theory. History has proved time and again that none but the working class can be the initiator, the inspirer, the main force in building socialism, that its Party alone, and no other, can organise and direct the energy of the mass of the people to building the new society.

Your country's working class, your Party, can be legitimately proud of the achievements of people's Poland. The four decades after the war, which is a relatively short period, have seen the deep-going social change and the gains that Polish patriots have aspired to for ages, namely, the country's guaranteed independence, and enduring just borders. Under the leadership of the PUWP, the workers, peasants and people's intelligentsia have raised Poland from the ashes, built an up-to-date industrial base, restored the historical monuments, and safeguarded and augmented the values of national culture. The allied parties are making a valuable contribution to this constructive effort.

As rightly noted at this congress, the Polish crisis was not a worker's protest against socialism. It was above all a disavowal by the aggrieved working class of the distortions of socialism in practice. The opponents of socialist Poland at home and abroad managed to exploit this disaffection for their own ends. We know all too well what they are after in the West who call themselves friends of the Polish people. They could not care less for the fate of the Polish nation. What they want is to dismantle socialism, to liquidate the socialist gains. Indeed, the worse it is in Poland, the better they like it.

And that, too, is a lesson, a reminder that socialism is a historically new undertaking, a difficult cause that has to overcome the resistance of the anti-socialist forces, and to contend with imperialism's economic, political, propagandist, and military pressures.

Lastly, the experience of the past period again showed the danger of mistakes and subjective deviations from the principles that lie at the root of socialism's political system, of neglecting the standards of Party and government life, of miscalculations in social and economic policy.

The most dependable guarantee against such deviations is the creative development and application of the Marxist-Leninist doctrine, and close links between the Party and the working class, the broad mass of the working people. Those links are alive and indestructible, if the Party has clear understanding of the people's needs, assesses the country's capabilities at each given stage in a realistic light, and blazes the trail to the future with bold confidence. Seen from the other angle, it means that every politically conscious worker, every citizen, must associate his expectations in life with the Party's policy, must conceive himself not simply as the doer of its will, but also as an active participant in elaborating and carrying out the Party's decisions.

And one more conclusion that we can draw is of universal, international relevance: the socialist revolution provides scope for society's all-round progress. This does not go to say that such progress is henceforth automatically assured, that the relations of production and the productive forces have been harmonised once and for all. The swift growth of production, science, technology, and culture, the very advancement of the human personality — all this sets new demands on how society is organised. It is on the order of the day to continuously renovate socialism upon its own basis. Lacking this, stagnation, a clotting up of the social organism may complicate the economic and social problems to a danger point.

The Communist Party of the Soviet Union said so clearly at its 27th Congress. The capacity for self-critical analysis, for sober assessment of its own activity and for drawing the due conclusions from past mistakes and miscalculations — that, too, is an important form of struggle for socialism, a fundamental principle making for the working-class party's success bequeathed to us by the great Lenin.

We have set our course resolutely on accelerating social and economic development, on renovating our life and clearing it of everything that hinders the full play of the socialist system's powerful political, economic, and spiritual potential.

In substance, all of us have one and the same aim, namely, learning as quickly as possible to fully utilize the immense potentialities of our system, and to find the optimum balance between the centre and the localities, the spheres belonging to the state and those belonging to society, between government and self-government. We must also learn to better stimulate the activity of people, to stimulate their labour and political involvement, their civic consciousness.

At present, pride of place goes of necessity to a deep-going and comprehensive improvement of the administrative mechanism. The main direction in this effort is clear to us. What we must do is resolve a dual problem: heighten the effectiveness of planning and organisation in determining the ways of our economic development, on the one hand, and afford the utmost scope to the initiative of work collectives, on the other.

As we know, the essence of socialism is expressed in the following formula: "From each according to his ability, to each according to his work." We are bent on confirming this formula by our everyday life, ruling out any wage leveling and seeing to it that conscientious and highly productive labour should be properly rewarded and social justice strictly abided by. For this we use economic levers, the power of persuasion, and the force of the law.

As you see, the reconstruction we have actively launched gathers into a tight knot a wide range of issues — from the functioning of the system, governmental and non-governmental institutions, down to the working and living conditions of people and the moral climate in our society....

We follow Lenin's approach: "What we need is more factual knowledge and fewer debates on ostensible communist principles. ...This calls for modesty and respect for the efficient 'specialists in science and technology,' and a business-like and careful analysis of our numerous *practical* mistakes, and their gradual but steady correction."

Our Parties face the historically important task of combining the social justice inherent in socialism with the highest possible economic efficiency. We must, we are simply obliged to make socialism stronger, more dynamic in its development, more successful in competing against capitalist society in all parameters. And that requires above all that we make full and effective use of the truly inexhaustible possibilities of the scientific and technological revolution.

Here, understandably, it is best for us to act together, to pool our efforts. That is needed, too, in face of the international political situation and, not least of all, in the interests of our economic security.

There is no denying that we were late in spotting the traps set along the trade routes to the West. You have mentioned here the damage sustained by Poland. And Poland is not the only one to sustain damage. The very idea that it is simpler buying in the capitalist market than producing at home, has been damaging. We are most decidedly shaking off such feelings in our country. Which does not mean, of course, that we are winding up economic contacts with the West. What we want is to use them rationally, to eliminate excesses, to prevent dependence....

Comrades, human civilization has come to a forking of the roads not only in questions of war and peace. We have entered an age where the indissoluble link between the right to life and the right to development is felt ever more strongly.

Can we reconcile ourselves with the fact that colossal financial means are being spent on weapons while hundreds of millions of people across the world are starving and millions die of hunger ever year? It is chiefly the peoples of developing countries who live in poverty. But the problem of poverty has not spared the advanced imperialist states either, including the United States. A country that allocates more than 300 billion dollars yearly on armaments, is unable or, what is worse, reluctant to feed its own undernourished, teach its own illiterates, and provide a roof for its own homeless.

The growing gap between the economically advanced and the underdeveloped countries is a most acute problem. But here, too, the imperialists' behaviour amounts to plain usury or, putting it more bluntly, to out-and-out plunder. The imperialists are drawing the noose of financial and technological dependence ever more tightly round the necks of dozens of countries. Nor do they shrink from the old methods, namely resort to brute force.

Everybody knows our attitude to this. All peoples have the sovereign right to shape their own future. There can be no normal international relations in the absence of that principle. We have always worked for the restructuring of the international political and economic order along reasonable and just lines, and have always supported anti-imperialist movements and organisations regardless of their social orientation.

This is an unusually complicated time, with conflicting tendencies interweaving and contending against one another on a global scale. We are witnessing social revolutions and the bitter resistance of the forces going off the state of history. We are witnessing a precipitous surge of scientific and technological progress, and also its other side imperiling the very survival of life on earth. We are witnessing extraordinary achievements in all areas of science and art, and, on the other hand, the degradations of the imperialist-inspired pop culture. We see wealth against a backdrop of poverty, and hunger amidst plenty. We see a powerful drive towards interdependence and closeness and, on the other hand, alienation and hostility among countries and groups of countries. In many people this breeds tergiversation and fear of the future.

Searching thought and its verification by social and political practice has become the motto for our parties at this responsible stage of history. We back everything that serves the true interests of the peoples, the cause of peace and social justice, and the progress of humankind. And we firmly reject anything that is contrary to these aims.

Source: Mikhail Gorbachev, Selected Speeches and Articles (Moscow: Progress Publishers, 1987), pp. 571-582.

32.2

✠

PERSONAL TESTIMONIALS, ETHNIC CLEANSING IN BOSNIA

The disintegration of the communist states was not always as peaceful as it was in the Soviet Union. In 1992 several Yugoslav republics proclaimed their independence, including Bosnia-Herzegovina and Croatia. The former communist party leader, Slobodan Milosevic, refused to accept their independence and used his control of the Serbian army (another state within Yugoslavia) to reclaim control of Bosnia. Milosevic promoted ethnic tensions between the predominantly Christian Serbs and the Muslim Bosnians. By 1995 over 200,000 Bosnians had been killed, many in campaigns of "ethnic cleansing." In retaliation, Croatian forces invaded Bosnia to push the Serbs out. A settlement was reached in 1995 that divided the territory into a separate Muslim Bosnian-Croatian state and a Serb state. A similar war broke out in Kosovo in 1999, and Milosevic remained in power until 2000.

The following personal accounts are taken from Helsinki Watch's investigations into Serb practices of ethnic cleansing (one of the most tragic legacies of the twentieth centuries). Helsinki Watch is an international organization that monitors human rights abuses.

------------ ✦ ------------

QUESTIONS

1. How are rape and castration weapons of ethnic cleansing?
2. If the Bosnian war began in 1992, why was Milosevic not forced from power until 2000?
3. How much is this a war between different cultures and how much a war between different religions?

After ten minutes, the bus stopped. The soldier on the bus said, "Now you'll be placed under UNPROFOR's [United Nations Protection Forces] control. Life for the living and for the dead...well, you know." They told us to get off the bus and line up in pairs, in a column. I was the last one in the column. We walked about fifty meters toward the back of the bus. I saw another bus in front of us, but I didn't know that people were inside.

They took us to the edge of the ravine. There were over one hundred meters between the edge of the ravine and Korĉanske Stijene. They told us to march [to the edge of the road] and to kneel. Then we heard gunfire. I was the last to have emerged from the bus and the first one facing the ravine. The hill wasn't too steep, so someone pushed me and I fell — rather rolled — into the canyon. There were dead people falling over us. People may have just been wounded, and then they may have thrown them into the ravine — I don't know. Some were wounded after they were pushed into the ravine, and others were still alive but the soldiers started shooting down into the canyon from above. More then ten but fewer than fifteen police officers did this [i.e., committed the massacre]....

I waited in my [hiding] spot until nightfall. Then I climbed up to see the dead. [In addition to those that had been executed that same day,] there were old corpses there as well. They were swollen, many were black and the bodies were rotting and the smell was bad. There were many corpses, but probably fewer than two hundred....

I was badly beaten. I was kneeling with my hands against the wall and they were hitting me from behind for two hours. After that first day, I was beaten at random. People were dying of internal injuries they had received from the beatings. I carried out the bodies. then trucks came and took them away....

From upstairs, I could see a couple of bodies every day in the field, but I'm not sure this was the only place where they threw away the bodies. It is horrible to say, but we were happy when new prisoners were brought in because then they did not beat us, but them....

One night, at about 1:15 a.m., men came into the hall in which we were detained. They were cocking their guns and demanding that we hand over any money we had [on our persons]. We did so but were then beaten mercilessly. The bestial beatings were a typical, daily occurrence....

The night the men were castrated, another three or four men were killed outside — we heard shots. The bodies were put on a little truck and driven away. Almost every night, between midnight and 2:00 a.m., drunken guards would take away approximately five men who never came back.

Prisoners were beaten every day, especially at night. The soldiers would pick out ten people, take them out [of the warehouse] and beat them. The wealthier or more educated persons [were usually the victims of such beatings]....

When we had to make the dash to eat, sometimes they would put oil on the floor to make us slip and fall, thereby making it easier for them to beat us. We would get about two finger-widths of bread a day.

Not one evening passed where four or five youths, between the ages of eighteen and twenty-five, weren't taken out and killed. There were also times when we had to lie down with our faces pressed against the courtyard floor and, if we were not lying closely enough, ten men would jump on us. They also used a hose to spray us with ice-cold water. They made us stand on one foot and those who couldn't were pulled out and beaten....

Soldiers would also take knives and twirl them around in prisoners' mouths. This was done mostly to men in their early twenties. During the time I was in Omarska, [prisoners] died of starvation....

Khoja Husein Granol, from Mujkanovići, was forced to eat ham, and they made him say that it was good. Faruk's — I forgot his last name — head was cracked open with a rifle butt. Dr. Esad Sadiković tied Faruk's hair in a knot so his skull would not open. Another prisoner picked maggots out of this wound. He survived Omarska, but he is now blind in one eye. Most of us, myself included, had maggot-infested wounds. One man was clubbed on the head with a rifle butt until his scalp was ripped off. They would let him heal for a few days and then do it again....

The commanding officer told me to make coffee for him and two other men present. One was a man named Babić who was the manager of the mine in Omarska, and he was serving his military duty and was in uniform. A second man was named Nedeljko Grabovac, and he was a reserve captain in the "Serbian Army." He said that the Muslims were raping Serbian women. Grabovac told me to get out of the room but then he grabbed me and took me into another office. He threw me on the floor, and someone else came into the room. During that period, the electricity would go on and off at intervals. When I was assaulted, there was no electricity in the building, and I could not identify the second man who had entered the room. Both Grabovac and the second man started to beat me. They said I was an Ustaša and that I needed to give birth to a Serb — that I would then be different. I was raped only by Grabovac; the other man had left the room. After he raped me, I was ordered to go back to my room with the other women.

The next evening, Grabovac came to my door and told me to get out and I did so. He said that I must have gotten a cold the night before, and he gave me some tea — but I didn't want to drink it. He then hit me in the head with the butt of this revolver. He grabbed my chest and dragged me to the bathroom, where he beat me. The commanding officer was present during this entire abuse. I should add that all the women were beaten at various points during our detention, but none of us was ever beaten in the face; they only beat our bodies.

On the third evening, Grabovac took me out again and started to excuse himself for his actions the previous evening, explaining that "our nationalities are at war." Then he started to show me what he called "instruments of torture used by the Muslims against the Serbs." He showed me a fishhook that he claimed was used to cut the veins of Serbian men and a ball-and-chain contraption which he claimed was used to strangle Serbs. But these instruments were covered with blood, and they must have been used very recently. It would have been virtually impossible for a Muslim to have done this to a Serb in Omarska and I thought to myself that those weapons had probably been used against the prisoners, not the Serbs but I said nothing. He then started to beat me again because I did not respond to his statements....

That day [i.e., August 11], two Serbian policemen came [to my door.] It was 9:30 p.m. I knew both of them — they worked in our [local] police station. They told me that I had to go to the police station with them to give a statement and that I'd go home immediately after I finished [giving a statement]. I was not very scared because I knew I was not guilty of anything. I was not politically active, I was not a member of any political party and I believed them when they said that I would only have to make a statement and then go home. I was so stupid....

They locked me in one of the big halls. Offices had earlier been in this building. There were office tables in the room. I was dark. I heard the screams of the men who were tortured and the shouts of their torturers. At about 2:00 a.m., I heard the door being unlocked and I saw the light of a flashlight. I recognized Zoran Sikirica, who was at that time the commander of Keraterm. He told me that inspectors were coming from Banja Luka in a few minutes and that they would have to ask me some questions. Only a crazy person would believe that any inspectors were coming to interrogate you at 2:00 in the morning. And then he did it. He raped me on one of the tables.

First, he started to insult me. He asked me if I had a husband…or a lover. Then he ordered me to take off my clothes. I started to cry, and I told him that I was menstruating. He said he didn't mind and that he would show me how a Serb does it. He tied my hands and then he raped me on the table….

While one of them was raping me, the other two were laughing, insulting me and cheering him [i.e., the rapist] on. They smelled of alcohol. It was terrible. They bit my legs, which were black and blue for the next couple of days. When they finished, one of them untied my hands, and they were gone. That night I cried a lot, but I never cried again [during my detention.]

Source: *War Crimes in Bosnia-Hercegovina, Volume II* (New York: Human Rights Watch, 1993), pp. 38-40, 98-101, 163-166.

32.3

✤

RACIAL TENSIONS: RAP SONGS

Racial tensions are typical of the West post-1970. The civil rights movement in the 1960s ended legal segregation in the United States and promoted integration across Europe, but de facto *separation of peoples based on race, ethnicity, and religion continues to exist throughout the West. Immigration of cheap labor from Africa and the Middle East has led to eruptions of racial violence in Germany, France, and Britain. Economic disparity, perceptions of legal bias, and cultural differences led to tension and violence in the United States in the 1990s.*

Popular culture has been a particularly fertile ground on which to explore racial differences and problems. The following four rap songs are from two American artists, the band Public Enemy and the performer Ice Cube. The latter released "Who Got the Camera?" and "It was a Good Day" in response to race riots in Los Angeles in 1992, which broke out after a white jury exonerated several members of the Los Angeles police of assault for beating a black man. The beating, the trial verdict, and the riots were filmed and played repeatedly on national television.

✤

QUESTIONS

1. How does the popularity of rap music in general depict the dominance of American culture in the world markets?
2. What is Ice Cube saying, in his music and by what he is, about the role of media in the late twentieth century?
3. What do these songs have in common with the testimonials about ethnic cleansing in the previous source?

911 IS A JOKE

Hit me
Going, going, gone
Now I dialed 911 a long time ago
Don't you see how late they're reactin'
They only come and they come when they wanna
So get the morgue embalm the goner
They don't care 'cause they stay paid anyway
They teach ya like an ace they can't be betrayed
I know you stumble with no use people
If your life is on the line they you're dead today
Late comings with the late comin' stretcher
That's a body bag in disguise y'all betcha
I call 'em body snatchers quick they come to fetch ya?
With an autopsy ambulance just to dissect ya
They are the kings 'cause they swing amputation
Lose your arms, your legs to them it's compilation
I can prove it to you watch the rotation
It all adds up to a funky situation
So get up get, get get down
911 is a joke in yo town
Get up, get, get, get down
Late 911 wears the late crown

911 is a joke

Everyday they don't never come correct
You can ask my man right here with the broken neck
He's a witness to the job never bein' done
He would've been in full in 8 9-11
Was a joke 'cause they always jokin'
They the token to your life when it's croakin'
They need to be in a pawn shop on a
911 is a joke we don't want 'em
I call a cab 'cause a cab will come quicker
The doctors huddle up and call a flea flicker
The reason that I say that 'cause they
Flick you off like fleas
They be laughin' at ya while you're crawlin' on your knees
And to the strength so go the length
Thinkin' you are first when you really are tenth
You better wake up and smell the real flavor
Cause 911 is a fake life saver

So get up, get, get get down
911 is a joke in yo town
Get up, get, get, get down
Late 911 wears the late crown

Ow, ow 911 is a joke

FIGHT THE POWER

1989 the number another summer (get down)
Sound of the funky drummer
Music hittin' your heart cause I know you got sould
(Brothers and sisters, hey)
Listen if you're missin' y'all
Swingin' while I'm singin'
Givin' whatcha gettin'
Knowin' what I know
While the Black bands sweatin'
And the rhythm rhymes rollin'
Got to give us what we want
Gotta give us what we need
Our freedom of speech is freedom or death
We got to fight the powers that be
Lemme hear you say
Fight the power

Chorus

As the rhythm designed to bounce
What counts is that the rhymes
Designed to fill your mind
Now that you've realized the prides arrived
We got to pump the stuff to make us tough
from the heart
It's a start, a work of art
To revolutionize make a change nothin's strange
People, people we are the same
No we're not the same
Cause we don't know the game
What we need is awareness, we can't get careless
You say what is this?
My beloved lets get down to business
Mental self defensive fitness
(Yo) bum rush the show
You gotta go for what you know
Make everybody see, in order to fight the powers that be
Lemme hear you say...
Fight the Power

Chorus

Elvis was a hero to most
But he never meant shit to me you see
Straight up racist that sucker was
Simple and plain
Mother fuck him and John Wayne
Cause I'm Black and I'm proud
I'm ready and hyped plus I'm amped
Most of my heroes don't appear on no stamps
Sample a look back you look and find
Nothing but rednecks for 400 years if you check
Don't worry be happy
Was a number one jam
Damn if I say it you can slap me right here
(Get it) lets get this party started right
Right on, c'mon
What we got to say
Power to the people no delay
To make everybody see
In order to fight the powers that be

(Fight the Power)

IT WAS A GOOD DAY

B reak 'em off somethin
Shit..
Yo..
Yo.. uhh..

[Verse One]

Just wakin up in the morning gotta thank God
I don't know but today seems kinda odd
No barkin from the dogs, no smog
And momma cooked a breakfast with no hog (damn)
I got my grub on, but didn't pig out
Finally got a call from a girl wanna dig out
(Whassup?) Hooked it up on later as I hit the do'
Thinkin will I live, another twenty-fo'
I gotta go cause I got me a drop top
And if I hit the switch, I can make the ass drop

Had to stop, at a red light
Looking in my mirror and not a jacker in sight
And everything is alright
I got a beep from Kim, and she can fuck all night
Called up the homies and I'm askin y'all
Which park, are y'all playin basketball?
Get me on the court and I'm trouble
Last week fucked around and got a triple double
Freaking niggaz everyway like M.J.
I can't believe, today was a good day (shit!)

[Verse Two]

Drove to the pad and hit the showers
Didn't even get no static from the cowards
Cause just yesterday them fools tried to blast me
Saw the police and they rolled right past me
No flexin, didn't even look in a nigga's direction
as I ran the intersection
Went to $hort Dog's house, they was watchin Yo! MTV Raps
What's the haps on the craps?
Shake 'em up, shake 'em up, shake 'em up, shake 'em
Roll 'em in a circle of niggaz and watch me break 'em
With the seven, seven-eleven, seven-eleven
Seven even back do' Lil' Joe
I picked up the cash flow
Then we played bones, and I'm yellin domino
Plus nobody I know got killed in South Central L.A.
Today was a good day (shit!)

[Verse Three]

Left my nigga's house paid (what)
Picked up a girl been tryin to fuck since the 12th grade
It's ironic, I had the brew she had the chronic
The Lakers beat the Supersonics
I felt on the big fat fanny
Pulled out the jammy, and killed the punanny
And my dick runs deep so deep
So deep put her ass to sleep
Woke her up around one
She didn't hesitate, to call Ice Cube the top gun
Drove her to the pad and I'm coasting
Took another sip of the potion hit the three-wheel motion

I was glad everything had worked out
Dropped her ass off, then I chirped out
Today was like one of those fly dreams
Didn't even see a berry flashing those high beams
No helicopter looking for a murder
Two in the mornin got the Fatburger
Even saw the lights of the Goodyear Blimp
And it read, "Ice Cube's a pimp" (yeah)
Drunk as hell but no throwing up
Half way home and my pager still blowin up
Today I didn't even have to use my A.K.
I got to say it was a good day (shit!)

[Ice Cube]
Hey wait, wait a minute Pooh, stop this shit
What the fuck I'm thinkin about?

WHO GOT THE CAMERA

[Verse One]

Drivin down the motherfuckin highway
The flyway hey bitch, you goin my way?
Now I got a passenger
I look at the miniskirt, now I'm askin her
Would you like to hit the fat bud,
Or perhaps should I run your name through the mud
I mean, are you giving up the nappy dugout?
She said no, well then get the fuck out
Cause I know where the hoes be feinin'
Plus your fat ass got my six-deuce leanin'
Bust a U on the avenue
Why oh why there ain't shit to do
But then sir jinx played his mix
And you thought that shit played out in eighty six
Lookin for my dogs
Looked up in the mirror being followed by the hogs
One time's on my motherfuckin line
Why the fuck the swine had to get behind a nigga like me
They must thind I'm a gee
They both walk up with the g. l. o. c.
(Freeze! There was a robbery and the nigger looked just like you. now
Get out of the car with your hands up and legs spread.)

Started they investigation
No driver's license no registration
When I stepped out the car they slammed me
Goddamn y'all who got the camera?

[Chorus]

Oh please, oh please, oh please, just gimme just one more hit
Oh please, oh please, oh please, just gimme just one more hit
Who got the camera?
[x2]

[Verse Two]

No lights no camera no action
And the pigs wouldn't believe that my slave name was Jackson
He said don't lie to me
I'm lookin for John, Matt, or Spike Lee
The motherfucker called for back up
I guess they planned to beat the mack up
He called me a b\silly ass thug
And pulled out his billy ass club
Tearin up my coupe lookin for the chronic
Goddamn nobody got a panasonic
Found an empty can of old gold
Came around and put my ass in a choke hold
Fucked around and broke my pager
Then they hit a nigga with the tazer
The motherfucking pigs were tryin to hurt me
I fell to the floor and yelled lord have mercy
Then they hit me in the face ya'll
But to them it ain't nuttin but (a friendly game of base ball)
Crowd stood around I said goddamn ya
Who got the camera

[Repeat Chorus]

[Verse Three]

I knew when I saw that deputy smirkin'
That they were gonna put some work in
Mr. law had to hit me in the jaw
Cause I called them faggots with guns and badges
They played rat-a-tat-tat on me head
But if I had the gatty-gat-gat they'd be dead

A victim of a big fat 187
And little devils don't go to heaven
Last night there were eleven but they were'nt scarin me
So they tried the flashlight therapy
I looked at the black one and called him a traitor
I don't give a fuck if you got a beta
Just take my fuckin picture
So I can go downtown and bitch and pitch ya (?)
The one that called me a spook
His name is officer david duke
If the crowd weren't around they would've shot me
Tried to play me out like my name was rodney
Fuckin police gettin badder
But if I had a camera the shit wouldn't matter
(bitch), uh who got my nine, who got my nine
Ya'll done did it this time, uh
Who the fuck got my nine

Sources: W. Drayton, K. Shocklee, and E. Sadler ("911 is a Joke") and K. Shocklee, E. Sadler, and C. Ridenhour ("Fight the Power"), from *Fear of a Black Planet*, Public Enemy (CBS Records, 1989, 1990); Ice Cube ("Who Got the Camera?" "It was a Good Day"), from *The Predator*, Ice Cube (Priority Records, 1992).

32.4

--- ✢ ---

THE NECESSITY FOR AN ISLAMIC GOVERNMENT, IMAM KHOMEINI

In 1979 the first conflict between a fundamentalist Muslim state and the West occurred in Iran. Iranian religious leaders (led by Khomeini) instigated a revolution against the king (shah) of Iran, and because the shah was viewed as a puppet of Western powers, the radicals in Iran turned against Westerners. The United States became a particular target of the fundamentalist Muslims when the Shah went to New York for medical treatment; American embassy workers were taken hostage and held until 1981. However, tensions between fundamentalist Muslim ideals and Western capitalist culture continues to this day; the most recent manifestation was the terrorist attacks on New York City and Washington, D.C. on September 11, 2001.

The causes of Islamic terrorism are not quite simple: religious purity, cultural independence, legacies of colonialism, and concerns about Western dominance of world markets are part of the issue. In 1970 Imam (a Muslim term for religious leader) Khomeini gave a series of lectures on the necessity of revolution. In the following lecture he discusses the need to create a pure Islamic government run according to the shari'a (the divine law of the Qu'ran).

---- ✦ ----

QUESTIONS

1. How does Khomeini explain the disparity between modern law and Islamic law?
2. Is Khomeini's vision of an Islamic state anti-materialism?
3. How does Khomeini characterize monarchy? How does this make his view of the state peculiarly twentieth century?

It is self-evident that the necessity for enactment of the law, which necessitated the formation of a government by the Prophet (upon whom be peace), was not confined or restricted to his time, but continues after his departure from this world. According to tone of the noble verses of the Qur'an, the ordinances of Islam are not limited with respect to time or place; they are permanent and must be enacted until the end of time. They were not revealed merely for the time of the Prophet, only to be abandoned thereafter, with retribution and the penal code of Islam no longer to be enacted, or the taxes prescribed by Islam no longer collected, and the defense of the lands and people of Islam suspended. The claim that the laws of Islam may remain in abeyance or are restricted to a particular time or place is contrary to the essential creedal bases of Islam. Since the enactment of laws, then, is necessary after the departure of the Prophet from this world, and indeed, will remain so until the end of time, the formation of a government and the establishment of executive and administrative organs are also necessary. Without the formation of a government and the establishment of such organs to ensure that through enactment of the law, all activities of the individual take place in the framework of a just system, chaos and anarchy and disorder will prevail and social, intellectual, and moral corruption will arise. The only way to prevent the emergence of anarchy and disorder and to protect society from corruption is to form a government and thus impact order to all the affairs of the country.

Both reason and divine law, then, demonstrate the necessity in our time for what was necessary during the lifetime of the Prophet and the age of the Commander of the Faithful, 'Ali ibn Abi Talib (peace be upon them) — namely the formation of a government and the establishment of executive and administrative organs....

No one can say it is no longer necessary to defend the frontiers and the territorial integrity of the Islamic homeland; that taxes such as the *jizya*, *khums* and *zakat* should no longer be collected; that the penal code of Islam, with its provisions for the payment of blood money and the exacting of requital, should be suspended. Any person who claims that the formation of an Islamic government is not necessary implicitly denies the necessity for the implementation of Islamic law, the universality and comprehensiveness of that law, and the eternal validity of the faith itself....

The nature and character of Islamic law and the divine ordinances of the *shari'a* furnish additional proof of the necessity for establishing government, for they indicate that the laws were laid down for the purpose of creating a state and administering the political, economic, and cultural affairs of society.

First, the laws of the *shari'a* embrace a diverse body of laws and regulations concerning war and peace and intercourse with other nations; penal and commercial law; and regulations pertaining to trade and agriculture. Islamic law contains provisions relating to the preliminaries of marriage and the form in which it should be contracted, and others relating to the development of the embryo in the womb and what food the parents should eat at the time of conception. It further stipulates the duties that are incumbent upon them while the infant is being suckled, and specifies how the child should be reared, and how the husband and the wife should relate to each other and to their children. Islam provides laws and instructions for all of these matters, aiming, as it does, to produce integrated and virtuous human beings who are walking embodiments of the law, or to put it differently the law's voluntary and instinctive executors. It is obvious, then, how much care Islam devotes to government and the political and economic relations of society, with the goal of creating conditions conducive to the production of morally upright and virtuous human beings.

The Glorious Qur'an and the Sunna contain all the laws and ordinances man needs in order to attain happiness and perfection of his state. The book *al-Kafi* has a chapter entitled, "All the Needs of Men Are Set Out in the Book and the Sunna," the "Book" meaning the Qur'an, which is, in its own words, "an exposition of all things." According to certain traditions, the Imam also swears that the Book and the Sunna contain without a doubt all that men need....

The ordinances pertaining to preservation of the Islamic order and defense of the territorial integrity and the independence of the Islamic *umma* also demanded the formation of a government. An example is the command: "Prepare against them whatever force you can muster and horses tethered" (Qur'an, 8:60), which enjoins the preparation of as much armed defensive force as possible and orders the Muslims to be always on the alert and at the ready, even in time of peace.

If the Muslims had acted in accordance with this command and, after forming a government, made the necessary extensive preparations to be in a state of full readiness for war, a handful of Jews would never have dared to occupy our lands, and to burn and destroy the Masjid al-Aqsa without the people's being capable of making an immediate response. All this has resulted from the failure of the Muslims to fulfill their duty of executing God's law and setting up a righteous and respectable government. If the rulers of the Muslim countries truly represented the believers and enacted God's ordinances, they would set aside their petty differences, abandon their subversive and divisive activities, and join together like the fingers of one hand. Then a handful of wretched Jews (the agents of America, Britain, and other foreign powers) would never have been able to accomplish what they have, no matter how much support they enjoyed from America an Britain. All this has happened because of the incompetence of those who rule over the Muslims.

The verse: "Prepare against them whatever force you can muster" commands you to be as strong and well-prepared as possible, so that your enemies will be unable to oppress you and transgress against you. It is because we have been lacking in unity, strength, and preparedness that we suffer oppression and are at the mercy of foreign aggressors....

After the death of the Most Noble Messenger (peace and blessings be upon him), the obstinate enemies of the faith, the Umayyads (God's curses be upon them) did not permit the Islamic state to attain stability with the rule of 'Ali ibn Abi Talib (upon whom be peace). They did not allow a form of government to exist that was pleasing to God, Exalted and Almighty, and to his Most Noble Messenger. They transformed the entire basis of government, and their policies were, for the most part, contradictory to Islam. The form of government of the Umayyads and the Abbasids, and the political and administrative policies they pursued, were anti-Islamic. The form of government was thoroughly perverted by being transformed into a monarchy, like those of the kings of Iran, the emperors of Rome, and the pharaohs of Egypt. For the most part, this non-Islamic form of government has persisted to the present day, as we can see.

Both law and reason require that we not permit governments to retain this non-Islamic and anti-Islamic character. The proofs are clear. First, the existence of a non-Islamic political order necessarily results in the non-implementation of the Islamic political order. Then, all non-Islamic systems of government are the systems of *kufr*, since the ruler in each case is an instance of *taghut*, and it is our duty to remove from the life of Muslim society all traces of *kufr* and destroy them. It is also our duty to create a favorable social environment for the education of believing and virtuous individuals, an environment that is in total contradiction with that produced by the rule of *taghut* and illegitimate power. The social environment created by *taghut* and *shirk* invariably brings about corruption such as you can now observe in Iran, the corruption termed "corruption on earth." This corruption must be swept away, and its instigators punished for their deeds. It is the same corruption that the Pharaoh generated in Egypt with his policies, so that the Qur'an says of him, "Truly he was among the corruptors" (28:4). A believing, pious, just individual cannot possibly exist in a socio-political environment of corruption. We have in reality, then, no choice but to destroy those systems of government that are corrupt in themselves and also entail the corruption of others, and to overthrow all treacherous, corrupt, oppressive, and criminal regimes.

This is a duty that all Muslims must fulfill, in every one of the Muslim countries, in order to achieve the triumphant political revolution of Islam.

Source: Imam Khomeini, *Islam and Revolution*, trans. Hamid Algar (London: KPI Limited, 1985), pp. 40-48.

— ✢ —

QUESTIONS FOR PART 32

1. Why did the dissolution of the communist states go so peacefully in some areas and so violently in others?
2. How much do these documents portray a feeling that the West is a threat to itself?
3. What examples of the positive development of the West would you list to counter these sources?